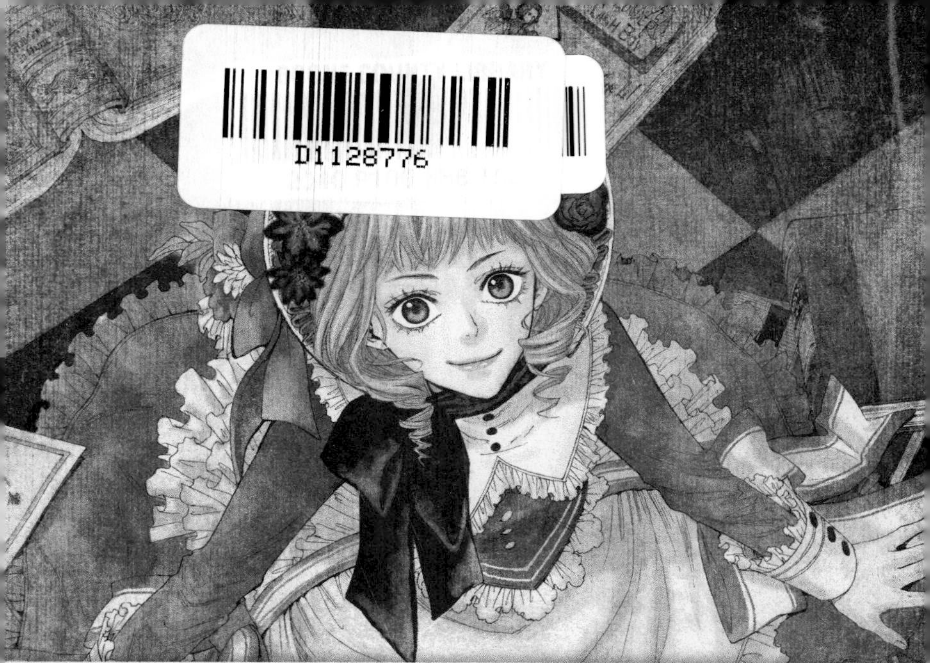

Lizzie Newton
Victorian Mysteries
VOLUME 1

Sto
Hey-jin Jeon

Art
Ki-ha Lee

Lizzie Newton
VICTORIAN MYSTERIES
VOLUME 1

art by **Hey-jin Jeon**
story by **Ki-ha Lee**

STAFF CREDITS

translation	**Lauren Na**
adaptation	**Janet Houck**
lettering & design	**Nicky Lim**
assistant editor	**Shanti Whitesides**
editor	**Adam Arnold**
publisher	**Jason DeAngelis** **Seven Seas Entertainment**

LIZZIE NEWTON: VICTORIAN MYSTERIES VOL. 1
©2011 by JEON Hey-jin, LEE Ki-ha, Daewon C.I. Inc.
All rights reserved. First published in Korea as A LADY DETECTIVE VOL. 1
in 2011 by Daewon C.I. Inc. English translation rights arranged by
Daewon C.I. Inc. through Topaz Agency Inc.

ISBN: 978-1-935934-80-6

Printed in the USA

First Printing: August 2012

10 9 8 7 6 5 4 3 2 1

FOLLOW US ONLINE: **www.gomanga.com**

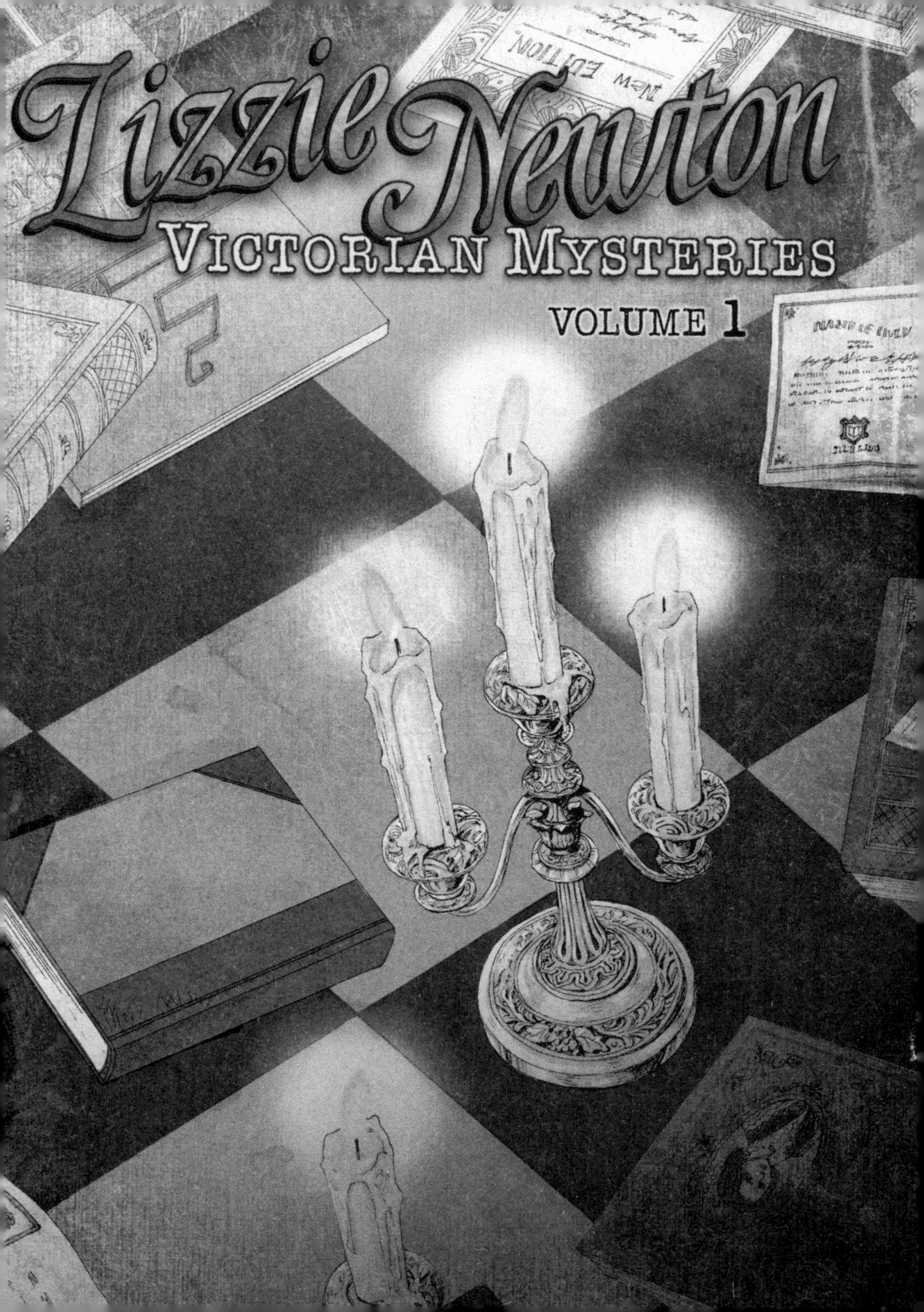
Lizzie Newton
VICTORIAN MYSTERIES
VOLUME 1
NEW EDITION

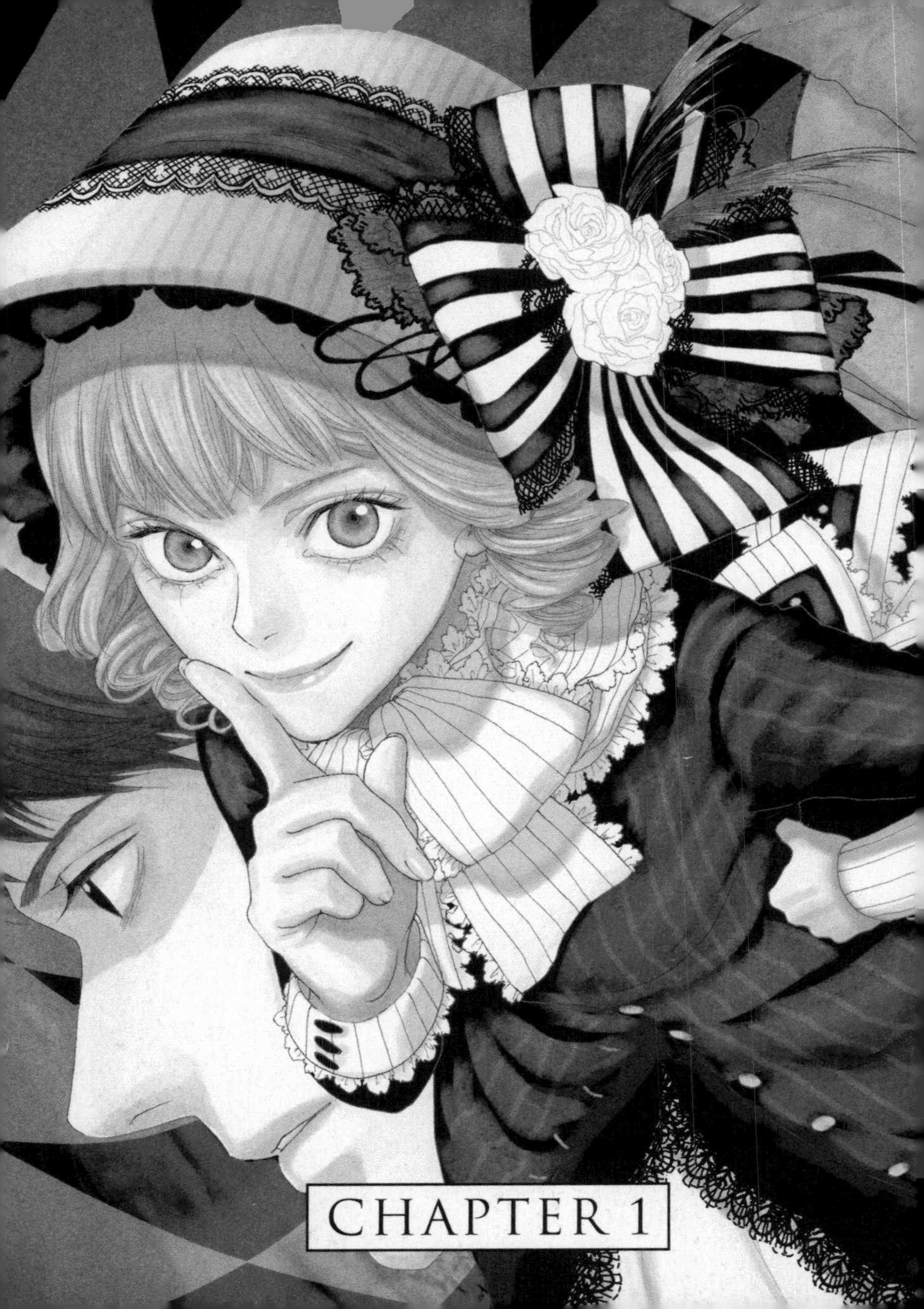
CHAPTER 1

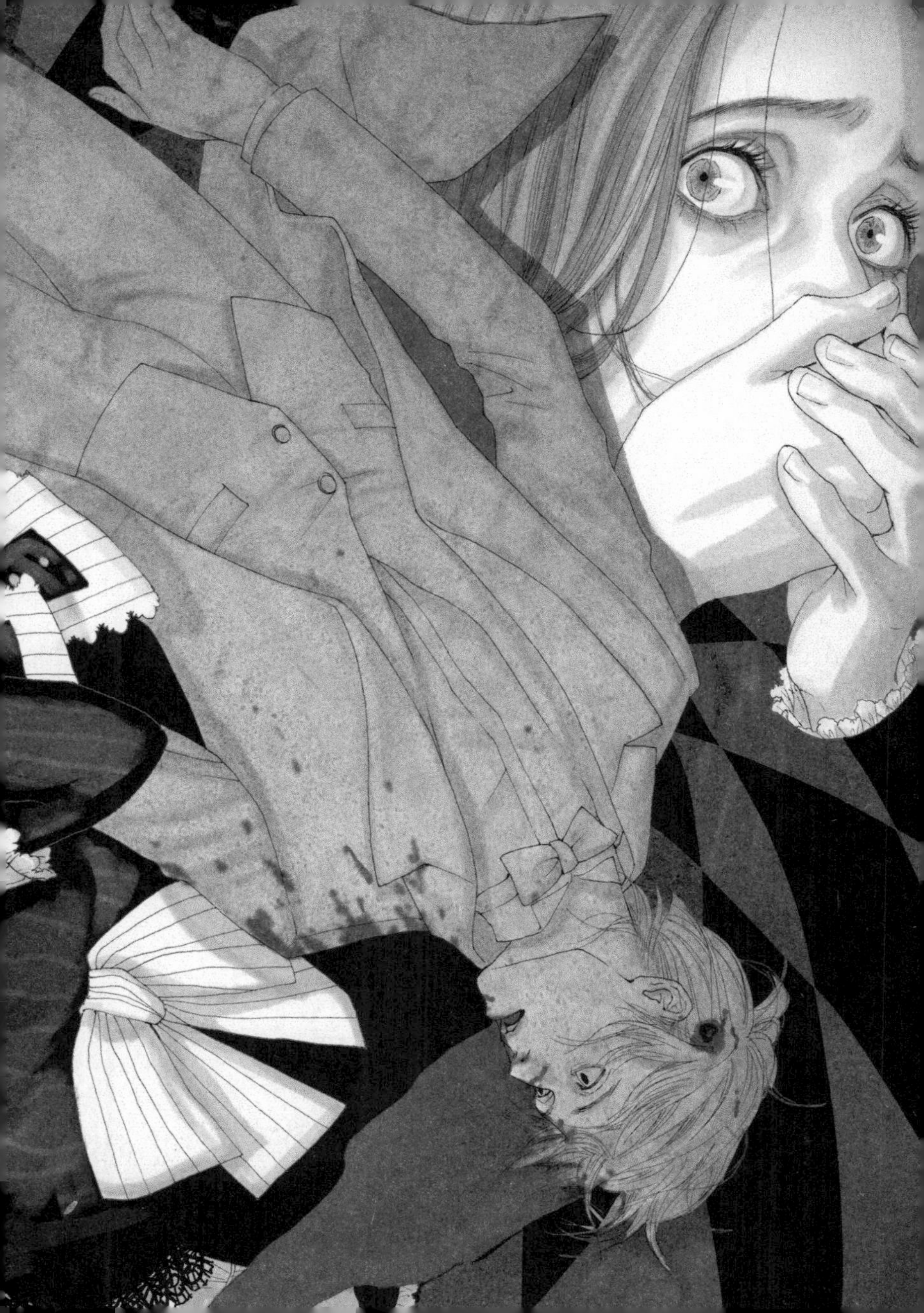

Lizzie Newton

VICTORIAN MYSTERIES

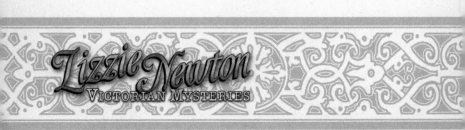

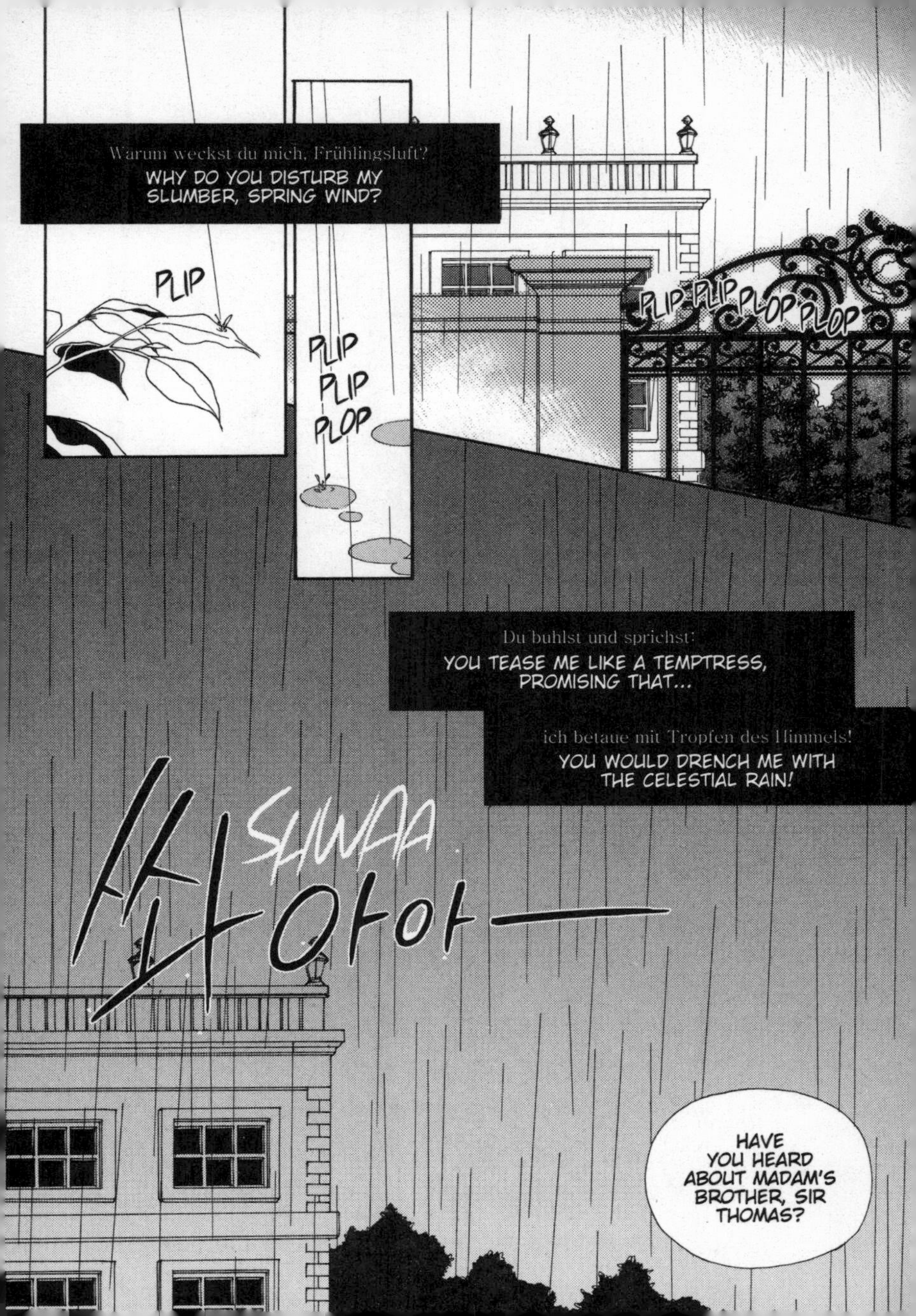
Warum weckst du mich, Frühlingsluft?
WHY DO YOU DISTURB MY SLUMBER, SPRING WIND?
PLIP
PLIP PLIP PLOP
PLIP PLIP PLOP PLOP
Du buhlst und sprichst:
YOU TEASE ME LIKE A TEMPTRESS, PROMISING THAT...
ich betaue mit Tropfen des Himmels!
YOU WOULD DRENCH ME WITH THE CELESTIAL RAIN!
SHWAA
HAVE YOU HEARD ABOUT MADAM'S BROTHER, SIR THOMAS?

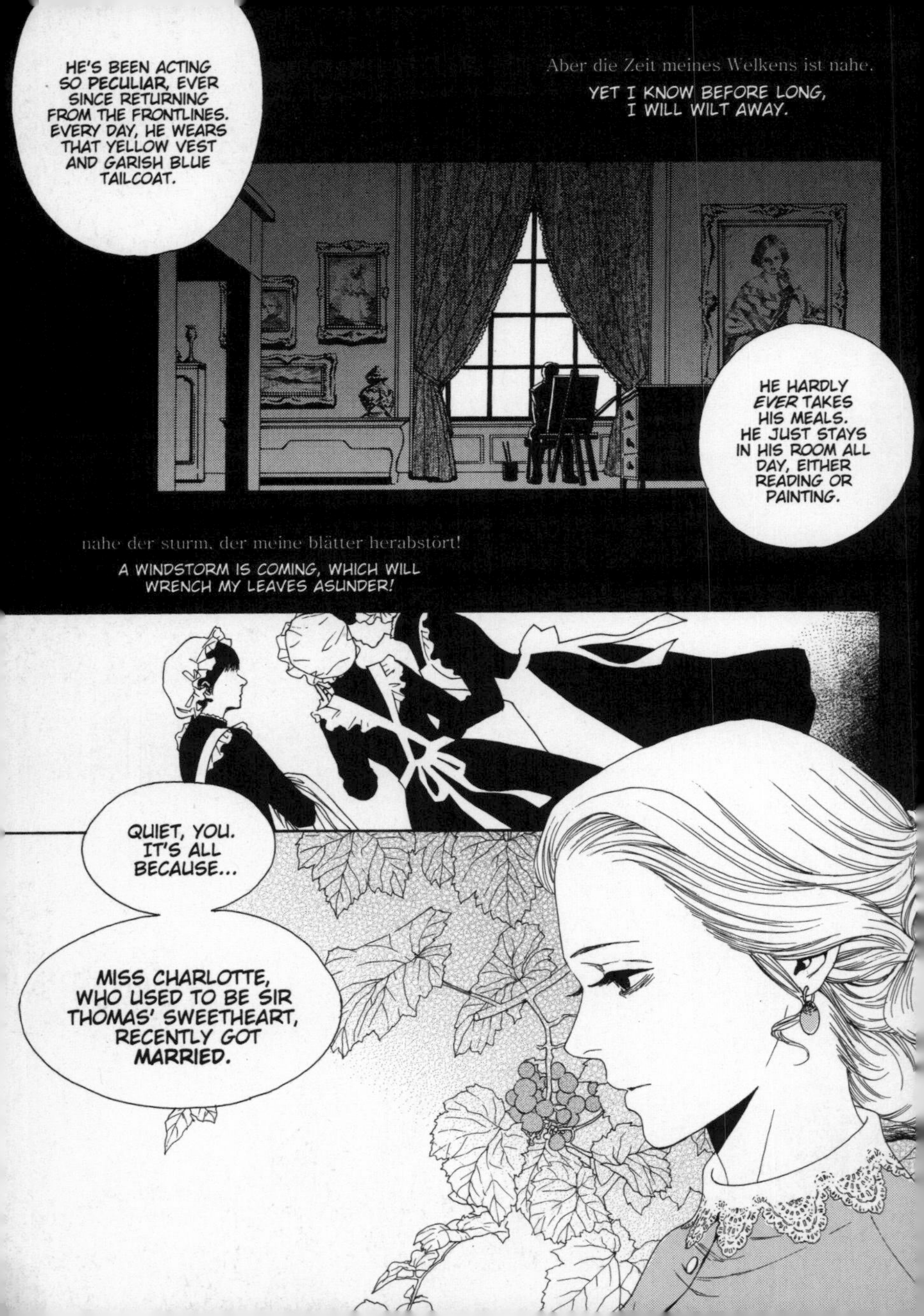
HE'S BEEN ACTING SO PECULIAR, EVER SINCE RETURNING FROM THE FRONTLINES. EVERY DAY, HE WEARS THAT YELLOW VEST AND GARISH BLUE TAILCOAT.
Aber die Zeit meines Welkens ist nahe.
YET I KNOW BEFORE LONG, I WILL WILT AWAY.
HE HARDLY EVER TAKES HIS MEALS. HE JUST STAYS IN HIS ROOM ALL DAY, EITHER READING OR PAINTING.
nahe der sturm, der meine blätter herabstört!
A WINDSTORM IS COMING, WHICH WILL WRENCH MY LEAVES ASUNDER!
QUIET, YOU. IT'S ALL BECAUSE...
MISS CHARLOTTE, WHO USED TO BE SIR THOMAS' SWEETHEART, RECENTLY GOT MARRIED.

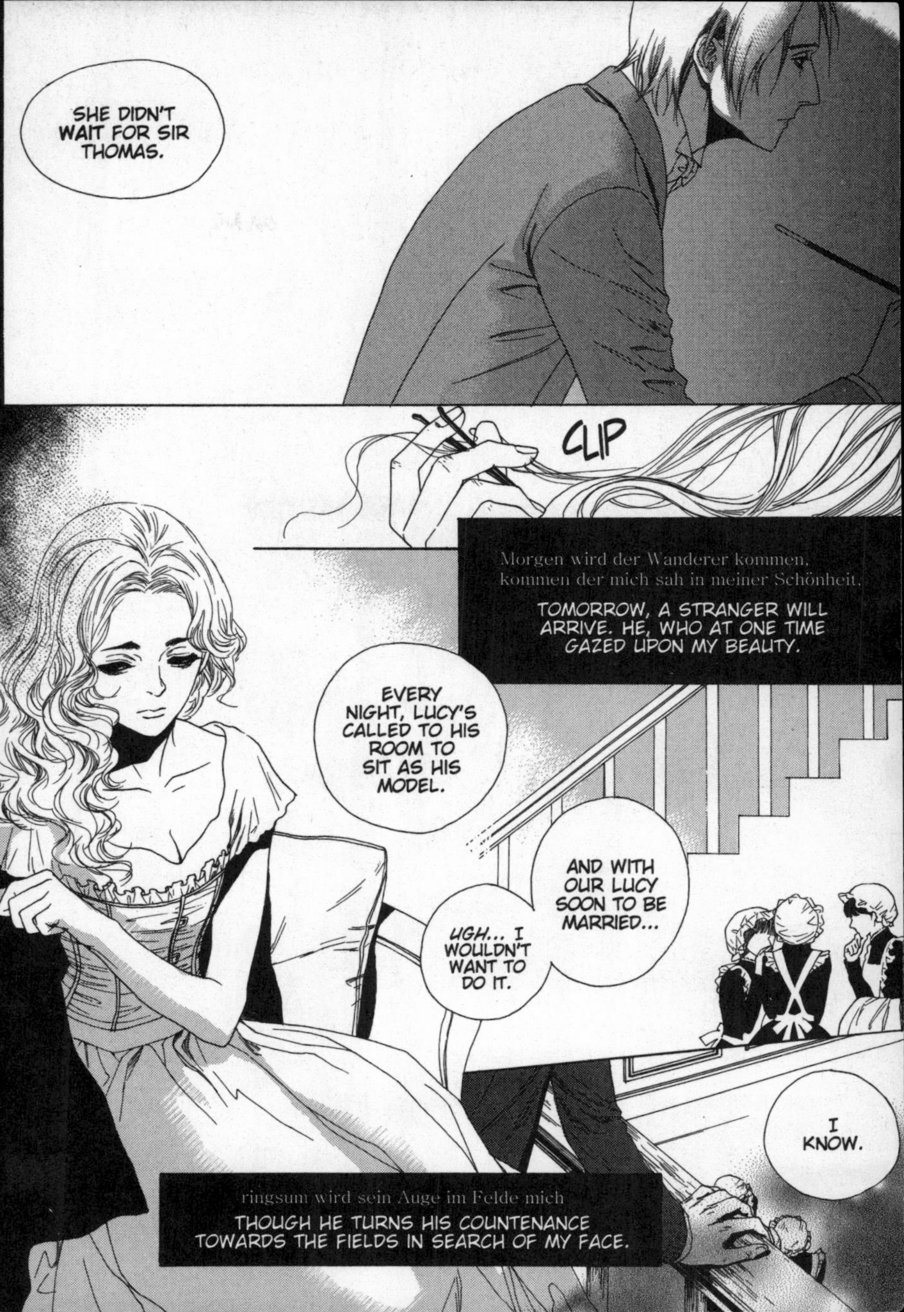
SHE DIDN'T WAIT FOR SIR THOMAS.
CLIP
Morgen wird der Wanderer kommen, kommen der mich sah in meiner Schönheit,
TOMORROW, A STRANGER WILL ARRIVE. HE, WHO AT ONE TIME GAZED UPON MY BEAUTY.
EVERY NIGHT, LUCY'S CALLED TO HIS ROOM TO SIT AS HIS MODEL.
UGH... I WOULDN'T WANT TO DO IT.
AND WITH OUR LUCY SOON TO BE MARRIED...
I KNOW.
ringsum wird sein Auge im Felde mich
THOUGH HE TURNS HIS COUNTENANCE TOWARDS THE FIELDS IN SEARCH OF MY FACE.

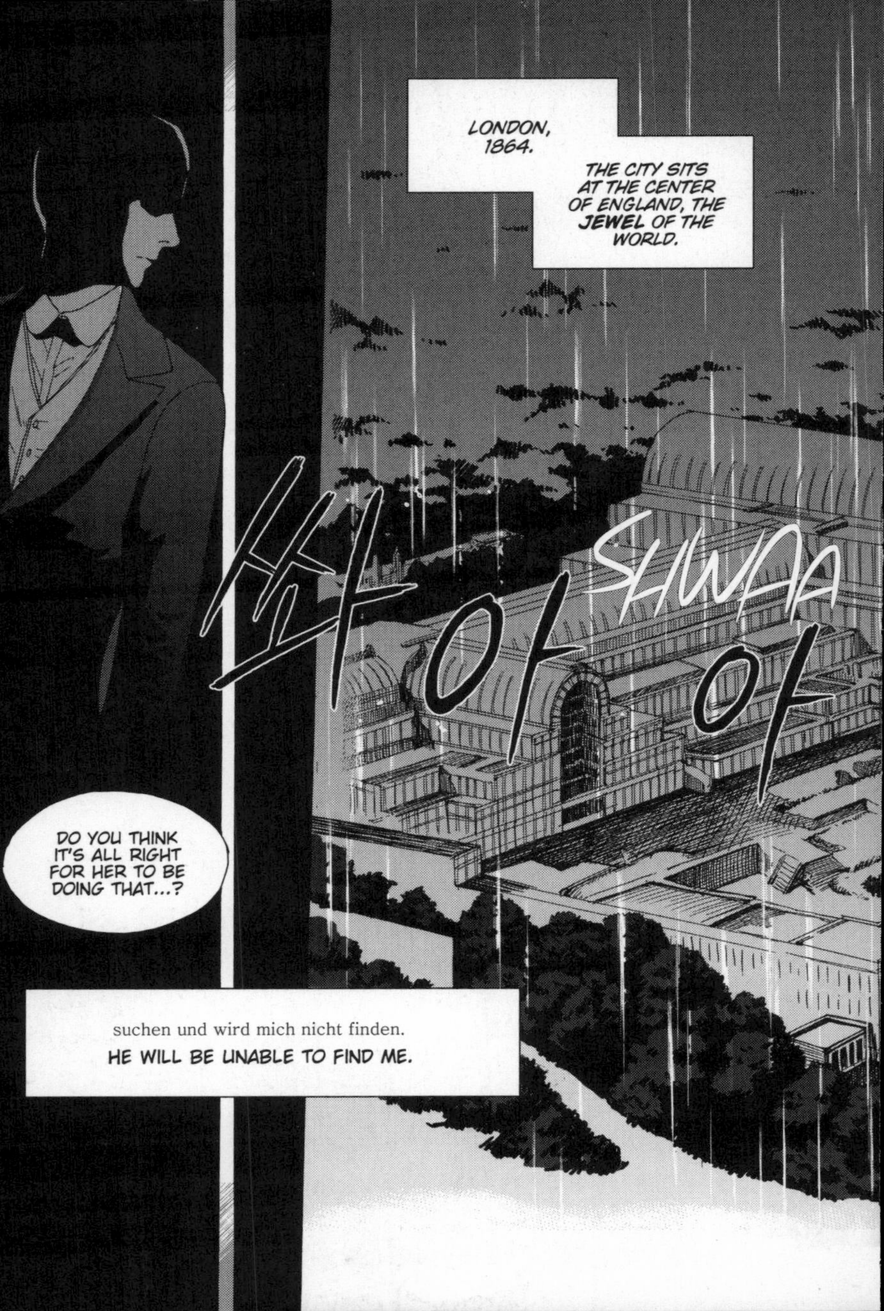
DO YOU THINK IT'S ALL RIGHT FOR HER TO BE DOING THAT...?
LONDON, 1864.
THE CITY SITS AT THE CENTER OF ENGLAND, THE **JEWEL** OF THE WORLD.
SHWAA
suchen und wird mich nicht finden.
HE WILL BE UNABLE TO FIND ME.

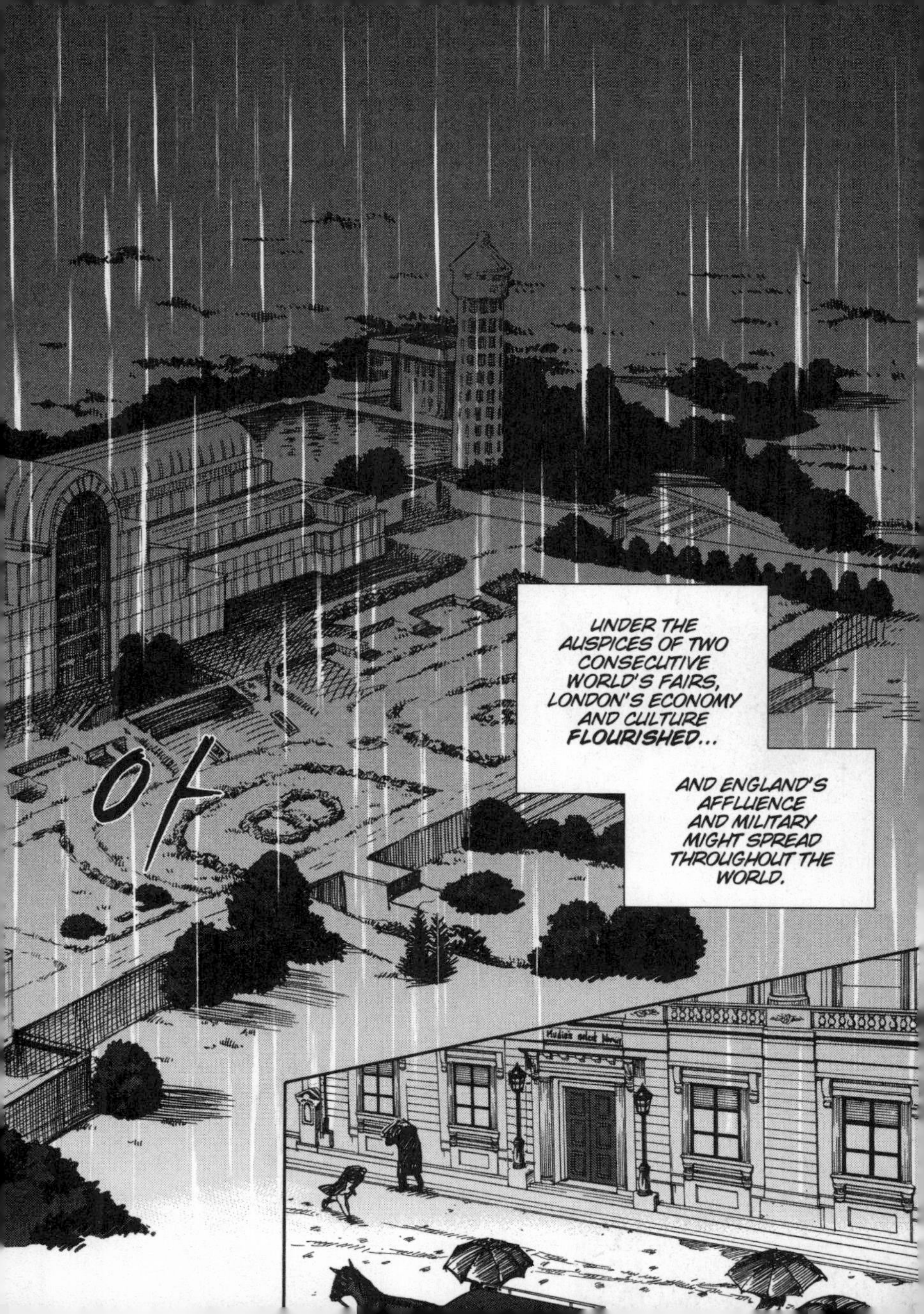
UNDER THE AUSPICES OF TWO CONSECUTIVE WORLD'S FAIRS, LONDON'S ECONOMY AND CULTURE FLOURISHED...
AND ENGLAND'S AFFLUENCE AND MILITARY MIGHT SPREAD THROUGHOUT THE WORLD.

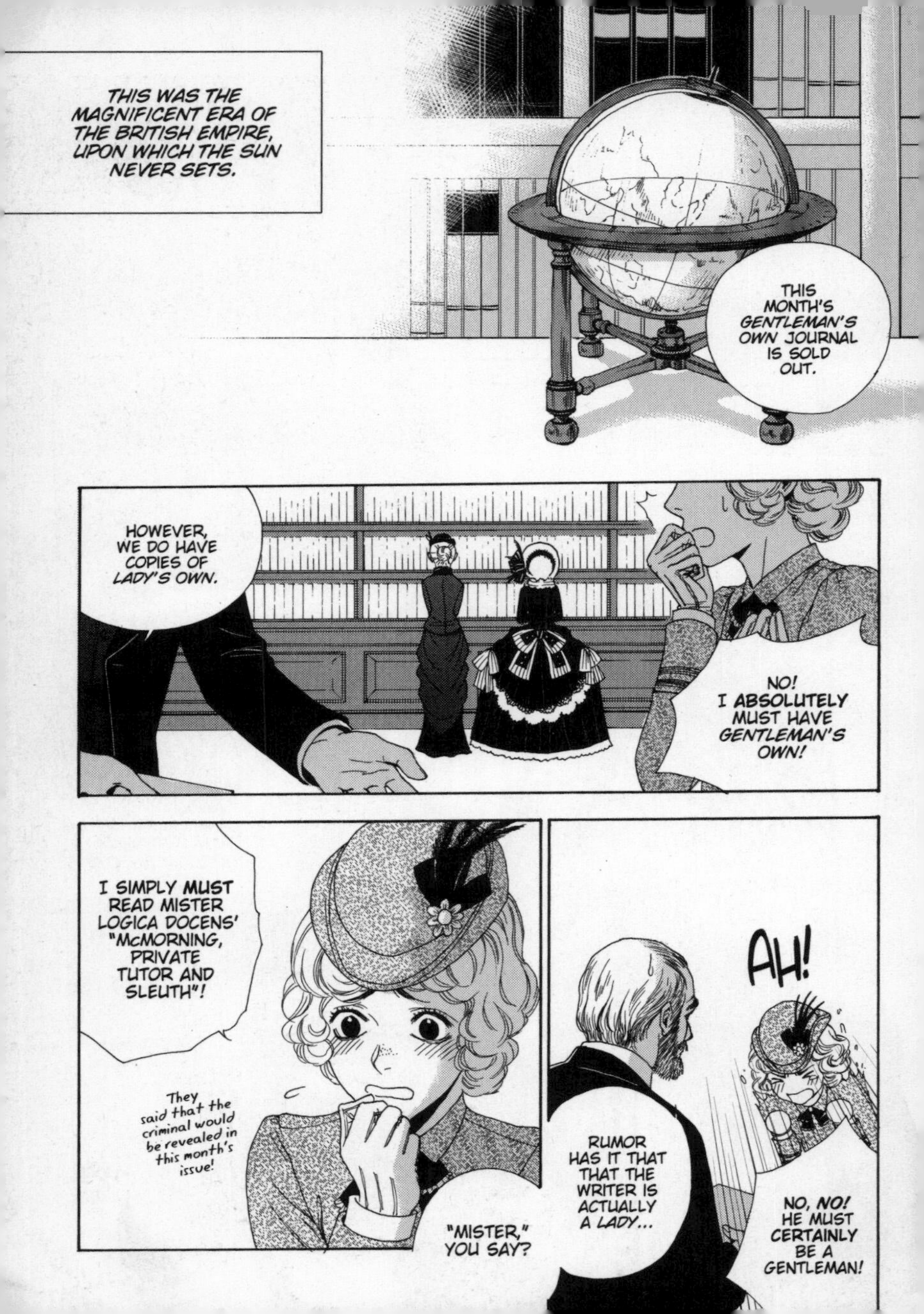
THIS WAS THE MAGNIFICENT ERA OF THE BRITISH EMPIRE, UPON WHICH THE SUN NEVER SETS.
THIS MONTH'S GENTLEMAN'S OWN JOURNAL IS SOLD OUT.
HOWEVER, WE DO HAVE COPIES OF LADY'S OWN.
NO! I ABSOLUTELY MUST HAVE GENTLEMAN'S OWN!
I SIMPLY MUST READ MISTER LOGICA DOCENS' "McMORNING, PRIVATE TUTOR AND SLEUTH"!
They said that the criminal would be revealed in this month's issue!
"MISTER," YOU SAY?
RUMOR HAS IT THAT THAT THE WRITER IS ACTUALLY A LADY...
AH!
NO, NO! HE MUST CERTAINLY BE A GENTLEMAN!

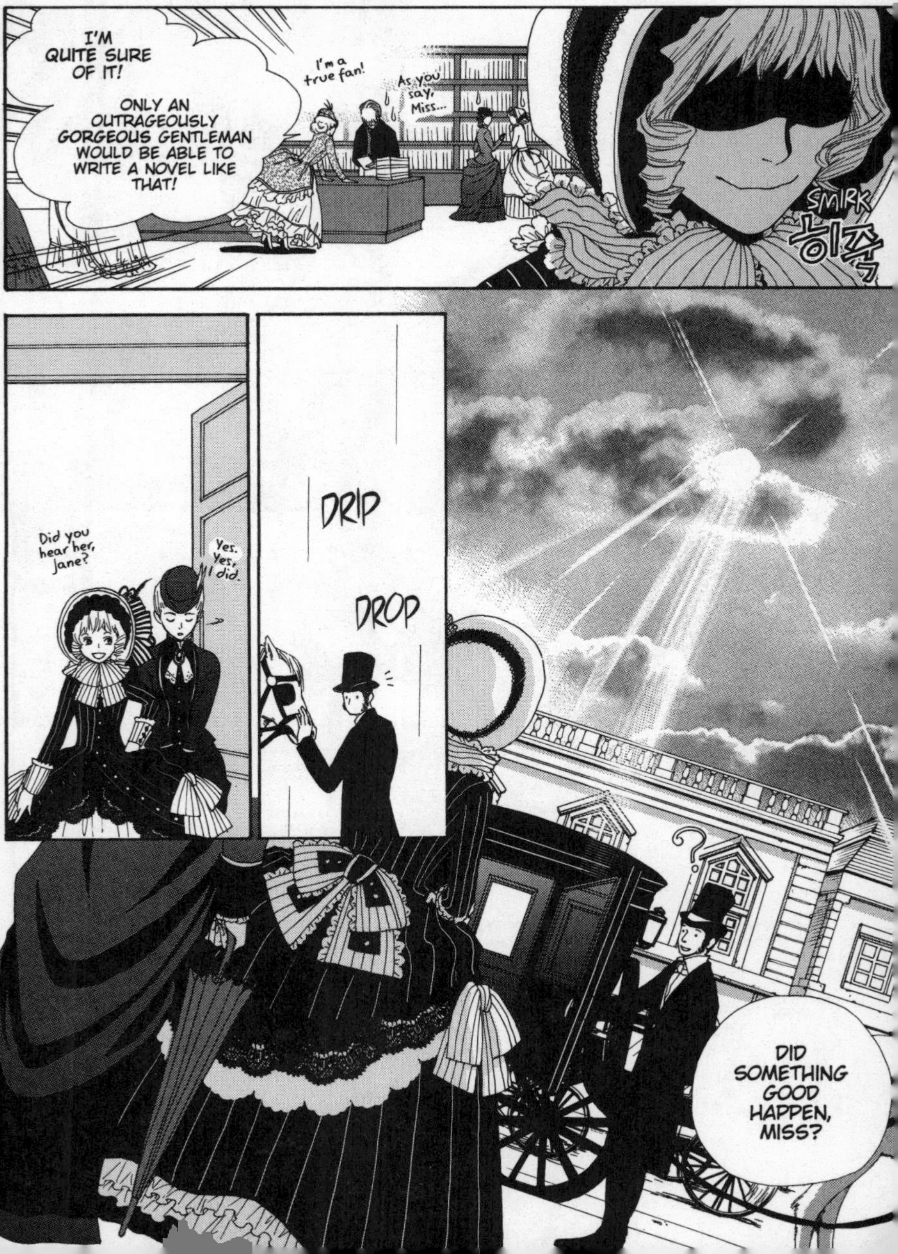
I'M QUITE SURE OF IT! ONLY AN OUTRAGEOUSLY GORGEOUS GENTLEMAN WOULD BE ABLE TO WRITE A NOVEL LIKE THAT!
I'm a true fan!
As you say, Miss...
SMIRK
히죽
Did you hear her, Jane?
Yes. Yes, I did.
DRIP
DROP
DID SOMETHING GOOD HAPPEN, MISS?

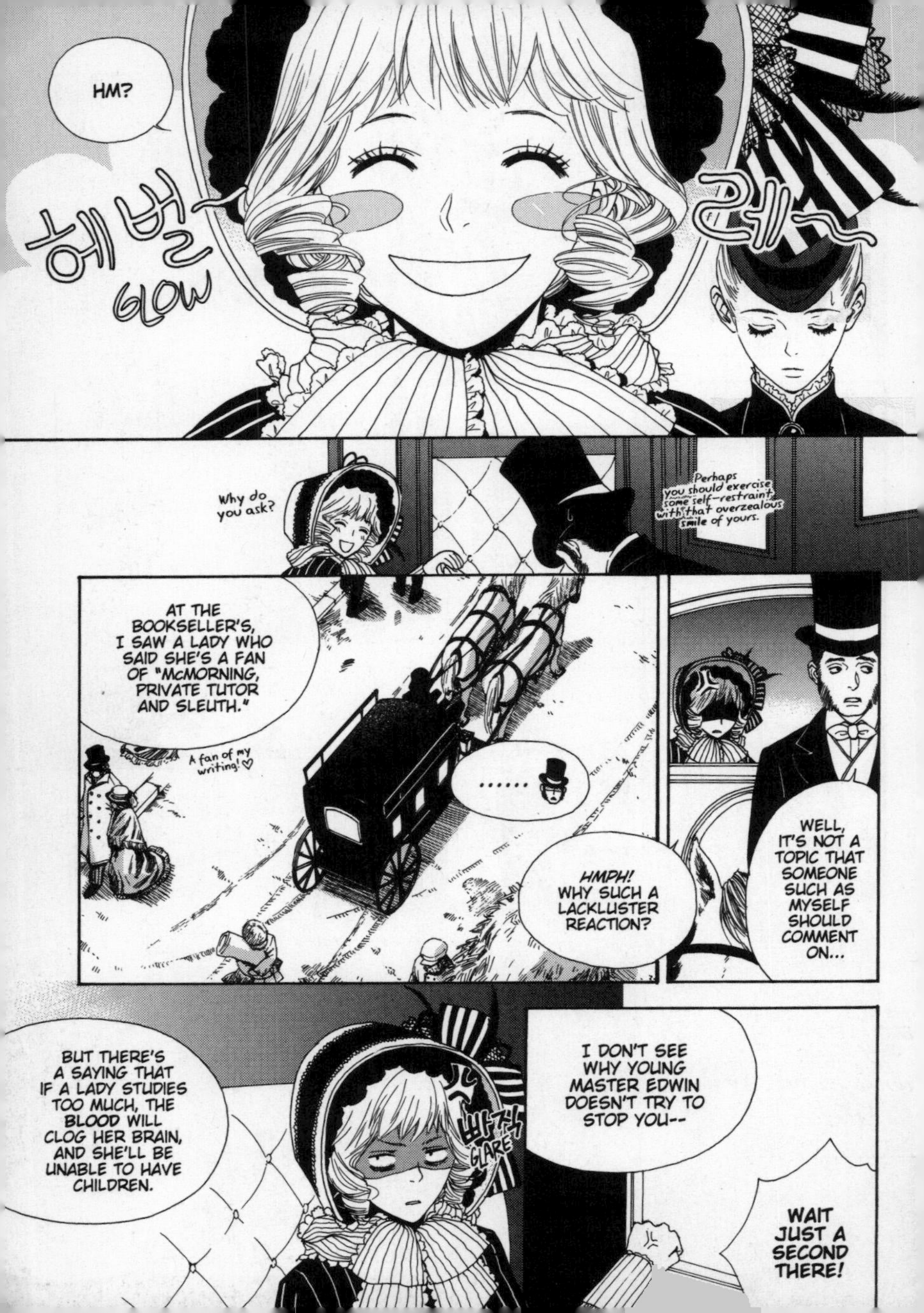
HM?
헤벌~
GLOW
레~~
Why do you ask?
Perhaps you should exercise some self-restraint with that overzealous smile of yours.
AT THE BOOKSELLER'S, I SAW A LADY WHO SAID SHE'S A FAN OF "McMORNING, PRIVATE TUTOR AND SLEUTH."
A fan of my writing! ♡
......
HMPH! WHY SUCH A LACKLUSTER REACTION?
WELL, IT'S NOT A TOPIC THAT SOMEONE SUCH AS MYSELF SHOULD COMMENT ON...
BUT THERE'S A SAYING THAT IF A LADY STUDIES TOO MUCH, THE BLOOD WILL CLOG HER BRAIN, AND SHE'LL BE UNABLE TO HAVE CHILDREN.
빠직
GLARE
I DON'T SEE WHY YOUNG MASTER EDWIN DOESN'T TRY TO STOP YOU--
WAIT JUST A SECOND THERE!

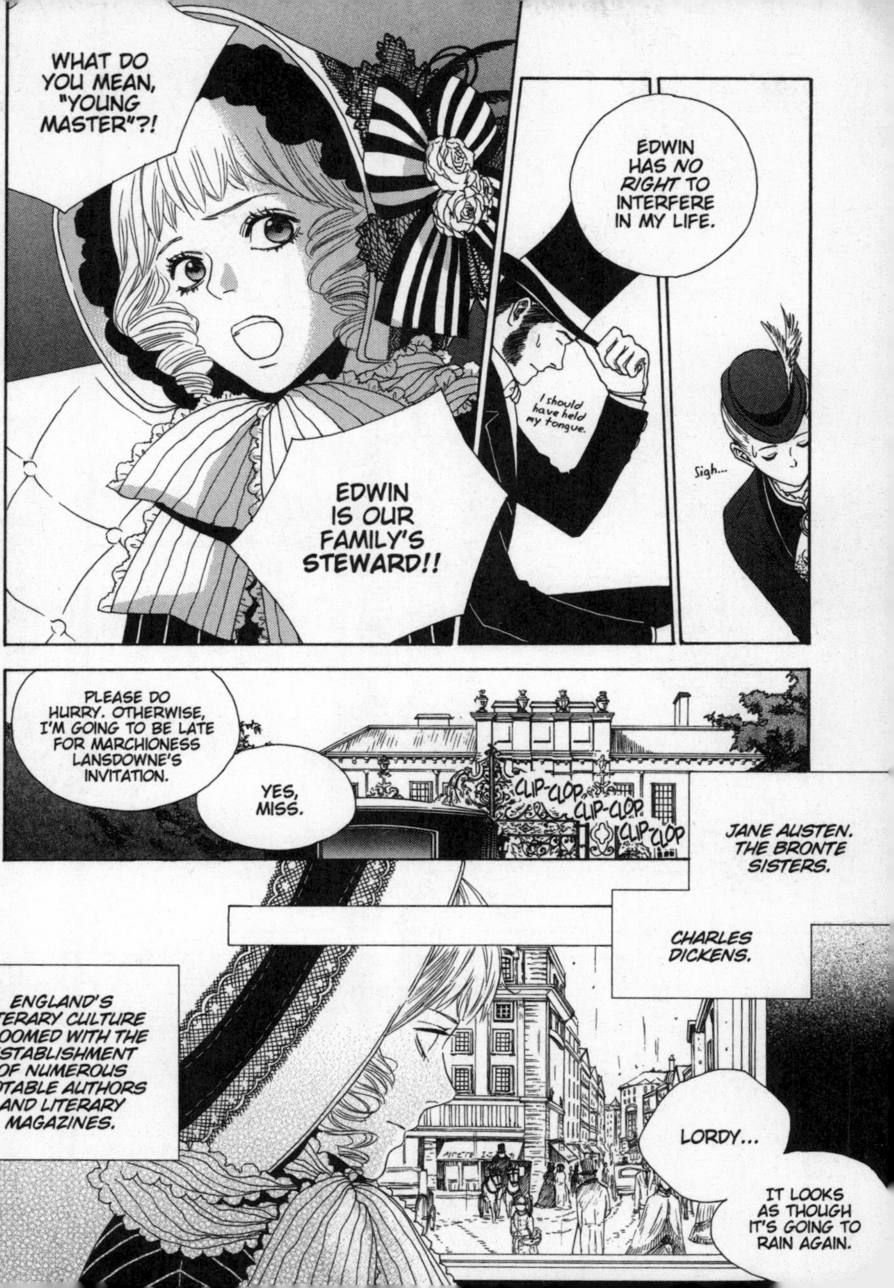
WHAT DO YOU MEAN, "YOUNG MASTER"?!
EDWIN IS OUR FAMILY'S STEWARD!!
EDWIN HAS NO RIGHT TO INTERFERE IN MY LIFE.
I should have held my tongue.
Sigh...
PLEASE DO HURRY. OTHERWISE, I'M GOING TO BE LATE FOR MARCHIONESS LANSDOWNE'S INVITATION.
YES, MISS.
CLIP-CLOP CLIP-CLOP CLIP-CLOP
JANE AUSTEN. THE BRONTE SISTERS.
CHARLES DICKENS.
ENGLAND'S LITERARY CULTURE BLOOMED WITH THE ESTABLISHMENT OF NUMEROUS NOTABLE AUTHORS AND LITERARY MAGAZINES.
LORDY...
IT LOOKS AS THOUGH IT'S GOING TO RAIN AGAIN.

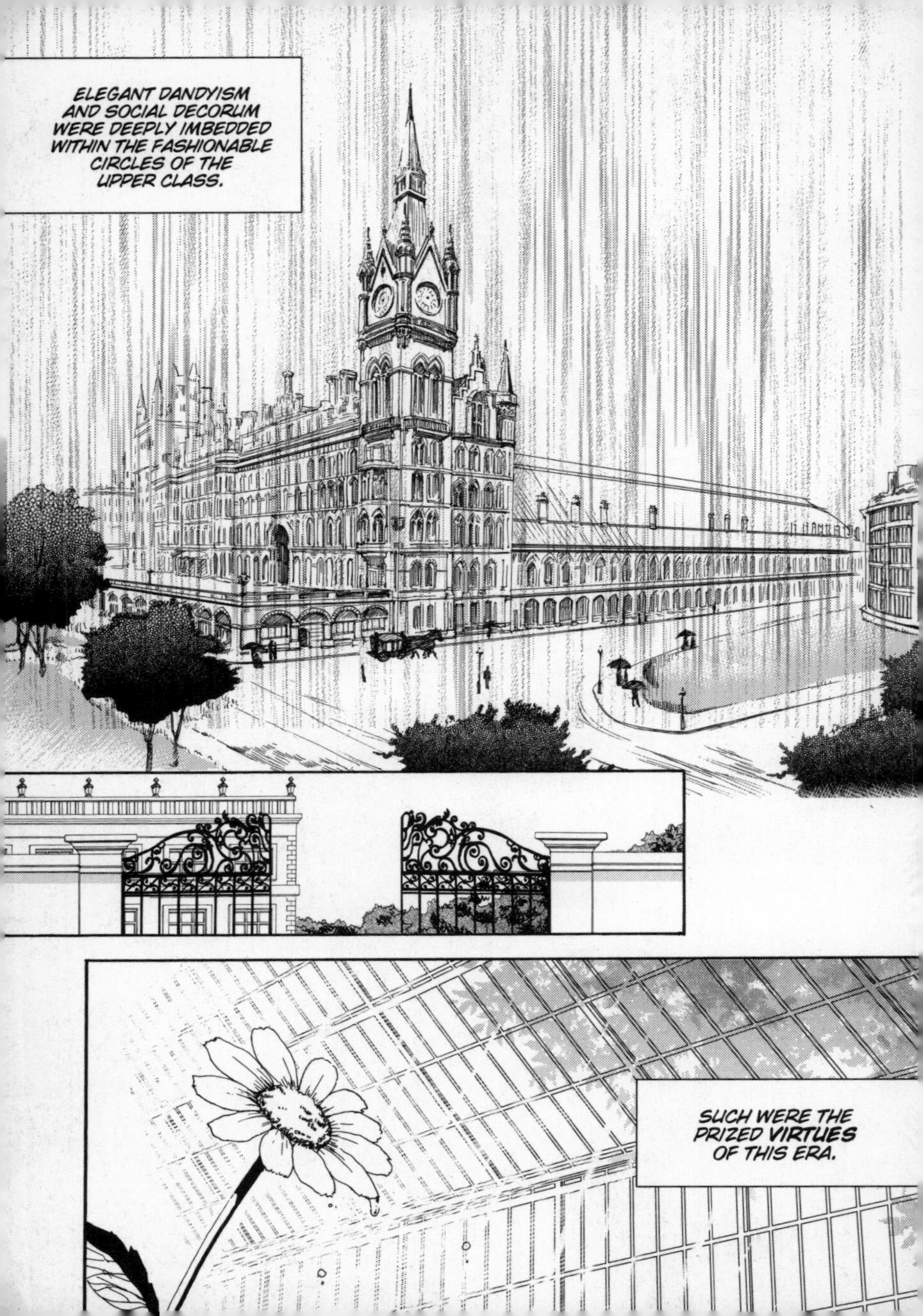
ELEGANT DANDYISM AND SOCIAL DECORUM WERE DEEPLY IMBEDDED WITHIN THE FASHIONABLE CIRCLES OF THE UPPER CLASS.
SUCH WERE THE PRIZED VIRTUES OF THIS ERA.

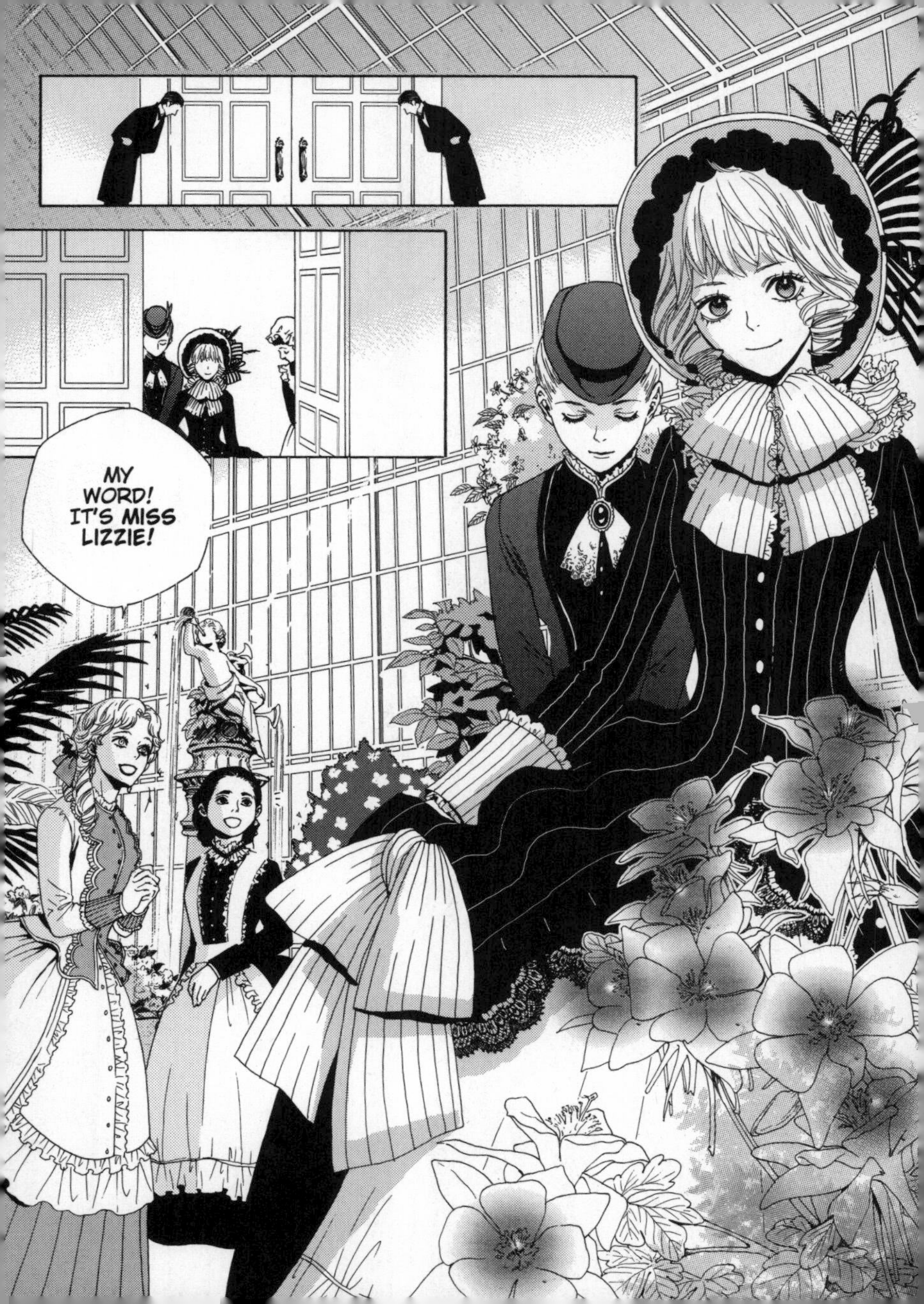
MY WORD! IT'S MISS LIZZIE!

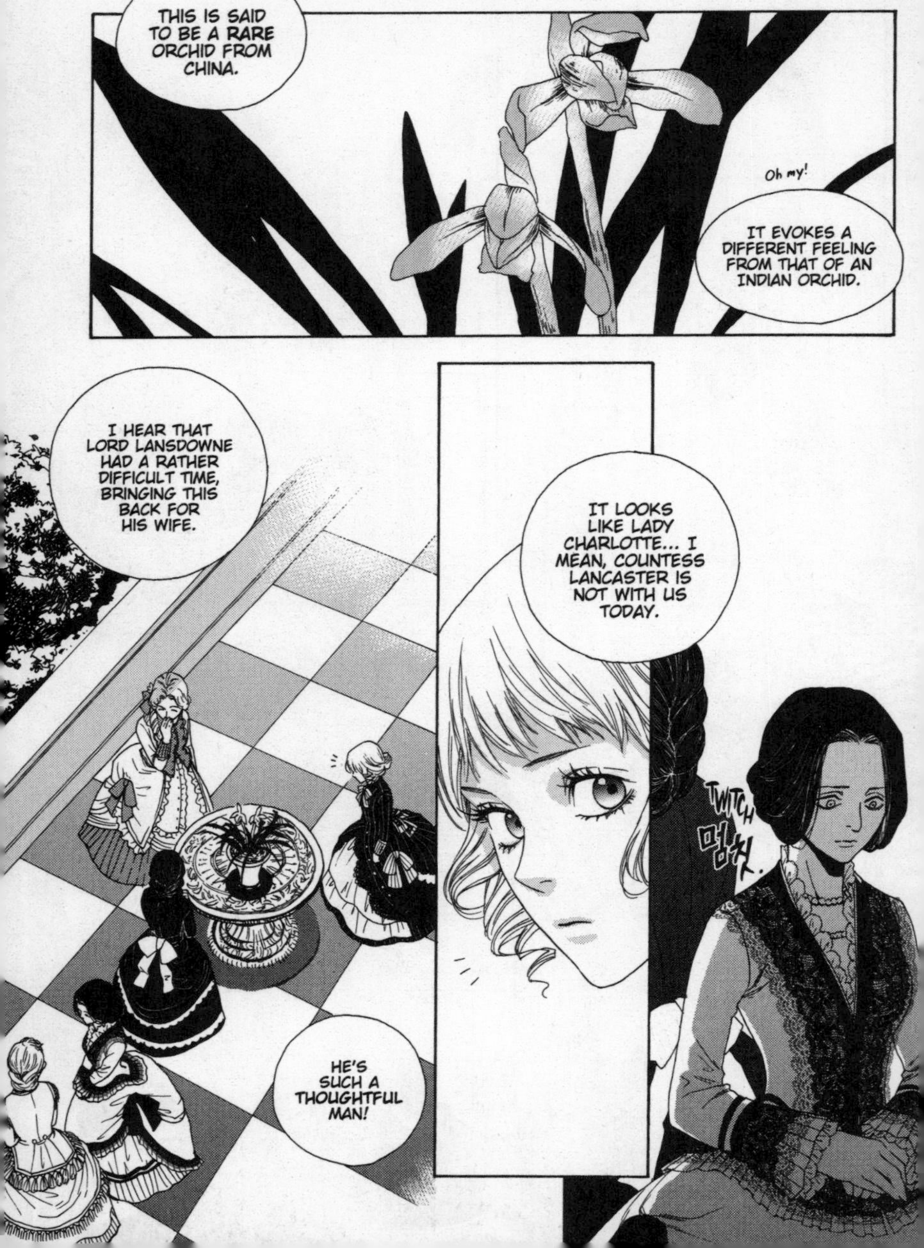
THIS IS SAID TO BE A RARE ORCHID FROM CHINA.
Oh my!
IT EVOKES A DIFFERENT FEELING FROM THAT OF AN INDIAN ORCHID.
I HEAR THAT LORD LANSDOWNE HAD A RATHER DIFFICULT TIME, BRINGING THIS BACK FOR HIS WIFE.
HE'S SUCH A THOUGHTFUL MAN!
IT LOOKS LIKE LADY CHARLOTTE... I MEAN, COUNTESS LANCASTER IS NOT WITH US TODAY.
TWITCH
멈칫.

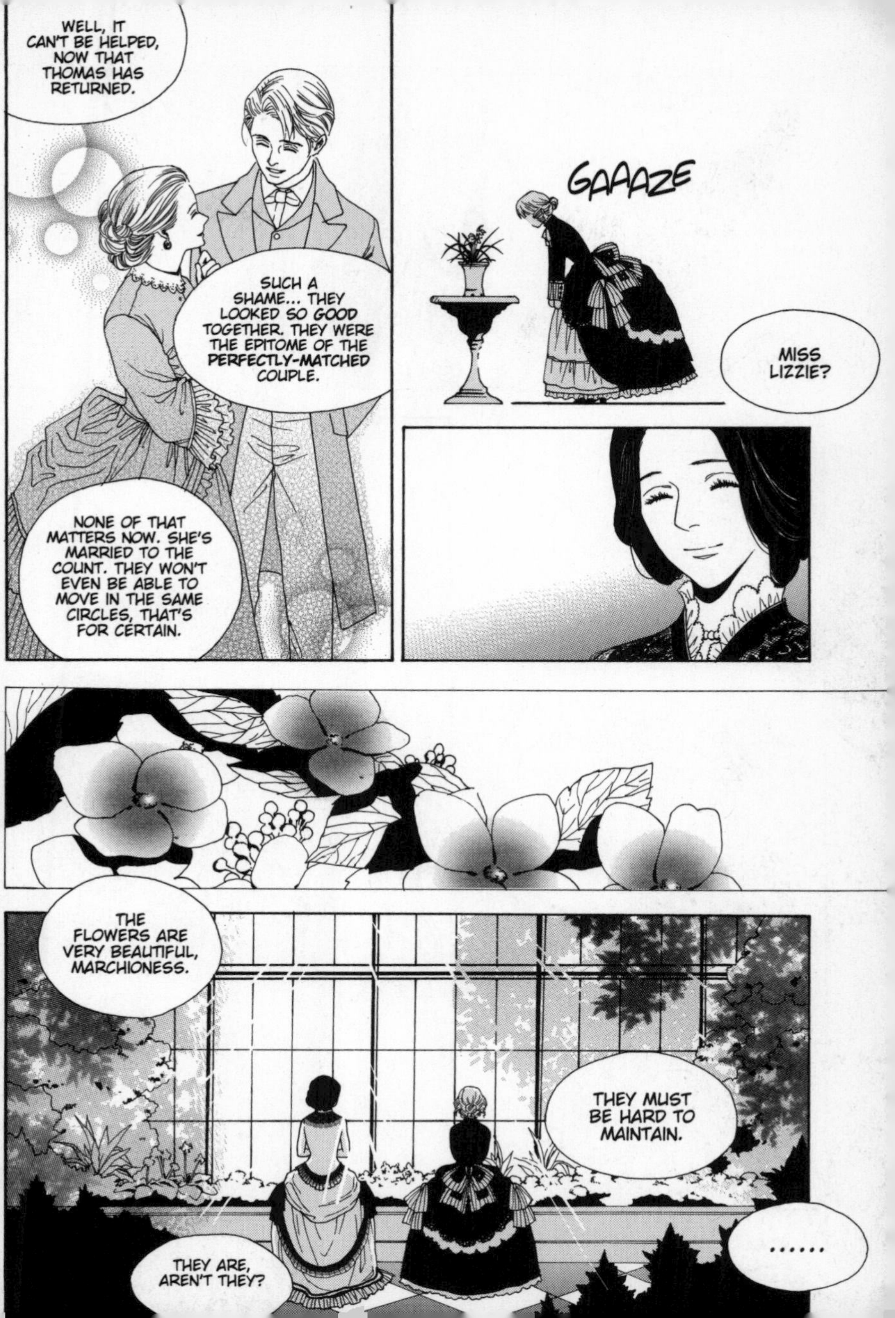
WELL, IT CAN'T BE HELPED, NOW THAT THOMAS HAS RETURNED.
SUCH A SHAME... THEY LOOKED SO GOOD TOGETHER. THEY WERE THE EPITOME OF THE PERFECTLY-MATCHED COUPLE.
NONE OF THAT MATTERS NOW. SHE'S MARRIED TO THE COUNT. THEY WON'T EVEN BE ABLE TO MOVE IN THE SAME CIRCLES, THAT'S FOR CERTAIN.
GAAAZE
MISS LIZZIE?
THE FLOWERS ARE VERY BEAUTIFUL, MARCHIONESS.
THEY MUST BE HARD TO MAINTAIN.
THEY ARE, AREN'T THEY?
......

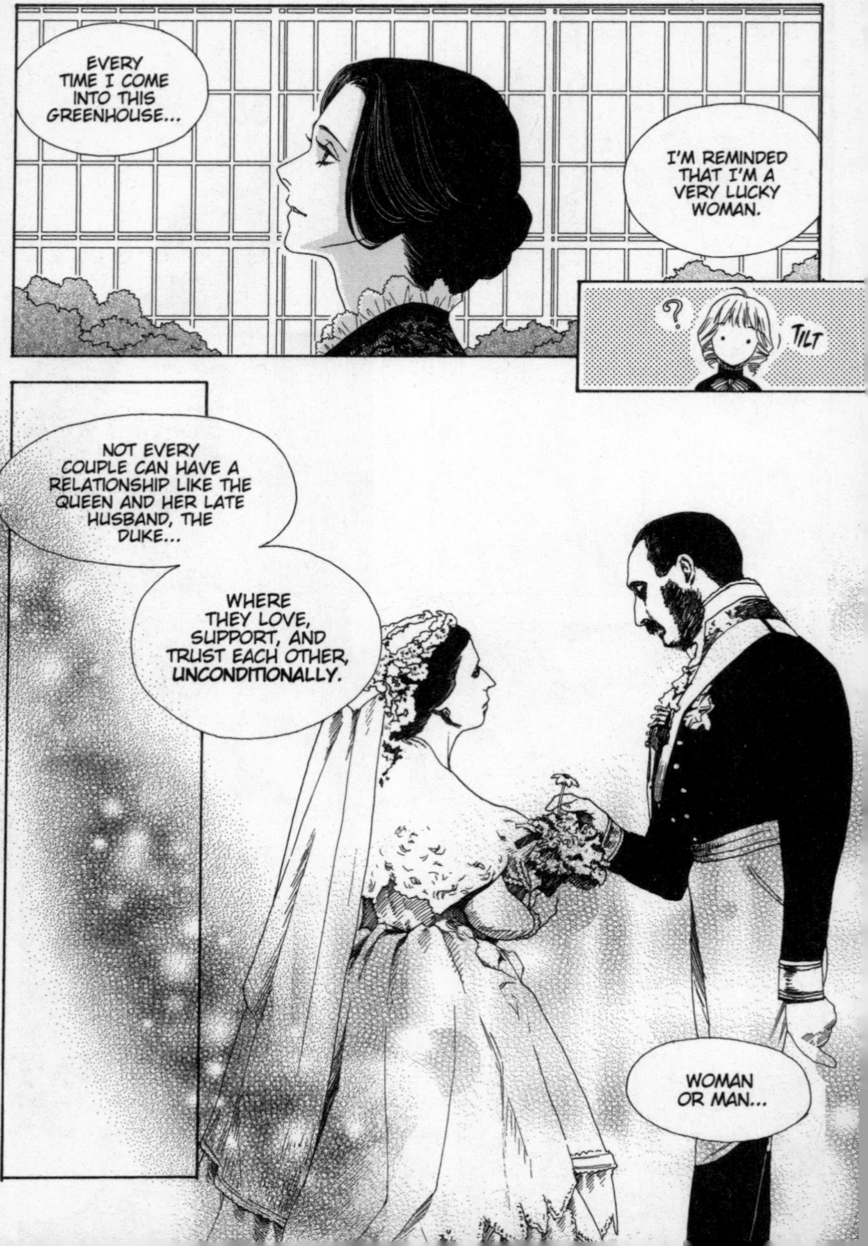
EVERY TIME I COME INTO THIS GREENHOUSE...
I'M REMINDED THAT I'M A VERY LUCKY WOMAN.
?
TILT
NOT EVERY COUPLE CAN HAVE A RELATIONSHIP LIKE THE QUEEN AND HER LATE HUSBAND, THE DUKE...
WHERE THEY LOVE, SUPPORT, AND TRUST EACH OTHER, UNCONDITIONALLY.
WOMAN OR MAN...

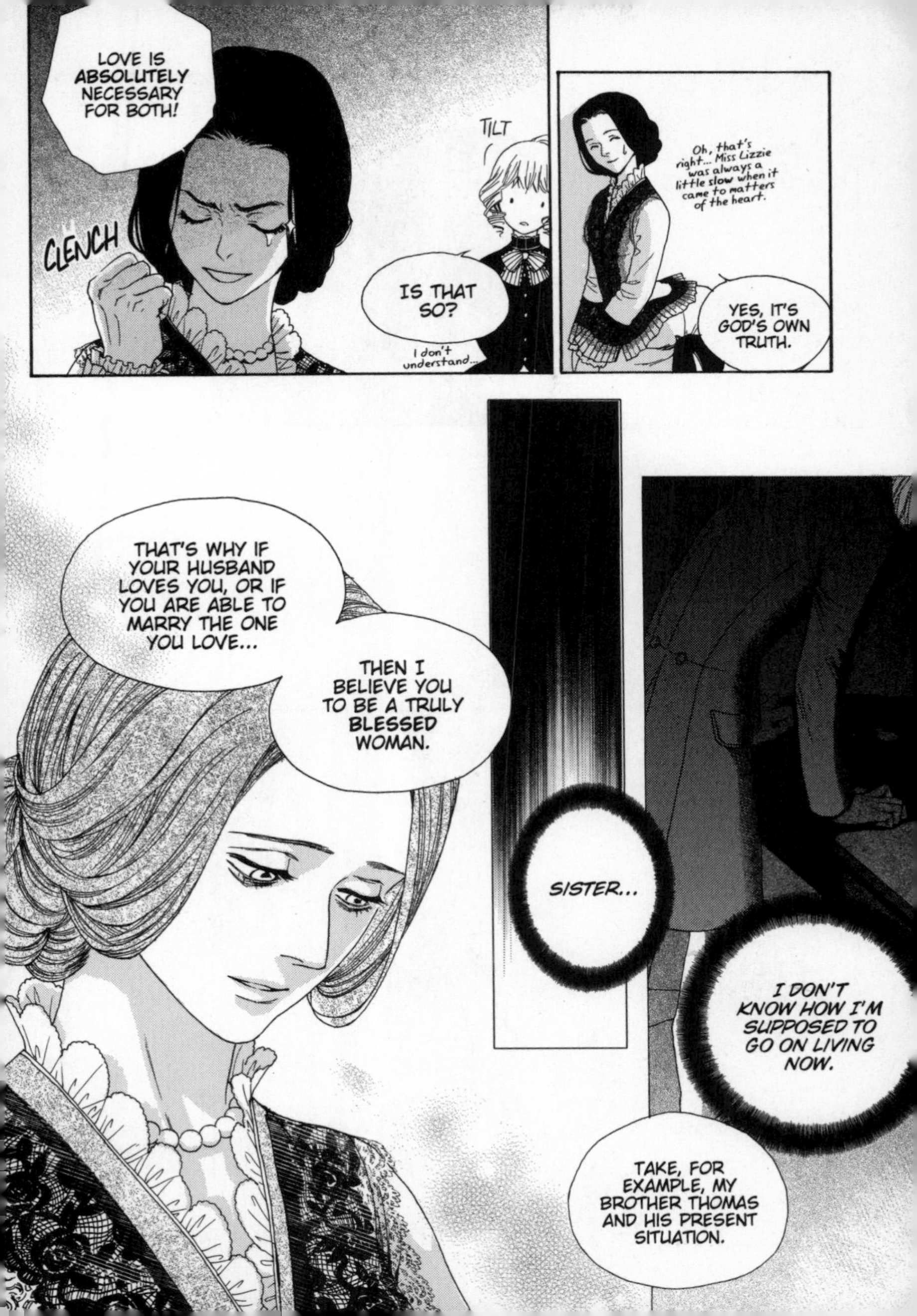
LOVE IS ABSOLUTELY NECESSARY FOR BOTH!
CLENCH
TILT
IS THAT SO?
I don't understand...
Oh, that's right... Miss Lizzie was always a little slow when it came to matters of the heart.
YES, IT'S GOD'S OWN TRUTH.
THAT'S WHY IF YOUR HUSBAND LOVES YOU, OR IF YOU ARE ABLE TO MARRY THE ONE YOU LOVE...
THEN I BELIEVE YOU TO BE A TRULY BLESSED WOMAN.
SISTER...
I DON'T KNOW HOW I'M SUPPOSED TO GO ON LIVING NOW.
TAKE, FOR EXAMPLE, MY BROTHER THOMAS AND HIS PRESENT SITUATION.

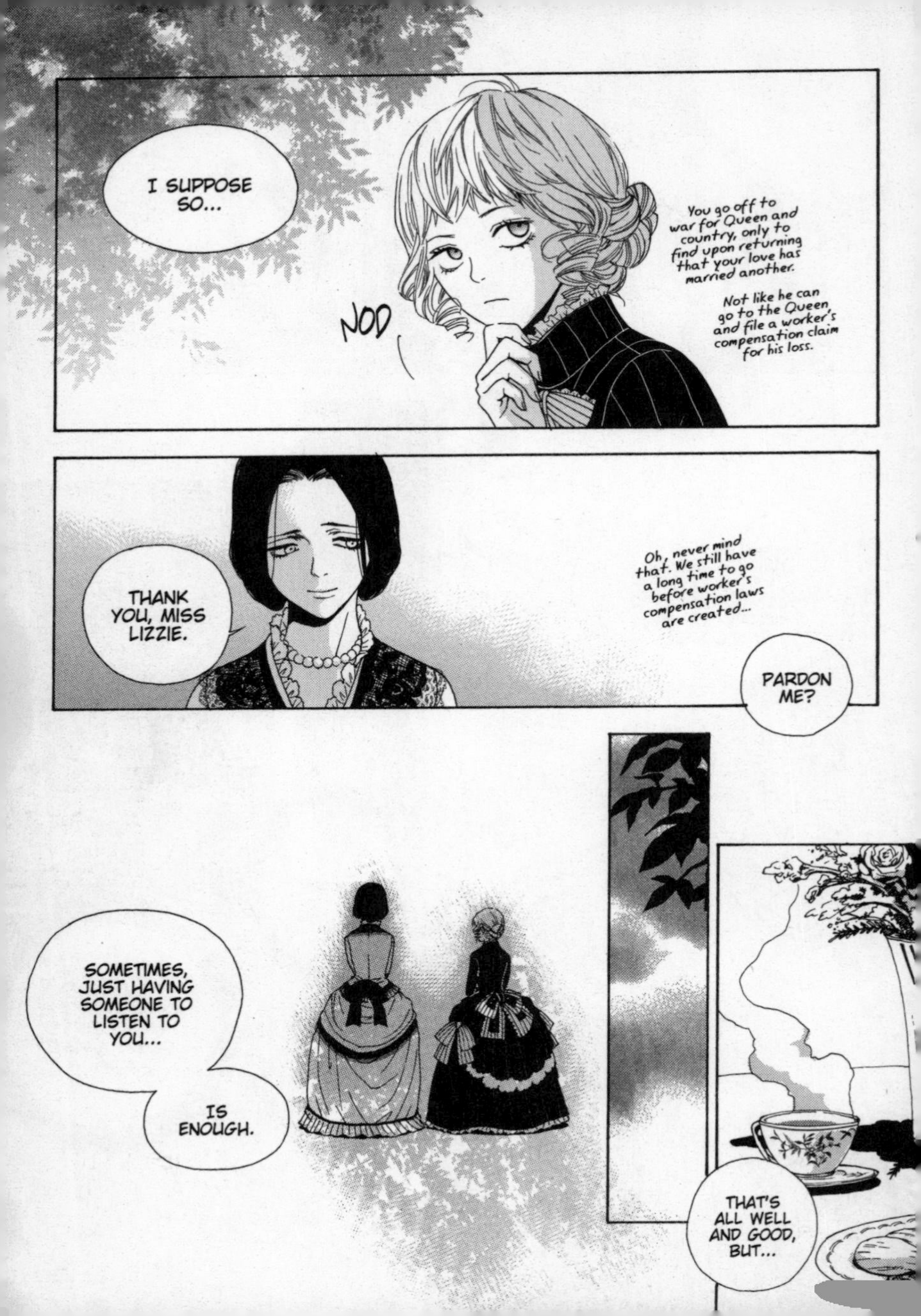
I SUPPOSE SO...
NOD
You go off to war for Queen and country, only to find upon returning that your love has married another.
Not like he can go to the Queen and file a worker's compensation claim for his loss.
THANK YOU, MISS LIZZIE.
Oh, never mind that. We still have a long time to go before worker's compensation laws are created...
PARDON ME?
SOMETIMES, JUST HAVING SOMEONE TO LISTEN TO YOU...
IS ENOUGH.
THAT'S ALL WELL AND GOOD, BUT...

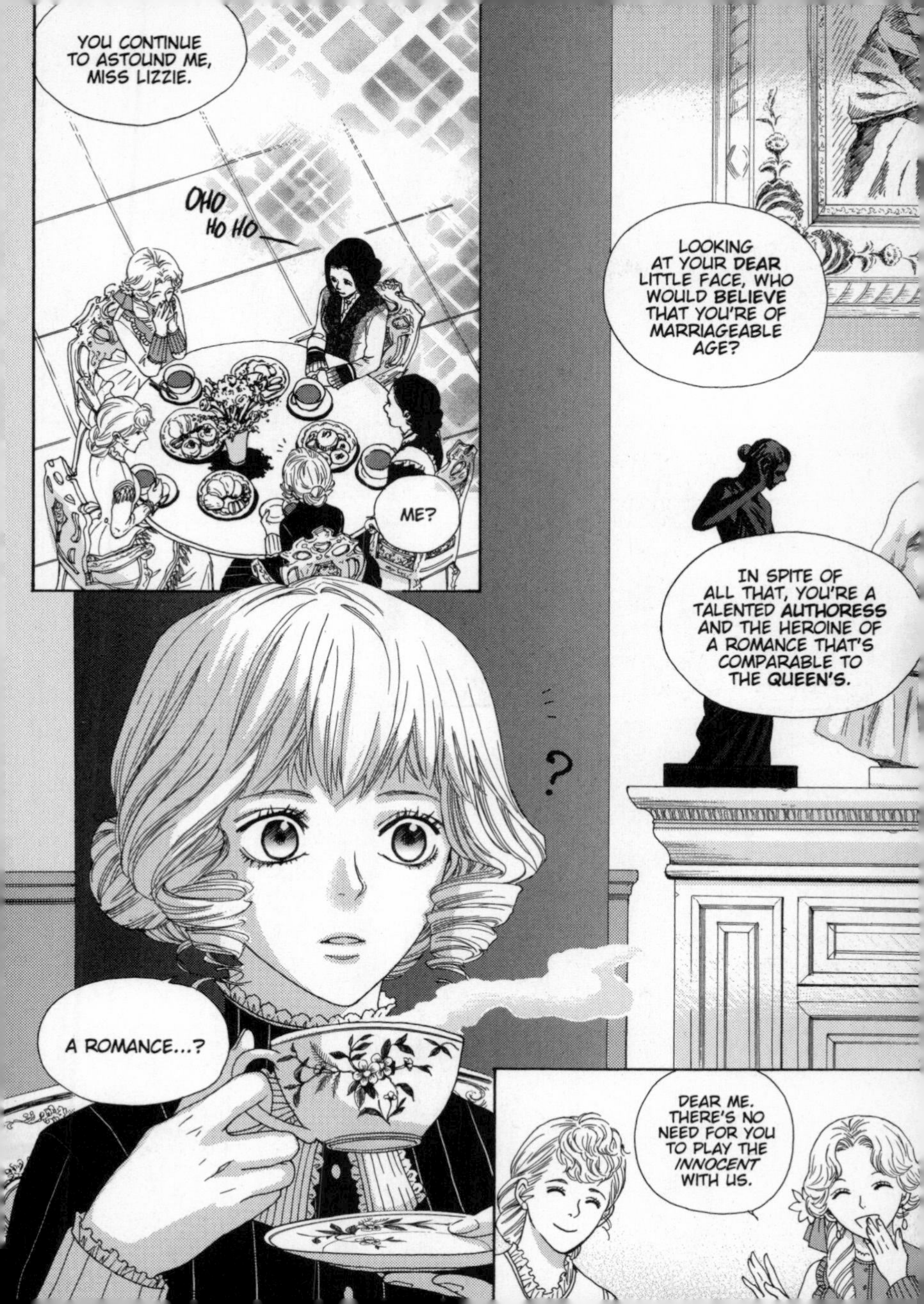
YOU CONTINUE TO ASTOUND ME, MISS LIZZIE.
OHO HO HO
ME?
LOOKING AT YOUR DEAR LITTLE FACE, WHO WOULD BELIEVE THAT YOU'RE OF MARRIAGEABLE AGE?
IN SPITE OF ALL THAT, YOU'RE A TALENTED AUTHORESS AND THE HEROINE OF A ROMANCE THAT'S COMPARABLE TO THE QUEEN'S.
?
A ROMANCE...?
DEAR ME. THERE'S NO NEED FOR YOU TO PLAY THE *INNOCENT* WITH US.

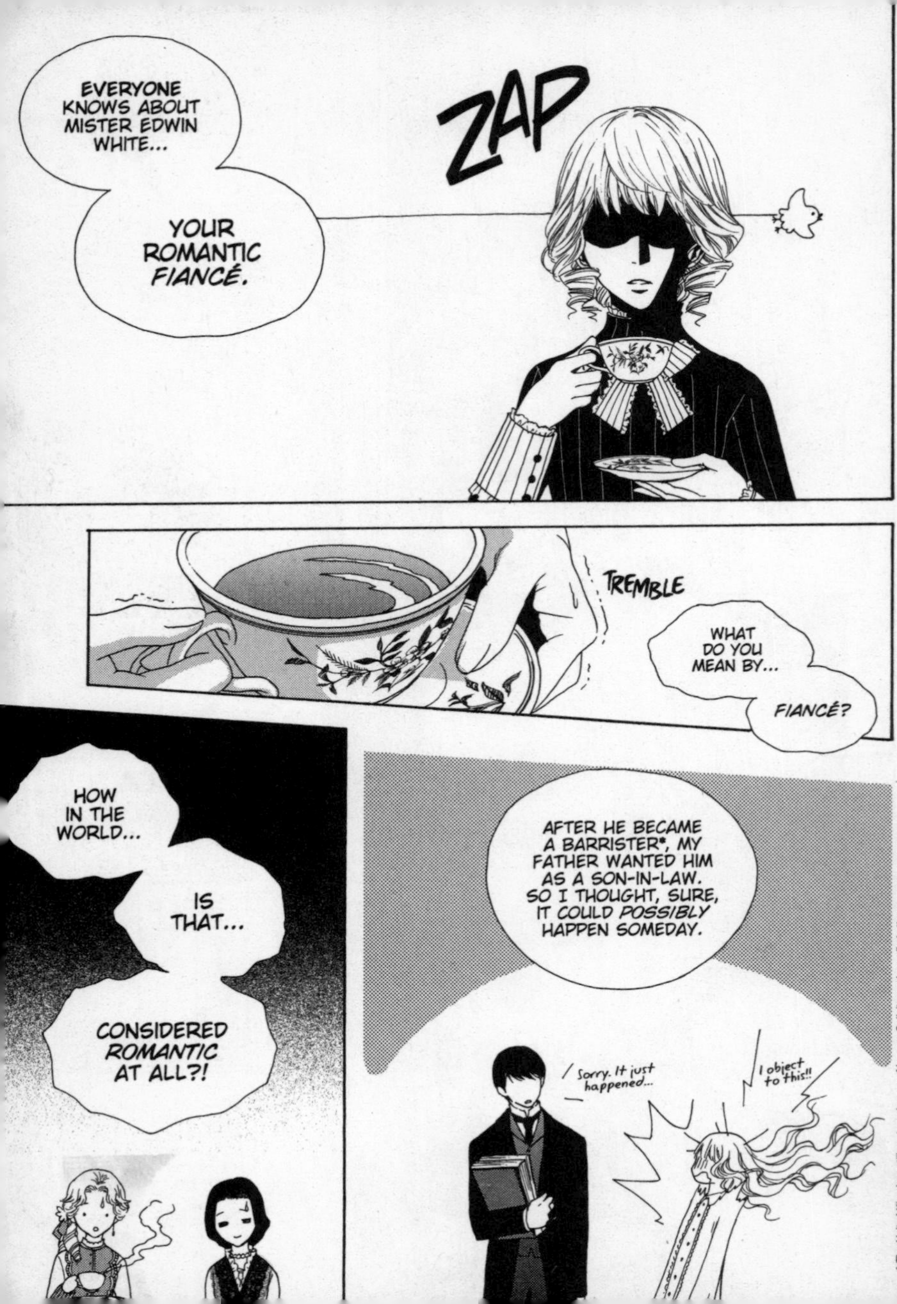
EVERYONE KNOWS ABOUT MISTER EDWIN WHITE...
YOUR ROMANTIC *FIANCÉ*.
ZAP
TREMBLE
WHAT DO YOU MEAN BY...
FIANCÉ?
HOW IN THE WORLD...
IS THAT...
CONSIDERED *ROMANTIC* AT ALL?!
AFTER HE BECAME A BARRISTER*, MY FATHER WANTED HIM AS A SON-IN-LAW. SO I THOUGHT, SURE, IT COULD *POSSIBLY* HAPPEN SOMEDAY.
Sorry. It just happened...
I object to this!!

* *The United Kingdom utilizes two classes of lawyer. Solicitors, also called attorneys, prepare cases by working directly with the client to take statements and affidavits. Barristers, thought of as "the gentlemen*

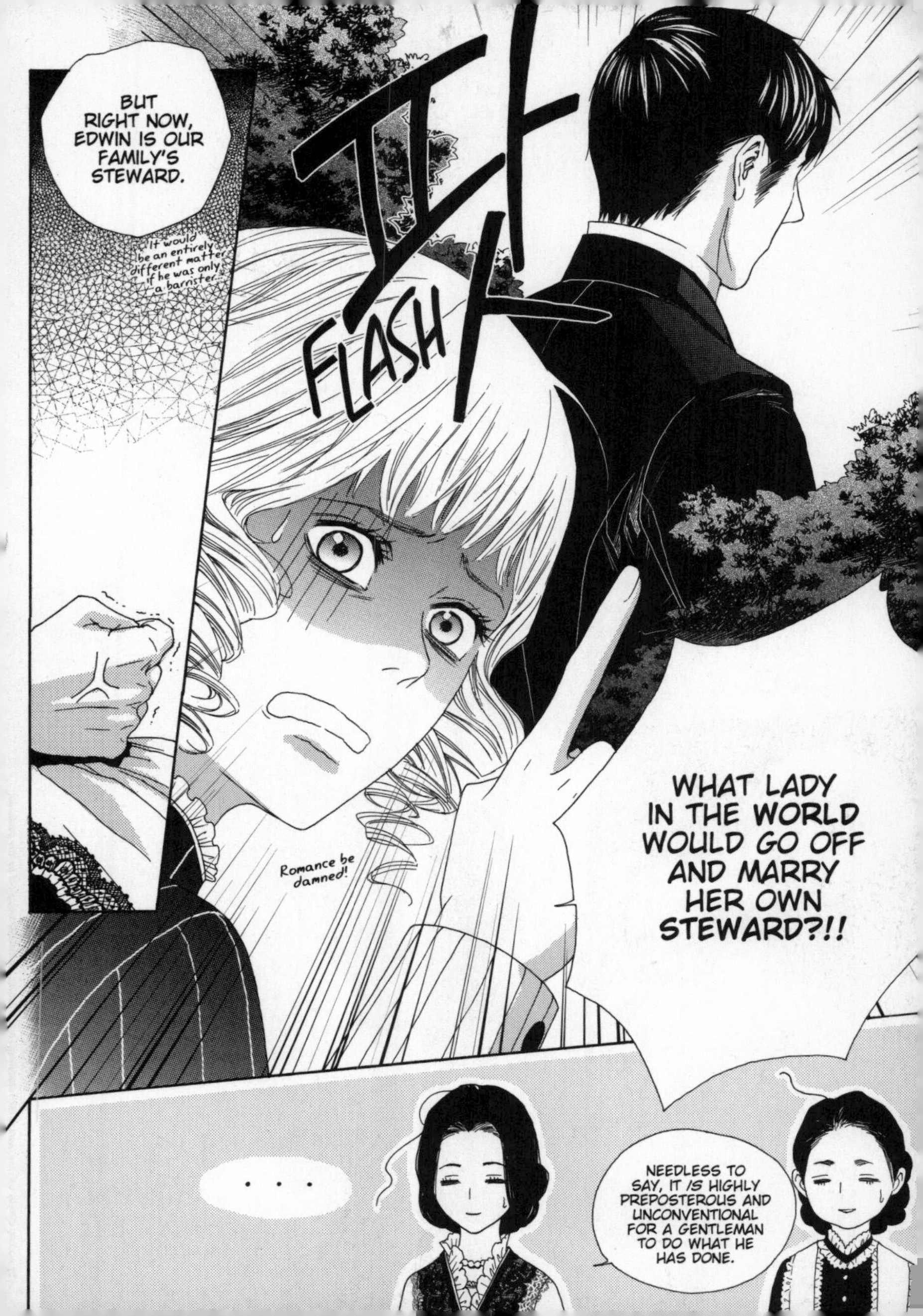
BUT RIGHT NOW, EDWIN IS OUR FAMILY'S STEWARD.
It would be an entirely different matter if he was only a barrister...
FLASH
Romance be damned!
WHAT LADY IN THE WORLD WOULD GO OFF AND MARRY HER OWN STEWARD?!!
. . .
NEEDLESS TO SAY, IT IS HIGHLY PREPOSTEROUS AND UNCONVENTIONAL FOR A GENTLEMAN TO DO WHAT HE HAS DONE.

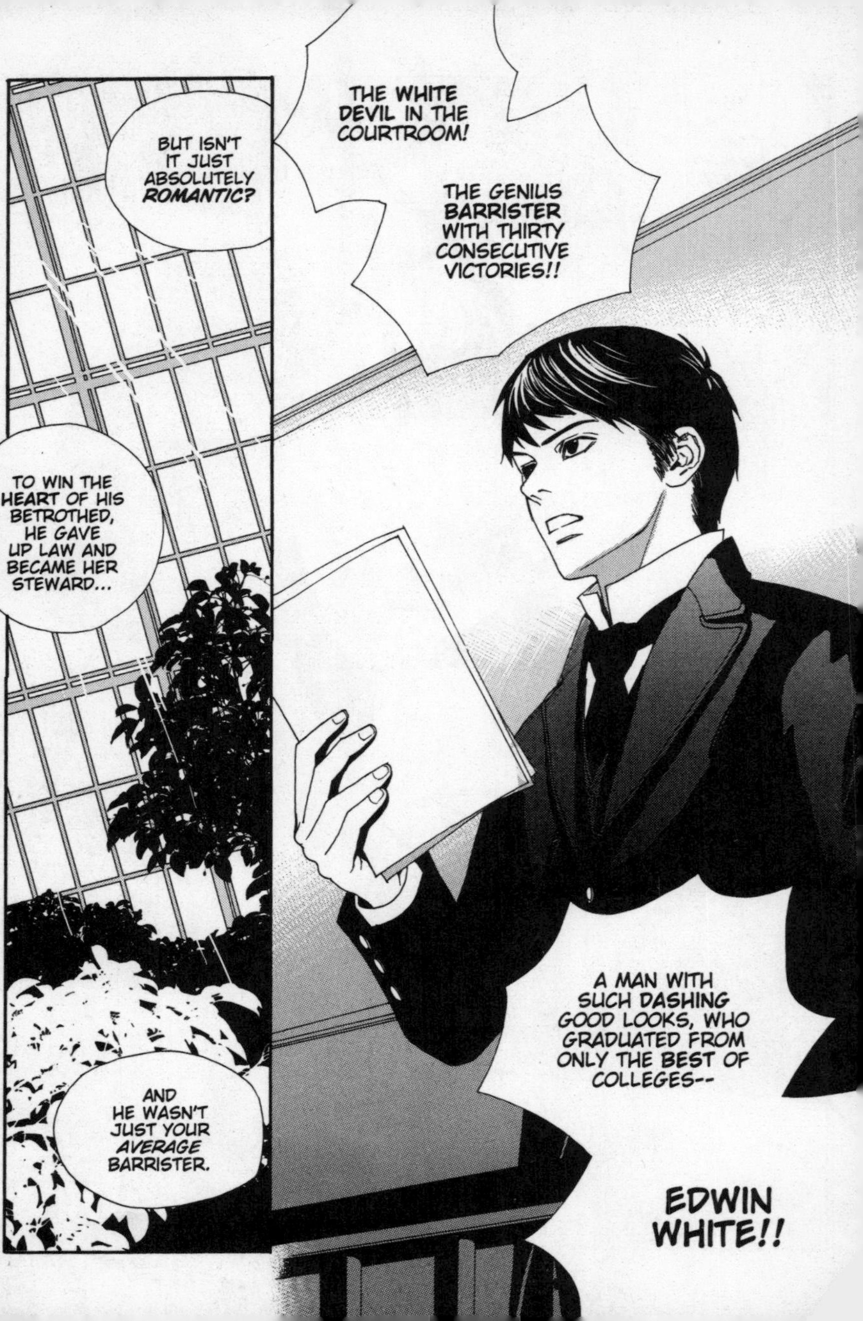
BUT ISN'T IT JUST ABSOLUTELY *ROMANTIC*?
TO WIN THE HEART OF HIS BETROTHED, HE GAVE UP LAW AND BECAME HER STEWARD...
AND HE WASN'T JUST YOUR *AVERAGE* BARRISTER.
THE WHITE DEVIL IN THE COURTROOM!
THE GENIUS BARRISTER WITH THIRTY CONSECUTIVE VICTORIES!!
A MAN WITH SUCH DASHING GOOD LOOKS, WHO GRADUATED FROM ONLY THE BEST OF COLLEGES--
EDWIN WHITE!!

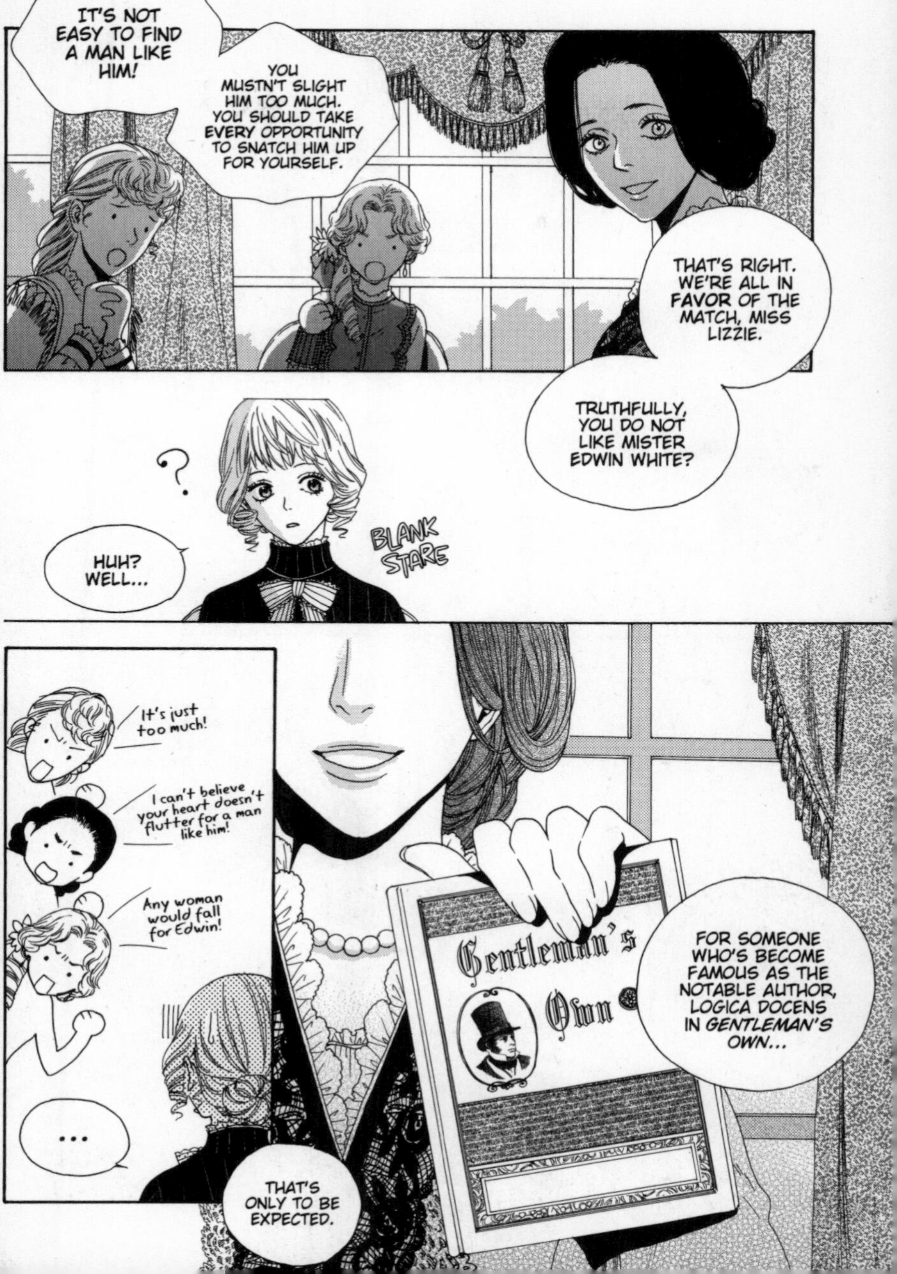
IT'S NOT EASY TO FIND A MAN LIKE HIM!
YOU MUSTN'T SLIGHT HIM TOO MUCH. YOU SHOULD TAKE EVERY OPPORTUNITY TO SNATCH HIM UP FOR YOURSELF.
THAT'S RIGHT. WE'RE ALL IN FAVOR OF THE MATCH, MISS LIZZIE.
TRUTHFULLY, YOU DO NOT LIKE MISTER EDWIN WHITE?
?
HUH? WELL...
BLANK STARE
It's just too much!
I can't believe your heart doesn't flutter for a man like him!
Any woman would fall for Edwin!
...
Gentleman's Own
FOR SOMEONE WHO'S BECOME FAMOUS AS THE NOTABLE AUTHOR, LOGICA DOCENS IN GENTLEMAN'S OWN...
THAT'S ONLY TO BE EXPECTED.

IT'S NOT UNREASONABLE FOR YOU TO HAVE SOME PRIDE IN YOURSELF.

May I see that for a moment, Marchioness?

Oh, yes, of course.

They were out of stock all over the city.

Gentleman's Oku

* Matthew Arnold (1822-1888): English poet and cultural critic. Professor at the University of Oxford.

HAVE YOU SEEN THE LITERARY REVIEW OF THIS ISSUE?

NO, NOT YET.

THE FAMOUS CRITIC, PROFESSOR ARNOLD* OF OXFORD UNIVERSITY WROTE A VERY FAVORABLE REVIEW OF "McMORNING, PRIVATE TUTOR AND SLEUTH."

HE ALSO WROTE THAT LOGICA DOCENS HAS TRUE TALENT AS A WRITER.

OH MY...

MISS LIZZIE, YOU REALLY ARE AMAZING.

타
BANG

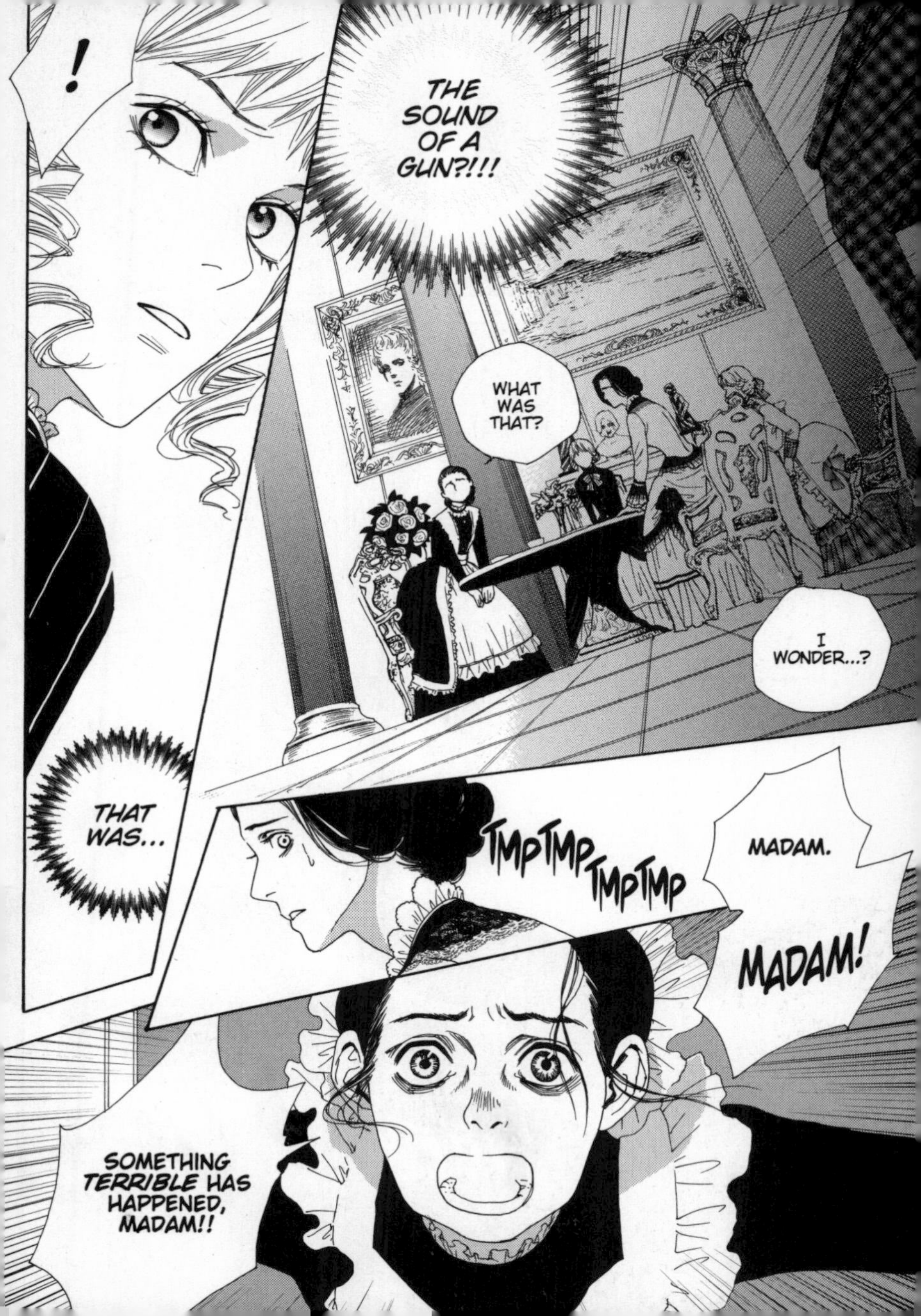
!
THE SOUND OF A GUN?!!!
WHAT WAS THAT?
I WONDER...?
THAT WAS...
TMPTMP TMPTMP
MADAM.
MADAM!
SOMETHING *TERRIBLE* HAS HAPPENED, MADAM!!

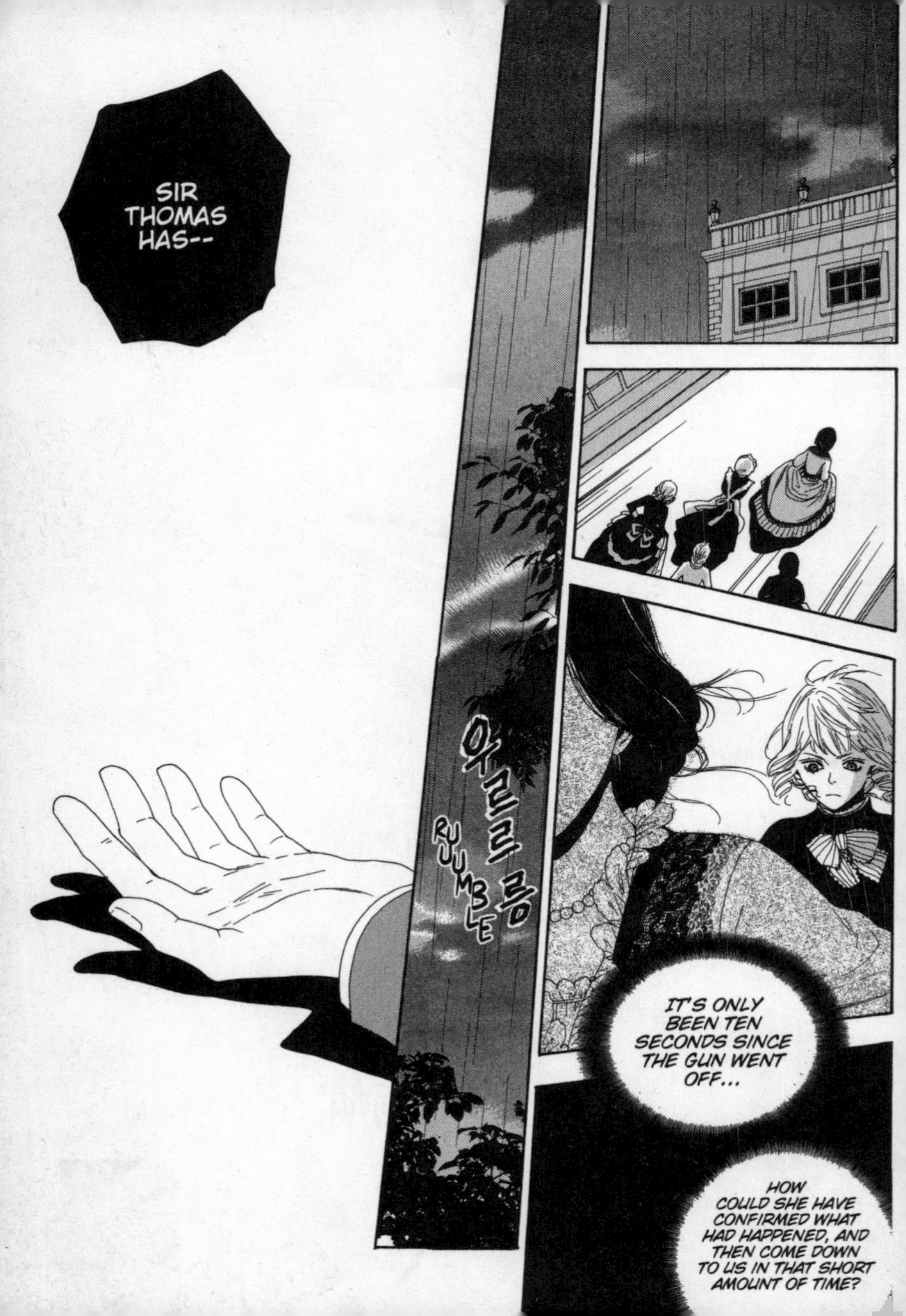
SIR THOMAS HAS--
우르르 릉
RUUMBLE
IT'S ONLY BEEN TEN SECONDS SINCE THE GUN WENT OFF...
HOW COULD SHE HAVE CONFIRMED WHAT HAD HAPPENED, AND THEN COME DOWN TO US IN THAT SHORT AMOUNT OF TIME?

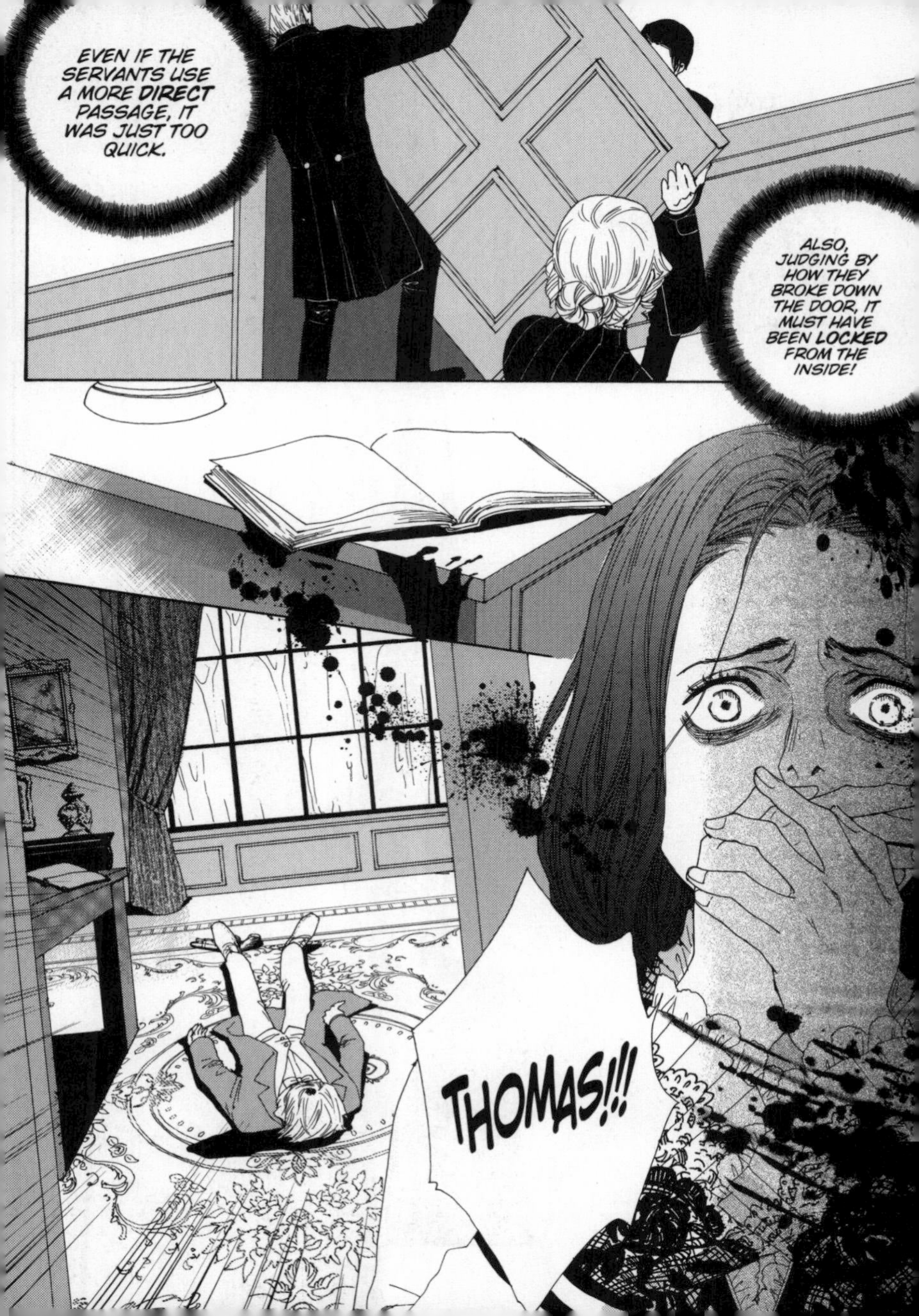
EVEN IF THE SERVANTS USE A MORE DIRECT PASSAGE, IT WAS JUST TOO QUICK.
ALSO, JUDGING BY HOW THEY BROKE DOWN THE DOOR, IT MUST HAVE BEEN LOCKED FROM THE INSIDE!
THOMAS!!!

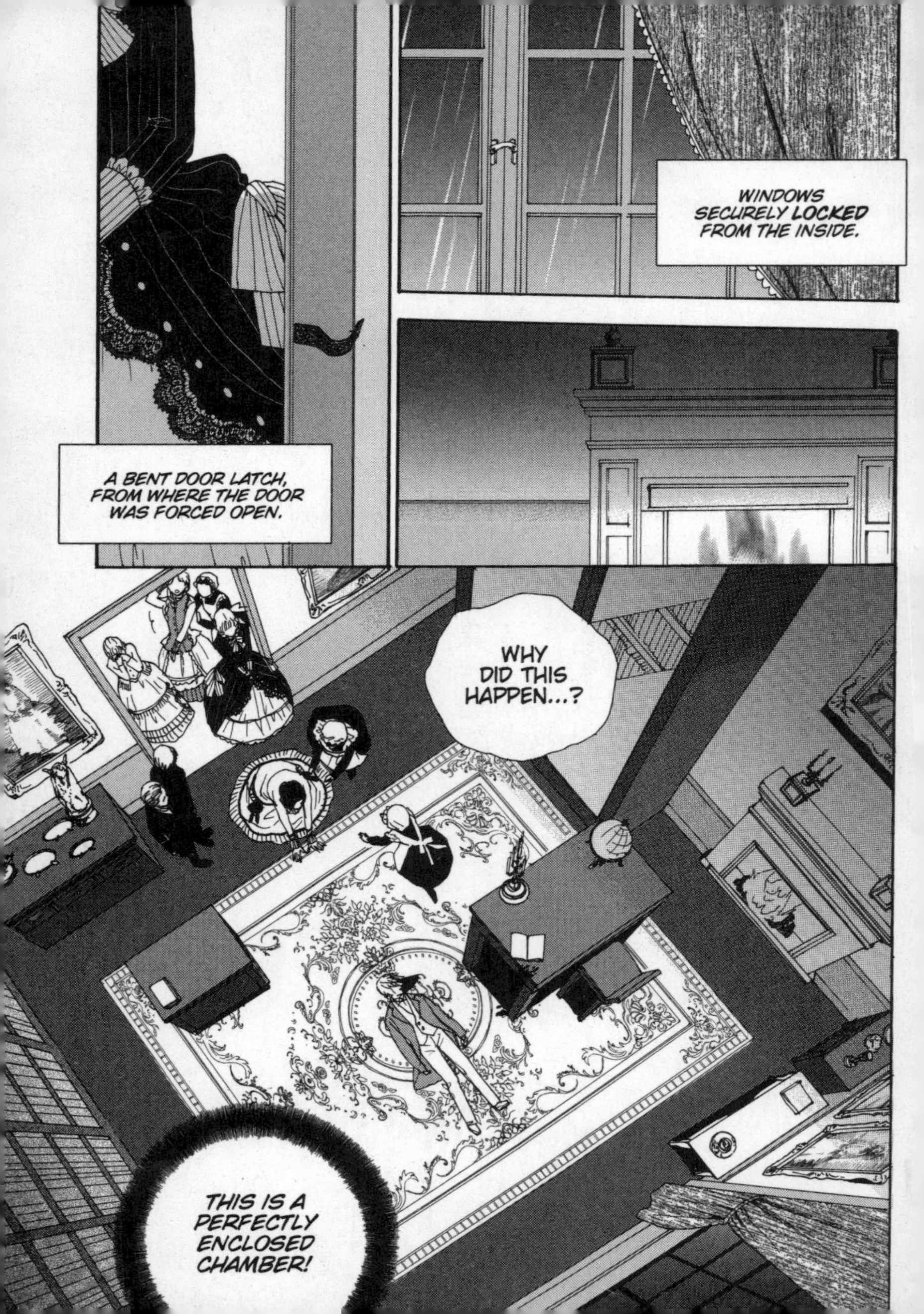

WINDOWS SECURELY LOCKED FROM THE INSIDE.
A BENT DOOR LATCH, FROM WHERE THE DOOR WAS FORCED OPEN.
WHY DID THIS HAPPEN...?
THIS IS A PERFECTLY ENCLOSED CHAMBER!

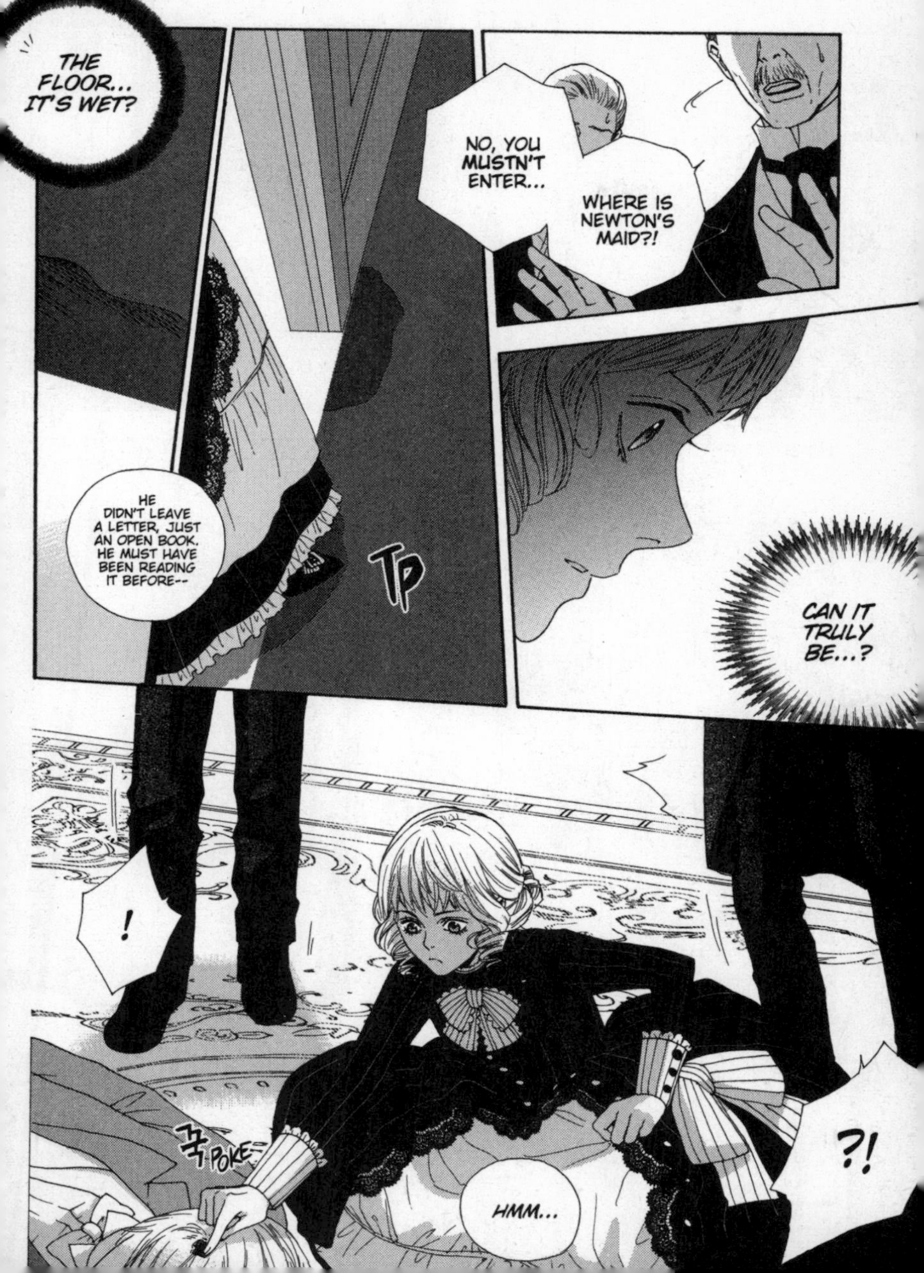
THE FLOOR... IT'S WET?
HE DIDN'T LEAVE A LETTER, JUST AN OPEN BOOK. HE MUST HAVE BEEN READING IT BEFORE--
TP
NO, YOU MUSTN'T ENTER...
WHERE IS NEWTON'S MAID?!
CAN IT TRULY BE...?
!
POKE
HMM...
?!

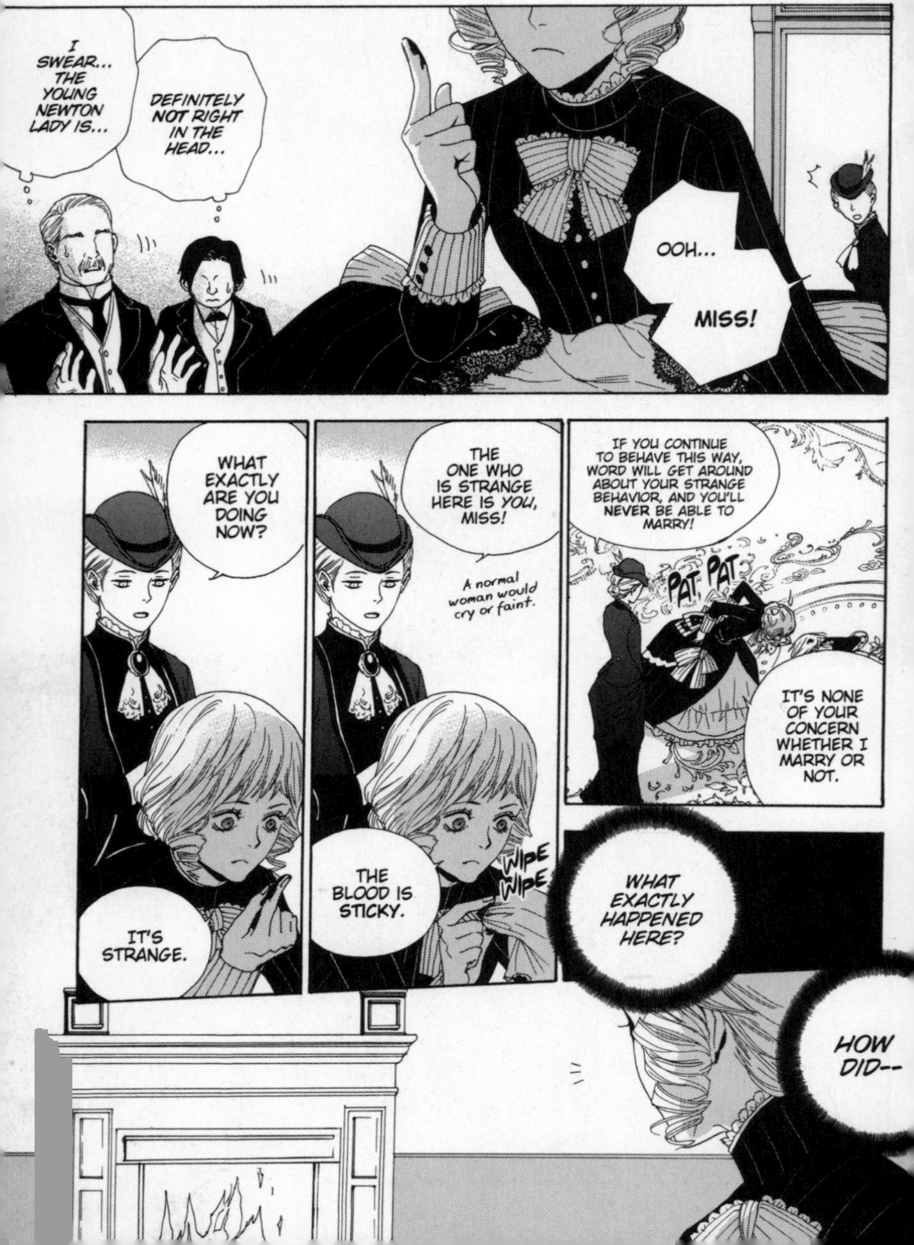
I SWEAR... THE YOUNG NEWTON LADY IS...
DEFINITELY NOT RIGHT IN THE HEAD...
OOH...
MISS!
WHAT EXACTLY ARE YOU DOING NOW?
IT'S STRANGE.
THE ONE WHO IS STRANGE HERE IS YOU, MISS!
A normal woman would cry or faint.
WIPE WIPE
THE BLOOD IS STICKY.
IF YOU CONTINUE TO BEHAVE THIS WAY, WORD WILL GET AROUND ABOUT YOUR STRANGE BEHAVIOR, AND YOU'LL NEVER BE ABLE TO MARRY!
PAT PAT
IT'S NONE OF YOUR CONCERN WHETHER I MARRY OR NOT.
WHAT EXACTLY HAPPENED HERE?
HOW DID--

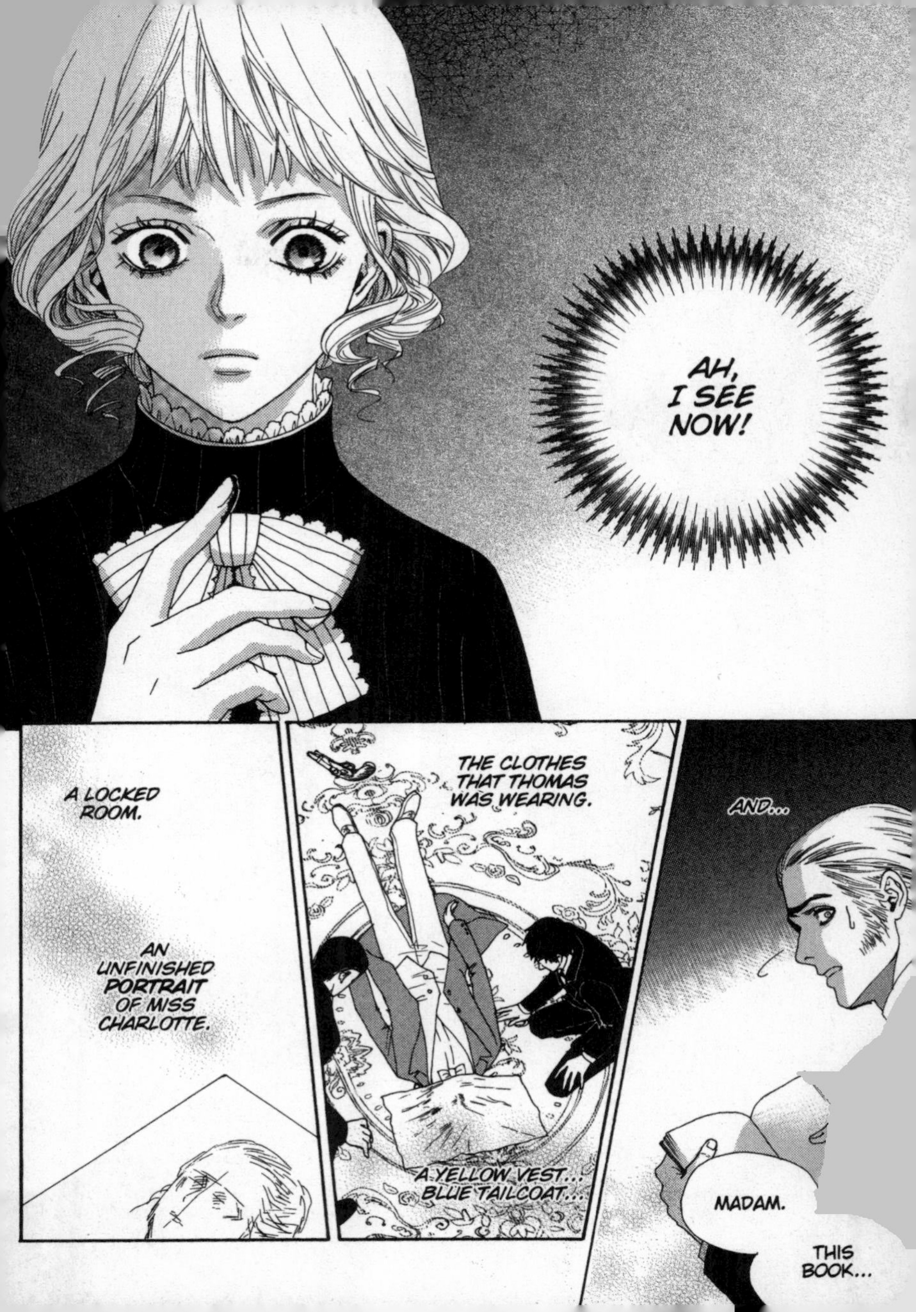
AH, I SEE NOW!
A LOCKED ROOM.
AN UNFINISHED PORTRAIT OF MISS CHARLOTTE.
THE CLOTHES THAT THOMAS WAS WEARING.
A YELLOW VEST... BLUE TAILCOAT...
AND...
MADAM.
THIS BOOK...

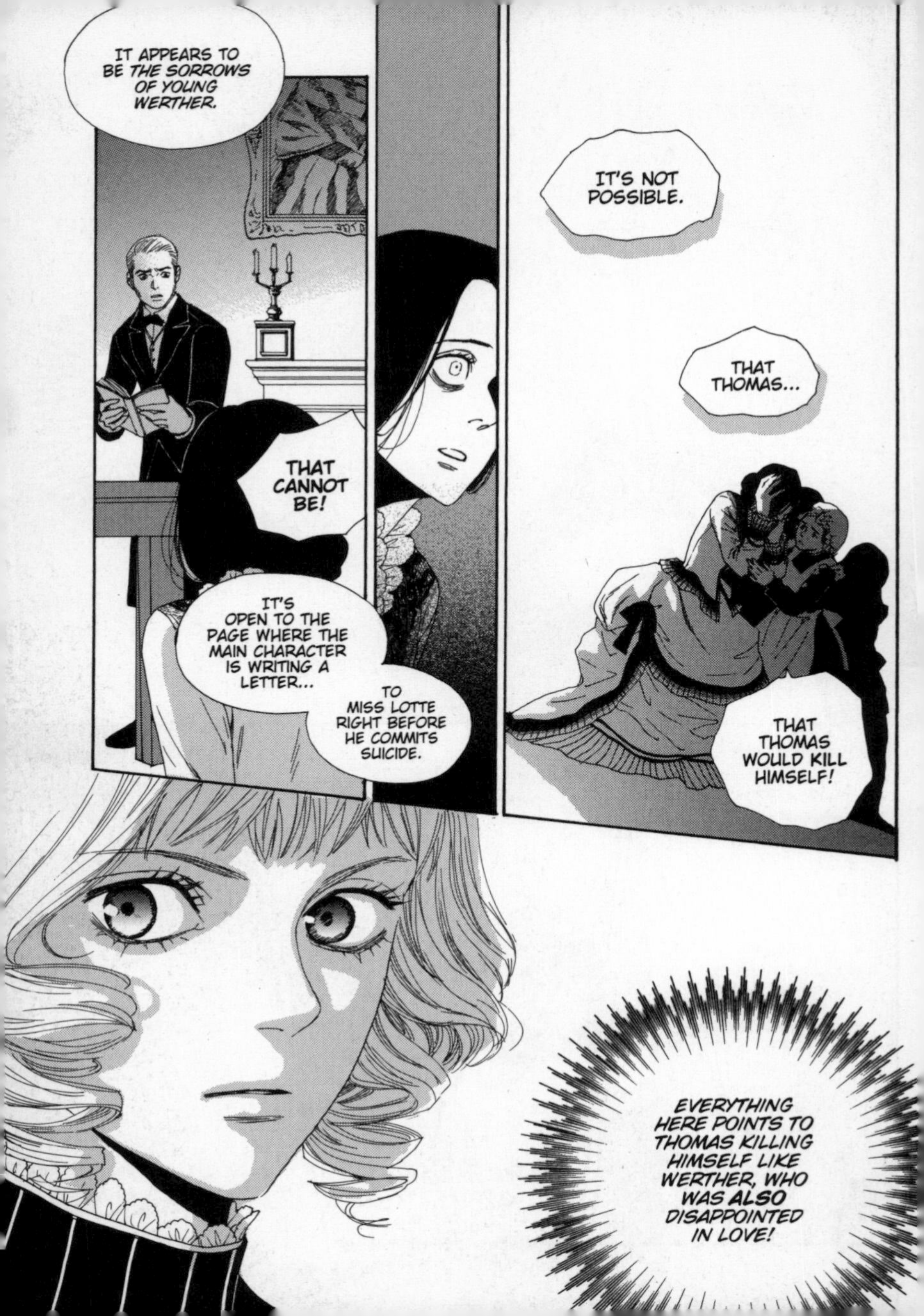
IT APPEARS TO BE *THE SORROWS OF YOUNG WERTHER.*
THAT CANNOT BE!
IT'S OPEN TO THE PAGE WHERE THE MAIN CHARACTER IS WRITING A LETTER...
TO MISS LOTTE RIGHT BEFORE HE COMMITS SUICIDE.
IT'S NOT POSSIBLE.
THAT THOMAS...
THAT THOMAS WOULD KILL HIMSELF!
EVERYTHING HERE POINTS TO THOMAS KILLING HIMSELF LIKE WERTHER, WHO WAS ***ALSO*** *DISAPPOINTED IN LOVE!*

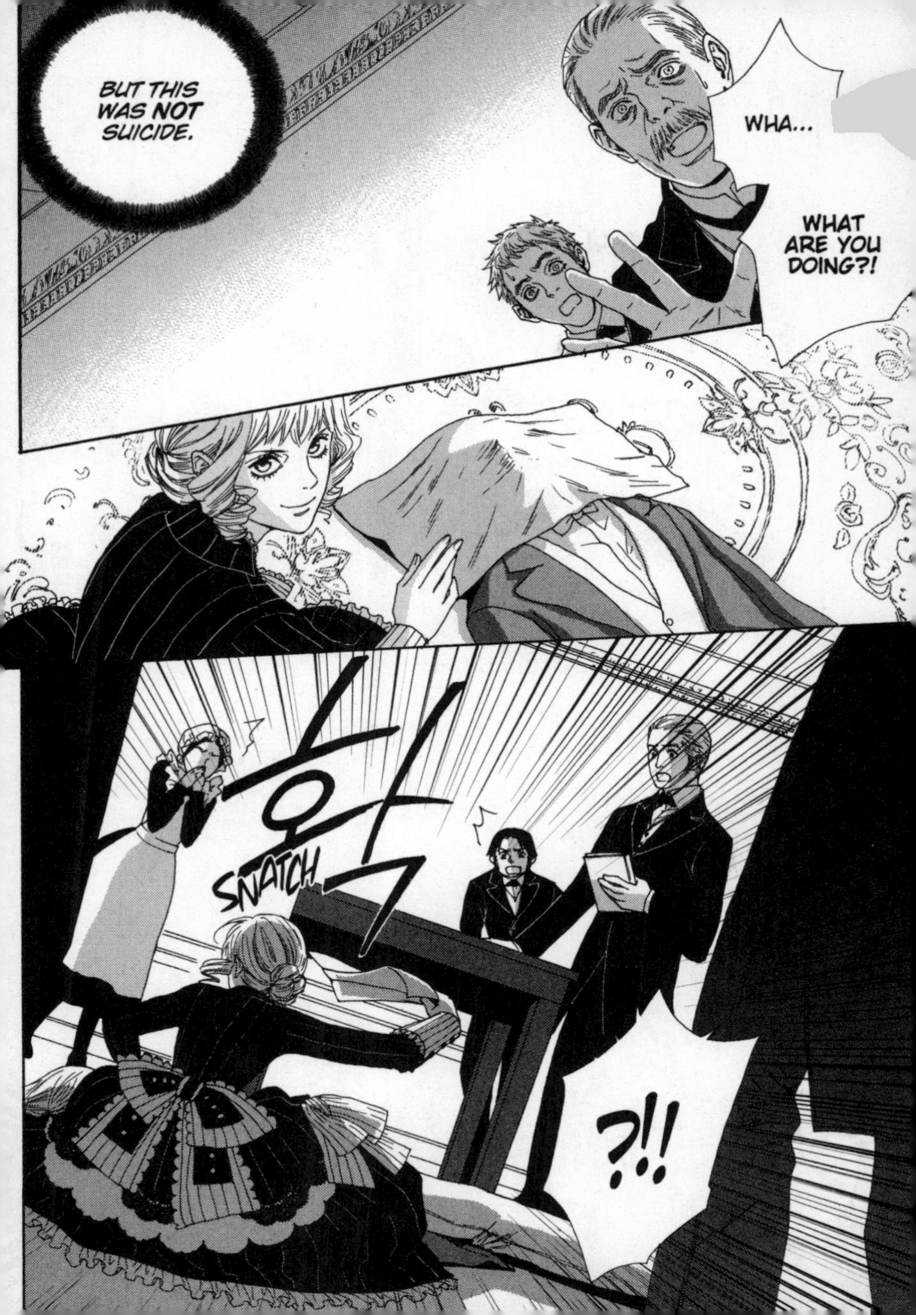
BUT THIS WAS NOT SUICIDE.
WHA...
WHAT ARE YOU DOING?!
SNATCH
?!!

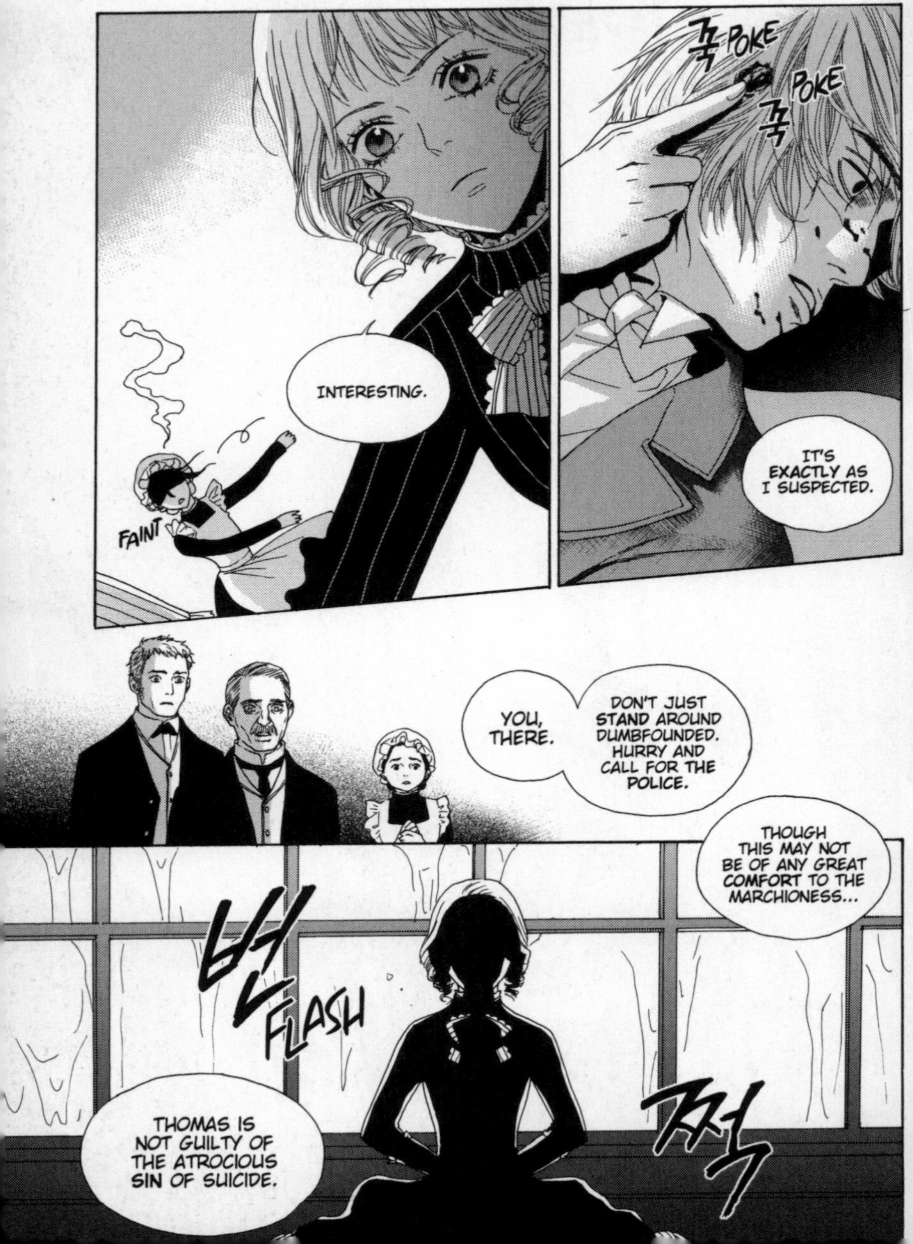
INTERESTING.
FAINT
꾹 POKE
POKE 꾹
IT'S EXACTLY AS I SUSPECTED.
YOU, THERE.
DON'T JUST STAND AROUND DUMBFOUNDED. HURRY AND CALL FOR THE POLICE.
THOUGH THIS MAY NOT BE OF ANY GREAT COMFORT TO THE MARCHIONESS...
번 FLASH
THOMAS IS NOT GUILTY OF THE ATROCIOUS SIN OF SUICIDE.
쫘악

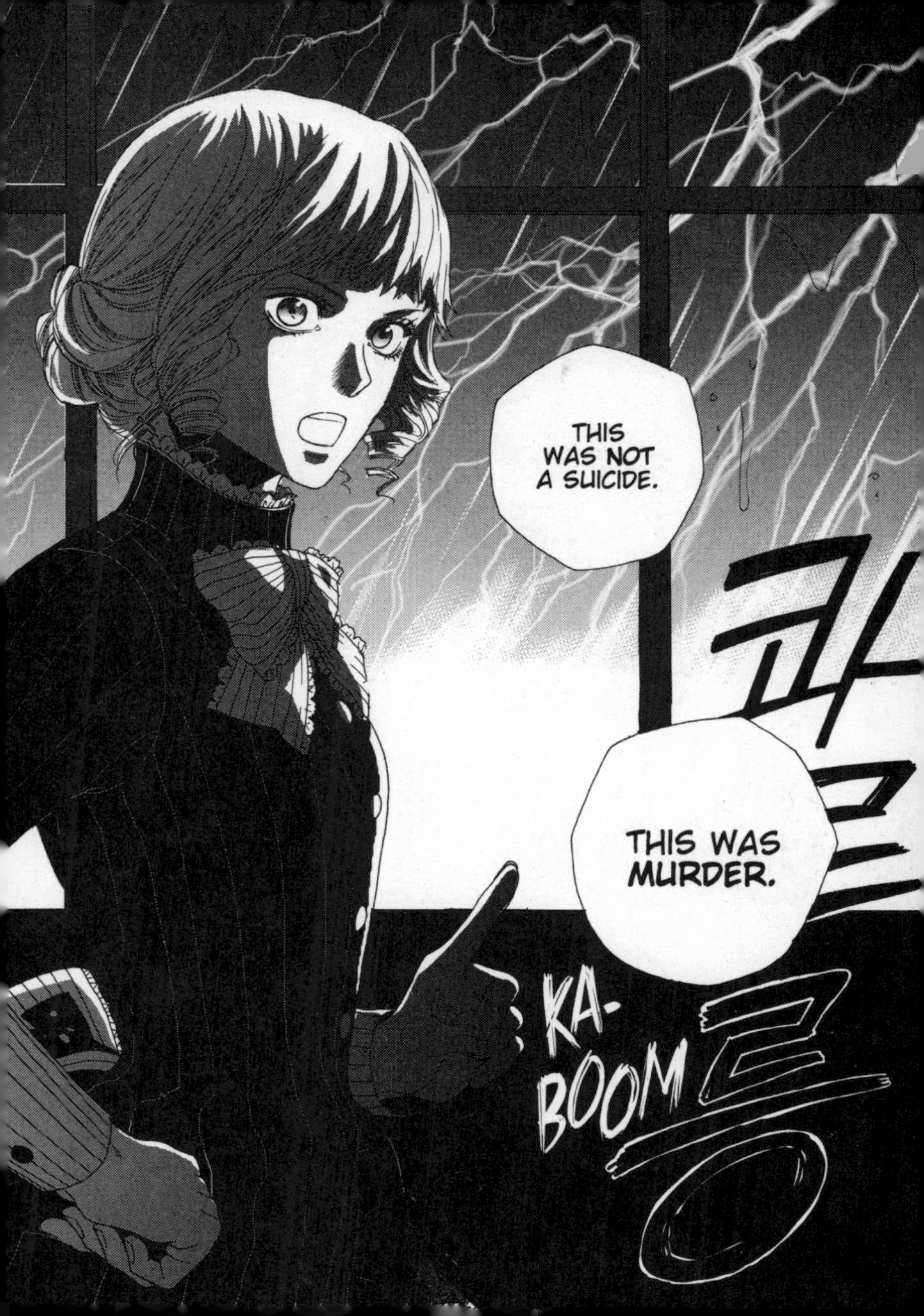
THIS WAS NOT A SUICIDE.
THIS WAS MURDER.
KA-BOOM

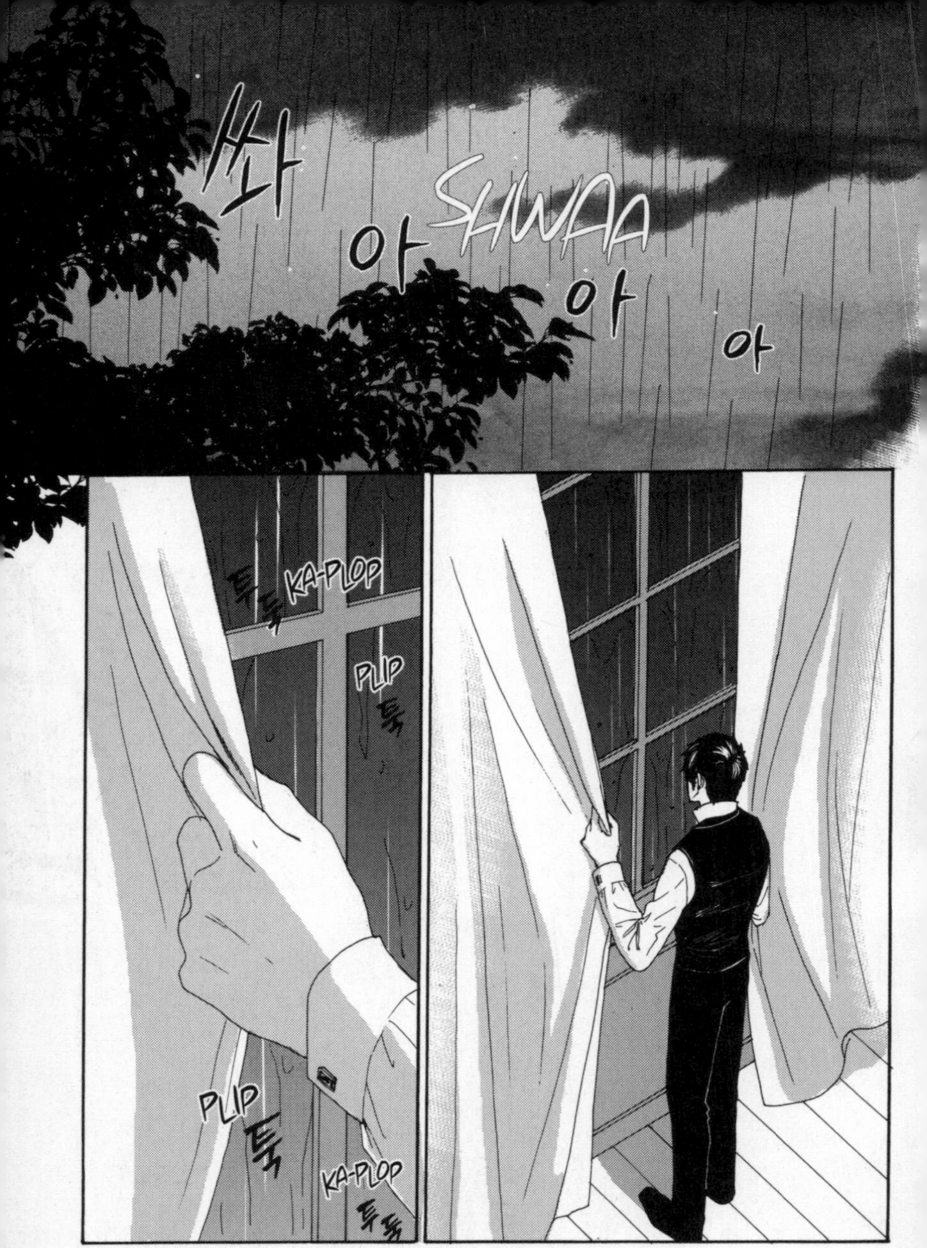
쏴아아아
SHWAA
투둑
KA-PLOP
PLIP
툭
PLIP
툭
KA-PLOP
투둑

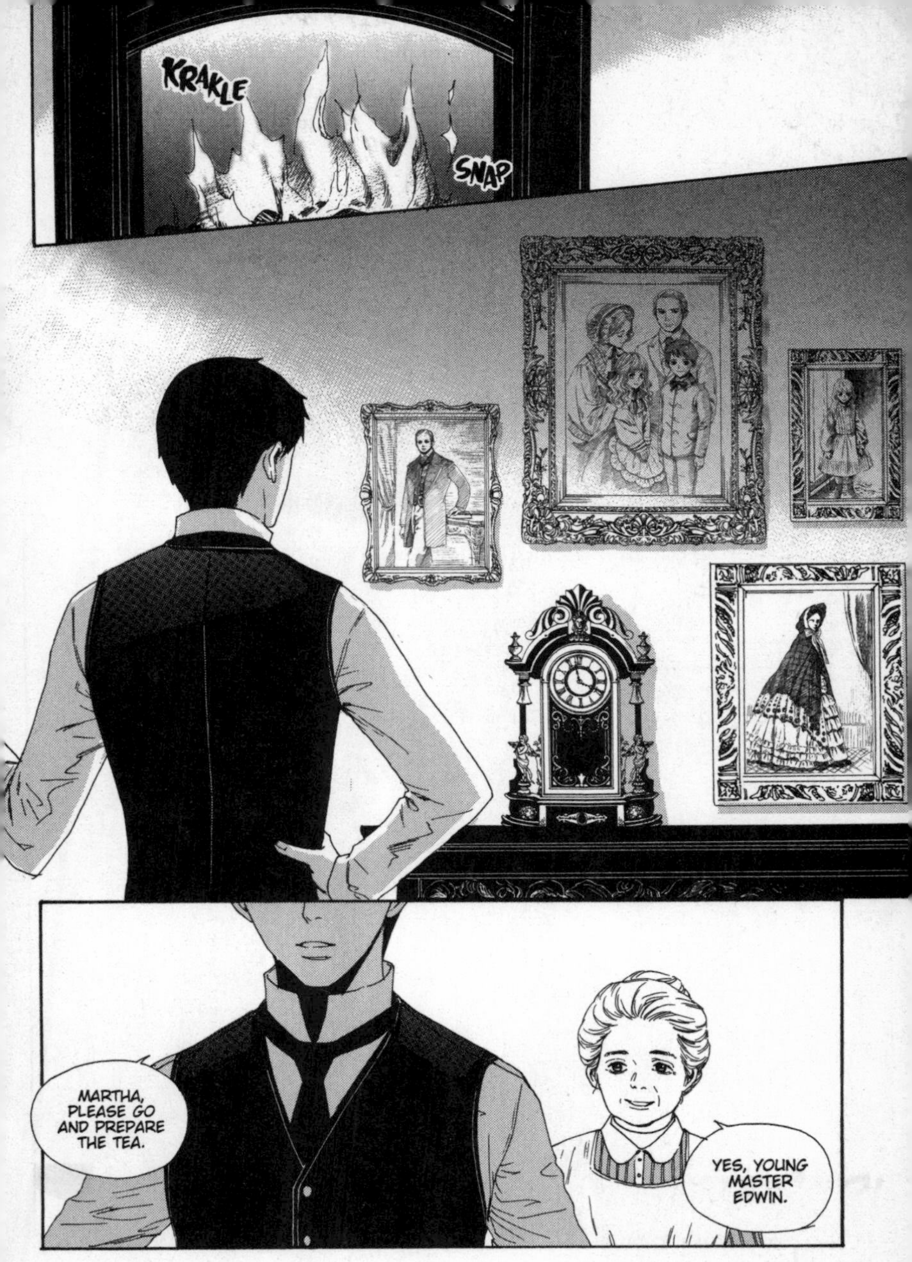
KRAKLE
SNAP
MARTHA, PLEASE GO AND PREPARE THE TEA.
YES, YOUNG MASTER EDWIN.

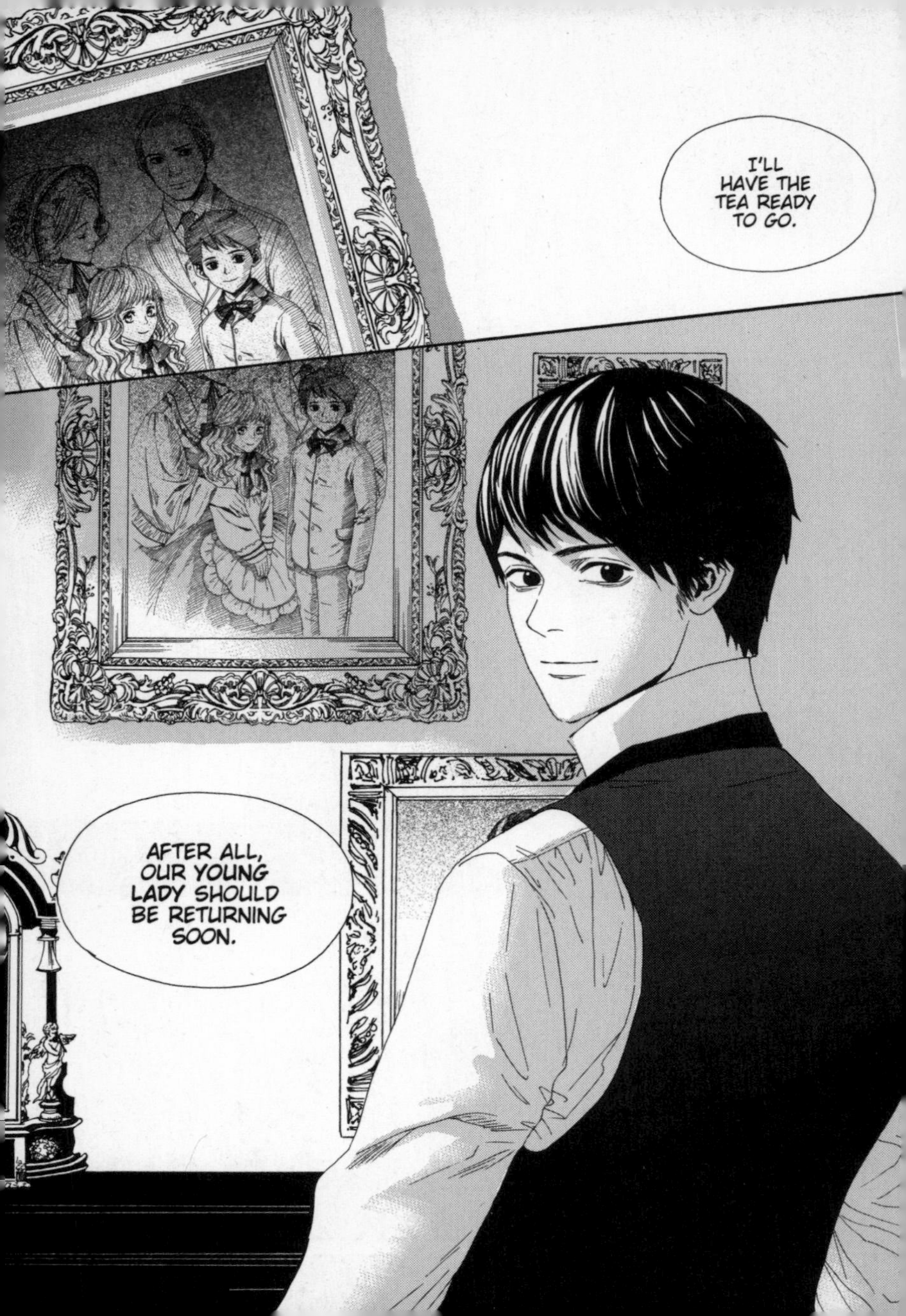
I'LL HAVE THE TEA READY TO GO.
AFTER ALL, OUR YOUNG LADY SHOULD BE RETURNING SOON.

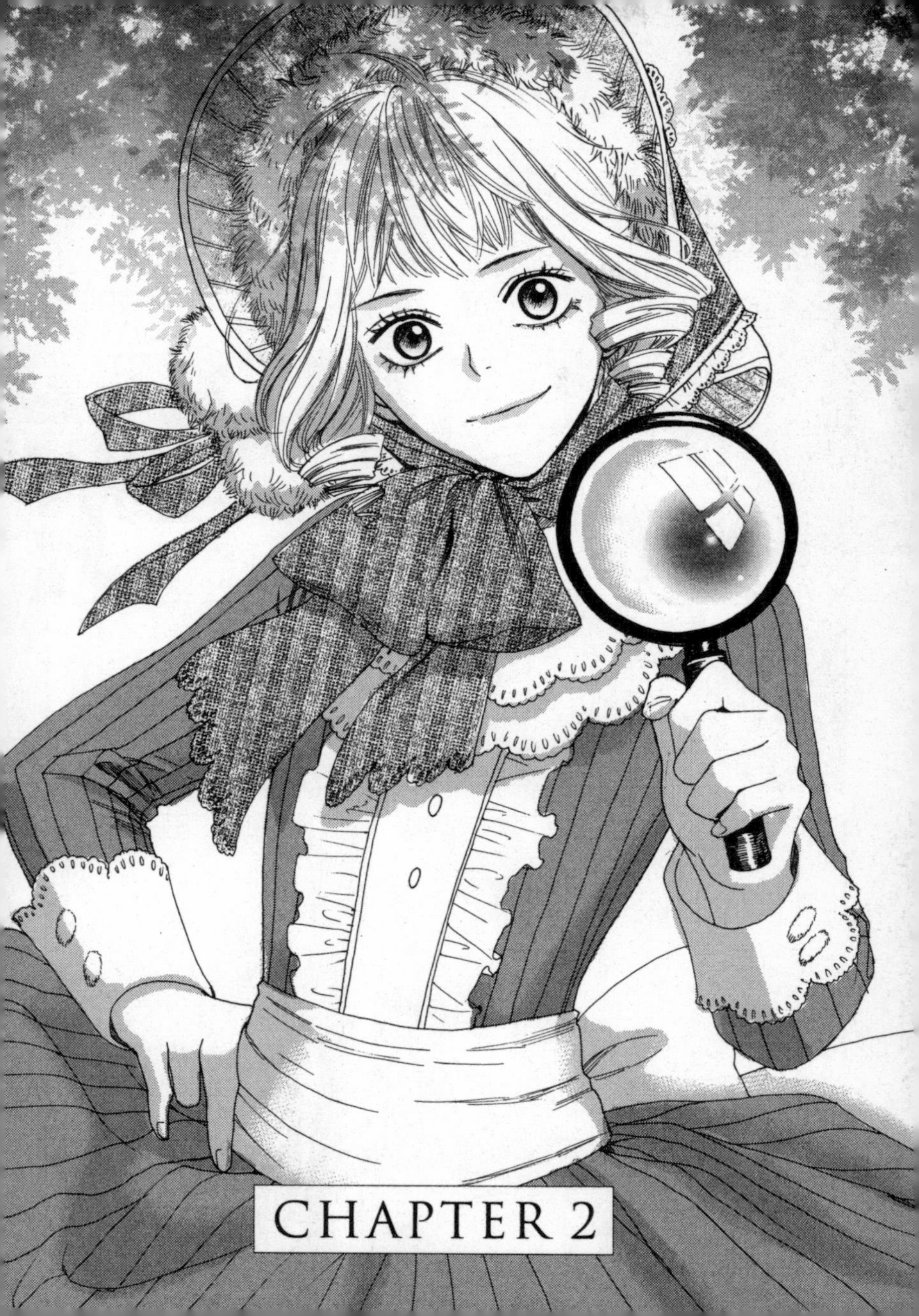

CHAPTER 2

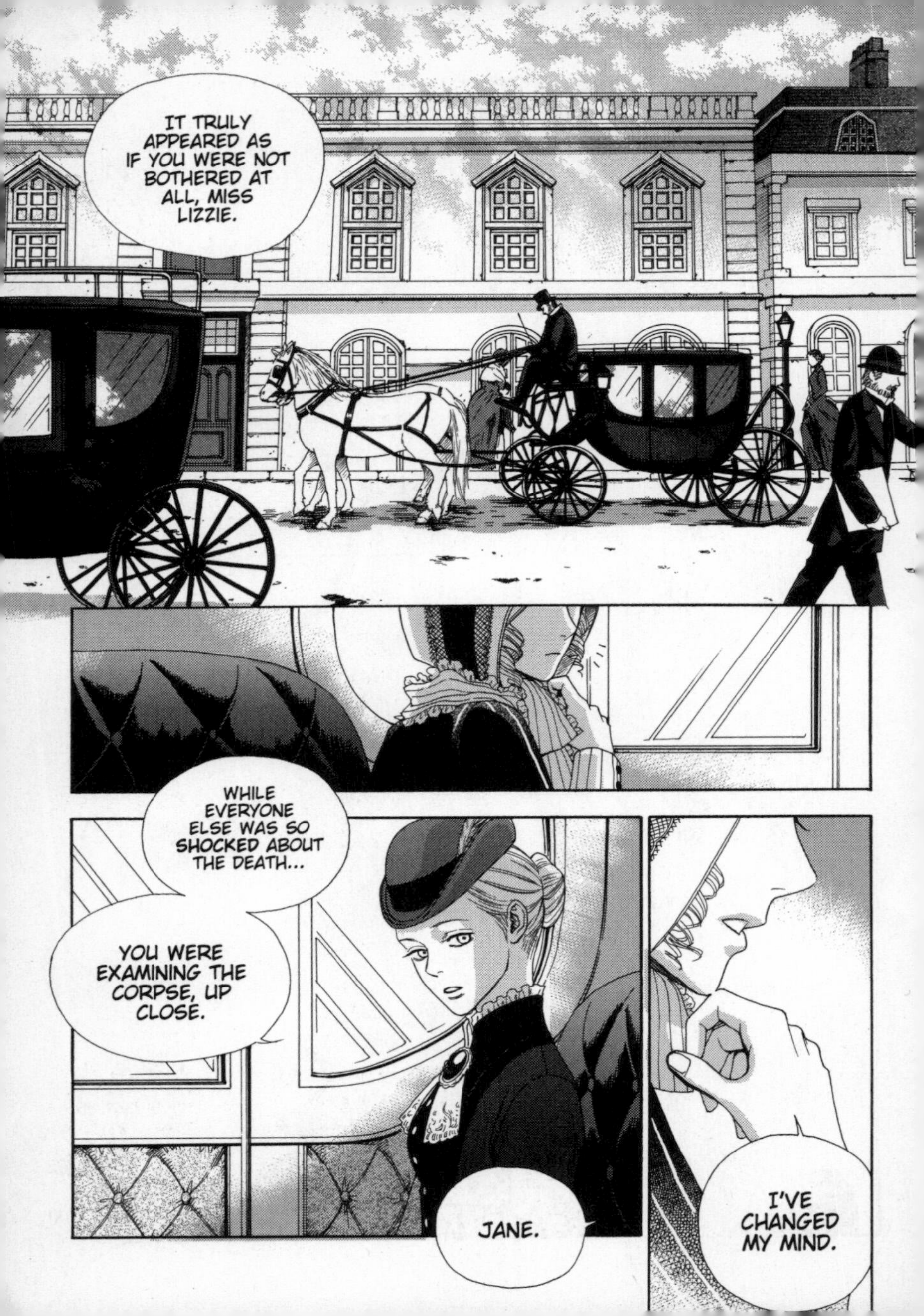
IT TRULY APPEARED AS IF YOU WERE NOT BOTHERED AT ALL, MISS LIZZIE.
WHILE EVERYONE ELSE WAS SO SHOCKED ABOUT THE DEATH...
YOU WERE EXAMINING THE CORPSE, UP CLOSE.
JANE.
I'VE CHANGED MY MIND.

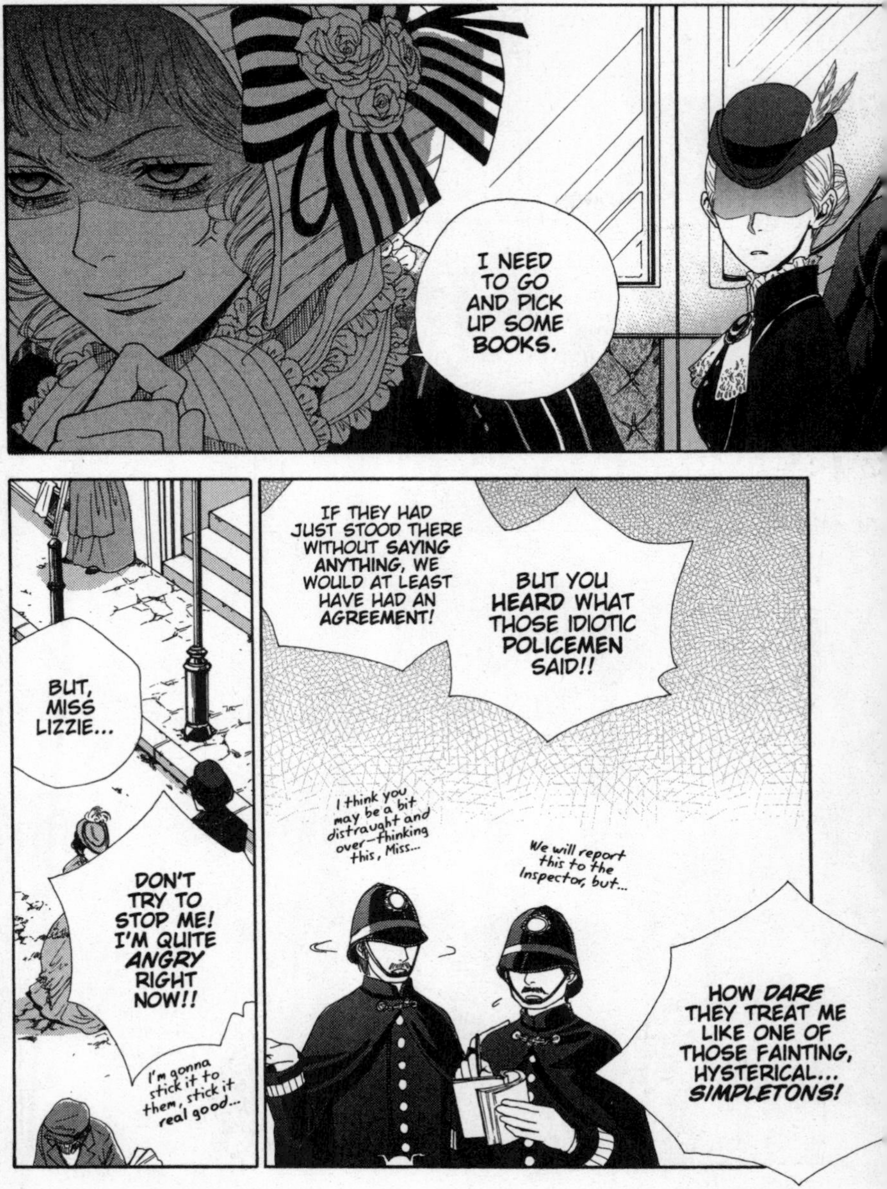
I NEED TO GO AND PICK UP SOME BOOKS.
BUT, MISS LIZZIE...
DON'T TRY TO STOP ME! I'M QUITE ANGRY RIGHT NOW!!
I'm gonna stick it to them, stick it real good...
IF THEY HAD JUST STOOD THERE WITHOUT SAYING ANYTHING, WE WOULD AT LEAST HAVE HAD AN AGREEMENT!
BUT YOU HEARD WHAT THOSE IDIOTIC POLICEMEN SAID!!
I think you may be a bit distraught and over-thinking this, Miss...
We will report this to the Inspector, but...
HOW DARE THEY TREAT ME LIKE ONE OF THOSE FAINTING, HYSTERICAL... SIMPLETONS!

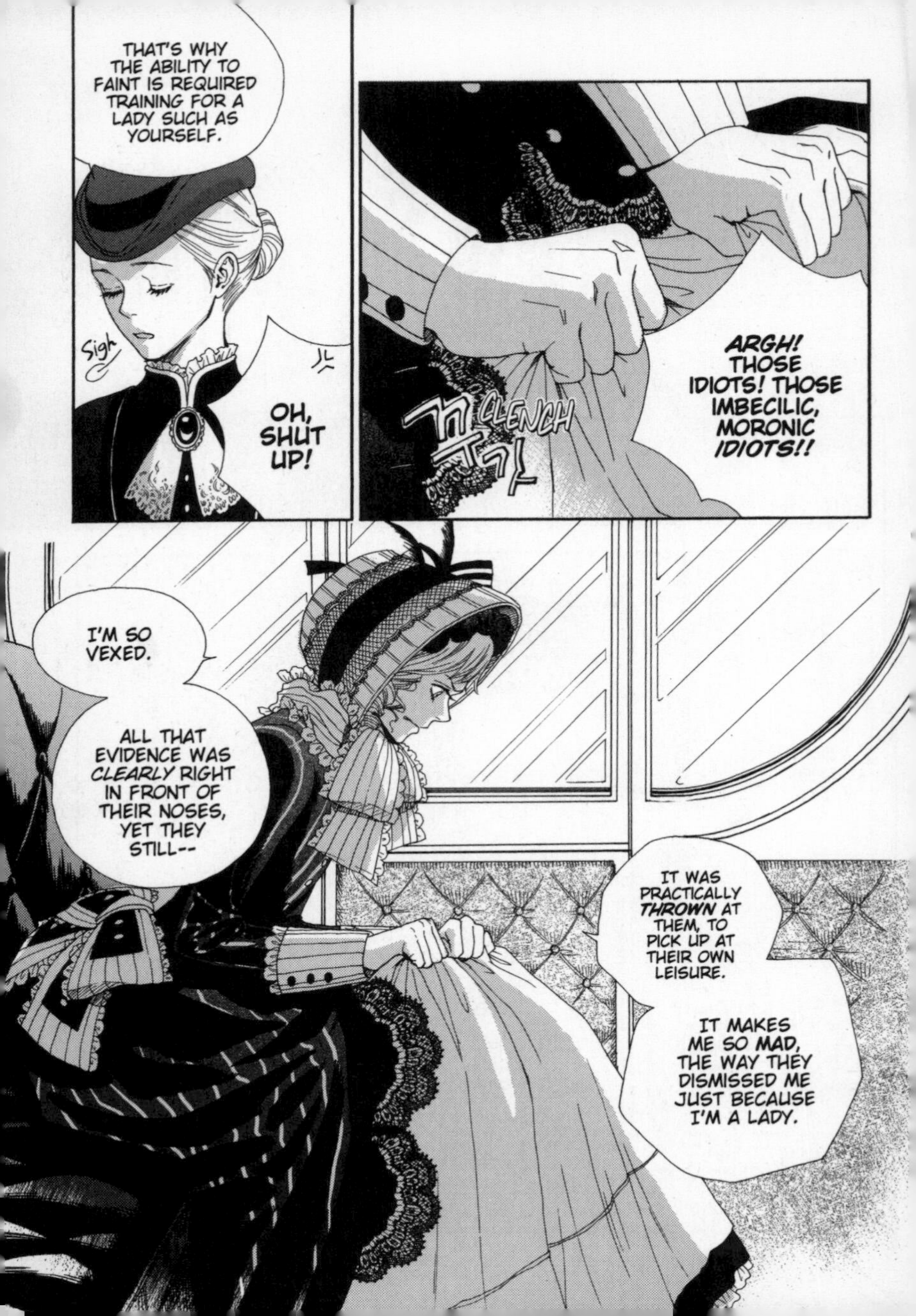

THAT'S WHY THE ABILITY TO FAINT IS REQUIRED TRAINING FOR A LADY SUCH AS YOURSELF.
Sigh
OH, SHUT UP!
CLENCH
ARGH! THOSE IDIOTS! THOSE IMBECILIC, MORONIC *IDIOTS!!*
I'M SO VEXED.
ALL THAT EVIDENCE WAS *CLEARLY* RIGHT IN FRONT OF THEIR NOSES, YET THEY STILL--
IT WAS PRACTICALLY ***THROWN*** AT THEM, TO PICK UP AT THEIR OWN LEISURE.
IT MAKES ME SO **MAD**, THE WAY THEY DISMISSED ME JUST BECAUSE I'M A LADY.

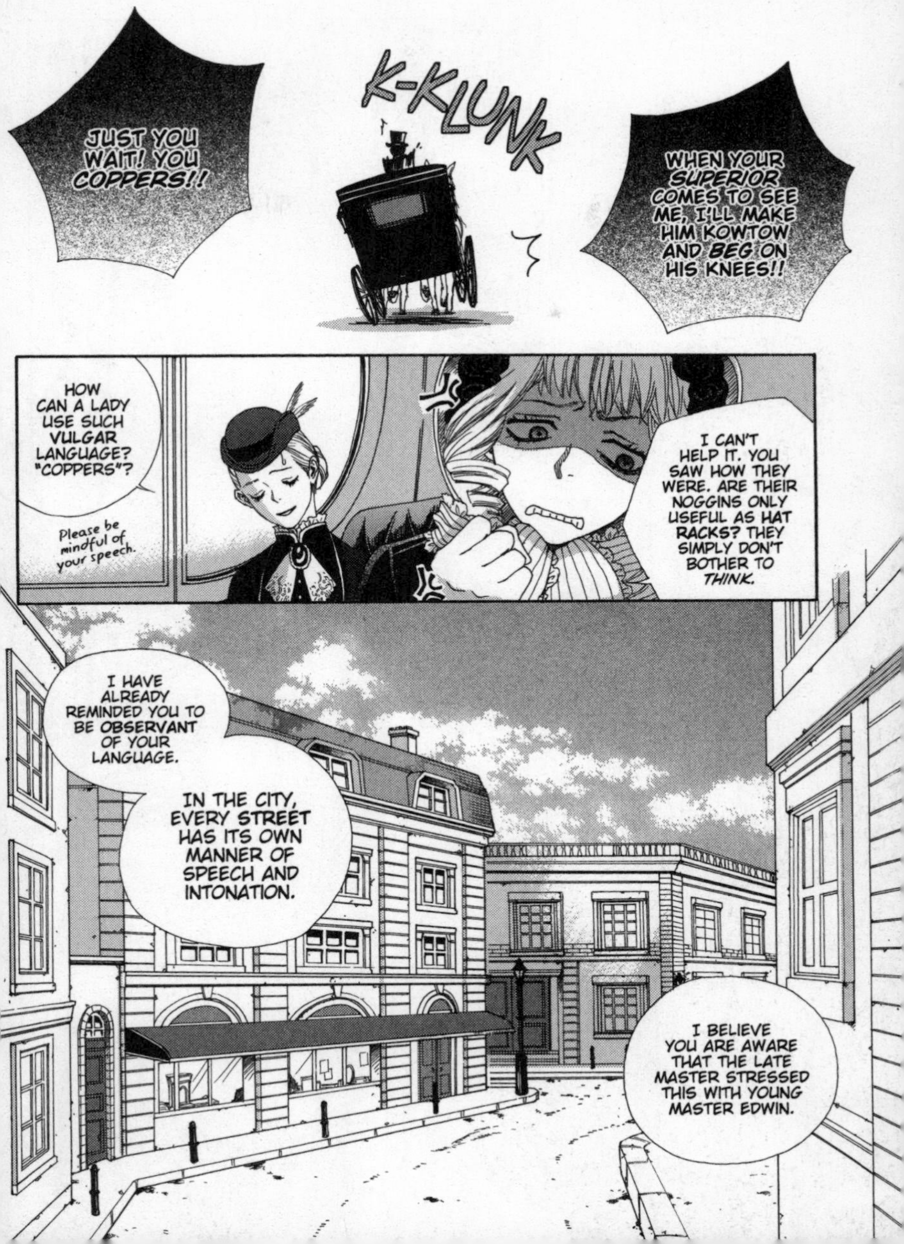
JUST YOU WAIT! YOU COPPERS!!
K-KLUNK
WHEN YOUR SUPERIOR COMES TO SEE ME, I'LL MAKE HIM KOWTOW AND BEG ON HIS KNEES!!
HOW CAN A LADY USE SUCH VULGAR LANGUAGE? "COPPERS"?
Please be mindful of your speech.
I CAN'T HELP IT. YOU SAW HOW THEY WERE. ARE THEIR NOGGINS ONLY USEFUL AS HAT RACKS? THEY SIMPLY DON'T BOTHER TO THINK.
I HAVE ALREADY REMINDED YOU TO BE OBSERVANT OF YOUR LANGUAGE.
IN THE CITY, EVERY STREET HAS ITS OWN MANNER OF SPEECH AND INTONATION.
I BELIEVE YOU ARE AWARE THAT THE LATE MASTER STRESSED THIS WITH YOUNG MASTER EDWIN.

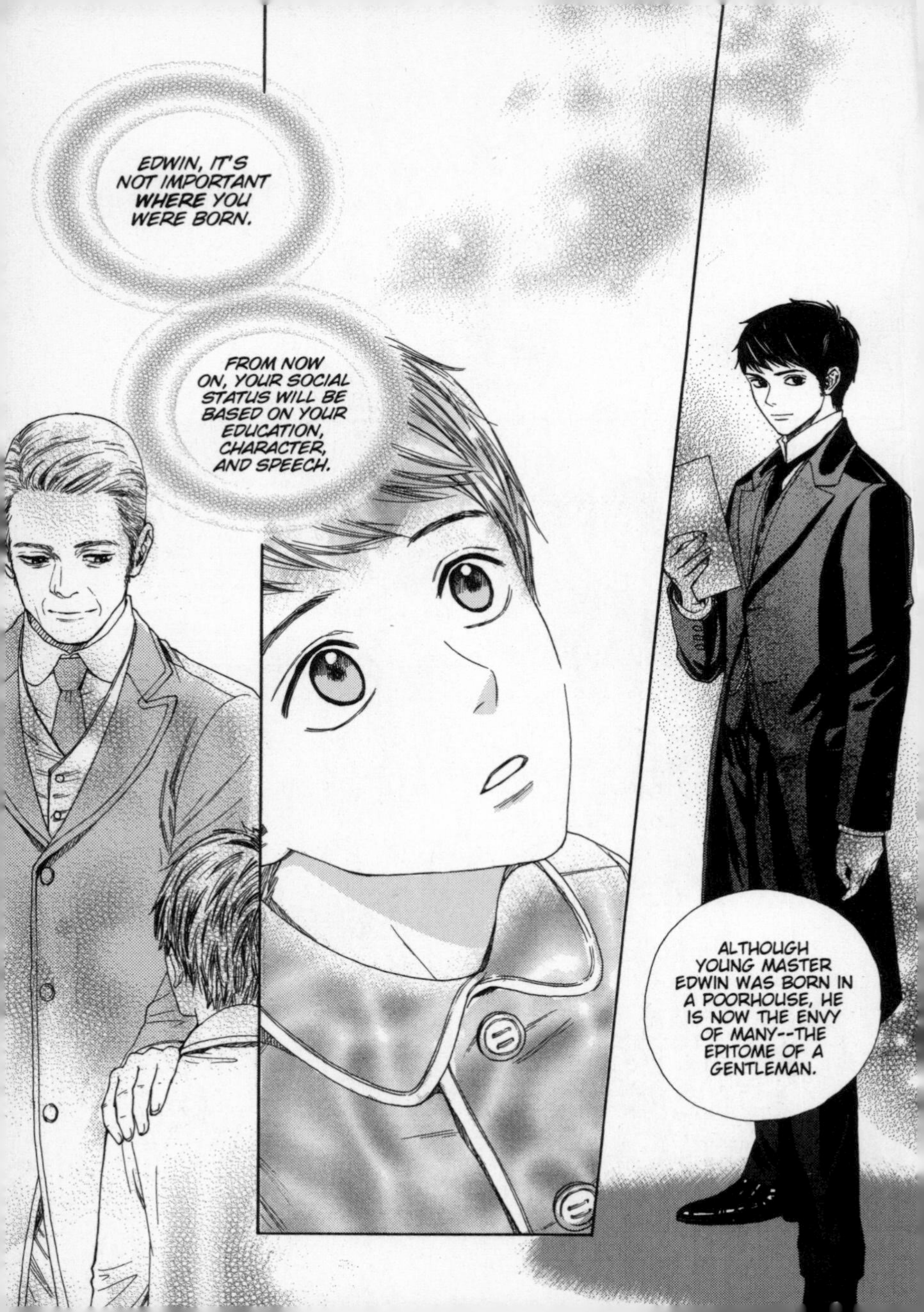
EDWIN, IT'S NOT IMPORTANT WHERE YOU WERE BORN.
FROM NOW ON, YOUR SOCIAL STATUS WILL BE BASED ON YOUR EDUCATION, CHARACTER, AND SPEECH.
ALTHOUGH YOUNG MASTER EDWIN WAS BORN IN A POORHOUSE, HE IS NOW THE ENVY OF MANY--THE EPITOME OF A GENTLEMAN.

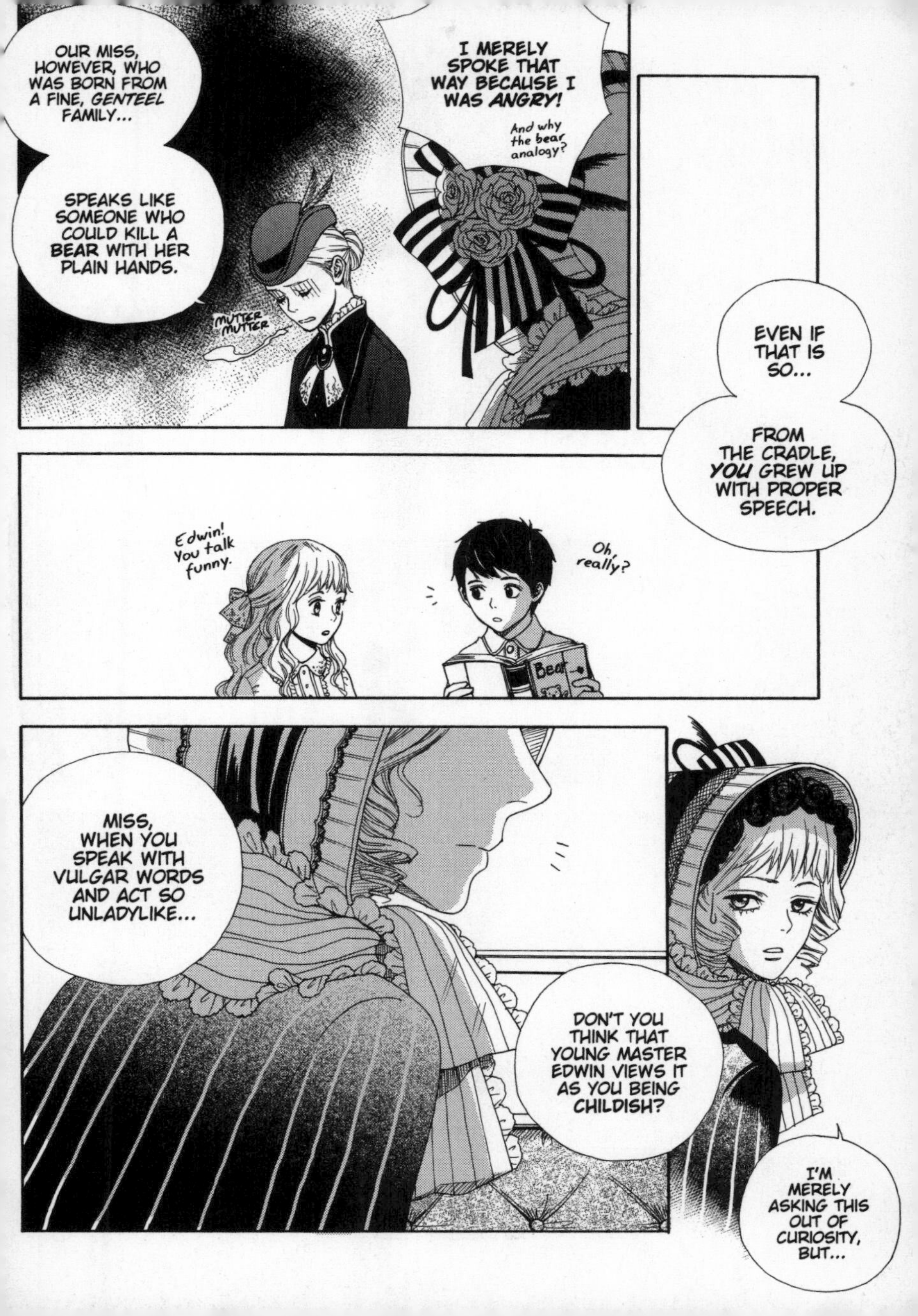

OUR MISS, HOWEVER, WHO WAS BORN FROM A FINE, GENTEEL FAMILY...
SPEAKS LIKE SOMEONE WHO COULD KILL A BEAR WITH HER PLAIN HANDS.
MUTTER MUTTER
I MERELY SPOKE THAT WAY BECAUSE I WAS ANGRY!
And why the bear analogy?
EVEN IF THAT IS SO...
FROM THE CRADLE, YOU GREW UP WITH PROPER SPEECH.
Edwin! You talk funny.
Oh, really?
Bear
MISS, WHEN YOU SPEAK WITH VULGAR WORDS AND ACT SO UNLADYLIKE...
DON'T YOU THINK THAT YOUNG MASTER EDWIN VIEWS IT AS YOU BEING CHILDISH?
I'M MERELY ASKING THIS OUT OF CURIOSITY, BUT...

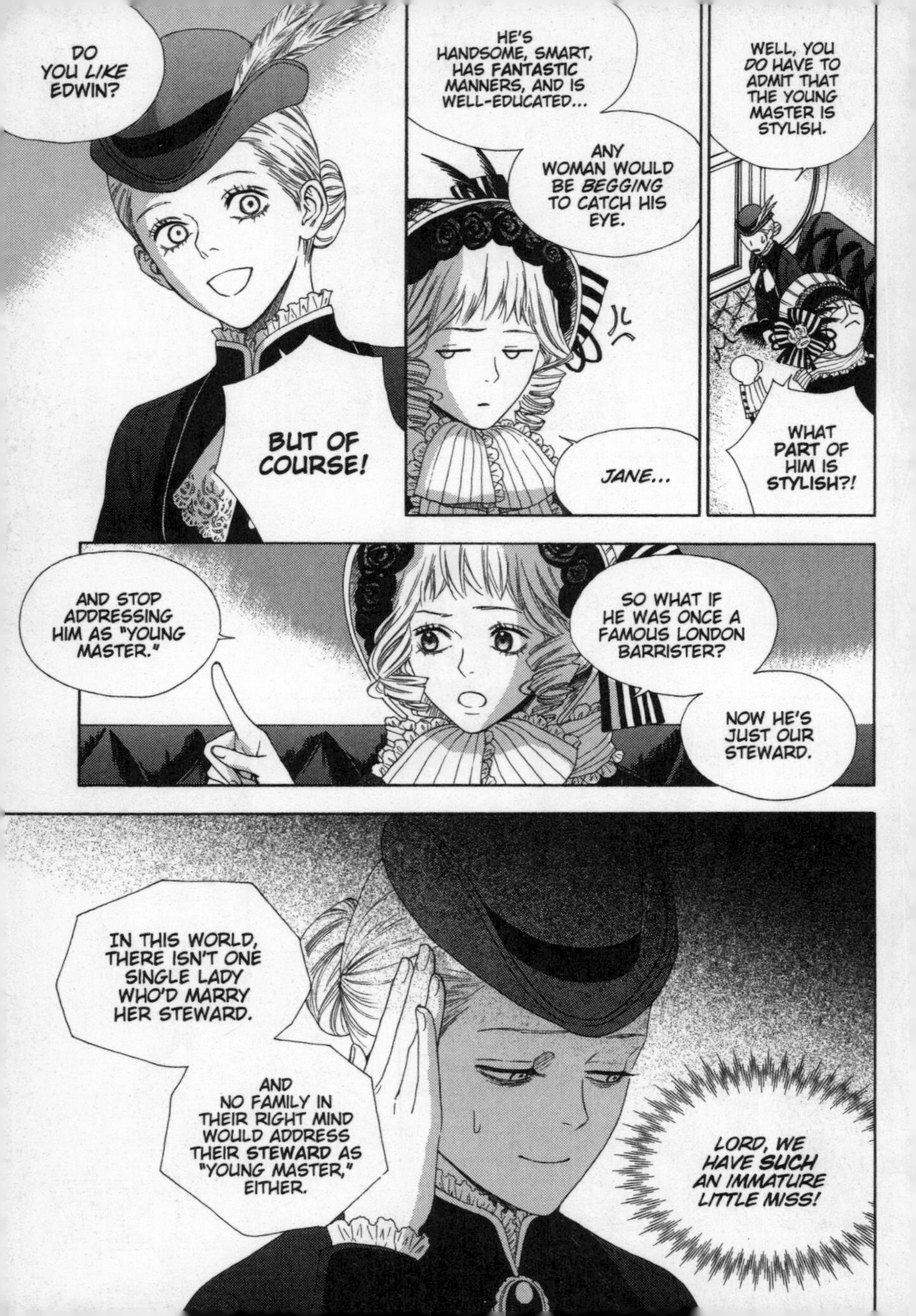
DO YOU *LIKE* EDWIN?
BUT OF COURSE!
HE'S HANDSOME, SMART, HAS FANTASTIC MANNERS, AND IS WELL-EDUCATED...
ANY WOMAN WOULD BE *BEGGING* TO CATCH HIS EYE.
JANE...
WELL, YOU *DO* HAVE TO ADMIT THAT THE YOUNG MASTER IS STYLISH.
WHAT PART OF HIM IS STYLISH?!
AND STOP ADDRESSING HIM AS "YOUNG MASTER."
SO WHAT IF HE WAS ONCE A FAMOUS LONDON BARRISTER?
NOW HE'S JUST OUR STEWARD.
IN THIS WORLD, THERE ISN'T ONE SINGLE LADY WHO'D MARRY HER STEWARD.
AND NO FAMILY IN THEIR RIGHT MIND WOULD ADDRESS THEIR STEWARD AS "YOUNG MASTER," EITHER.
LORD, WE HAVE SUCH *AN IMMATURE LITTLE MISS!*

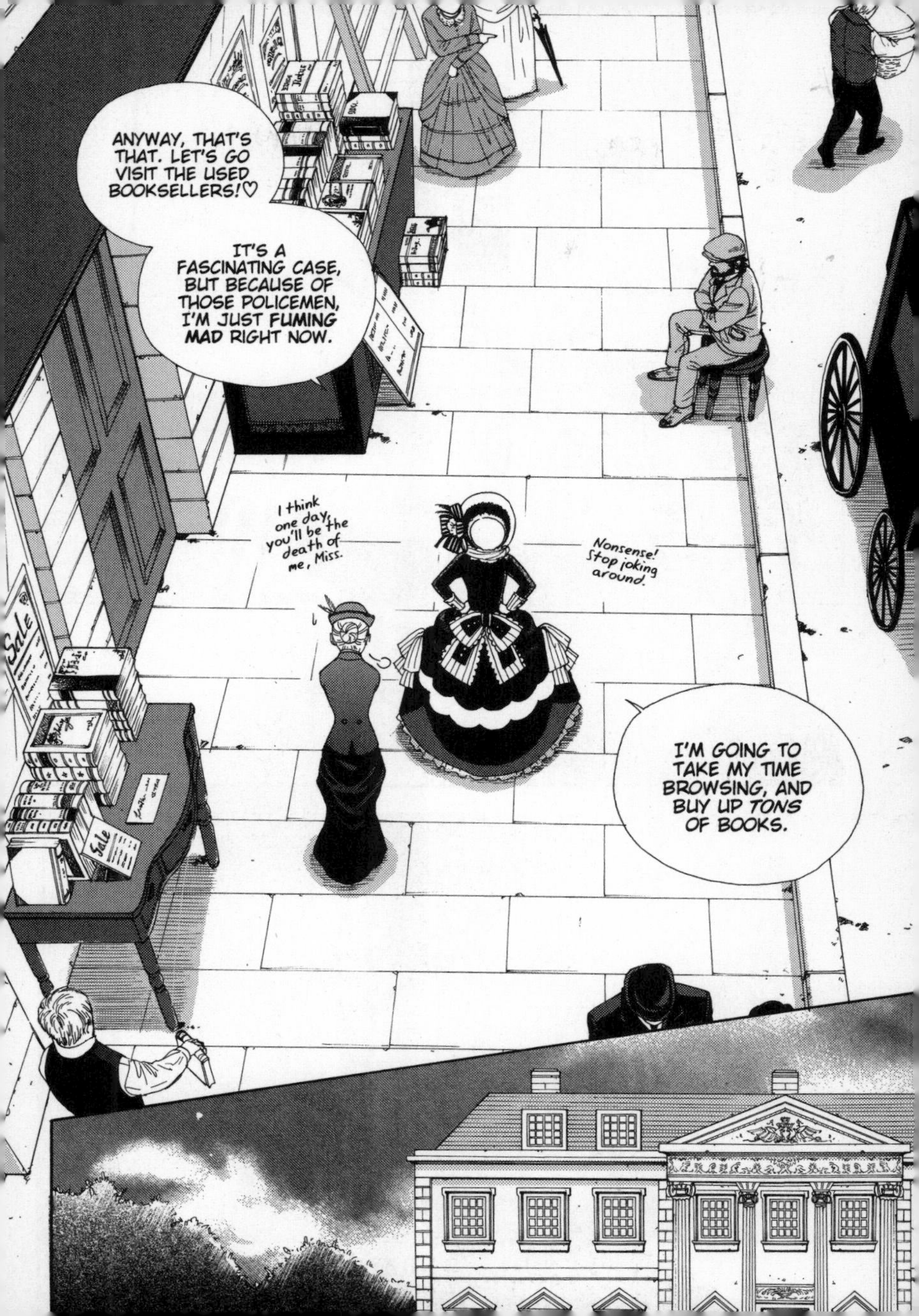
ANYWAY, THAT'S THAT. LET'S GO VISIT THE USED BOOKSELLERS!♡
IT'S A FASCINATING CASE, BUT BECAUSE OF THOSE POLICEMEN, I'M JUST FUMING MAD RIGHT NOW.
I think one day, you'll be the death of me, Miss.
Nonsense! Stop joking around.
Sale
Sale
I'M GOING TO TAKE MY TIME BROWSING, AND BUY UP TONS OF BOOKS.

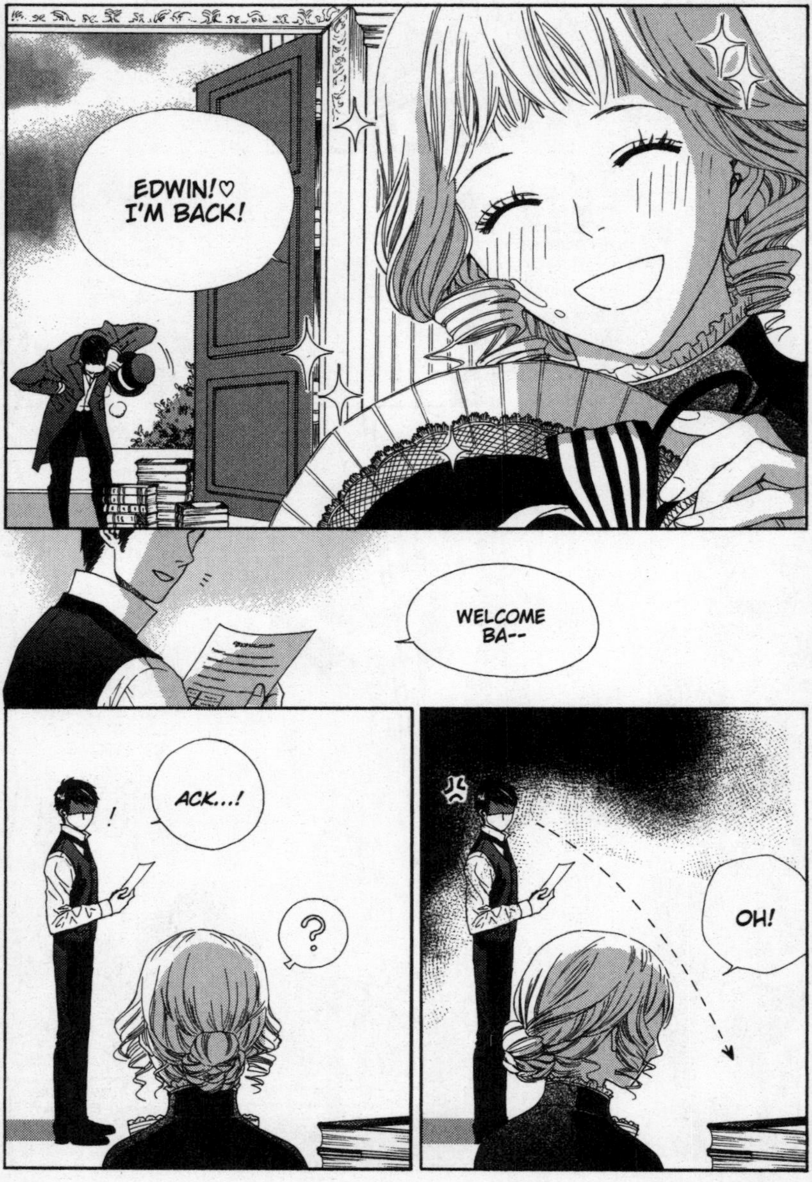
EDWIN!♡
I'M BACK!
WELCOME
BA--
ACK...!
!
?
OH!

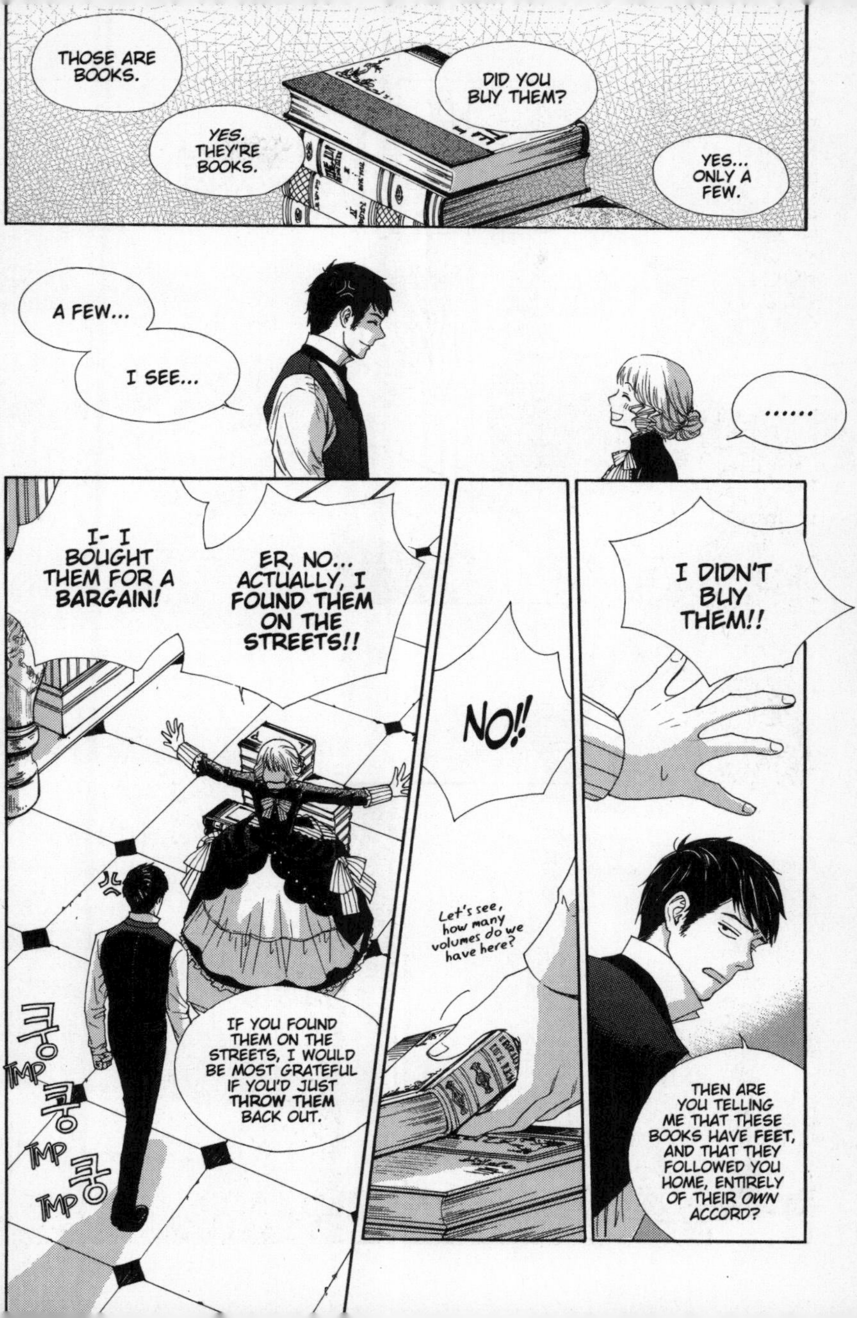
THOSE ARE BOOKS.
YES. THEY'RE BOOKS.
DID YOU BUY THEM?
YES... ONLY A FEW.
A FEW...
I SEE...
......
I- I BOUGHT THEM FOR A BARGAIN!
ER, NO... ACTUALLY, I FOUND THEM ON THE STREETS!!
IF YOU FOUND THEM ON THE STREETS, I WOULD BE MOST GRATEFUL IF YOU'D JUST THROW THEM BACK OUT.
쿵 TMP
쿵 TMP
쿵 TMP
NO!!
Let's see, how many volumes do we have here?
I DIDN'T BUY THEM!!
THEN ARE YOU TELLING ME THAT THESE BOOKS HAVE FEET, AND THAT THEY FOLLOWED YOU HOME, ENTIRELY OF THEIR *OWN* ACCORD?

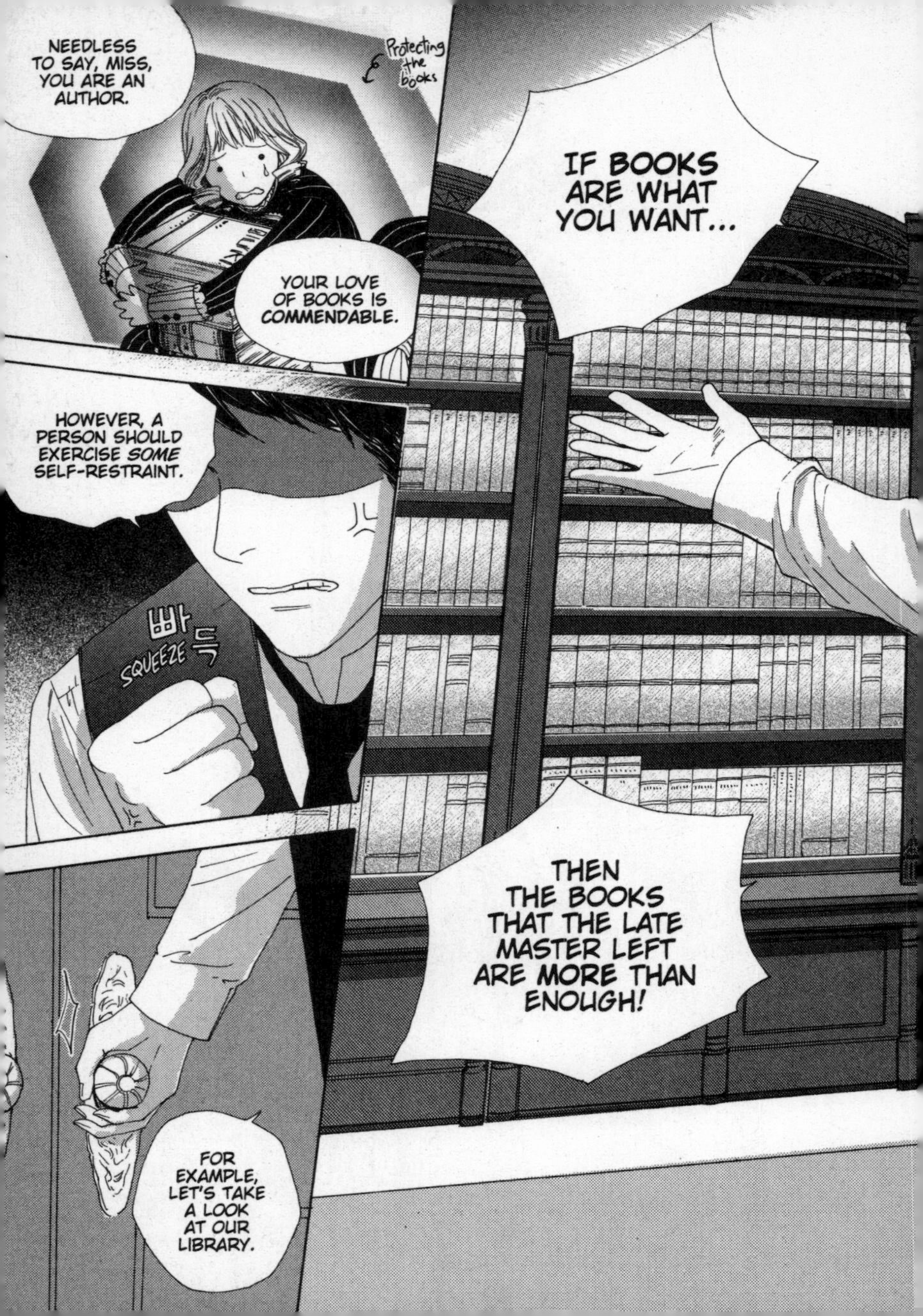
NEEDLESS TO SAY, MISS, YOU ARE AN AUTHOR.
Protecting the books
YOUR LOVE OF BOOKS IS COMMENDABLE.
IF BOOKS ARE WHAT YOU WANT...
HOWEVER, A PERSON SHOULD EXERCISE SOME SELF-RESTRAINT.
빠득
SQUEEZE
THEN THE BOOKS THAT THE LATE MASTER LEFT ARE MORE THAN ENOUGH!
FOR EXAMPLE, LET'S TAKE A LOOK AT OUR LIBRARY.

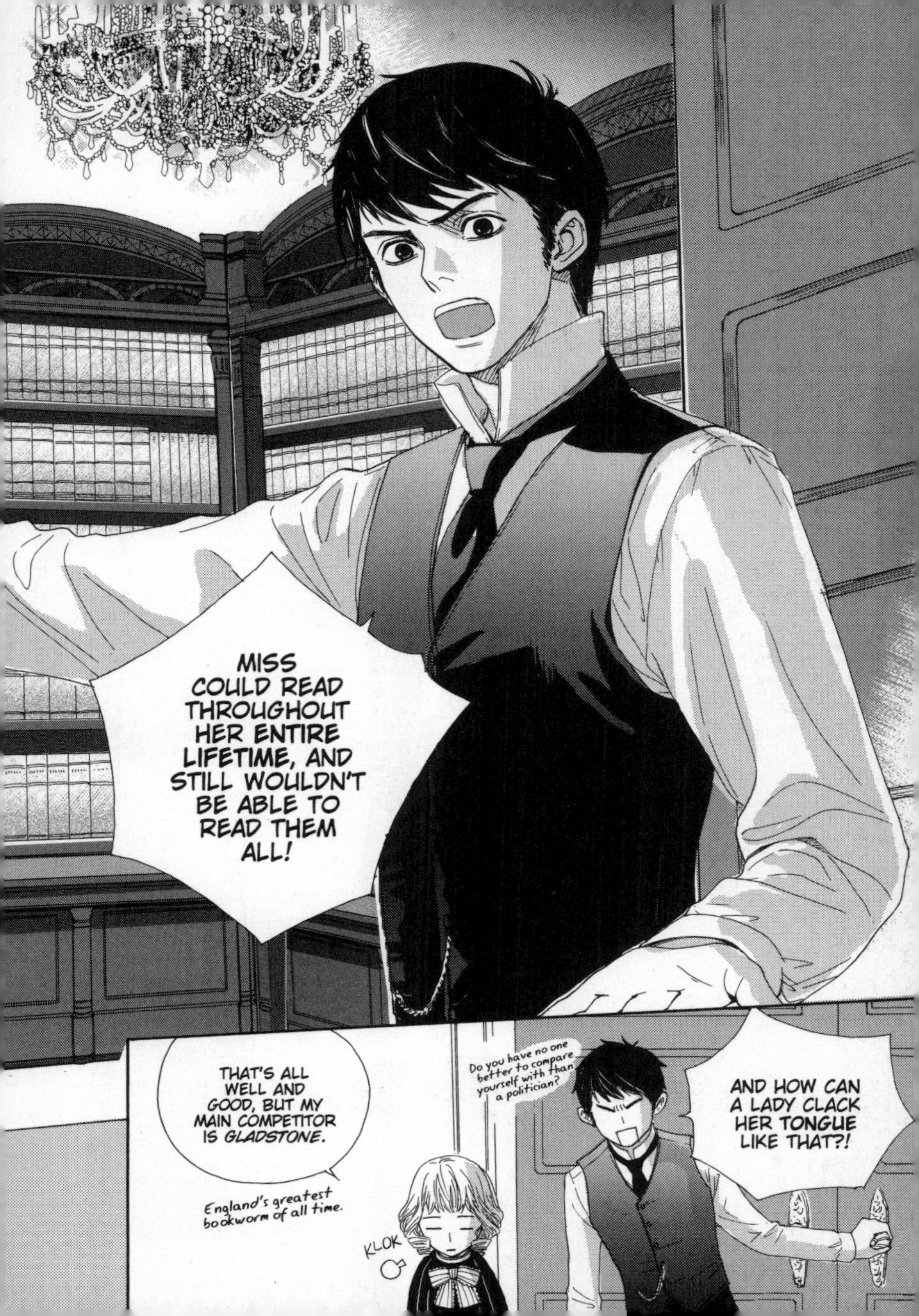
MISS COULD READ THROUGHOUT HER ENTIRE LIFETIME, AND STILL WOULDN'T BE ABLE TO READ THEM ALL!
THAT'S ALL WELL AND GOOD, BUT MY MAIN COMPETITOR IS *GLADSTONE*.
England's greatest bookworm of all time.
Do you have no one better to compare yourself with than a politician?
AND HOW CAN A LADY CLACK HER TONGUE LIKE THAT?!
KLOK

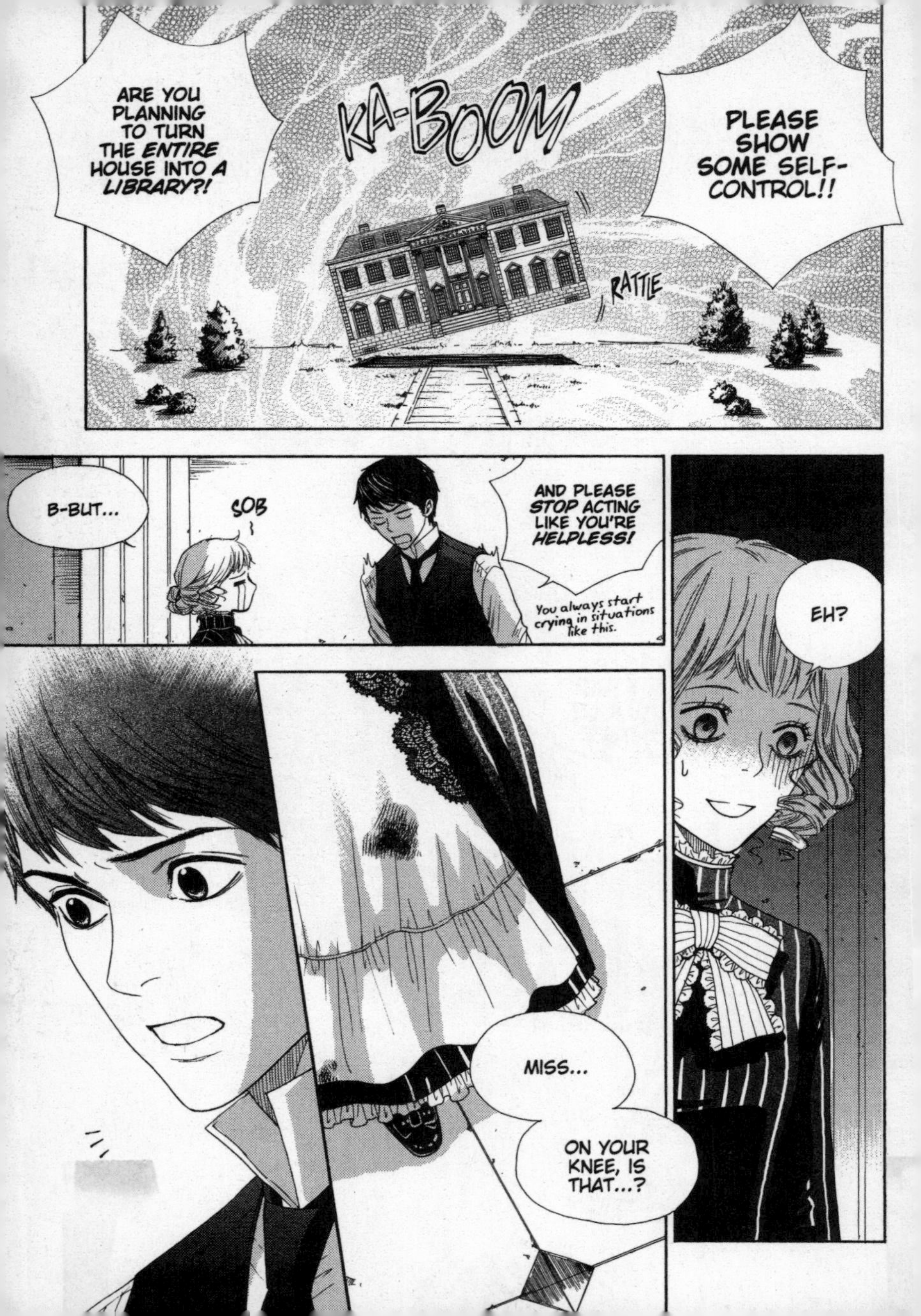

ARE YOU PLANNING TO TURN THE *ENTIRE* HOUSE INTO A *LIBRARY?!*
KA-BOOM
PLEASE SHOW SOME SELF-CONTROL!!
RATTLE
B-BUT...
SOB
AND PLEASE *STOP* ACTING LIKE YOU'RE *HELPLESS!*
You always start crying in situations like this.
EH?
MISS...
ON YOUR KNEE, IS THAT...?

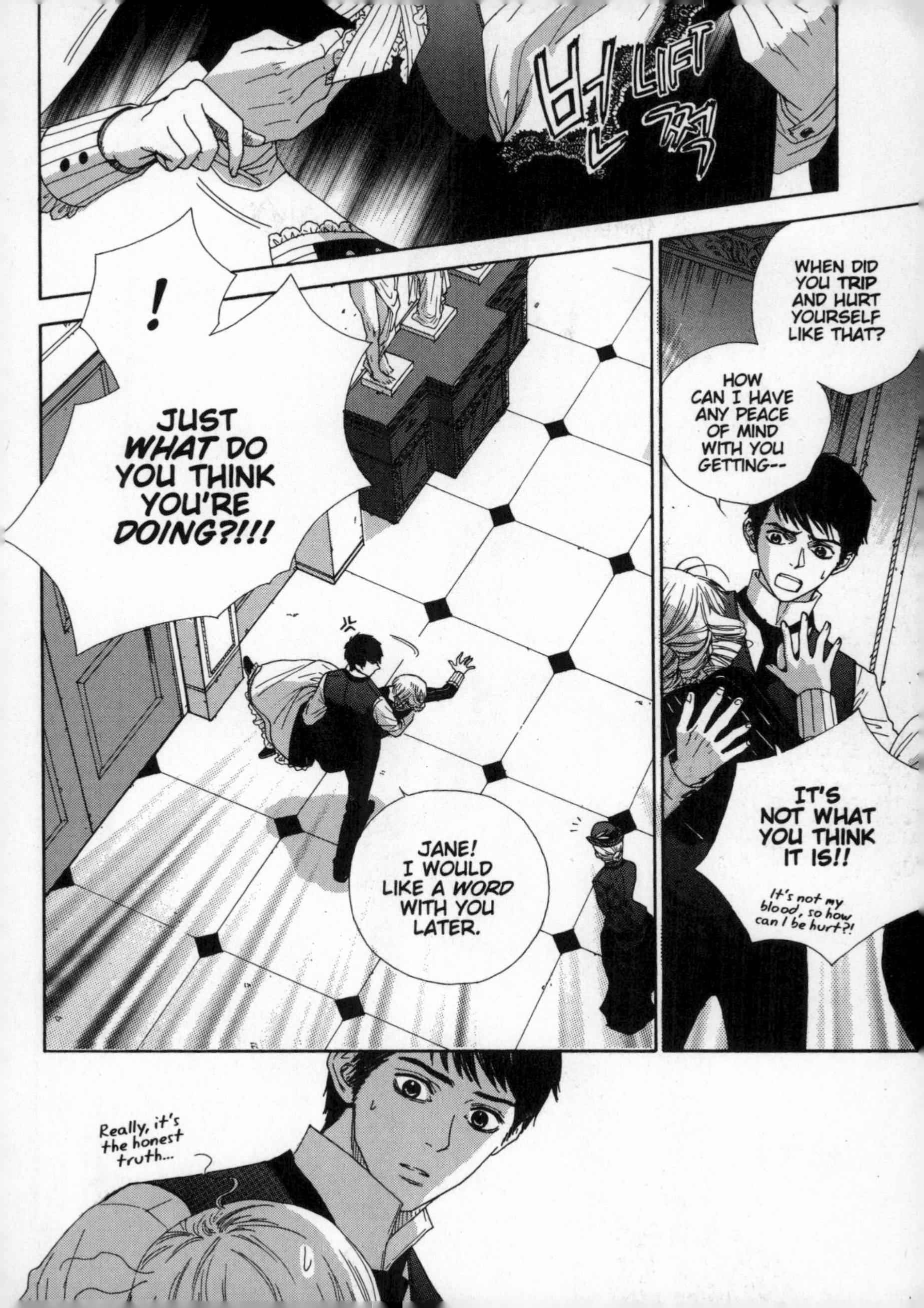
LIFT
!
JUST WHAT DO YOU THINK YOU'RE DOING?!!!
JANE! I WOULD LIKE A WORD WITH YOU LATER.
WHEN DID YOU TRIP AND HURT YOURSELF LIKE THAT?
HOW CAN I HAVE ANY PEACE OF MIND WITH YOU GETTING--
IT'S NOT WHAT YOU THINK IT IS!!
It's not my blood, so how can I be hurt?!
Really, it's the honest truth...

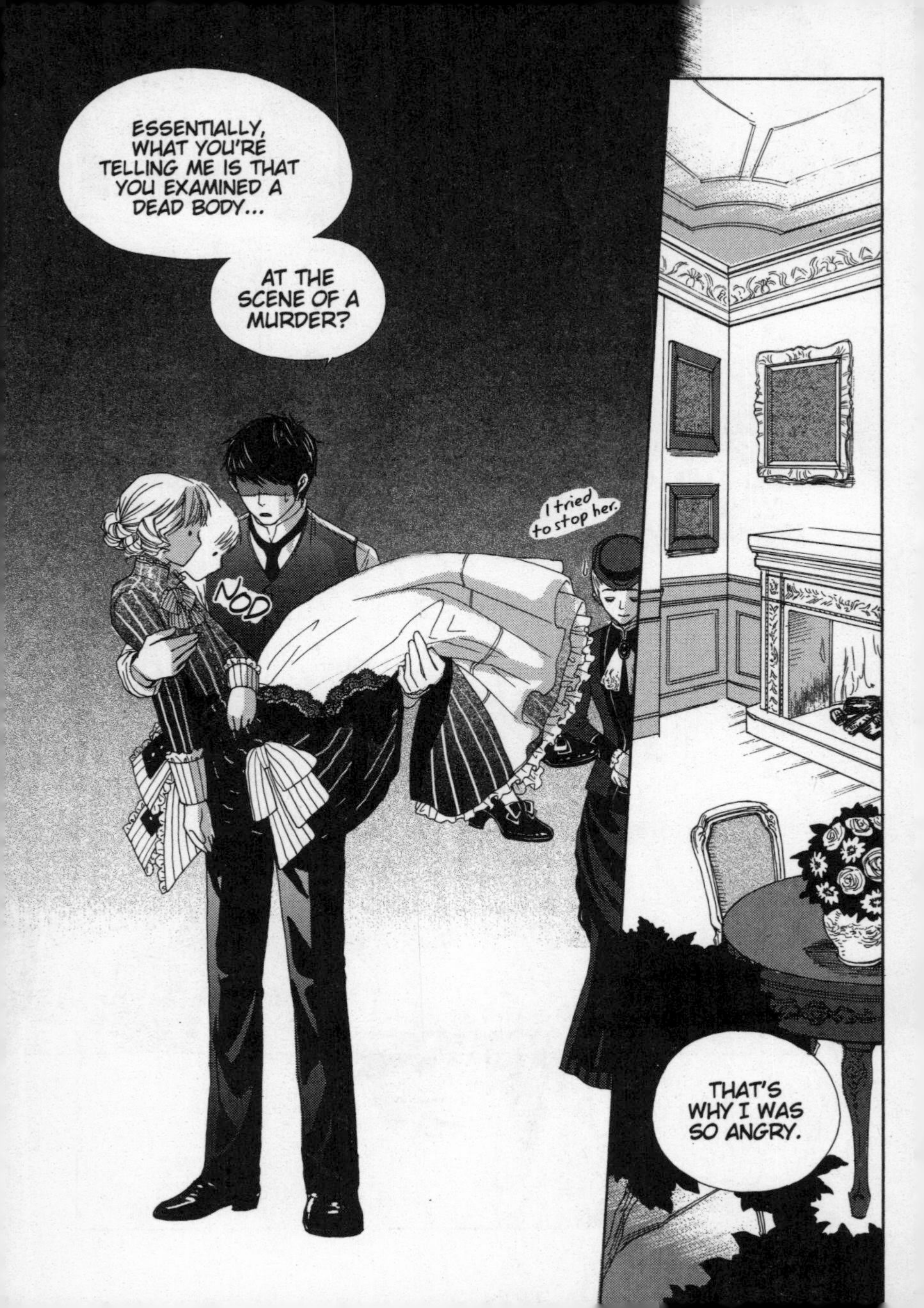
ESSENTIALLY, WHAT YOU'RE TELLING ME IS THAT YOU EXAMINED A DEAD BODY...
AT THE SCENE OF A MURDER?
NOD
I tried to stop her.
THAT'S WHY I WAS SO ANGRY.

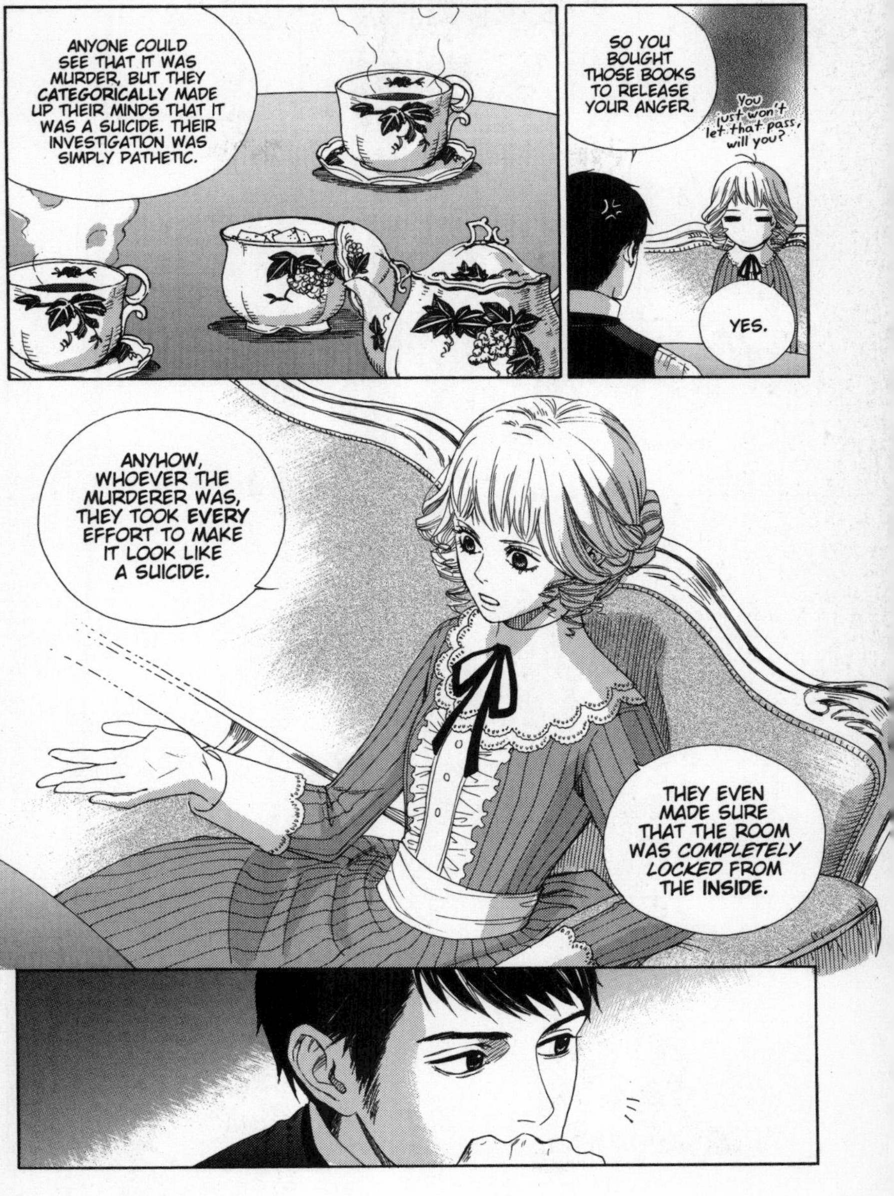
ANYONE COULD SEE THAT IT WAS MURDER, BUT THEY CATEGORICALLY MADE UP THEIR MINDS THAT IT WAS A SUICIDE. THEIR INVESTIGATION WAS SIMPLY PATHETIC.
SO YOU BOUGHT THOSE BOOKS TO RELEASE YOUR ANGER.
You just won't let that pass, will you?
YES.
ANYHOW, WHOEVER THE MURDERER WAS, THEY TOOK EVERY EFFORT TO MAKE IT LOOK LIKE A SUICIDE.
THEY EVEN MADE SURE THAT THE ROOM WAS COMPLETELY LOCKED FROM THE INSIDE.

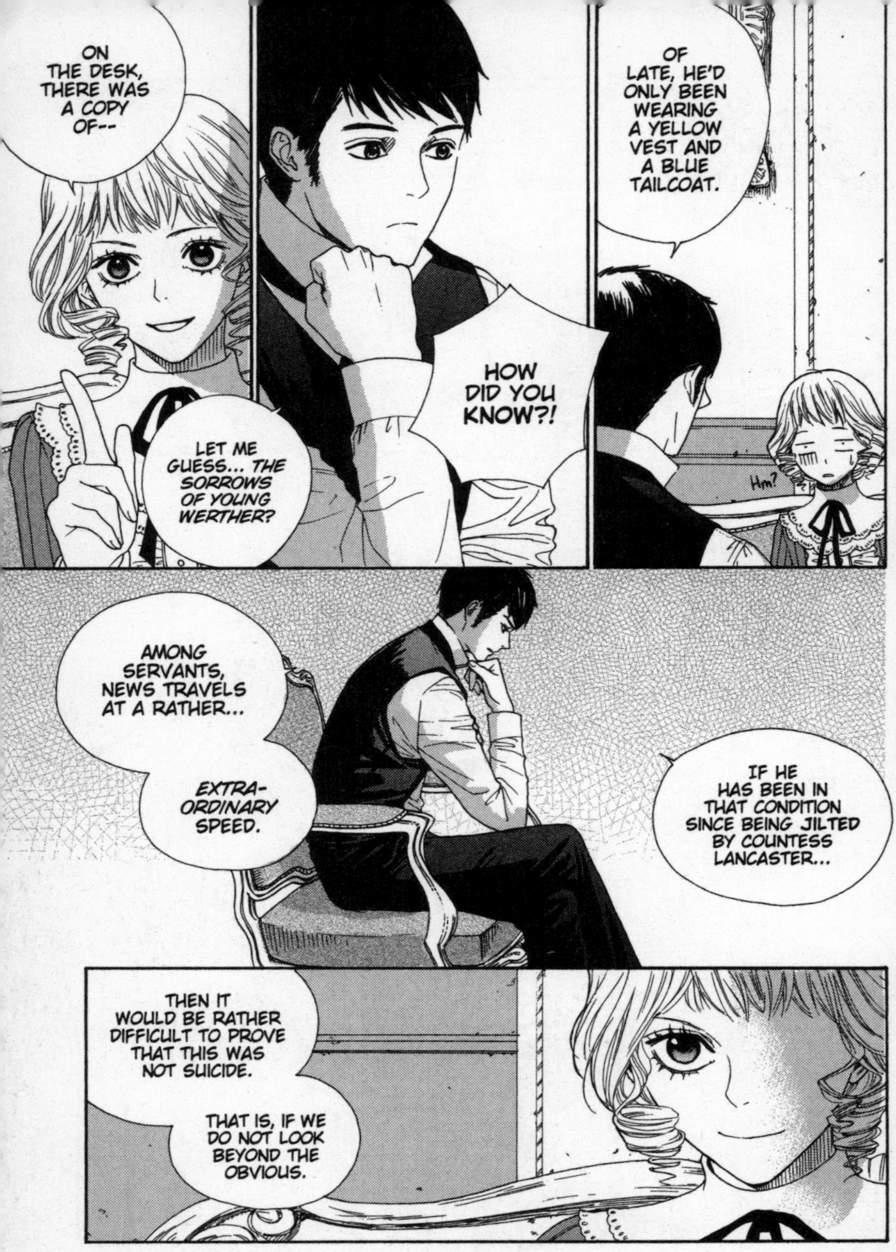
ON THE DESK, THERE WAS A COPY OF--
LET ME GUESS... THE SORROWS OF YOUNG WERTHER?
HOW DID YOU KNOW?!
OF LATE, HE'D ONLY BEEN WEARING A YELLOW VEST AND A BLUE TAILCOAT.
Hm?
AMONG SERVANTS, NEWS TRAVELS AT A RATHER...
EXTRA-ORDINARY SPEED.
IF HE HAS BEEN IN THAT CONDITION SINCE BEING JILTED BY COUNTESS LANCASTER...
THEN IT WOULD BE RATHER DIFFICULT TO PROVE THAT THIS WAS NOT SUICIDE.
THAT IS, IF WE DO NOT LOOK BEYOND THE OBVIOUS.

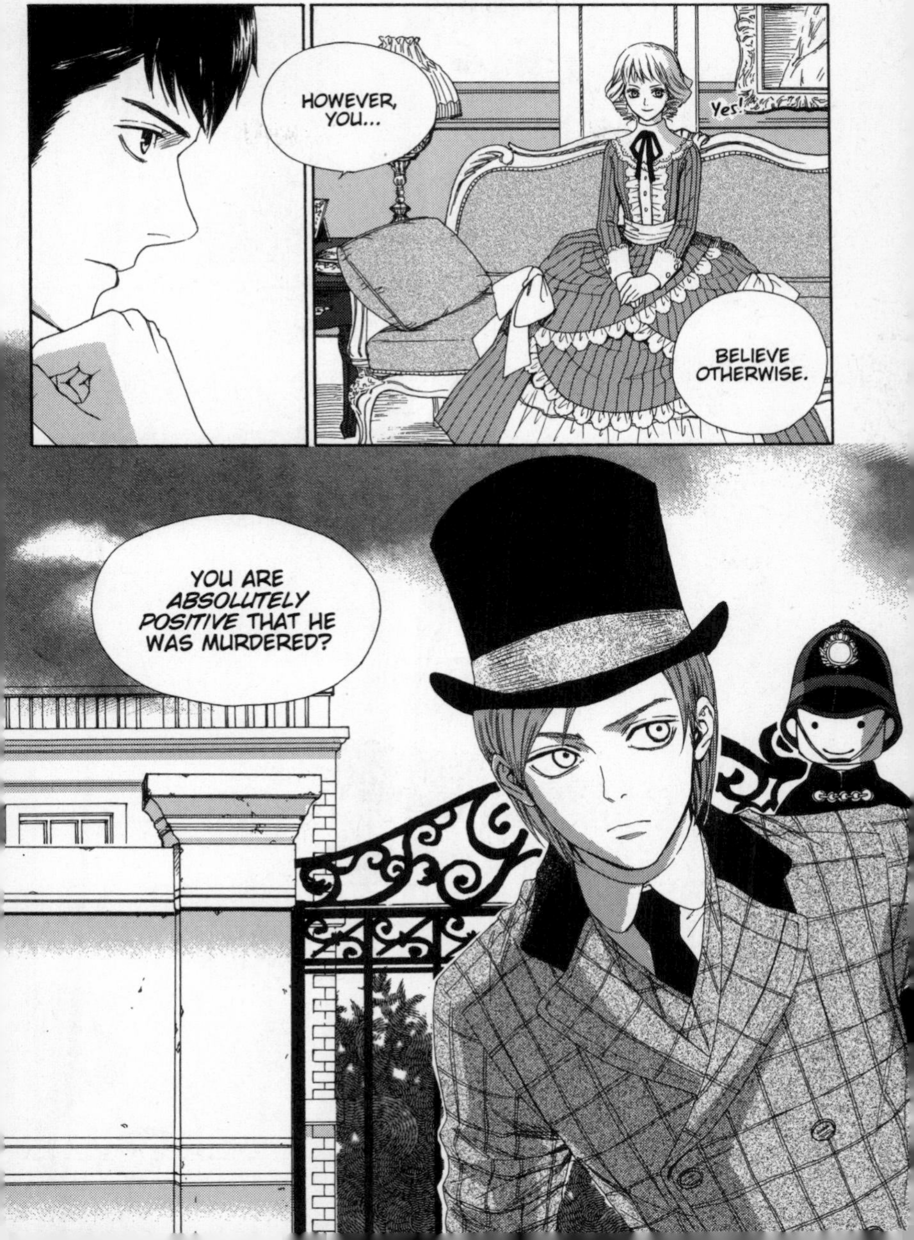
HOWEVER, YOU...
Yes!
BELIEVE OTHERWISE.
YOU ARE *ABSOLUTELY POSITIVE* THAT HE WAS MURDERED?

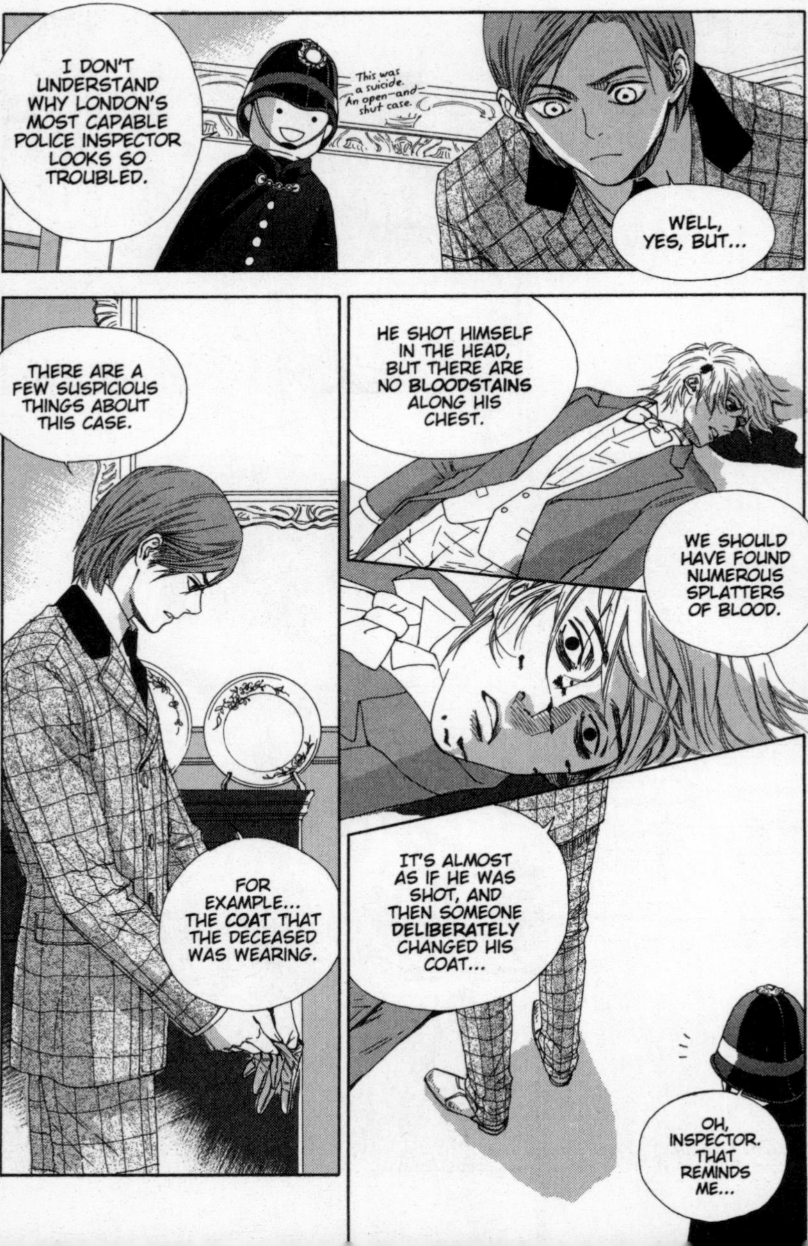
I DON'T UNDERSTAND WHY LONDON'S MOST CAPABLE POLICE INSPECTOR LOOKS SO TROUBLED.
This was a suicide. An open-and-shut case.
WELL, YES, BUT...
THERE ARE A FEW SUSPICIOUS THINGS ABOUT THIS CASE.
FOR EXAMPLE... THE COAT THAT THE DECEASED WAS WEARING.
HE SHOT HIMSELF IN THE HEAD, BUT THERE ARE NO BLOODSTAINS ALONG HIS CHEST.
WE SHOULD HAVE FOUND NUMEROUS SPLATTERS OF BLOOD.
IT'S ALMOST AS IF HE WAS SHOT, AND THEN SOMEONE DELIBERATELY CHANGED HIS COAT...
OH, INSPECTOR. THAT REMINDS ME...

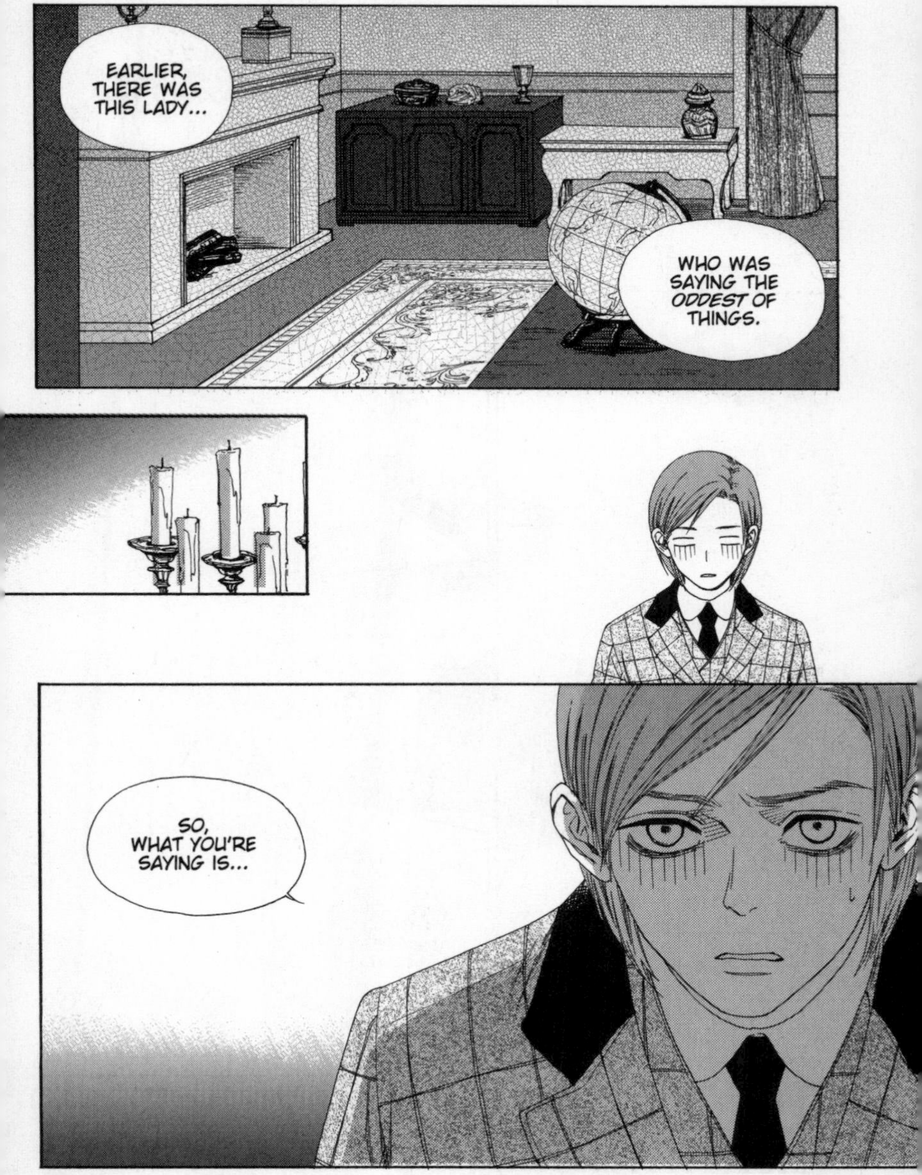
EARLIER, THERE WAS THIS LADY...
WHO WAS SAYING THE *ODDEST* OF THINGS.
SO, WHAT YOU'RE SAYING IS...

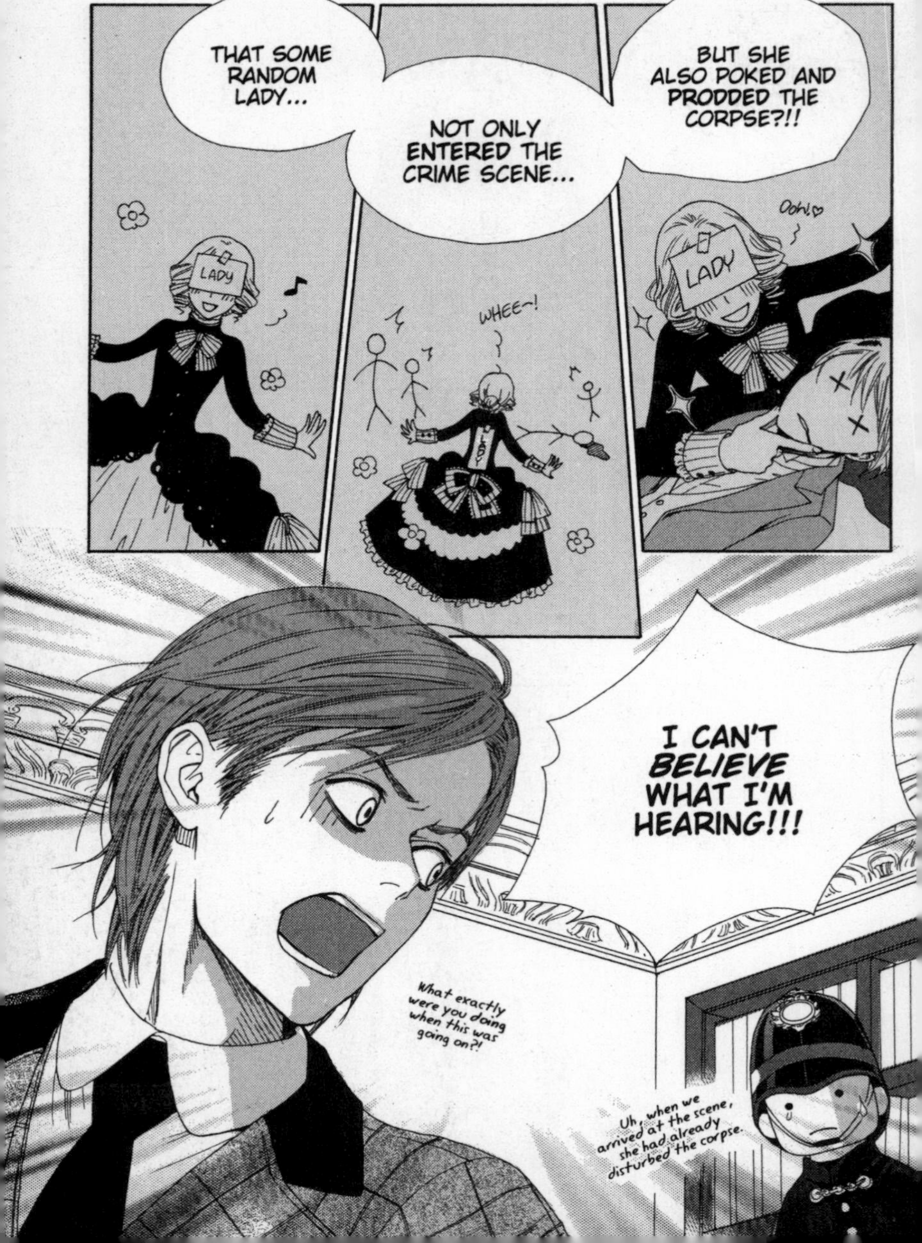
THAT SOME RANDOM LADY...
LADY
NOT ONLY ENTERED THE CRIME SCENE...
WHEE~!
LADY
BUT SHE ALSO POKED AND PRODDED THE CORPSE?!!
Ooh!♡
LADY
I CAN'T *BELIEVE* WHAT I'M HEARING!!!
What exactly were you doing when this was going on?!
Uh, when we arrived at the scene, she had already disturbed the corpse.

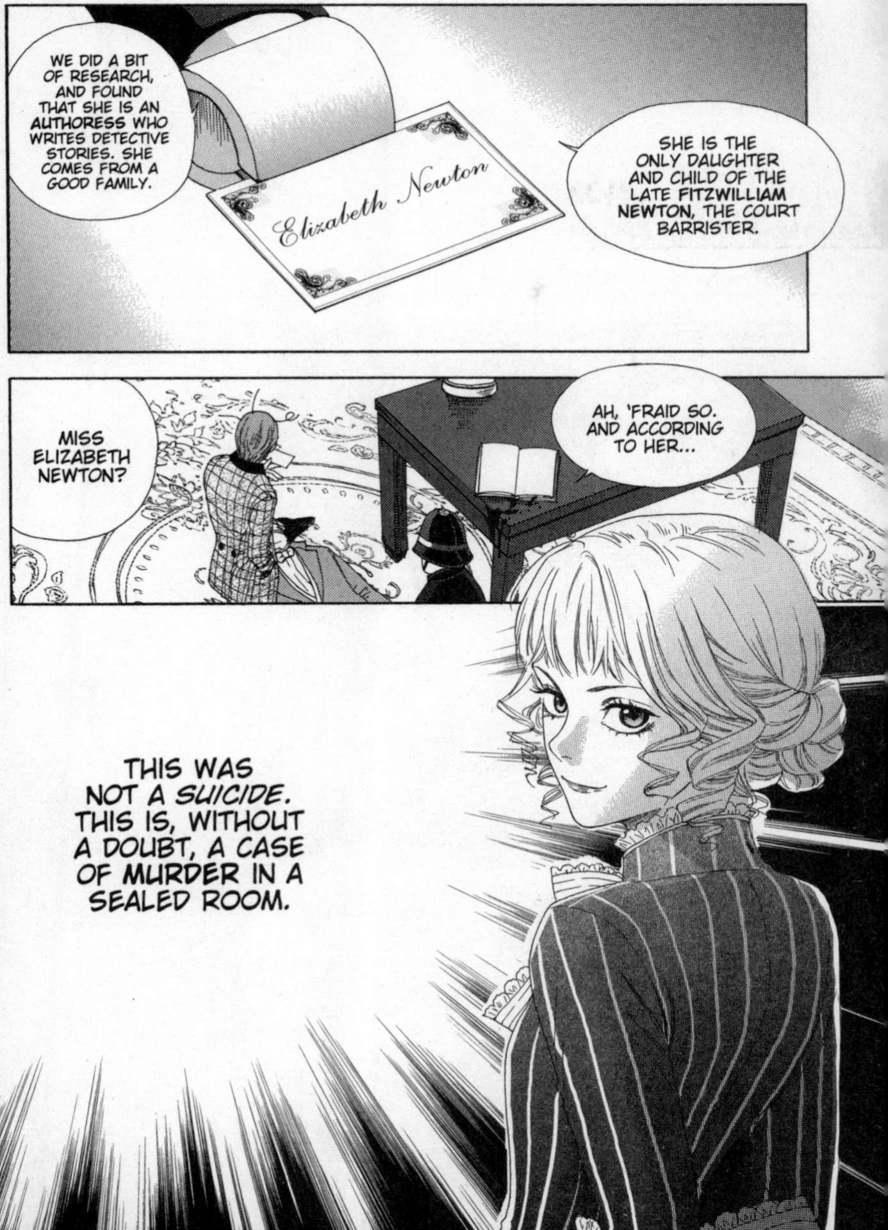
WE DID A BIT OF RESEARCH, AND FOUND THAT SHE IS AN AUTHORESS WHO WRITES DETECTIVE STORIES. SHE COMES FROM A GOOD FAMILY.
Elizabeth Newton
SHE IS THE ONLY DAUGHTER AND CHILD OF THE LATE FITZWILLIAM NEWTON, THE COURT BARRISTER.
MISS ELIZABETH NEWTON?
AH, 'FRAID SO. AND ACCORDING TO HER...
THIS WAS NOT A *SUICIDE*. THIS IS, WITHOUT A DOUBT, A CASE OF MURDER IN A SEALED ROOM.

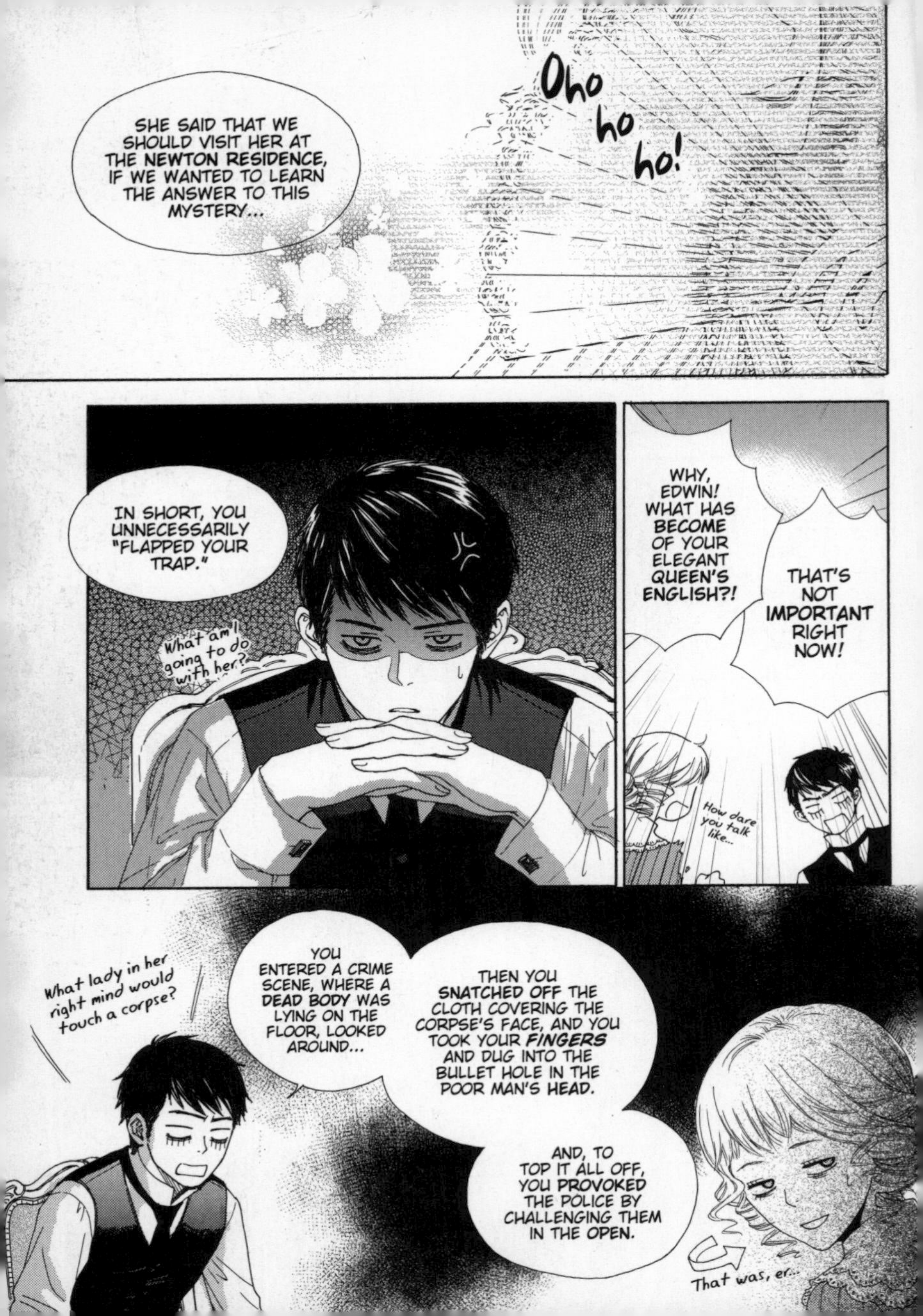
SHE SAID THAT WE SHOULD VISIT HER AT THE NEWTON RESIDENCE, IF WE WANTED TO LEARN THE ANSWER TO THIS MYSTERY...
Oho ho ho!
IN SHORT, YOU UNNECESSARILY "FLAPPED YOUR TRAP."
What am I going to do with her?
WHY, EDWIN! WHAT HAS BECOME OF YOUR ELEGANT QUEEN'S ENGLISH?!
THAT'S NOT IMPORTANT RIGHT NOW!
How dare you talk like...
What lady in her right mind would touch a corpse?
YOU ENTERED A CRIME SCENE, WHERE A DEAD BODY WAS LYING ON THE FLOOR, LOOKED AROUND...
THEN YOU SNATCHED OFF THE CLOTH COVERING THE CORPSE'S FACE, AND YOU TOOK YOUR FINGERS AND DUG INTO THE BULLET HOLE IN THE POOR MAN'S HEAD.
AND, TO TOP IT ALL OFF, YOU PROVOKED THE POLICE BY CHALLENGING THEM IN THE OPEN.
That was, er...

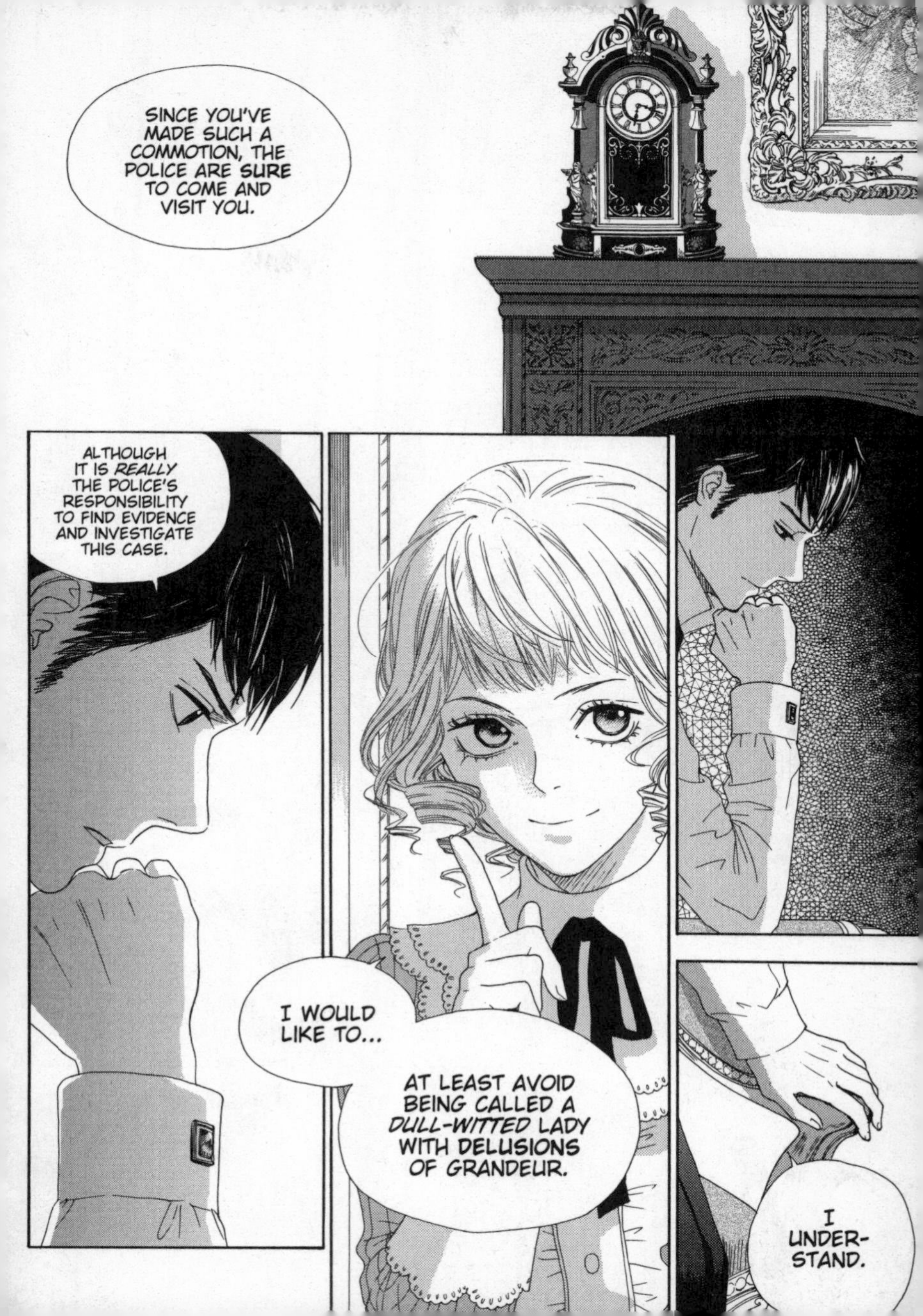
SINCE YOU'VE MADE SUCH A COMMOTION, THE POLICE ARE SURE TO COME AND VISIT YOU.
ALTHOUGH IT IS *REALLY* THE POLICE'S RESPONSIBILITY TO FIND EVIDENCE AND INVESTIGATE THIS CASE.
I WOULD LIKE TO...
AT LEAST AVOID BEING CALLED A *DULL-WITTED* LADY WITH DELUSIONS OF GRANDEUR.
I UNDER-STAND.

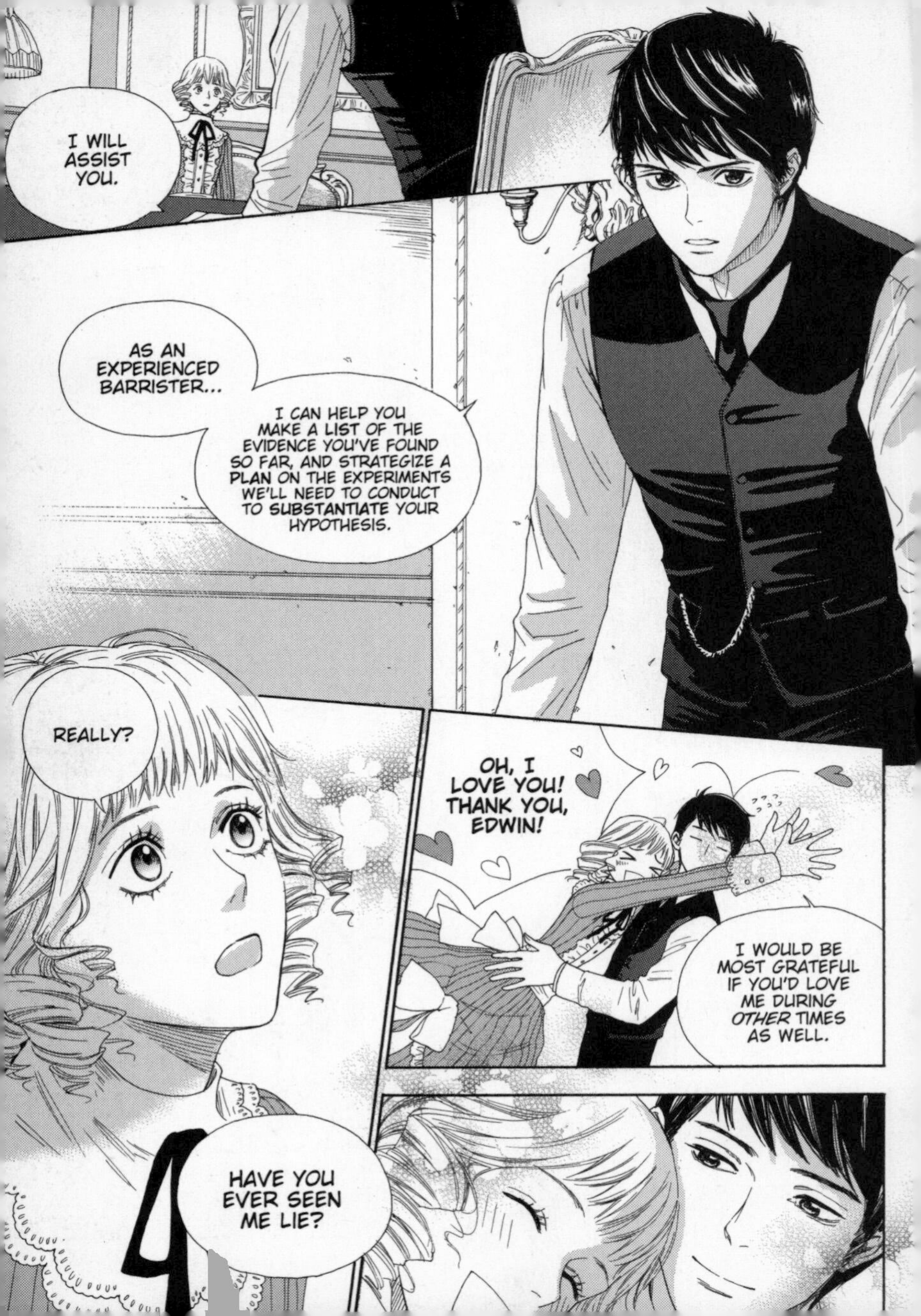
I WILL ASSIST YOU.
AS AN EXPERIENCED BARRISTER...
I CAN HELP YOU MAKE A LIST OF THE EVIDENCE YOU'VE FOUND SO FAR, AND STRATEGIZE A PLAN ON THE EXPERIMENTS WE'LL NEED TO CONDUCT TO SUBSTANTIATE YOUR HYPOTHESIS.
REALLY?
OH, I LOVE YOU! THANK YOU, EDWIN!
I WOULD BE MOST GRATEFUL IF YOU'D LOVE ME DURING *OTHER* TIMES AS WELL.
HAVE YOU EVER SEEN ME LIE?

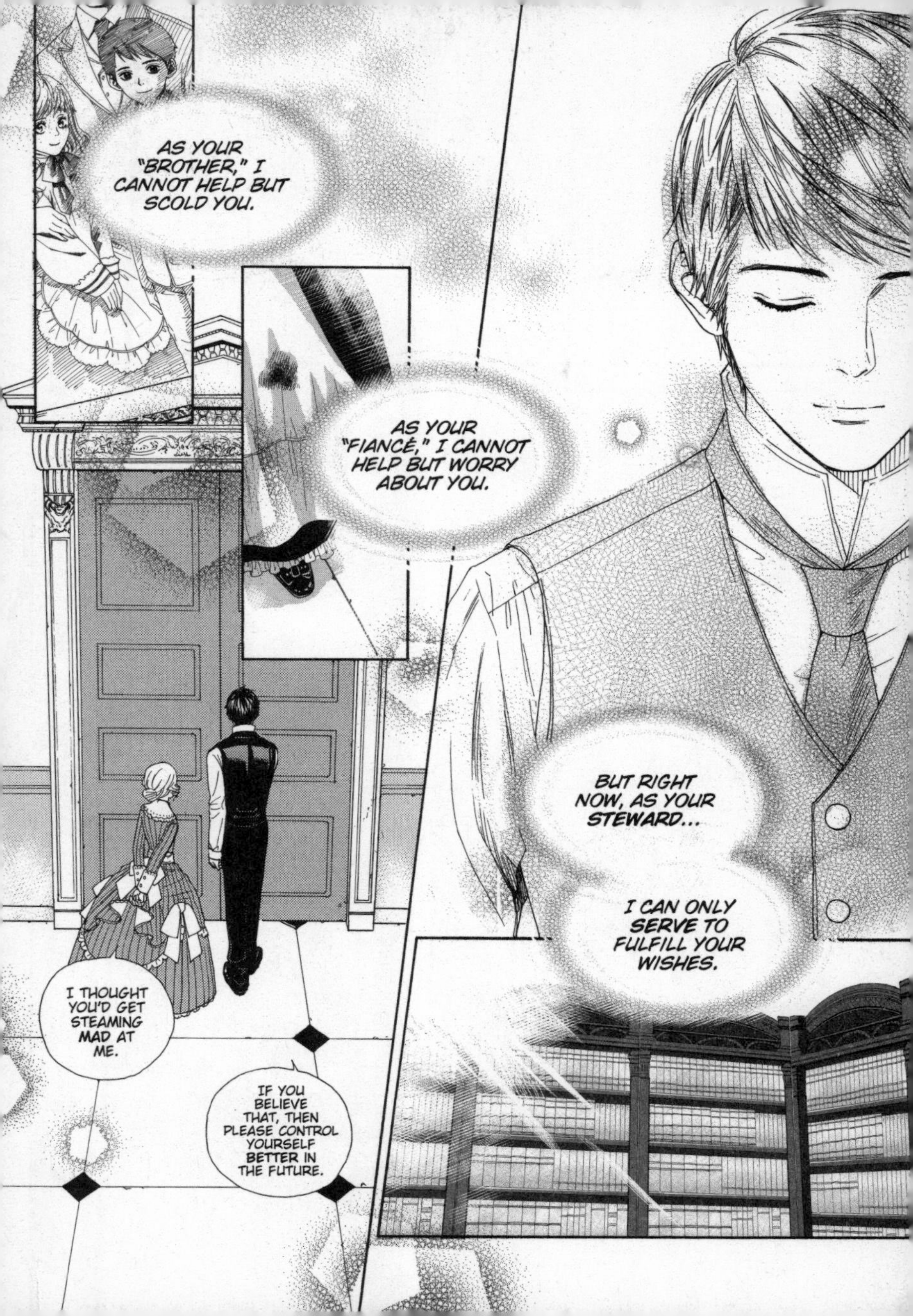
AS YOUR "BROTHER," I CANNOT HELP BUT SCOLD YOU.
AS YOUR "FIANCÉ," I CANNOT HELP BUT WORRY ABOUT YOU.
I THOUGHT YOU'D GET STEAMING MAD AT ME.
IF YOU BELIEVE THAT, THEN PLEASE CONTROL YOURSELF BETTER IN THE FUTURE.
BUT RIGHT NOW, AS YOUR STEWARD...
I CAN ONLY SERVE TO FULFILL YOUR WISHES.

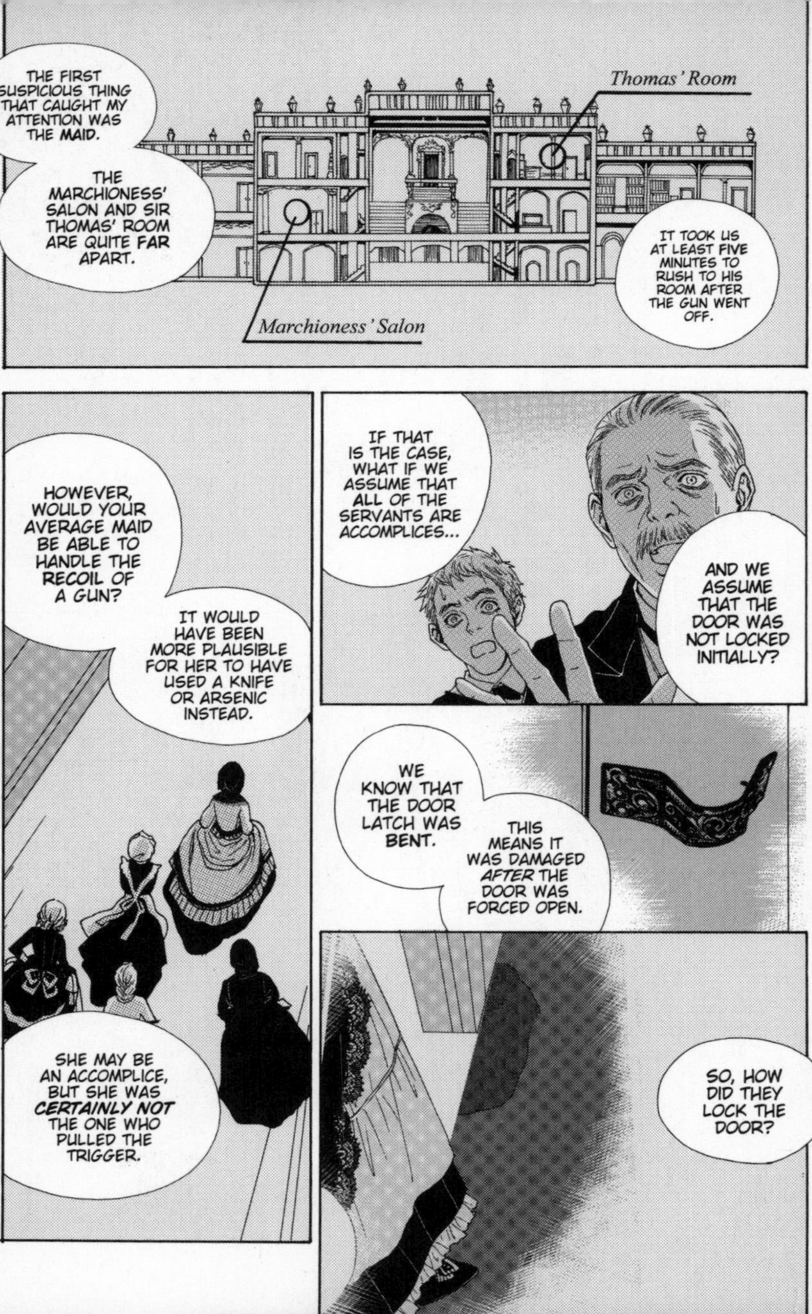
THE FIRST SUSPICIOUS THING THAT CAUGHT MY ATTENTION WAS THE MAID.
THE MARCHIONESS' SALON AND SIR THOMAS' ROOM ARE QUITE FAR APART.
Thomas' Room
Marchioness' Salon
IT TOOK US AT LEAST FIVE MINUTES TO RUSH TO HIS ROOM AFTER THE GUN WENT OFF.
HOWEVER, WOULD YOUR AVERAGE MAID BE ABLE TO HANDLE THE RECOIL OF A GUN?
IT WOULD HAVE BEEN MORE PLAUSIBLE FOR HER TO HAVE USED A KNIFE OR ARSENIC INSTEAD.
SHE MAY BE AN ACCOMPLICE, BUT SHE WAS CERTAINLY NOT THE ONE WHO PULLED THE TRIGGER.
IF THAT IS THE CASE, WHAT IF WE ASSUME THAT ALL OF THE SERVANTS ARE ACCOMPLICES...
AND WE ASSUME THAT THE DOOR WAS NOT LOCKED INITIALLY?
WE KNOW THAT THE DOOR LATCH WAS BENT.
THIS MEANS IT WAS DAMAGED AFTER THE DOOR WAS FORCED OPEN.
SO, HOW DID THEY LOCK THE DOOR?

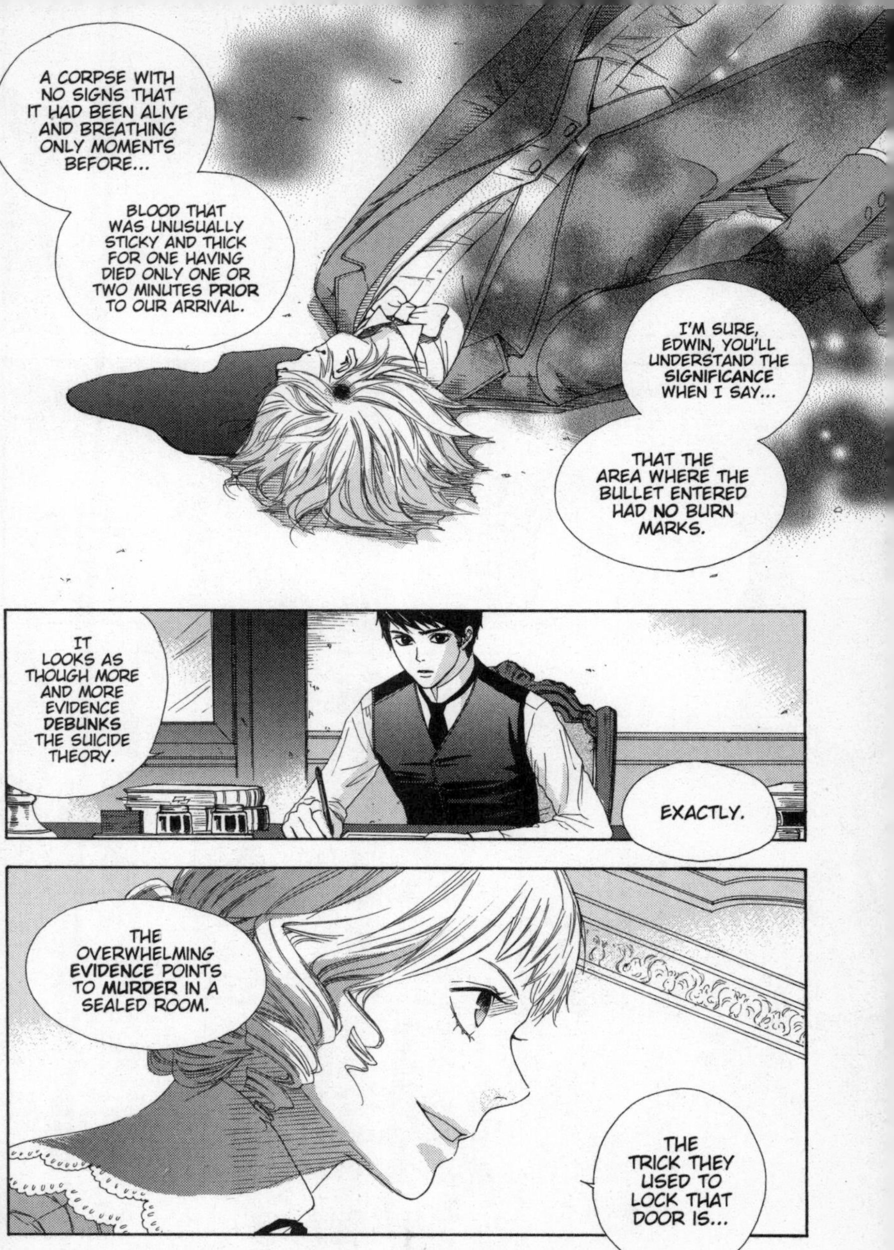
A CORPSE WITH NO SIGNS THAT IT HAD BEEN ALIVE AND BREATHING ONLY MOMENTS BEFORE...
BLOOD THAT WAS UNUSUALLY STICKY AND THICK FOR ONE HAVING DIED ONLY ONE OR TWO MINUTES PRIOR TO OUR ARRIVAL.
I'M SURE, EDWIN, YOU'LL UNDERSTAND THE SIGNIFICANCE WHEN I SAY...
THAT THE AREA WHERE THE BULLET ENTERED HAD NO BURN MARKS.
IT LOOKS AS THOUGH MORE AND MORE EVIDENCE DEBUNKS THE SUICIDE THEORY.
EXACTLY.
THE OVERWHELMING EVIDENCE POINTS TO MURDER IN A SEALED ROOM.
THE TRICK THEY USED TO LOCK THAT DOOR IS...

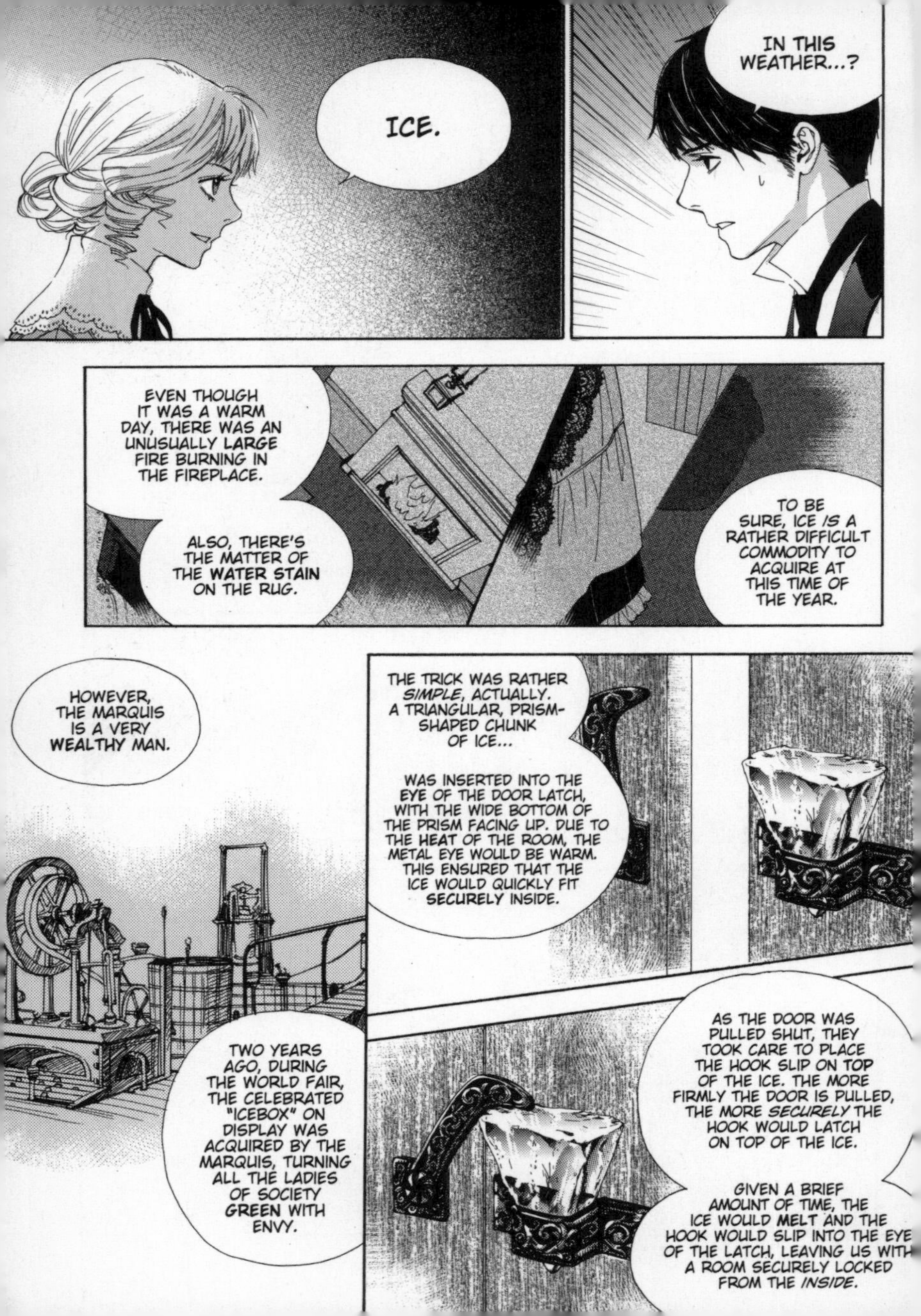
ICE.
IN THIS WEATHER...?
EVEN THOUGH IT WAS A WARM DAY, THERE WAS AN UNUSUALLY LARGE FIRE BURNING IN THE FIREPLACE.
ALSO, THERE'S THE MATTER OF THE WATER STAIN ON THE RUG.
TO BE SURE, ICE IS A RATHER DIFFICULT COMMODITY TO ACQUIRE AT THIS TIME OF THE YEAR.
HOWEVER, THE MARQUIS IS A VERY WEALTHY MAN.
TWO YEARS AGO, DURING THE WORLD FAIR, THE CELEBRATED "ICEBOX" ON DISPLAY WAS ACQUIRED BY THE MARQUIS, TURNING ALL THE LADIES OF SOCIETY GREEN WITH ENVY.
THE TRICK WAS RATHER SIMPLE, ACTUALLY. A TRIANGULAR, PRISM-SHAPED CHUNK OF ICE...
WAS INSERTED INTO THE EYE OF THE DOOR LATCH, WITH THE WIDE BOTTOM OF THE PRISM FACING UP. DUE TO THE HEAT OF THE ROOM, THE METAL EYE WOULD BE WARM. THIS ENSURED THAT THE ICE WOULD QUICKLY FIT SECURELY INSIDE.
AS THE DOOR WAS PULLED SHUT, THEY TOOK CARE TO PLACE THE HOOK SLIP ON TOP OF THE ICE. THE MORE FIRMLY THE DOOR IS PULLED, THE MORE SECURELY THE HOOK WOULD LATCH ON TOP OF THE ICE.
GIVEN A BRIEF AMOUNT OF TIME, THE ICE WOULD MELT AND THE HOOK WOULD SLIP INTO THE EYE OF THE LATCH, LEAVING US WITH A ROOM SECURELY LOCKED FROM THE INSIDE.

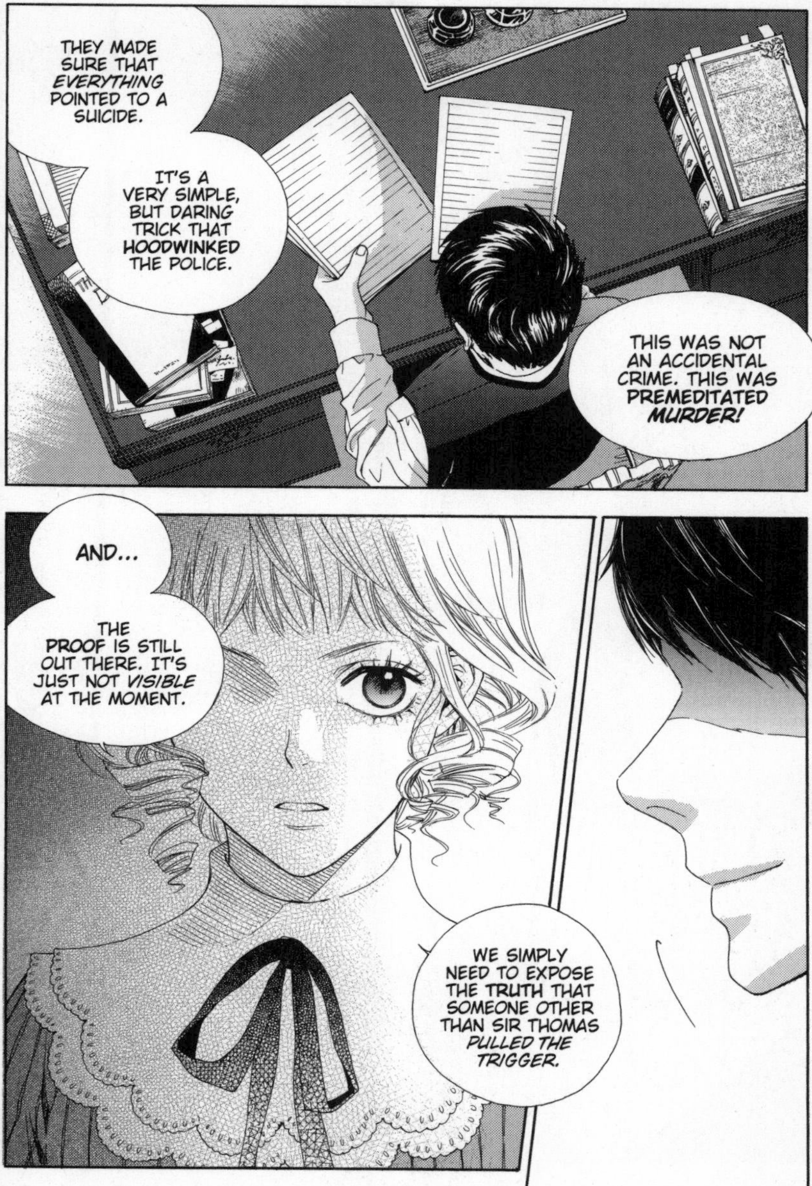
THEY MADE SURE THAT *EVERYTHING* POINTED TO A SUICIDE.
IT'S A VERY SIMPLE, BUT DARING TRICK THAT HOODWINKED THE POLICE.
THIS WAS NOT AN ACCIDENTAL CRIME. THIS WAS PREMEDITATED ***MURDER!***
AND...
THE PROOF IS STILL OUT THERE. IT'S JUST NOT *VISIBLE* AT THE MOMENT.
WE SIMPLY NEED TO EXPOSE THE TRUTH THAT SOMEONE OTHER THAN SIR THOMAS *PULLED THE TRIGGER.*

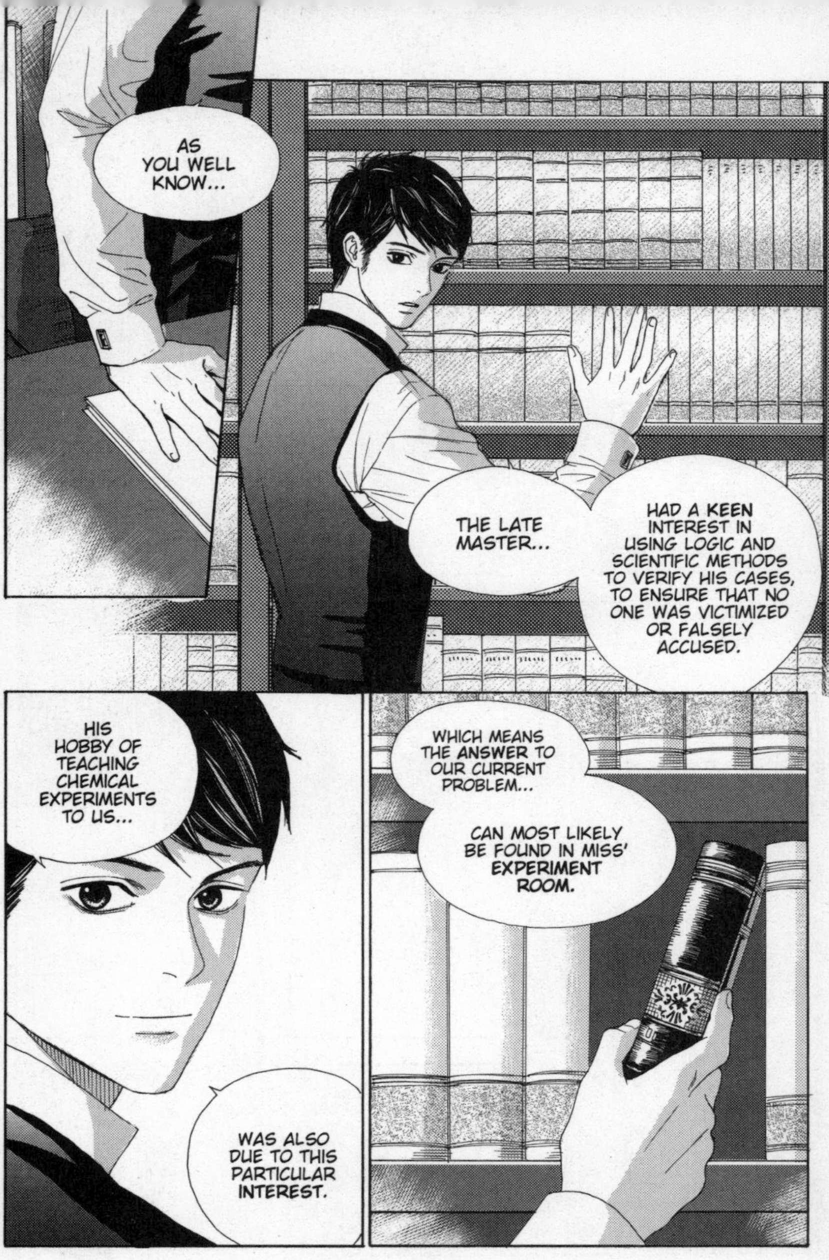
AS YOU WELL KNOW...
THE LATE MASTER...
HAD A KEEN INTEREST IN USING LOGIC AND SCIENTIFIC METHODS TO VERIFY HIS CASES, TO ENSURE THAT NO ONE WAS VICTIMIZED OR FALSELY ACCUSED.
HIS HOBBY OF TEACHING CHEMICAL EXPERIMENTS TO US...
WAS ALSO DUE TO THIS PARTICULAR INTEREST.
WHICH MEANS THE ANSWER TO OUR CURRENT PROBLEM...
CAN MOST LIKELY BE FOUND IN MISS' EXPERIMENT ROOM.

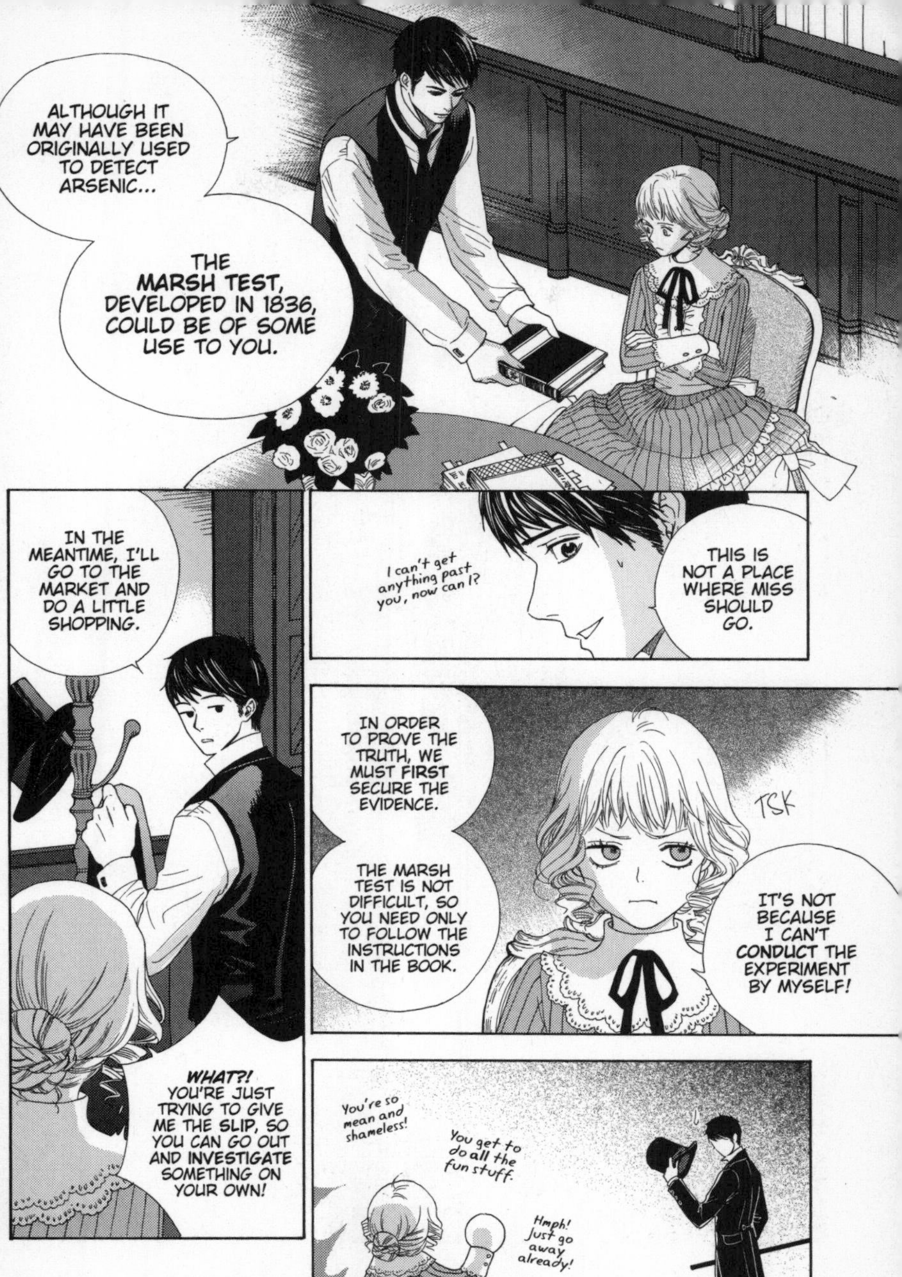
ALTHOUGH IT MAY HAVE BEEN ORIGINALLY USED TO DETECT ARSENIC...
THE MARSH TEST, DEVELOPED IN 1836, COULD BE OF SOME USE TO YOU.
IN THE MEANTIME, I'LL GO TO THE MARKET AND DO A LITTLE SHOPPING.
WHAT?! YOU'RE JUST TRYING TO GIVE ME THE SLIP, SO YOU CAN GO OUT AND INVESTIGATE SOMETHING ON YOUR OWN!
I can't get anything past you, now can I?
THIS IS NOT A PLACE WHERE MISS SHOULD GO.
IN ORDER TO PROVE THE TRUTH, WE MUST FIRST SECURE THE EVIDENCE.
THE MARSH TEST IS NOT DIFFICULT, SO YOU NEED ONLY TO FOLLOW THE INSTRUCTIONS IN THE BOOK.
TSK
IT'S NOT BECAUSE I CAN'T CONDUCT THE EXPERIMENT BY MYSELF!
You're so mean and shameless!
You get to do all the fun stuff.
Hmph! Just go away already!

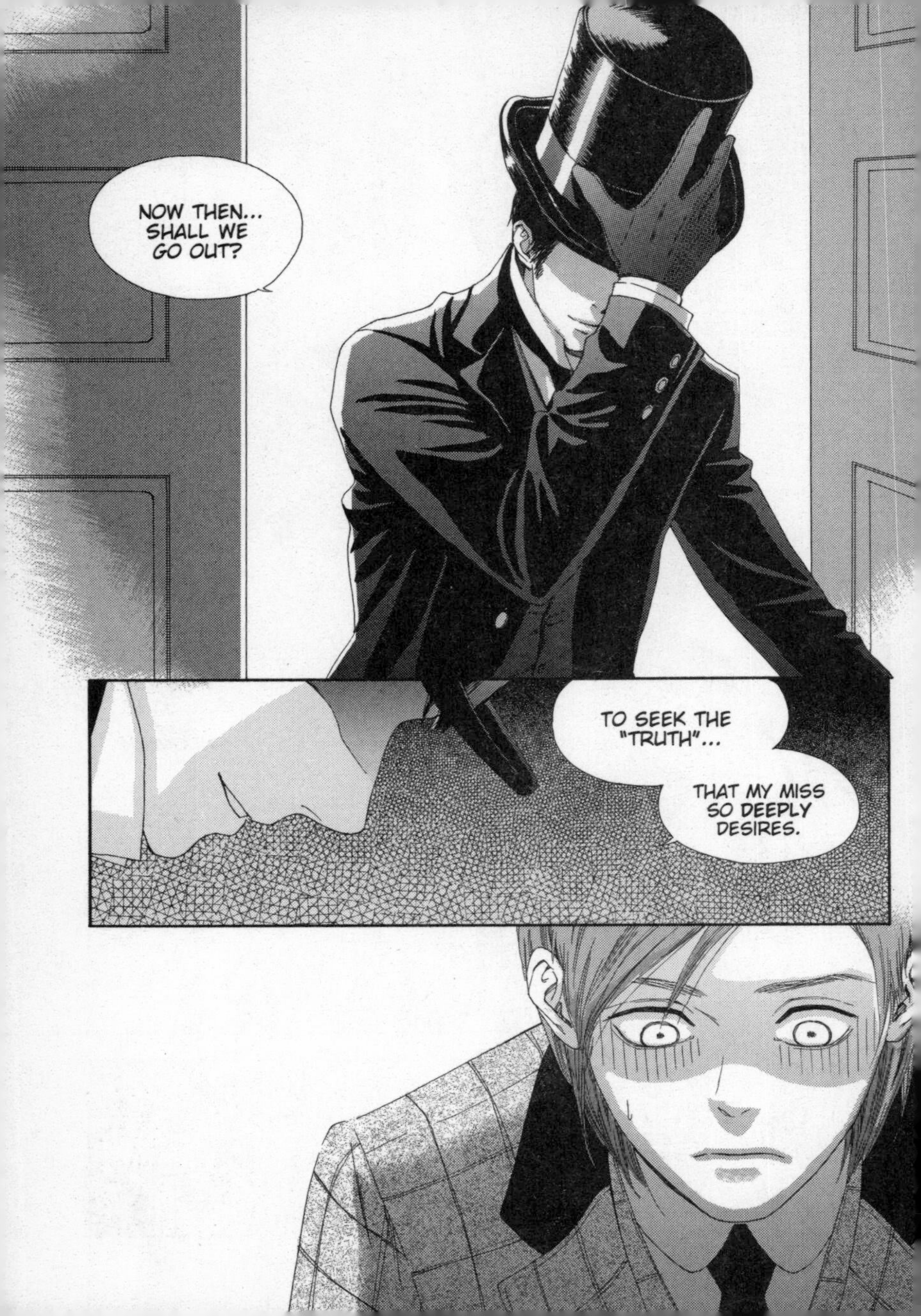
NOW THEN... SHALL WE GO OUT?
TO SEEK THE "TRUTH"...
THAT MY MISS SO DEEPLY DESIRES.

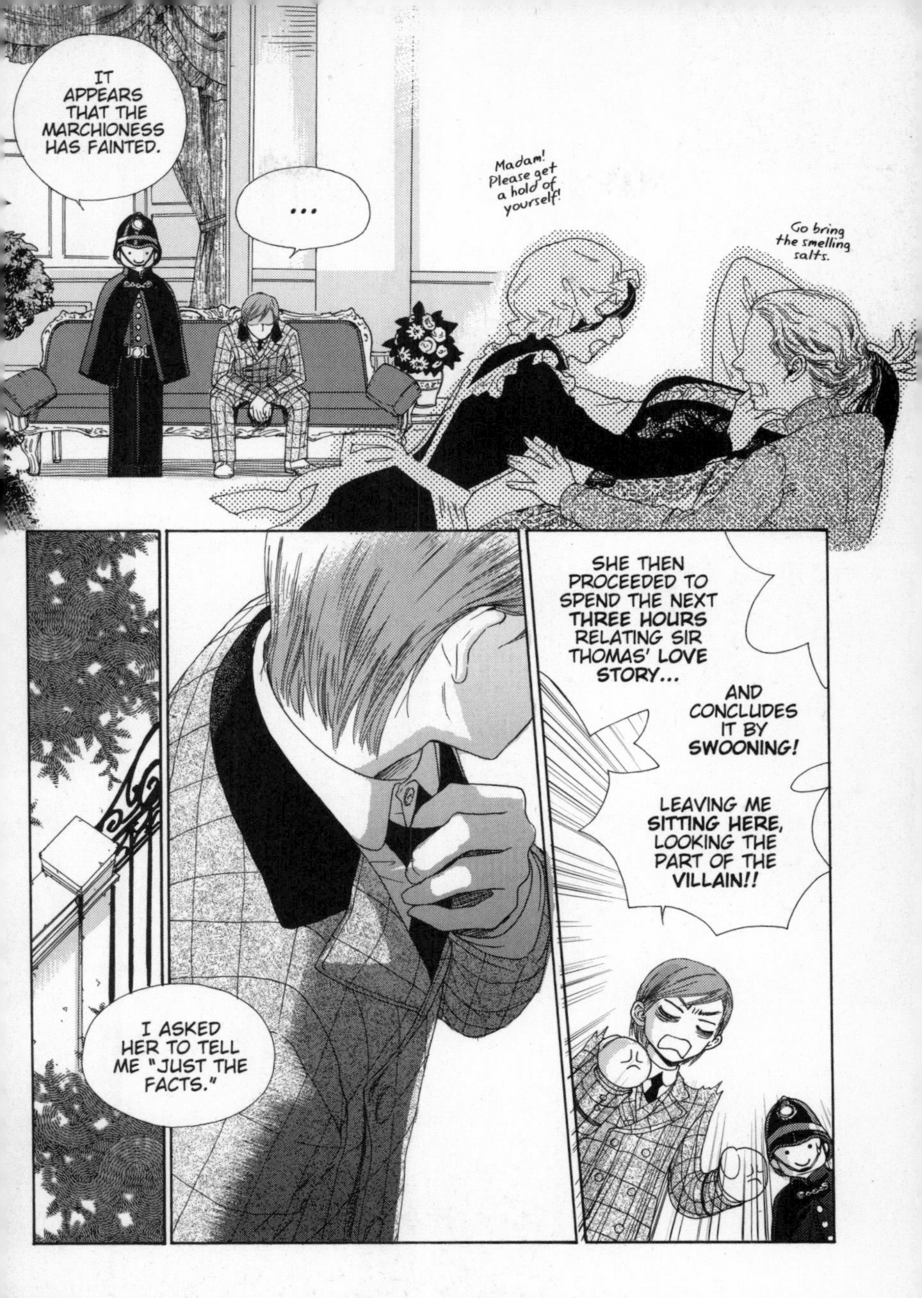
IT APPEARS THAT THE MARCHIONESS HAS FAINTED.
...
Madam! Please get a hold of yourself!
Go bring the smelling salts.
I ASKED HER TO TELL ME "JUST THE FACTS."
SHE THEN PROCEEDED TO SPEND THE NEXT THREE HOURS RELATING SIR THOMAS' LOVE STORY...
AND CONCLUDES IT BY SWOONING!
LEAVING ME SITTING HERE, LOOKING THE PART OF THE VILLAIN!!

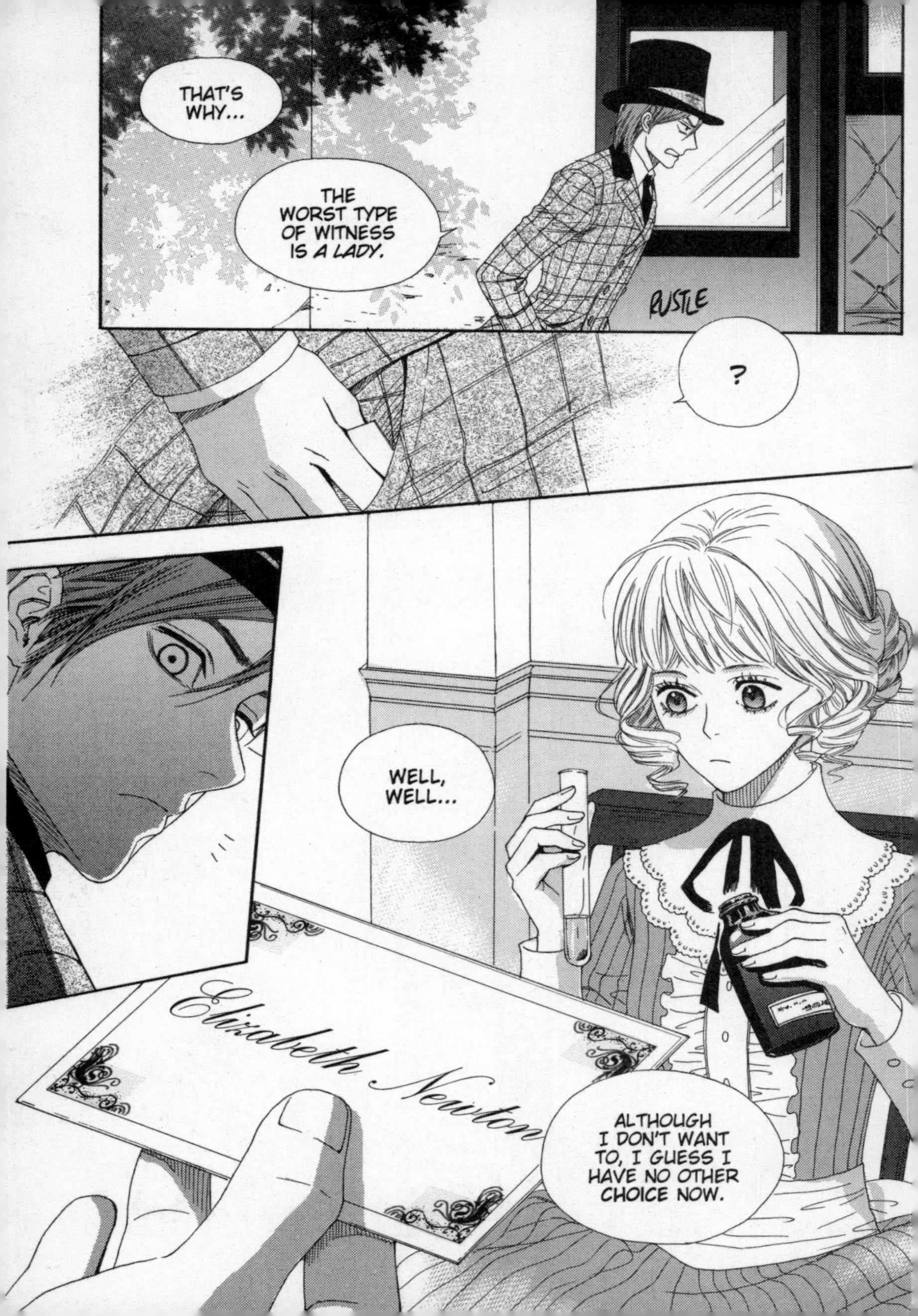
THAT'S WHY...
THE WORST TYPE OF WITNESS IS A LADY.
RUSTLE
?
WELL, WELL...
Elizabeth Newton
ALTHOUGH I DON'T WANT TO, I GUESS I HAVE NO OTHER CHOICE NOW.

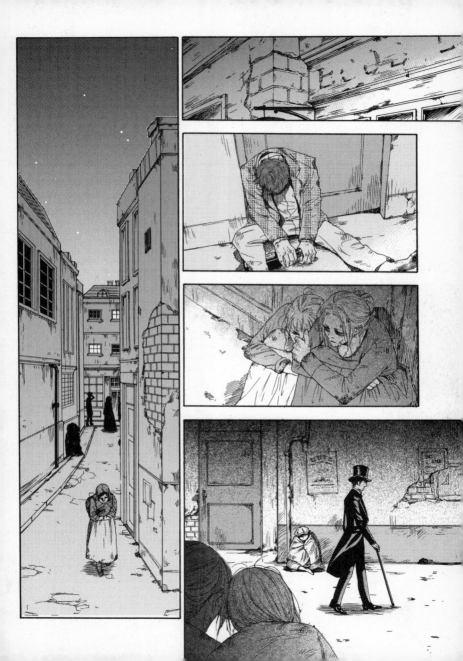

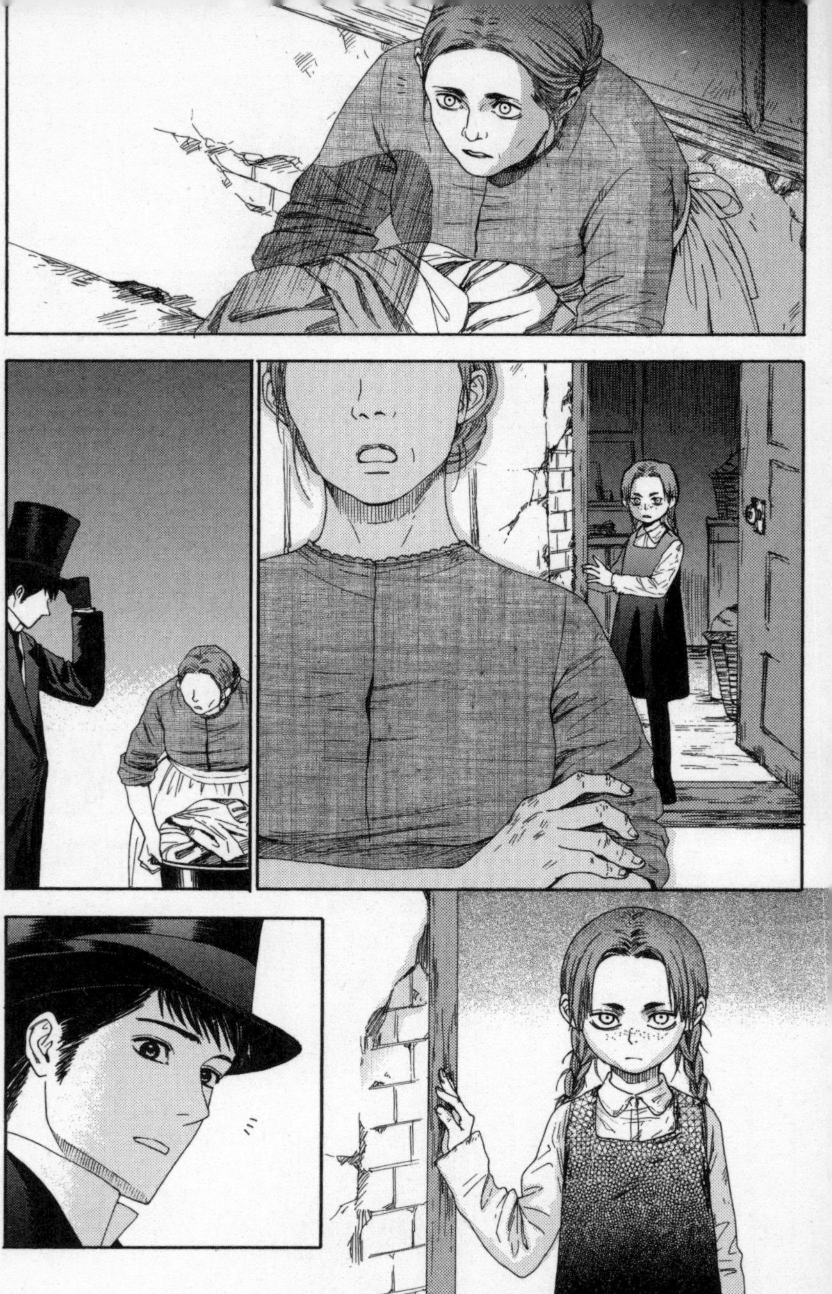

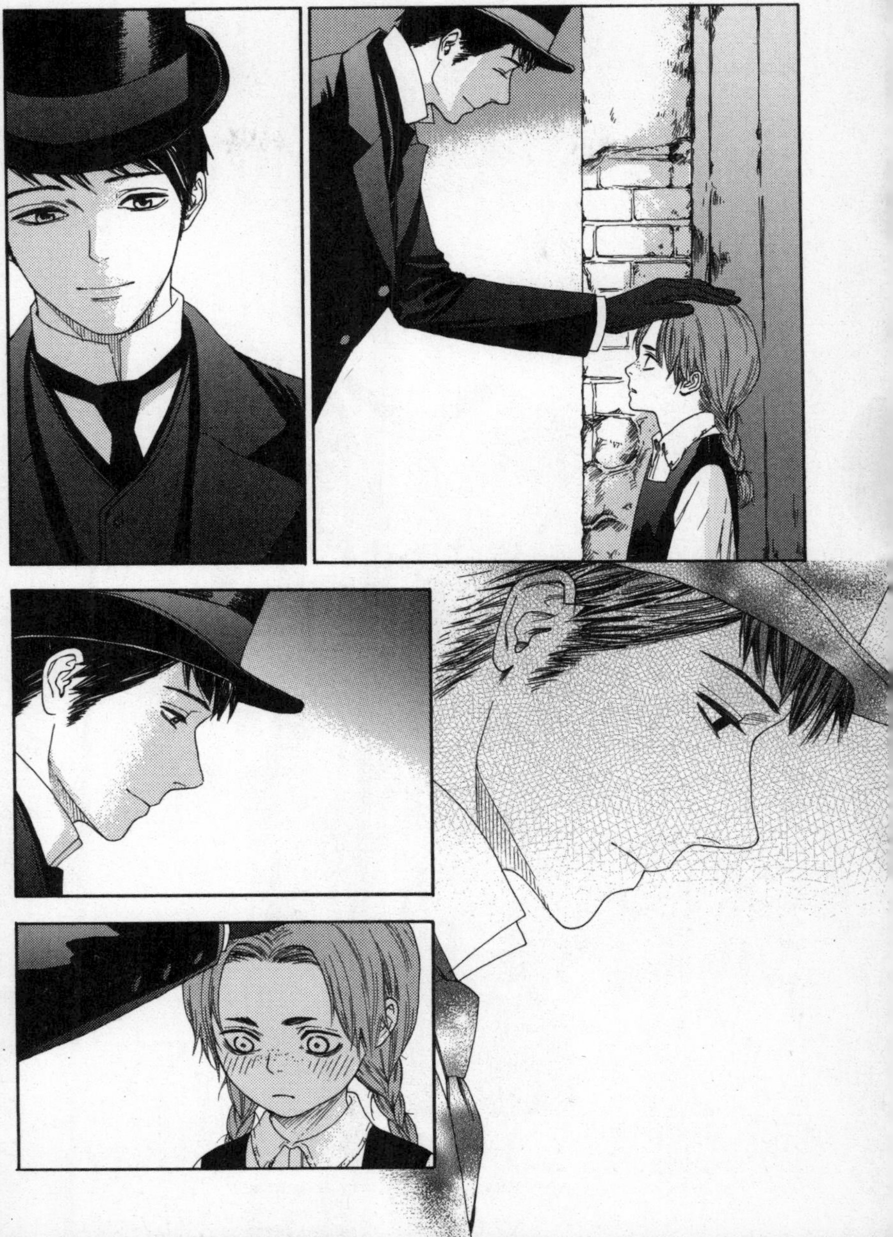

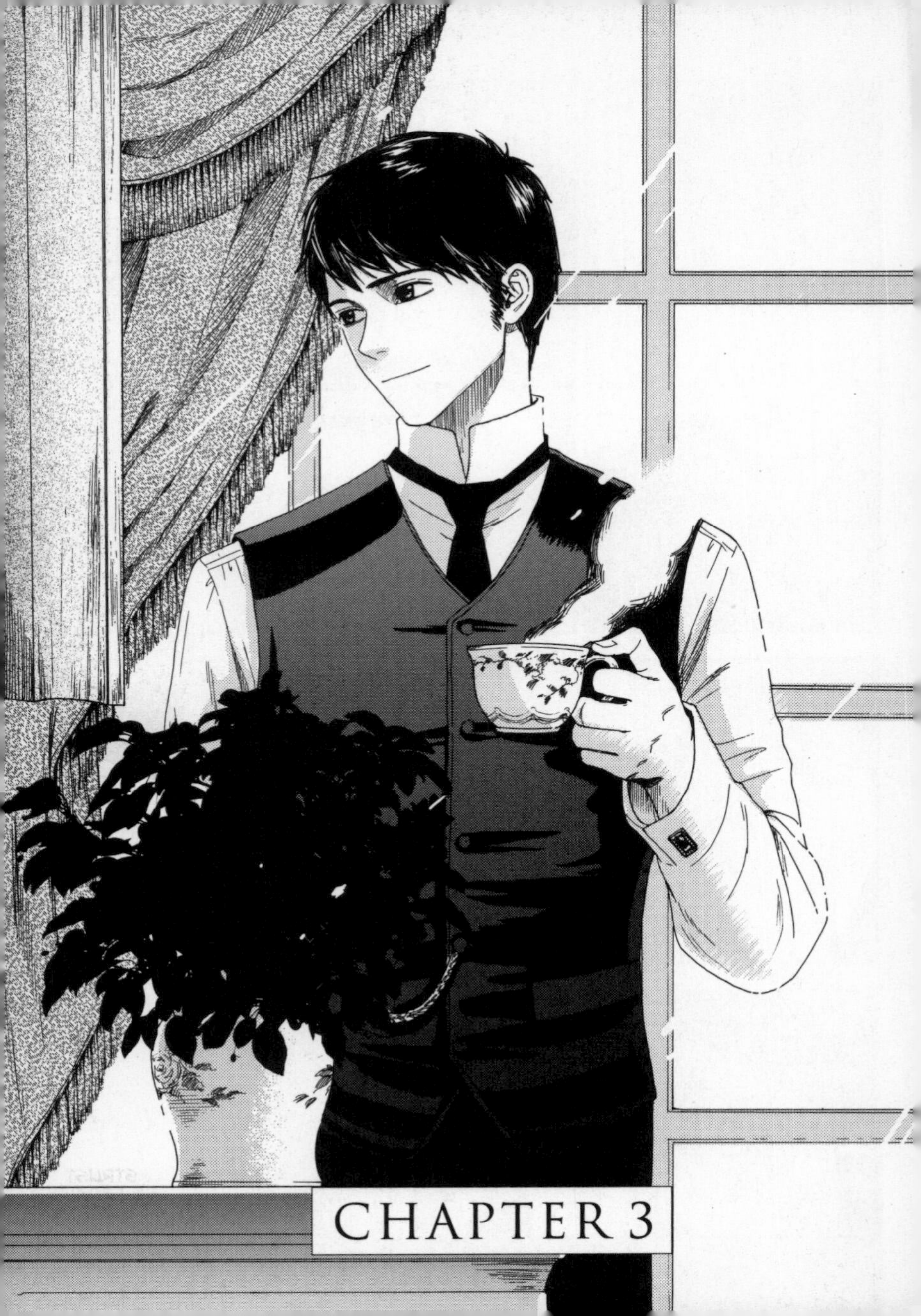
CHAPTER 3

YOU'RE...

NOT MARRIED YET, ARE YOU?

SIR...?

NO, I'M NOT. YOU'RE UNMARRIED AS WELL, IF I'M RIGHT, INSPECTOR.

I...

I AM *NEVER GOING* TO MARRY.

OH, I SEE! IT'S BECAUSE YOU'RE *MARRIED TO CRIME!*

OH, DO SHUT UP.

THE REASON WHY I WON'T MARRY IS EASY TO UNDERSTAND.

I SIMPLY...

What do you mean, "married to crime"? What am I, some kind of crime addict?

DISTRUST THE FEMALE PERSUASION *ENTIRELY.*

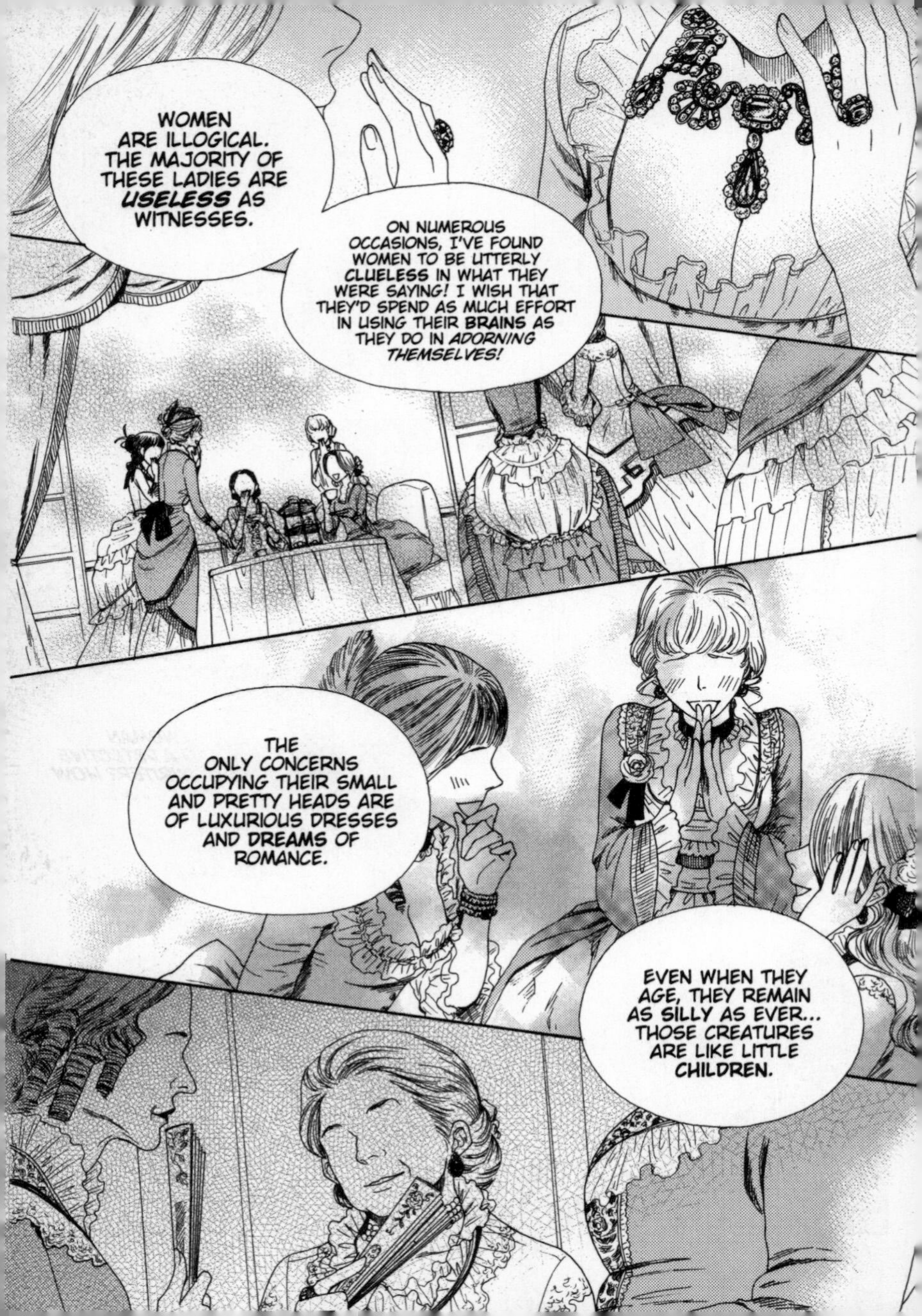
WOMEN ARE ILLOGICAL. THE MAJORITY OF THESE LADIES ARE ***USELESS*** AS WITNESSES.
ON NUMEROUS OCCASIONS, I'VE FOUND WOMEN TO BE UTTERLY **CLUELESS** IN WHAT THEY WERE SAYING! I WISH THAT THEY'D SPEND AS MUCH EFFORT IN USING THEIR **BRAINS** AS THEY DO IN *ADORNING THEMSELVES!*
THE ONLY CONCERNS OCCUPYING THEIR SMALL AND PRETTY HEADS ARE OF LUXURIOUS DRESSES AND **DREAMS** OF ROMANCE.
EVEN WHEN THEY AGE, THEY REMAIN AS SILLY AS EVER... THOSE CREATURES ARE LIKE LITTLE **CHILDREN.**

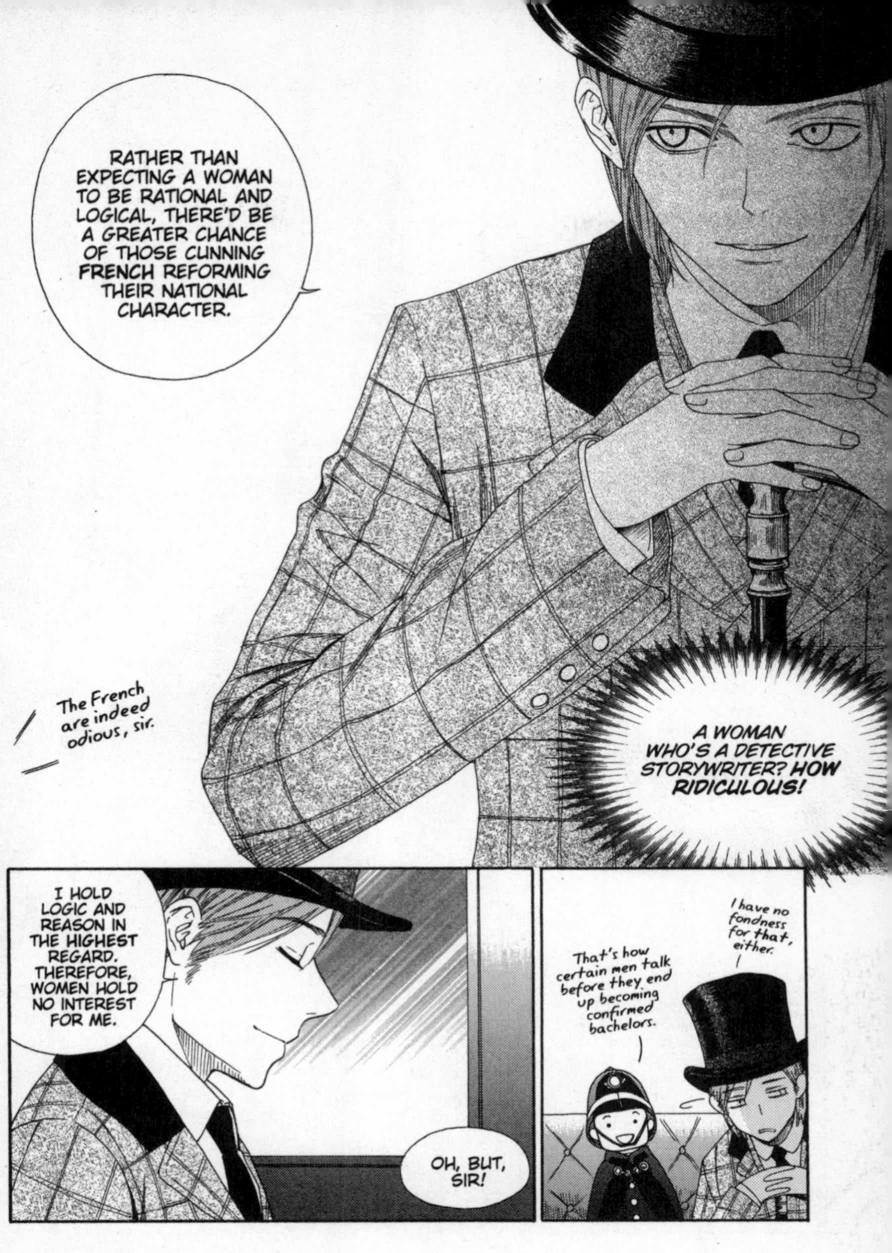
RATHER THAN EXPECTING A WOMAN TO BE RATIONAL AND LOGICAL, THERE'D BE A GREATER CHANCE OF THOSE CUNNING FRENCH REFORMING THEIR NATIONAL CHARACTER.
The French are indeed odious, sir.
A WOMAN WHO'S A DETECTIVE STORYWRITER? HOW RIDICULOUS!
I HOLD LOGIC AND REASON IN THE HIGHEST REGARD. THEREFORE, WOMEN HOLD NO INTEREST FOR ME.
OH, BUT, SIR!
That's how certain men talk before they end up becoming confirmed bachelors.
I have no fondness for that, either.

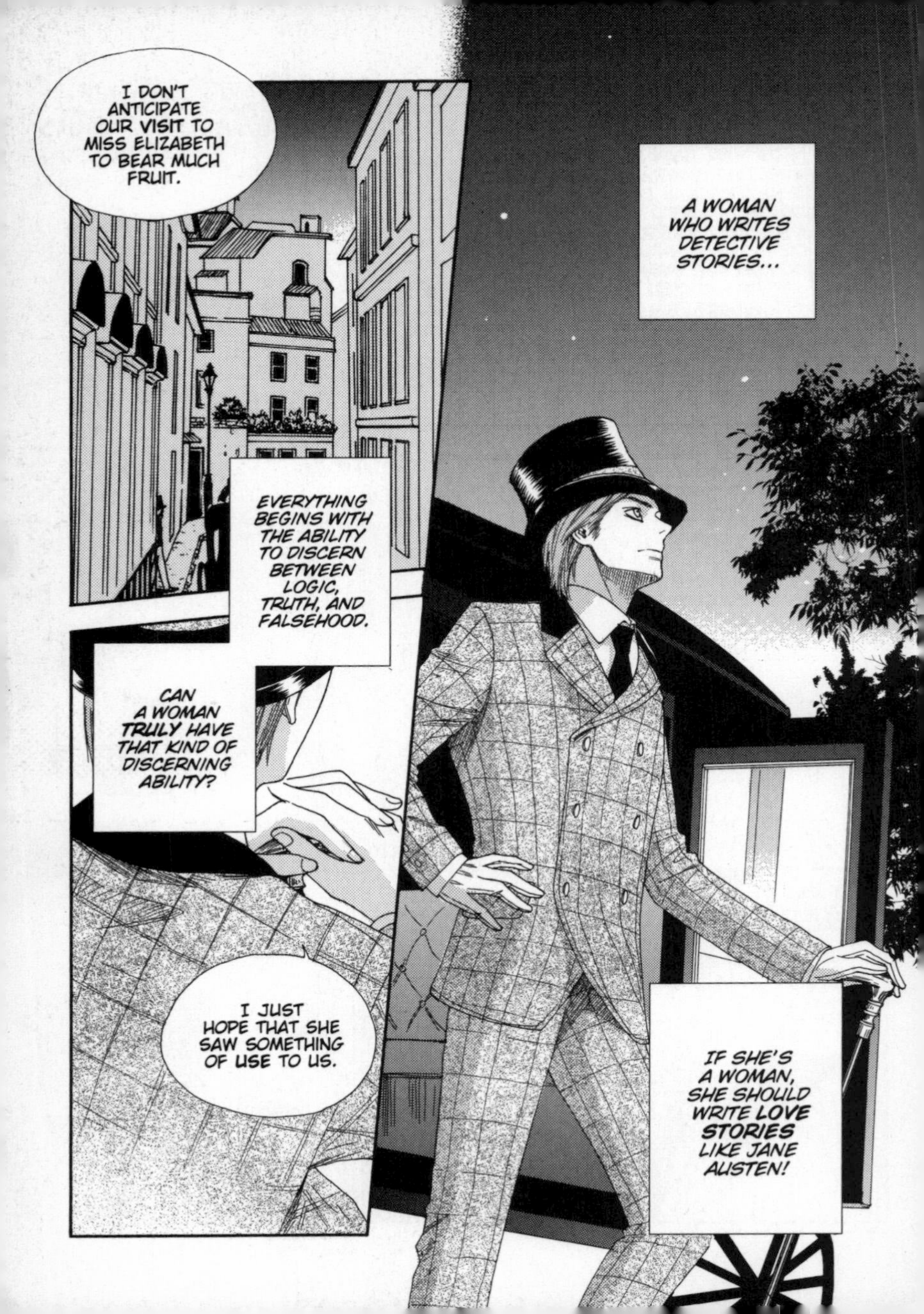
I DON'T ANTICIPATE OUR VISIT TO MISS ELIZABETH TO BEAR MUCH FRUIT.
A WOMAN WHO WRITES DETECTIVE STORIES...
EVERYTHING BEGINS WITH THE ABILITY TO DISCERN BETWEEN LOGIC, TRUTH, AND FALSEHOOD.
CAN A WOMAN TRULY HAVE THAT KIND OF DISCERNING ABILITY?
I JUST HOPE THAT SHE SAW SOMETHING OF USE TO US.
IF SHE'S A WOMAN, SHE SHOULD WRITE LOVE STORIES LIKE JANE AUSTEN!

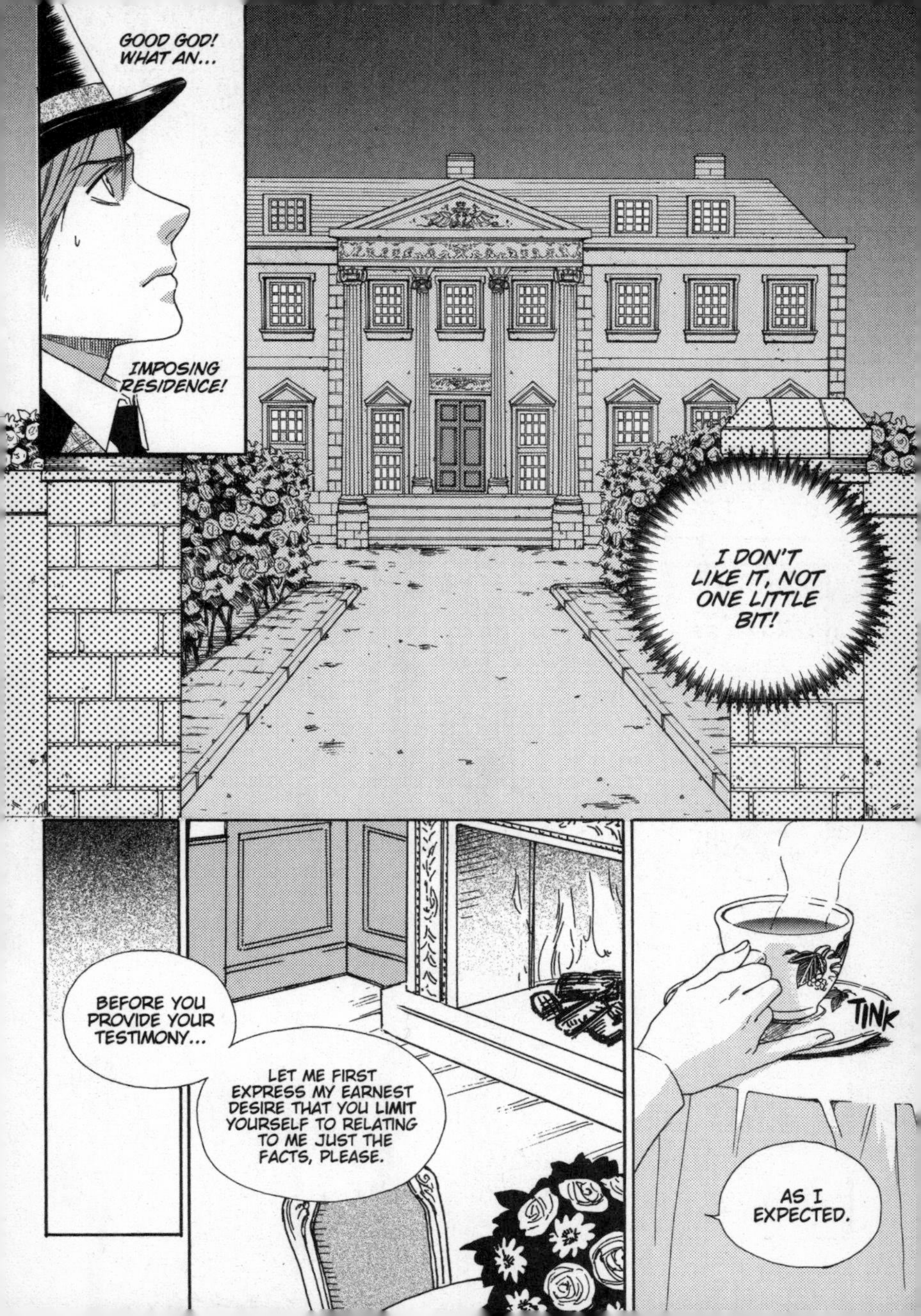
GOOD GOD! WHAT AN...
IMPOSING RESIDENCE!
I DON'T LIKE IT, NOT ONE LITTLE BIT!
BEFORE YOU PROVIDE YOUR TESTIMONY...
LET ME FIRST EXPRESS MY EARNEST DESIRE THAT YOU LIMIT YOURSELF TO RELATING TO ME JUST THE FACTS, PLEASE.
TINK
AS I EXPECTED.

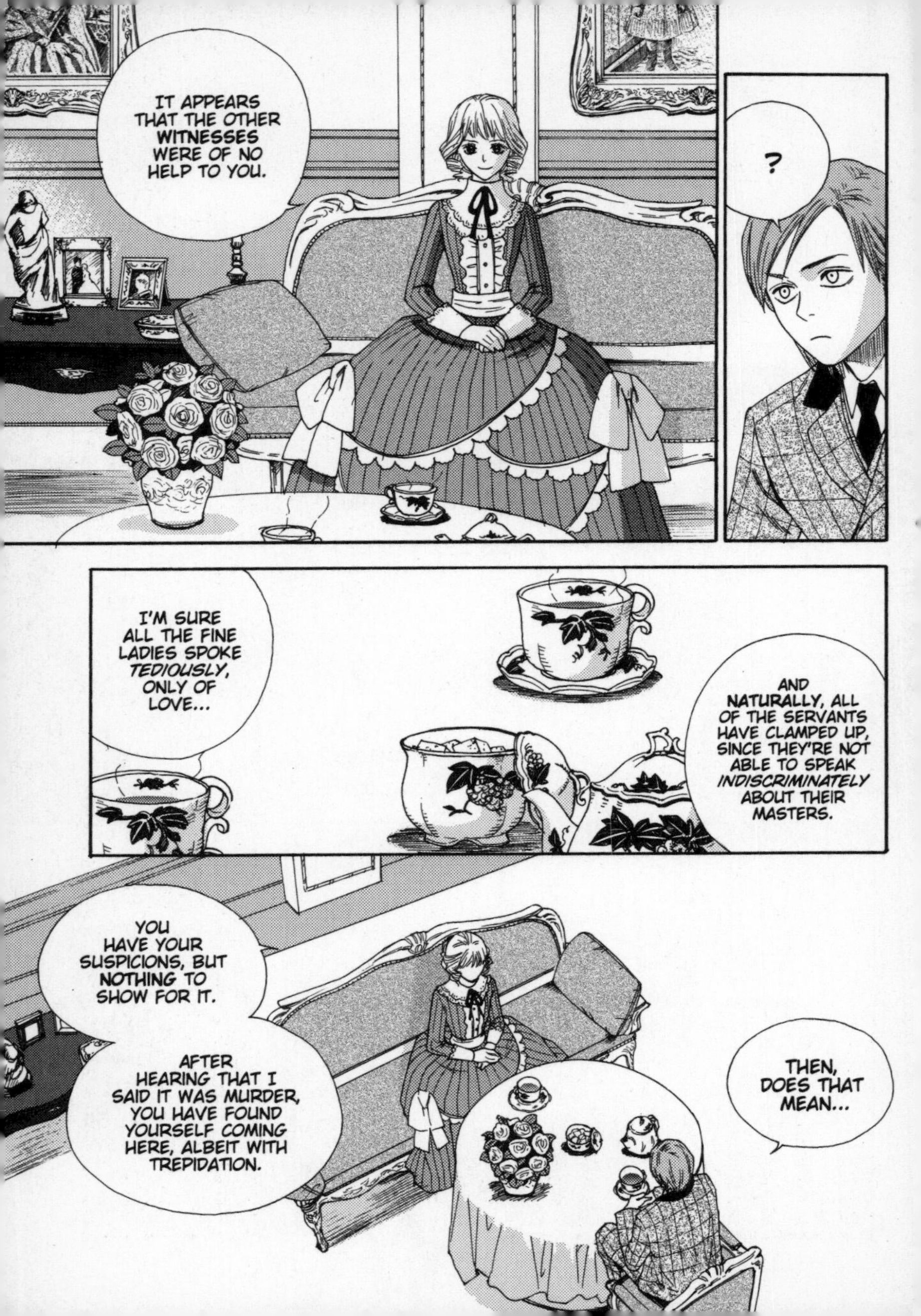
IT APPEARS THAT THE OTHER WITNESSES WERE OF NO HELP TO YOU.
?
I'M SURE ALL THE FINE LADIES SPOKE *TEDIOUSLY*, ONLY OF LOVE...
AND NATURALLY, ALL OF THE SERVANTS HAVE CLAMPED UP, SINCE THEY'RE NOT ABLE TO SPEAK *INDISCRIMINATELY* ABOUT THEIR MASTERS.
YOU HAVE YOUR SUSPICIONS, BUT NOTHING TO SHOW FOR IT.
AFTER HEARING THAT I SAID IT WAS MURDER, YOU HAVE FOUND YOURSELF COMING HERE, ALBEIT WITH TREPIDATION.
THEN, DOES THAT MEAN...

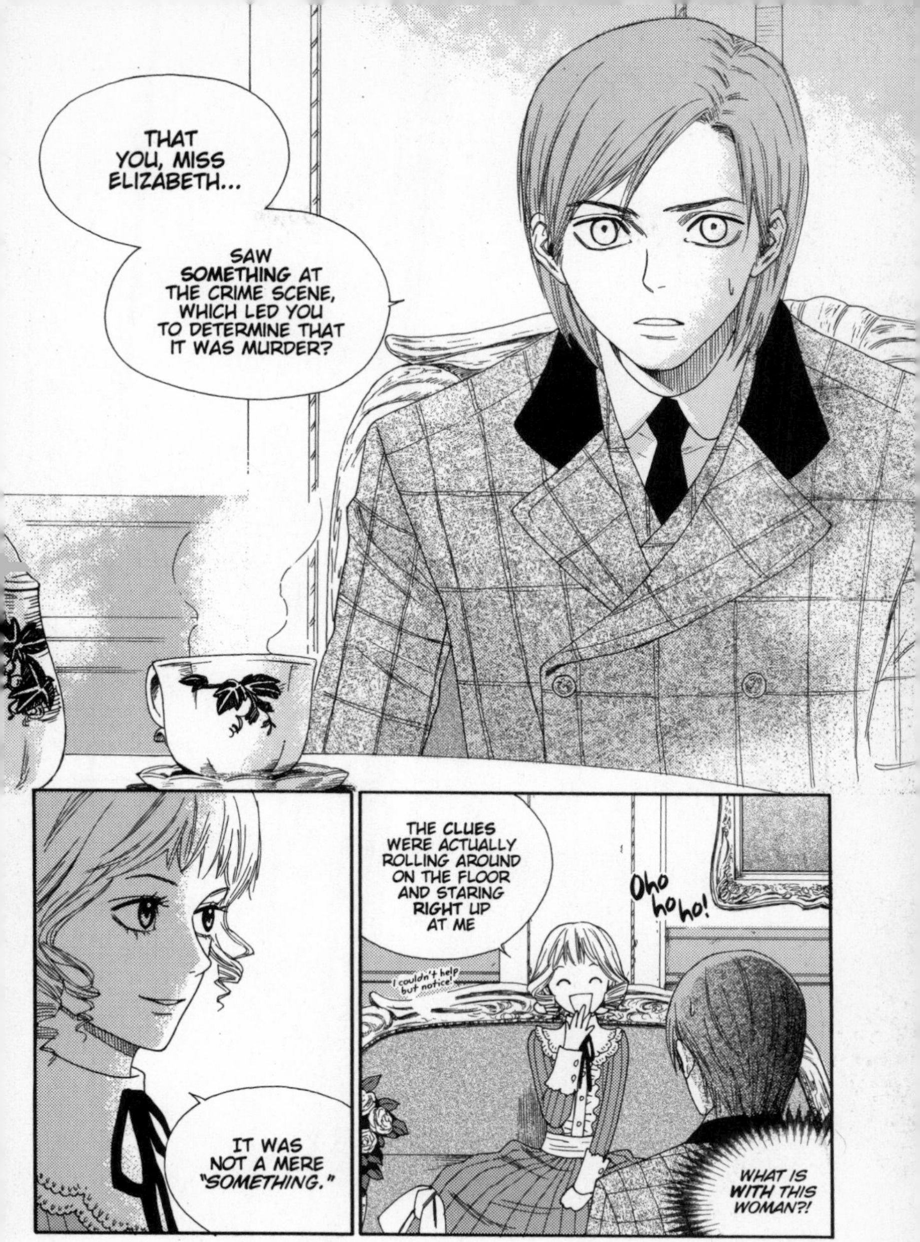
THAT YOU, MISS ELIZABETH...
SAW SOMETHING AT THE CRIME SCENE, WHICH LED YOU TO DETERMINE THAT IT WAS MURDER?
IT WAS NOT A MERE "SOMETHING."
THE CLUES WERE ACTUALLY ROLLING AROUND ON THE FLOOR AND STARING RIGHT UP AT ME
Oho ho ho!
I couldn't help but notice!
WHAT IS WITH THIS WOMAN?!

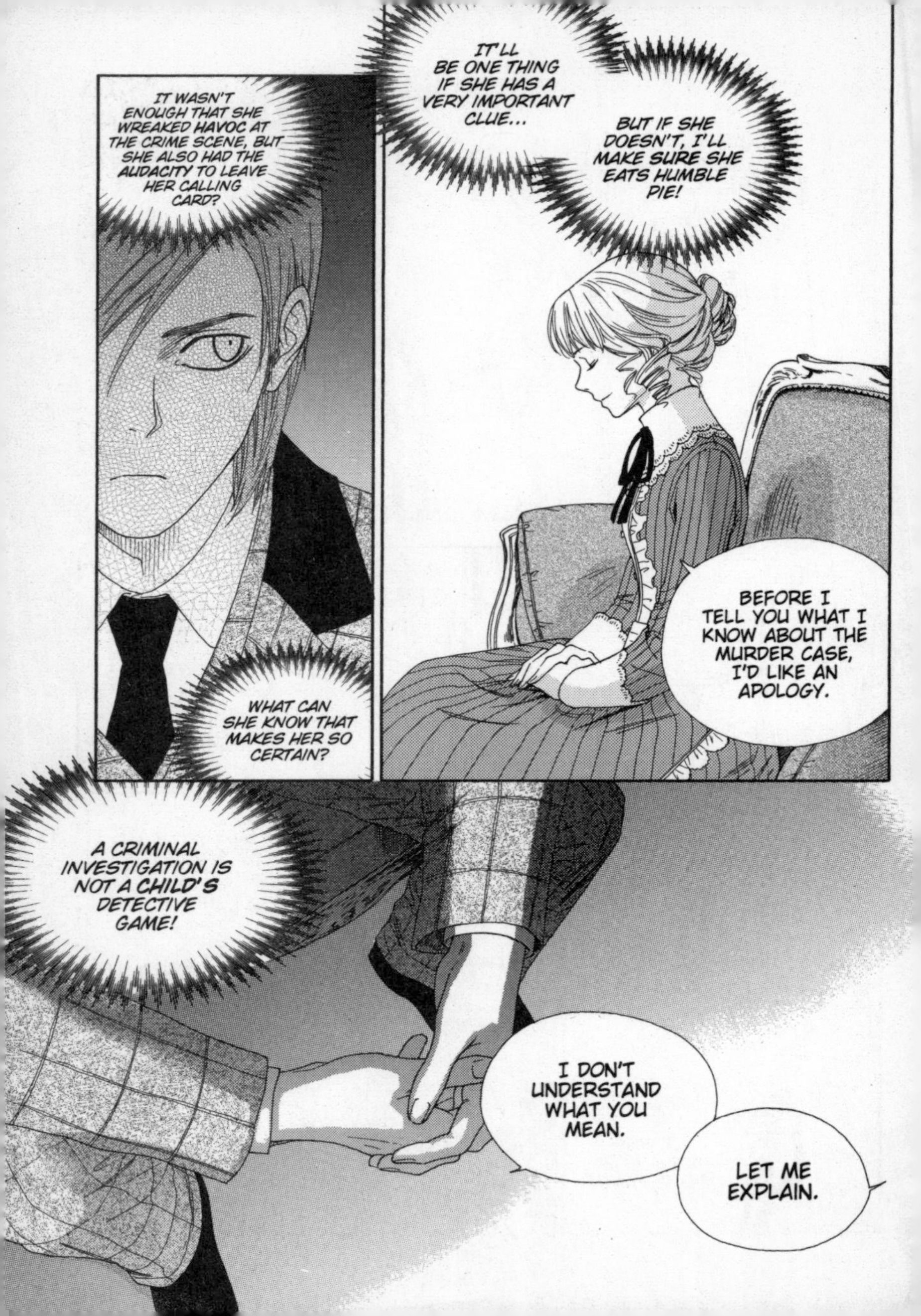
IT WASN'T ENOUGH THAT SHE WREAKED HAVOC AT THE CRIME SCENE, BUT SHE ALSO HAD THE AUDACITY TO LEAVE HER CALLING CARD?
WHAT CAN SHE KNOW THAT MAKES HER SO CERTAIN?
IT'LL BE ONE THING IF SHE HAS A VERY IMPORTANT CLUE...
BUT IF SHE DOESN'T, I'LL MAKE SURE SHE EATS HUMBLE PIE!
BEFORE I TELL YOU WHAT I KNOW ABOUT THE MURDER CASE, I'D LIKE AN APOLOGY.
A CRIMINAL INVESTIGATION IS NOT A CHILD'S DETECTIVE GAME!
I DON'T UNDERSTAND WHAT YOU MEAN.
LET ME EXPLAIN.

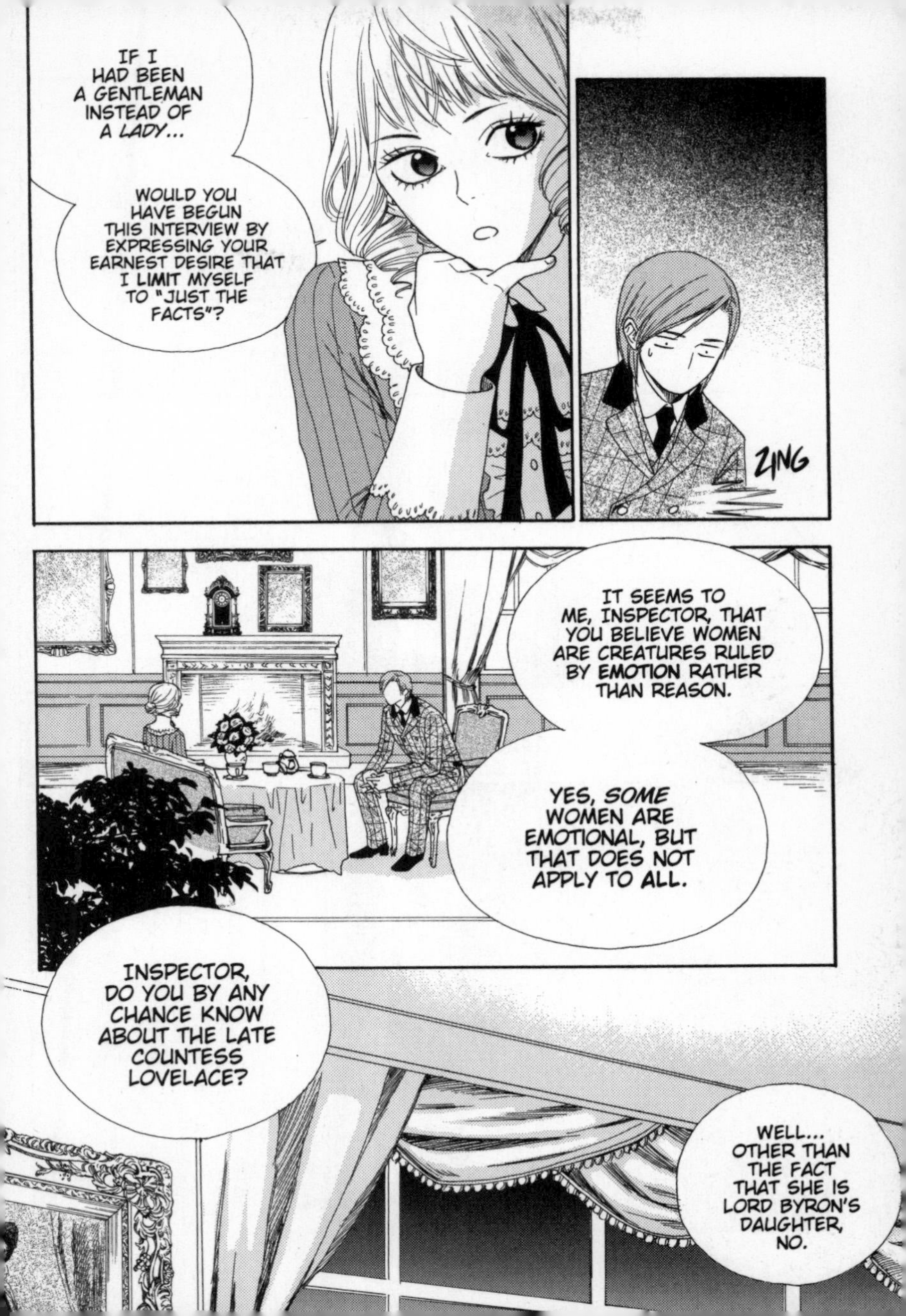
IF I HAD BEEN A GENTLEMAN INSTEAD OF A *LADY*...
WOULD YOU HAVE BEGUN THIS INTERVIEW BY EXPRESSING YOUR EARNEST DESIRE THAT I LIMIT MYSELF TO "JUST THE FACTS"?
ZING
IT SEEMS TO ME, INSPECTOR, THAT YOU BELIEVE WOMEN ARE CREATURES RULED BY EMOTION RATHER THAN REASON.
YES, *SOME* WOMEN ARE EMOTIONAL, BUT THAT DOES NOT APPLY TO ALL.
INSPECTOR, DO YOU BY ANY CHANCE KNOW ABOUT THE LATE COUNTESS LOVELACE?
WELL... OTHER THAN THE FACT THAT SHE IS LORD BYRON'S DAUGHTER, NO.

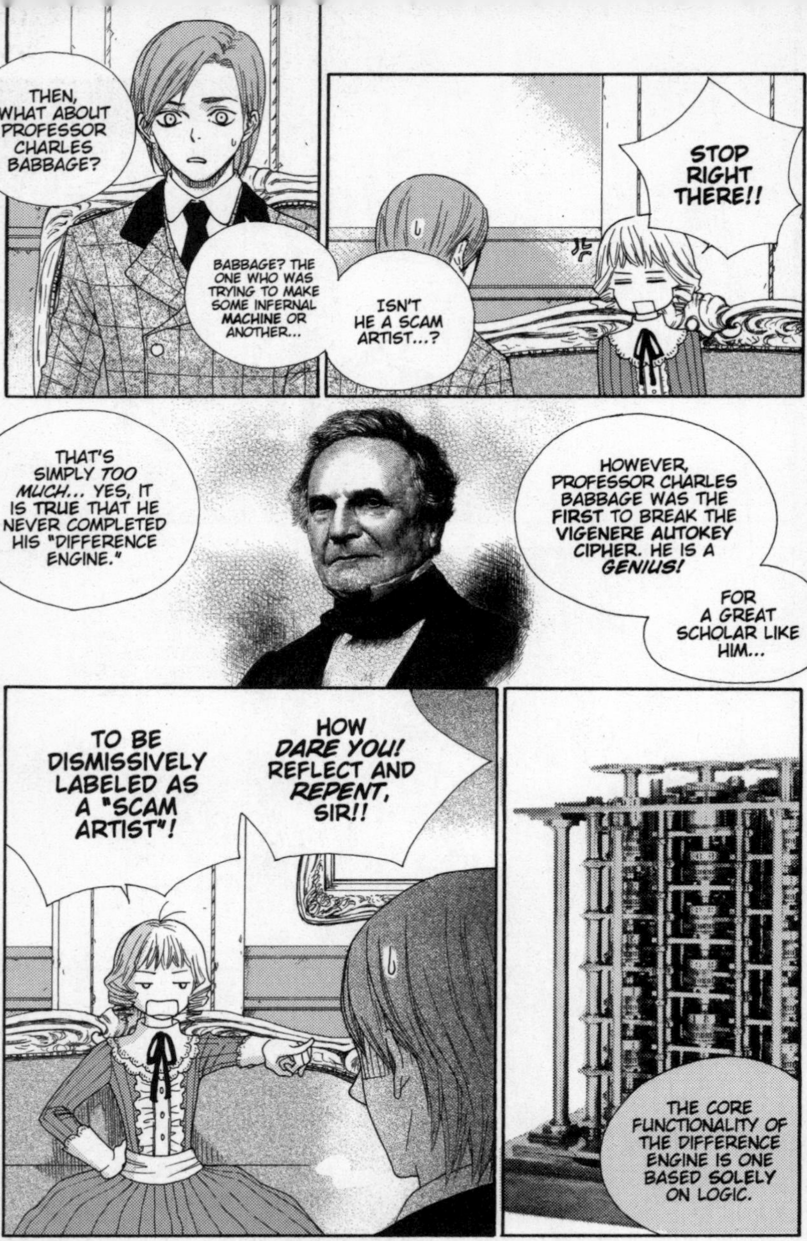
THEN, WHAT ABOUT PROFESSOR CHARLES BABBAGE?
BABBAGE? THE ONE WHO WAS TRYING TO MAKE SOME INFERNAL MACHINE OR ANOTHER...
ISN'T HE A SCAM ARTIST...?
STOP RIGHT THERE!!
THAT'S SIMPLY *TOO MUCH*... YES, IT IS TRUE THAT HE NEVER COMPLETED HIS "DIFFERENCE ENGINE."
HOWEVER, PROFESSOR CHARLES BABBAGE WAS THE FIRST TO BREAK THE VIGENERE AUTOKEY CIPHER. HE IS A *GENIUS!*
FOR A GREAT SCHOLAR LIKE HIM...
TO BE DISMISSIVELY LABELED AS A "SCAM ARTIST"!
HOW *DARE YOU!* REFLECT AND *REPENT,* SIR!!
THE CORE FUNCTIONALITY OF THE DIFFERENCE ENGINE IS ONE BASED SOLELY ON LOGIC.

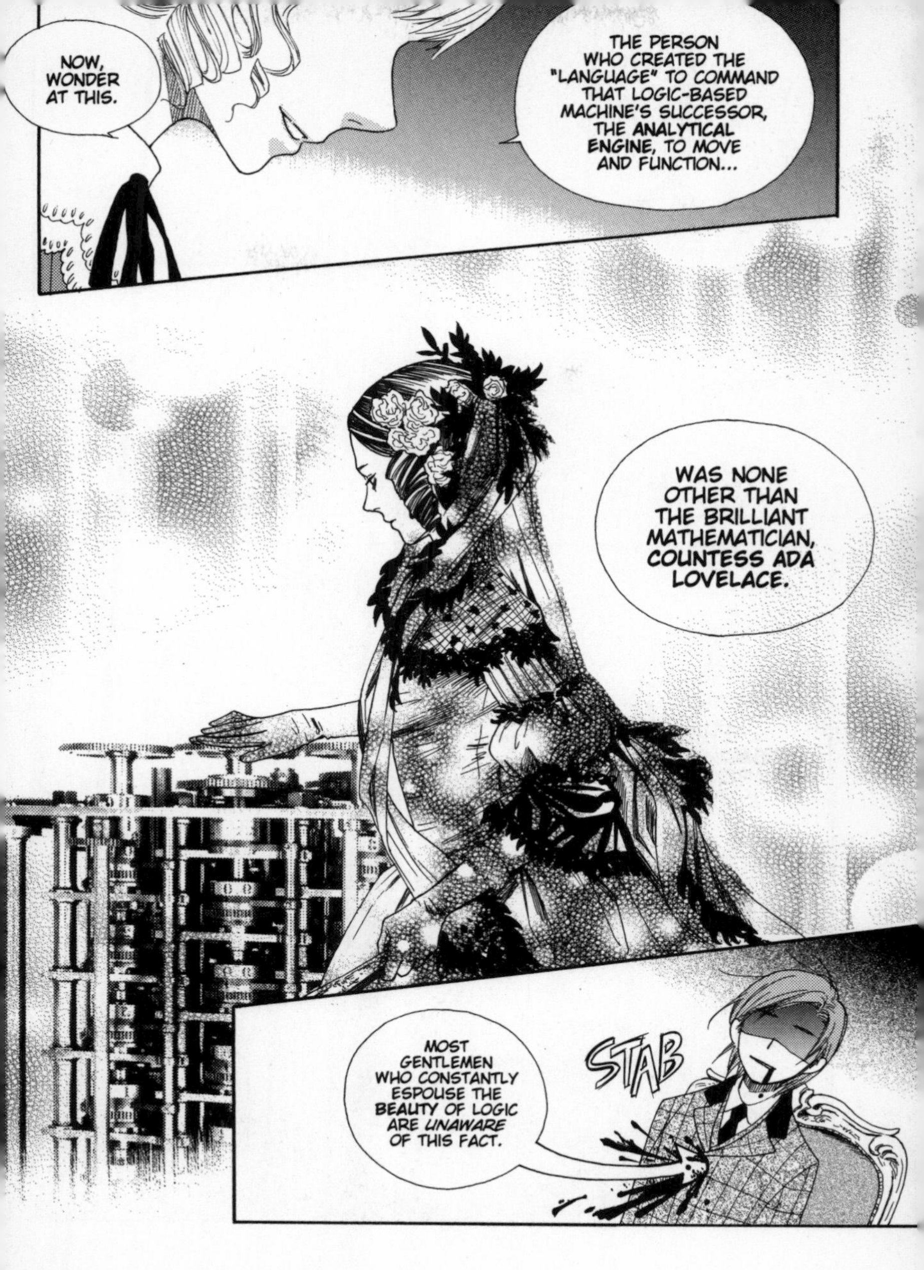
NOW, WONDER AT THIS.
THE PERSON WHO CREATED THE "LANGUAGE" TO COMMAND THAT LOGIC-BASED MACHINE'S SUCCESSOR, THE ANALYTICAL ENGINE, TO MOVE AND FUNCTION...
WAS NONE OTHER THAN THE BRILLIANT MATHEMATICIAN, COUNTESS ADA LOVELACE.
MOST GENTLEMEN WHO CONSTANTLY ESPOUSE THE BEAUTY OF LOGIC ARE *UNAWARE* OF THIS FACT.
STAB

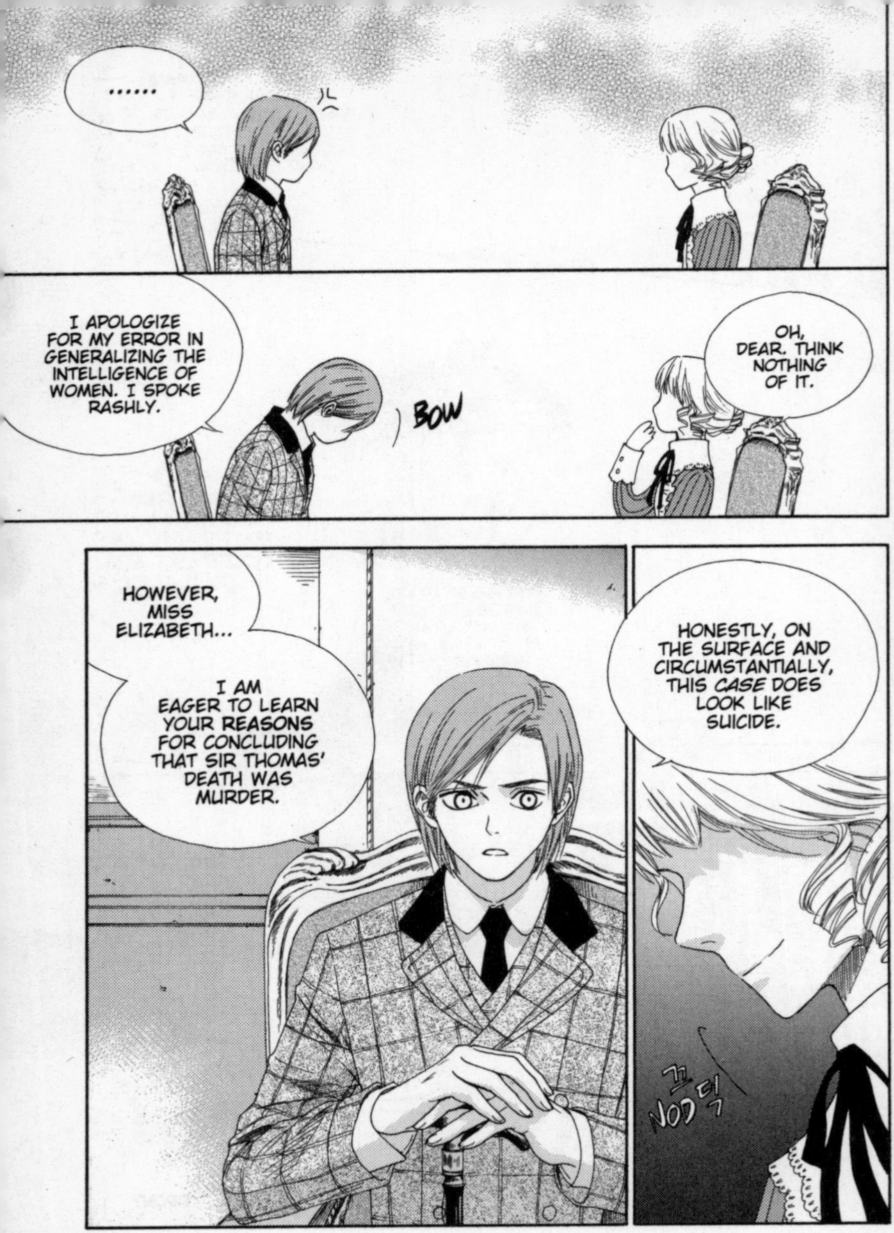
......
I APOLOGIZE FOR MY ERROR IN GENERALIZING THE INTELLIGENCE OF WOMEN. I SPOKE RASHLY.
BOW
OH, DEAR. THINK NOTHING OF IT.
HOWEVER, MISS ELIZABETH...
I AM EAGER TO LEARN YOUR REASONS FOR CONCLUDING THAT SIR THOMAS' DEATH WAS MURDER.
HONESTLY, ON THE SURFACE AND CIRCUMSTANTIALLY, THIS *CASE* DOES LOOK LIKE SUICIDE.
NOD

FOR THE LOVE OF HIS COUNTRY, HE WENT INTO THE BATTLEFIELD, RISKING HIS LIFE AS A SOLDIER, ONLY TO RETURN HOME AND FIND THAT HIS LOVE HAS BECOME ANOTHER MAN'S WIFE.

COINCIDENTALLY, HE READS *THE SORROWS OF YOUNG WERTHER.*

AS IT IS WITH THE MAIN CHARACTER OF THE BOOK, SIR THOMAS IS PESSIMISTIC ABOUT THE WORLD, AND CO--

UNDER THESE CIRCUMSTANCES, *ANYONE* WOULD BE RIGHTFULLY DESPONDENT, WOULD YOU NOT AGREE?

COMMITTING SUICIDE WOULD ONLY BE LOGICAL... IT MAKES FOR A VERY SIMPLE AND PAT EXPLANATION IN THIS CASE.

IT SEEMS TO ME THAT *YOU*, INSPECTOR, ARE THE ONE BEING SWEPT AWAY BY EMOTION, NOT I.

IF IT IS NOT TOO IMPOLITE OF ME, MAY I ASK YOUR AGE?

PARDON?

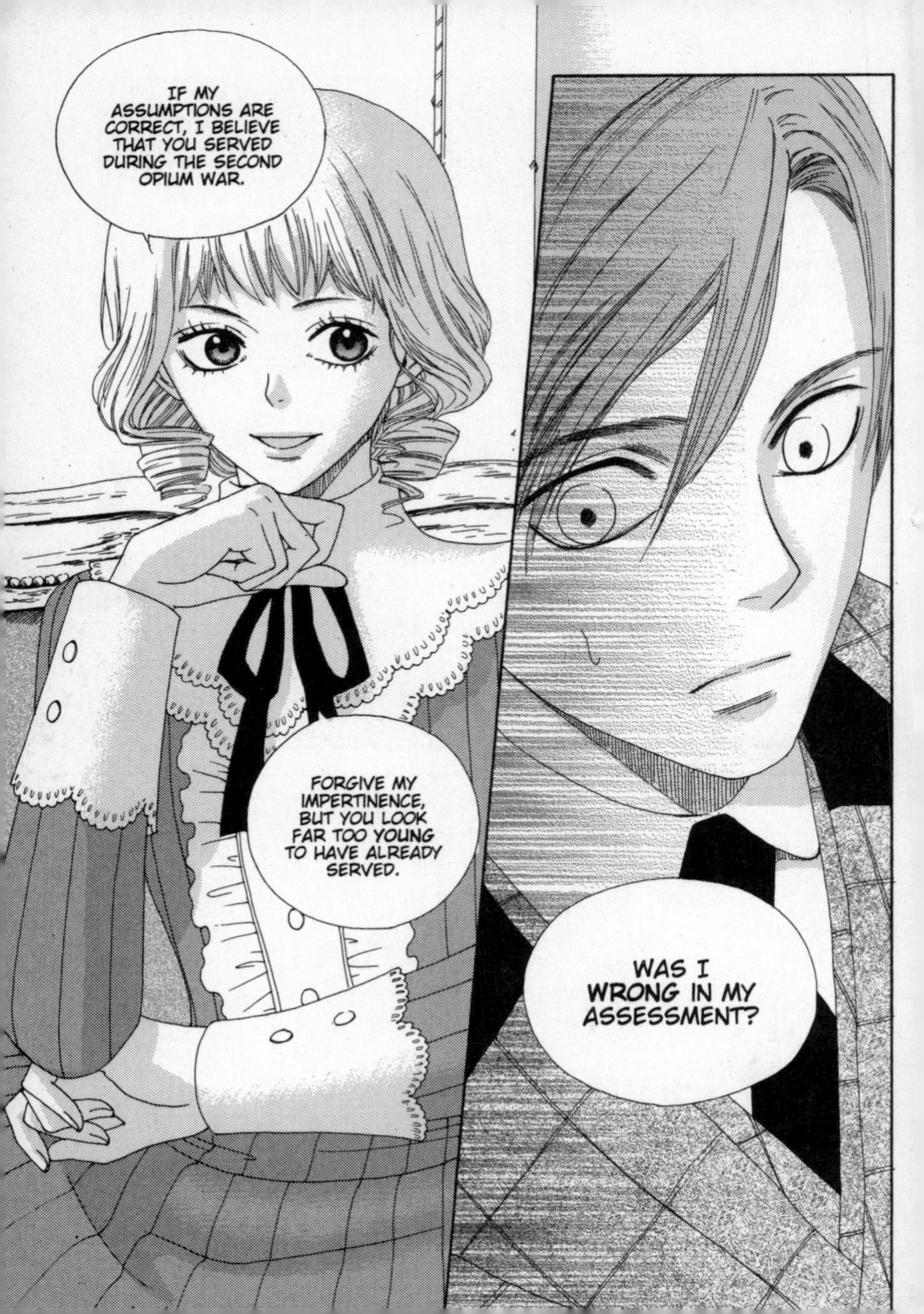
IF MY ASSUMPTIONS ARE CORRECT, I BELIEVE THAT YOU SERVED DURING THE SECOND OPIUM WAR.
FORGIVE MY IMPERTINENCE, BUT YOU LOOK FAR TOO YOUNG TO HAVE ALREADY SERVED.
WAS I WRONG IN MY ASSESSMENT?

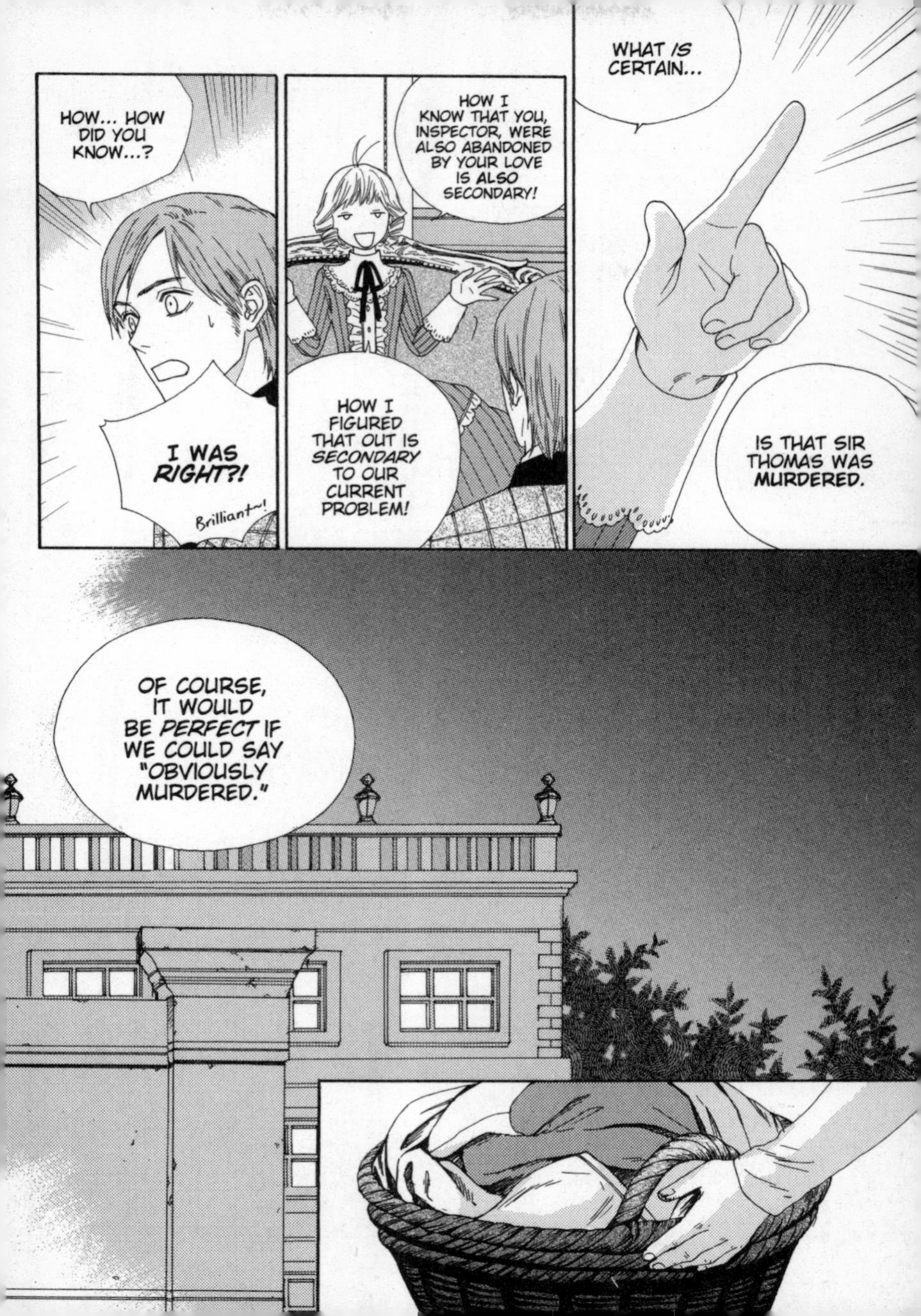
HOW... HOW DID YOU KNOW...?
I WAS *RIGHT?!*
Brilliant~!
HOW I KNOW THAT YOU, INSPECTOR, WERE ALSO ABANDONED BY YOUR LOVE IS ALSO SECONDARY!
HOW I FIGURED THAT OUT IS *SECONDARY* TO OUR CURRENT PROBLEM!
WHAT *IS* CERTAIN...
IS THAT SIR THOMAS WAS MURDERED.
OF COURSE, IT WOULD BE *PERFECT* IF WE COULD SAY "OBVIOUSLY MURDERED."

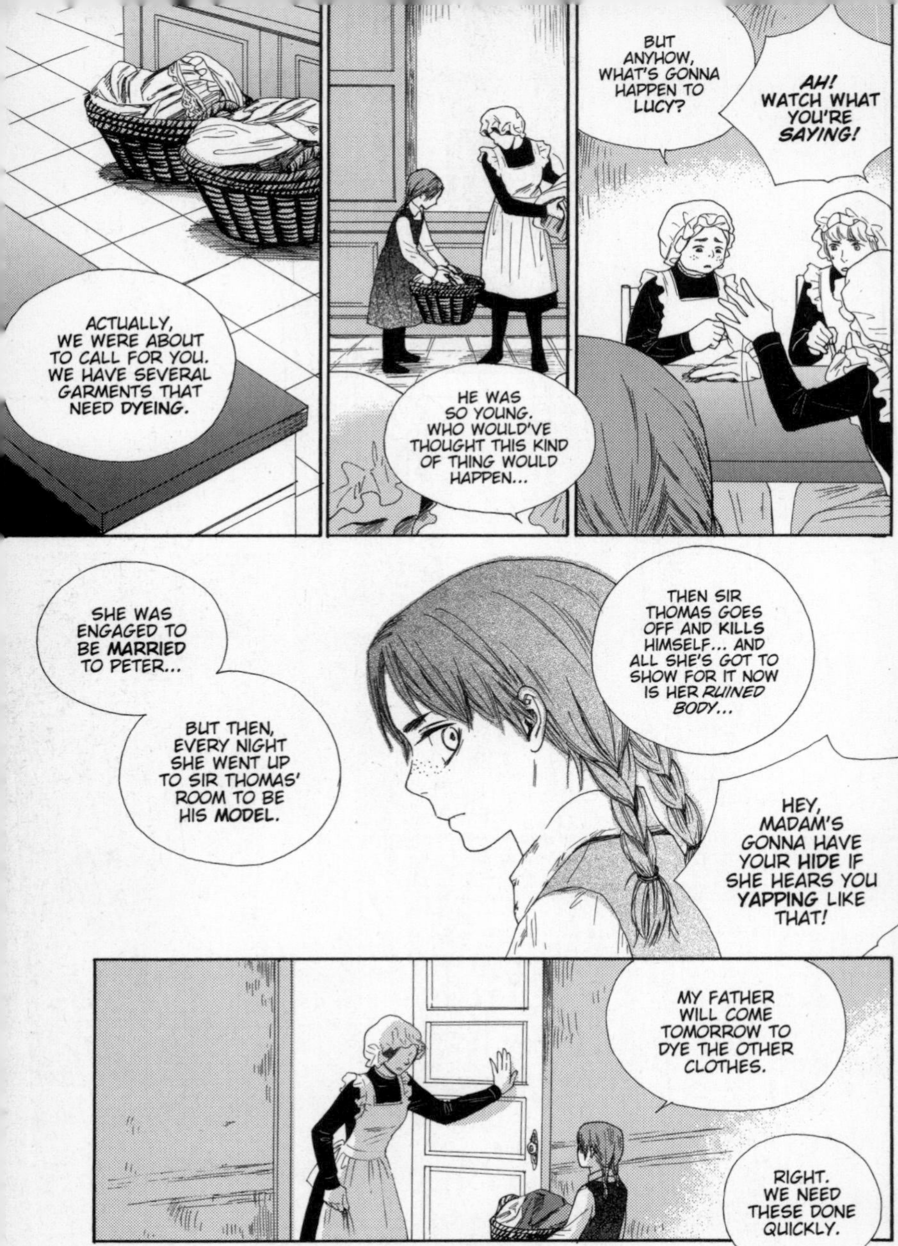
ACTUALLY, WE WERE ABOUT TO CALL FOR YOU. WE HAVE SEVERAL GARMENTS THAT NEED DYEING.
HE WAS SO YOUNG. WHO WOULD'VE THOUGHT THIS KIND OF THING WOULD HAPPEN...
BUT ANYHOW, WHAT'S GONNA HAPPEN TO LUCY?
AH! WATCH WHAT YOU'RE SAYING!
SHE WAS ENGAGED TO BE MARRIED TO PETER...
BUT THEN, EVERY NIGHT SHE WENT UP TO SIR THOMAS' ROOM TO BE HIS MODEL.
THEN SIR THOMAS GOES OFF AND KILLS HIMSELF... AND ALL SHE'S GOT TO SHOW FOR IT NOW IS HER RUINED BODY...
HEY, MADAM'S GONNA HAVE YOUR HIDE IF SHE HEARS YOU YAPPING LIKE THAT!
MY FATHER WILL COME TOMORROW TO DYE THE OTHER CLOTHES.
RIGHT. WE NEED THESE DONE QUICKLY.

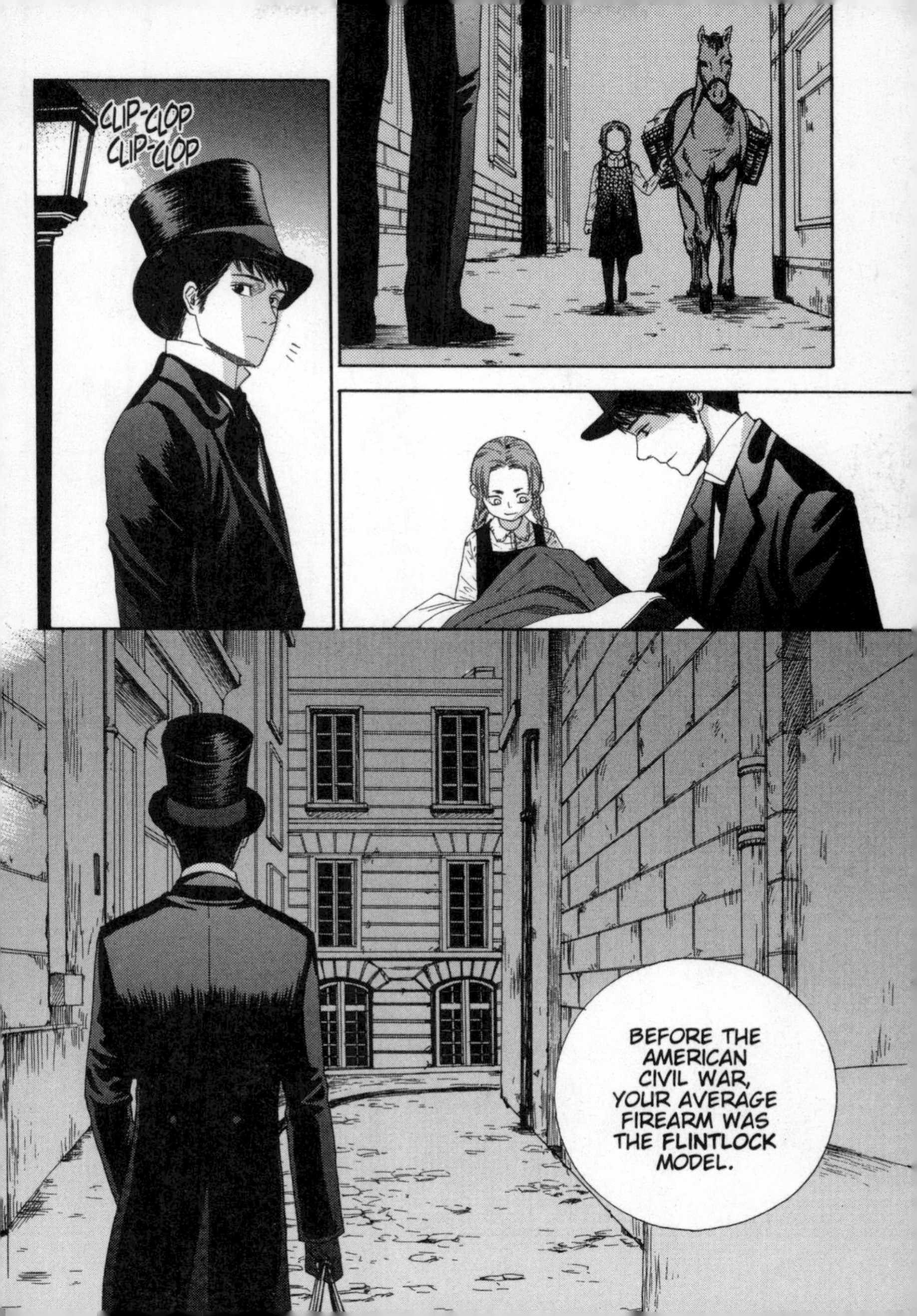
CLIP-CLOP
CLIP-CLOP
BEFORE THE AMERICAN CIVIL WAR, YOUR AVERAGE FIREARM WAS THE FLINTLOCK MODEL.

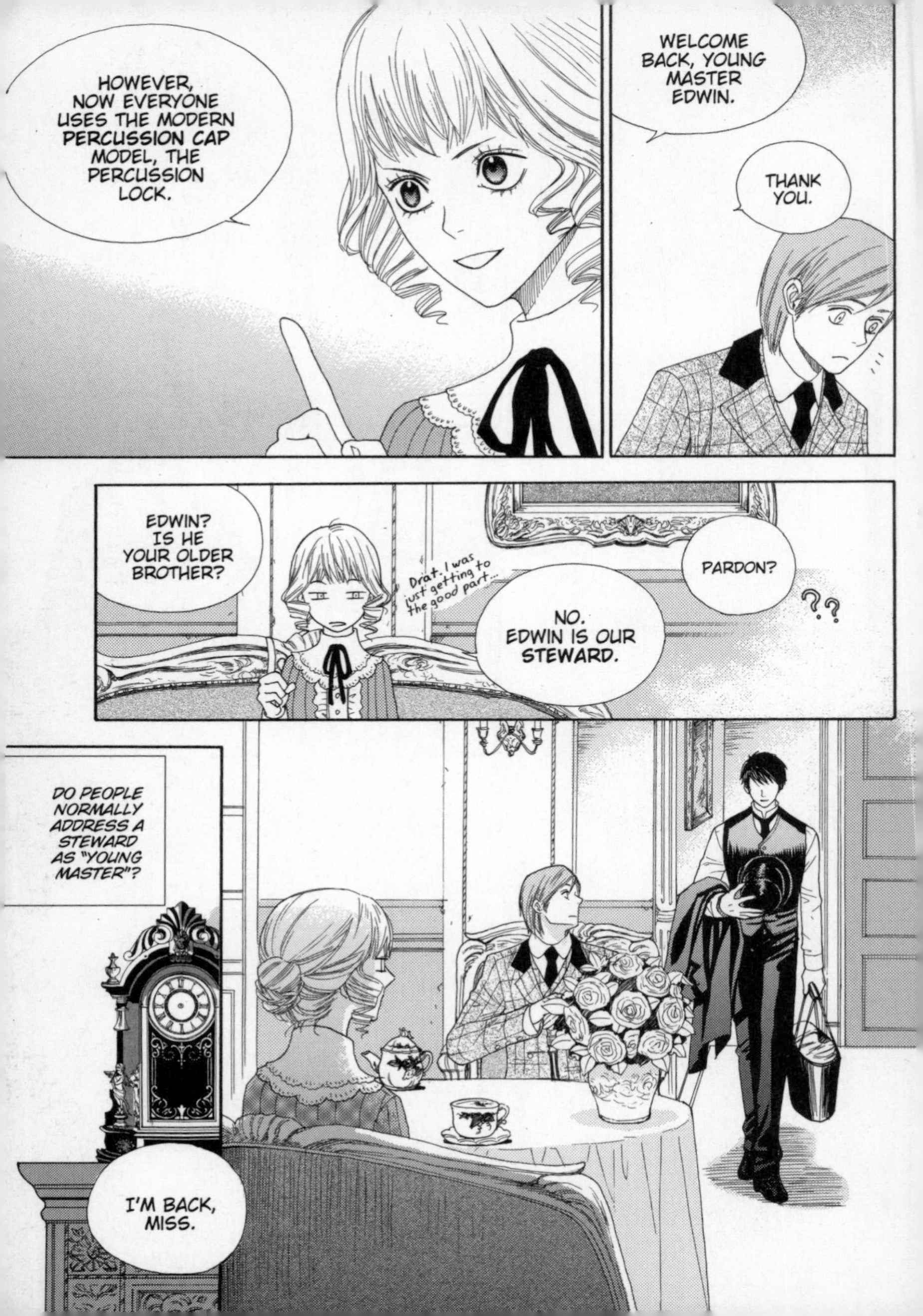
HOWEVER, NOW EVERYONE USES THE MODERN PERCUSSION CAP MODEL, THE PERCUSSION LOCK.
WELCOME BACK, YOUNG MASTER EDWIN.
THANK YOU.
EDWIN? IS HE YOUR OLDER BROTHER?
Drat. I was just getting to the good part...
NO. EDWIN IS OUR STEWARD.
PARDON?
??
DO PEOPLE NORMALLY ADDRESS A STEWARD AS "YOUNG MASTER"?
I'M BACK, MISS.

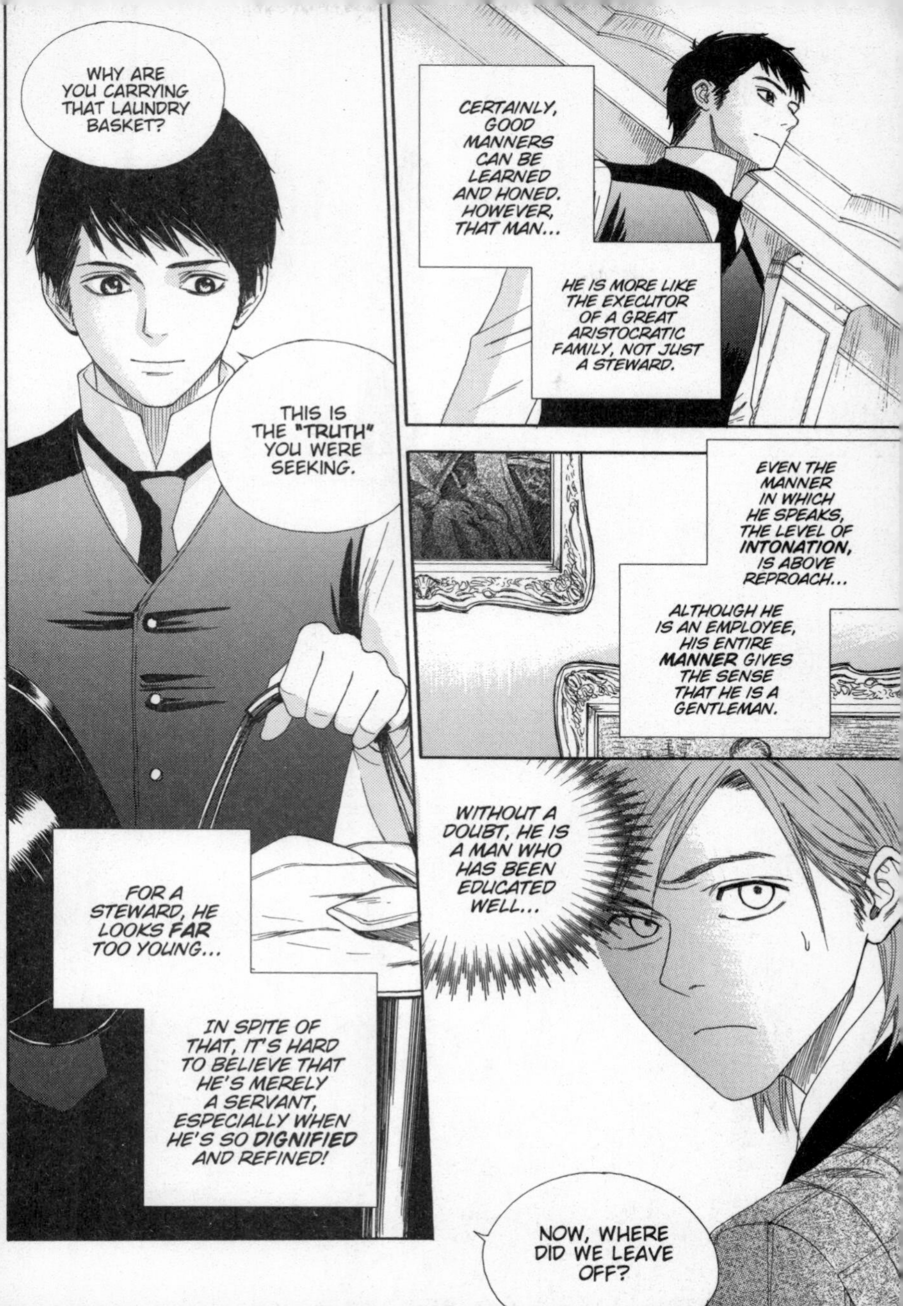
WHY ARE YOU CARRYING THAT LAUNDRY BASKET?
THIS IS THE "TRUTH" YOU WERE SEEKING.
FOR A STEWARD, HE LOOKS FAR TOO YOUNG...
IN SPITE OF THAT, IT'S HARD TO BELIEVE THAT HE'S MERELY A SERVANT, ESPECIALLY WHEN HE'S SO DIGNIFIED AND REFINED!
CERTAINLY, GOOD MANNERS CAN BE LEARNED AND HONED. HOWEVER, THAT MAN...
HE IS MORE LIKE THE EXECUTOR OF A GREAT ARISTOCRATIC FAMILY, NOT JUST A STEWARD.
EVEN THE MANNER IN WHICH HE SPEAKS, THE LEVEL OF INTONATION, IS ABOVE REPROACH...
ALTHOUGH HE IS AN EMPLOYEE, HIS ENTIRE MANNER GIVES THE SENSE THAT HE IS A GENTLEMAN.
WITHOUT A DOUBT, HE IS A MAN WHO HAS BEEN EDUCATED WELL...
NOW, WHERE DID WE LEAVE OFF?

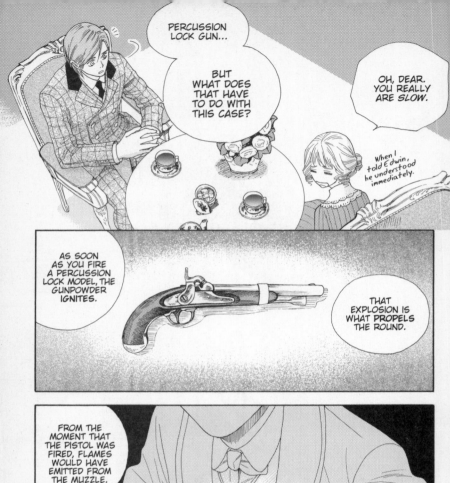

PERCUSSION LOCK GUN...

BUT WHAT DOES THAT HAVE TO DO WITH THIS CASE?

OH, DEAR. YOU REALLY ARE SLOW.

When I told Edwin, he understood immediately.

AS SOON AS YOU FIRE A PERCUSSION LOCK MODEL, THE GUNPOWDER IGNITES.

THAT EXPLOSION IS WHAT PROPELS THE ROUND.

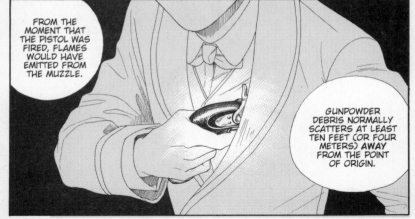

FROM THE MOMENT THAT THE PISTOL WAS FIRED, FLAMES WOULD HAVE EMITTED FROM THE MUZZLE.

GUNPOWDER DEBRIS NORMALLY SCATTERS AT LEAST TEN FEET (OR FOUR METERS) AWAY FROM THE POINT OF ORIGIN.

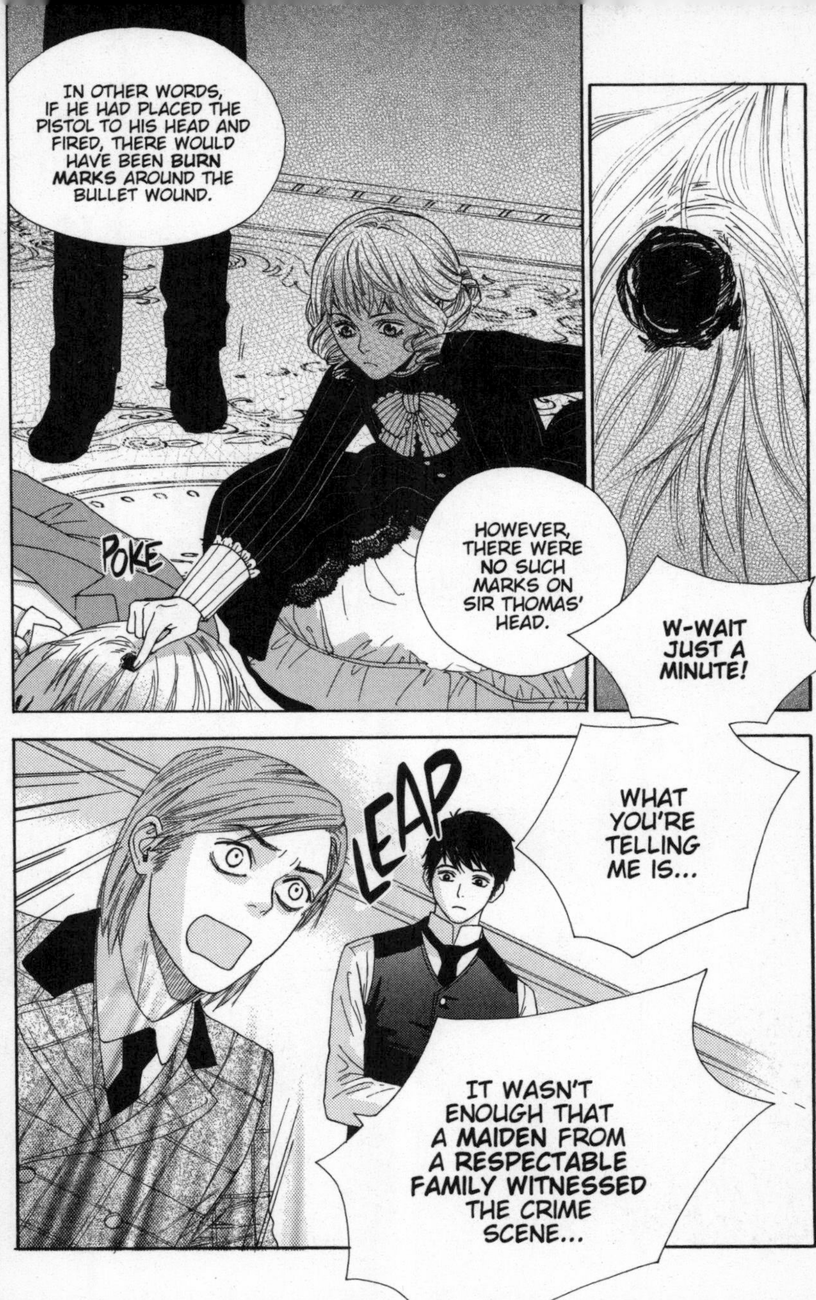
IN OTHER WORDS, IF HE HAD PLACED THE PISTOL TO HIS HEAD AND FIRED, THERE WOULD HAVE BEEN BURN MARKS AROUND THE BULLET WOUND.
POKE
HOWEVER, THERE WERE NO SUCH MARKS ON SIR THOMAS' HEAD.
W-WAIT JUST A MINUTE!
LEAP
WHAT YOU'RE TELLING ME IS...
IT WASN'T ENOUGH THAT A MAIDEN FROM A RESPECTABLE FAMILY WITNESSED THE CRIME SCENE...

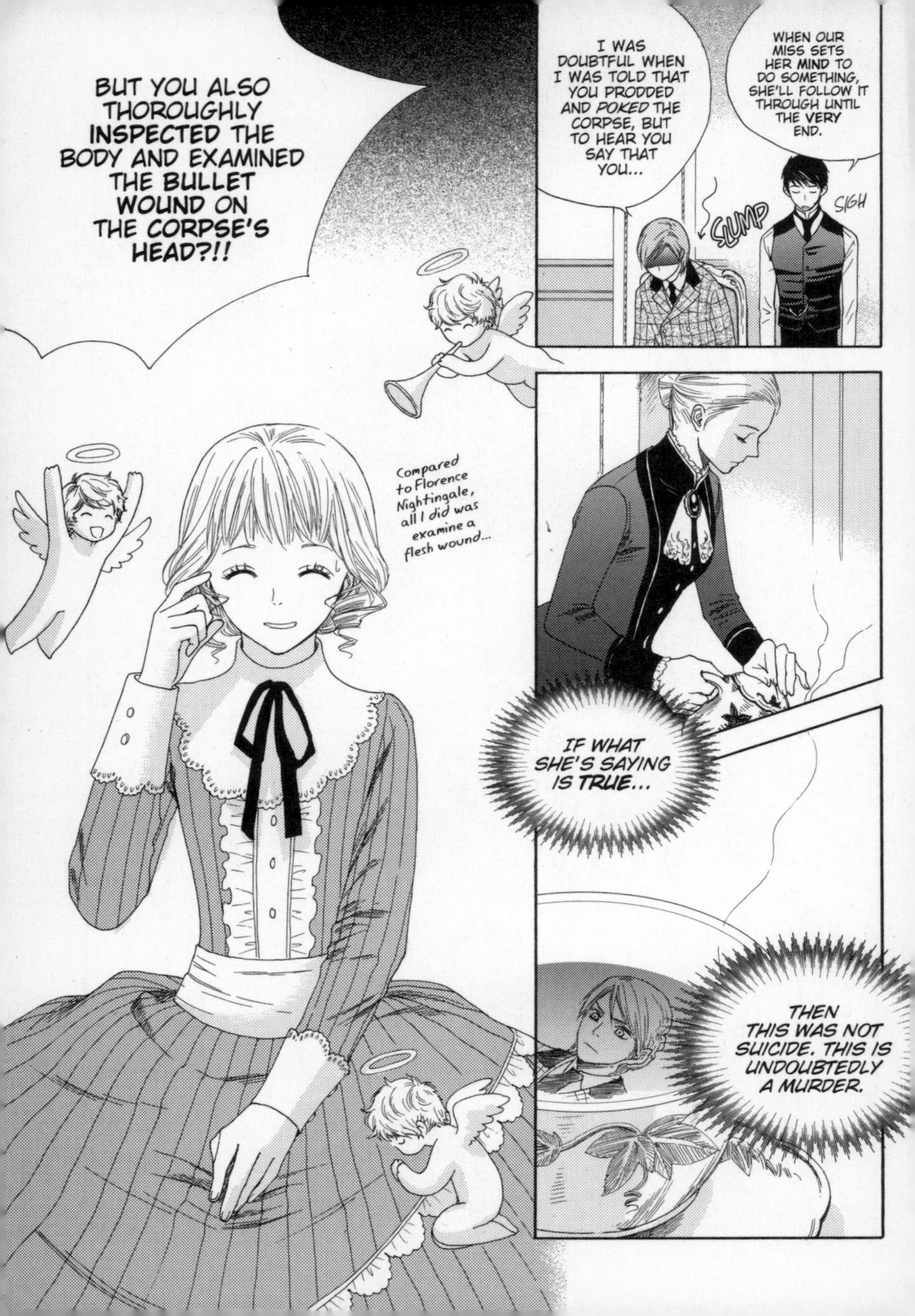
BUT YOU ALSO THOROUGHLY INSPECTED THE BODY AND EXAMINED THE BULLET WOUND ON THE CORPSE'S HEAD?!!
Compared to Florence Nightingale, all I did was examine a flesh wound...
I WAS DOUBTFUL WHEN I WAS TOLD THAT YOU PRODDED AND POKED THE CORPSE, BUT TO HEAR YOU SAY THAT YOU...
WHEN OUR MISS SETS HER MIND TO DO SOMETHING, SHE'LL FOLLOW IT THROUGH UNTIL THE VERY END.
SLUMP
SIGH
IF WHAT SHE'S SAYING IS TRUE...
THEN THIS WAS NOT SUICIDE. THIS IS UNDOUBTEDLY A MURDER.

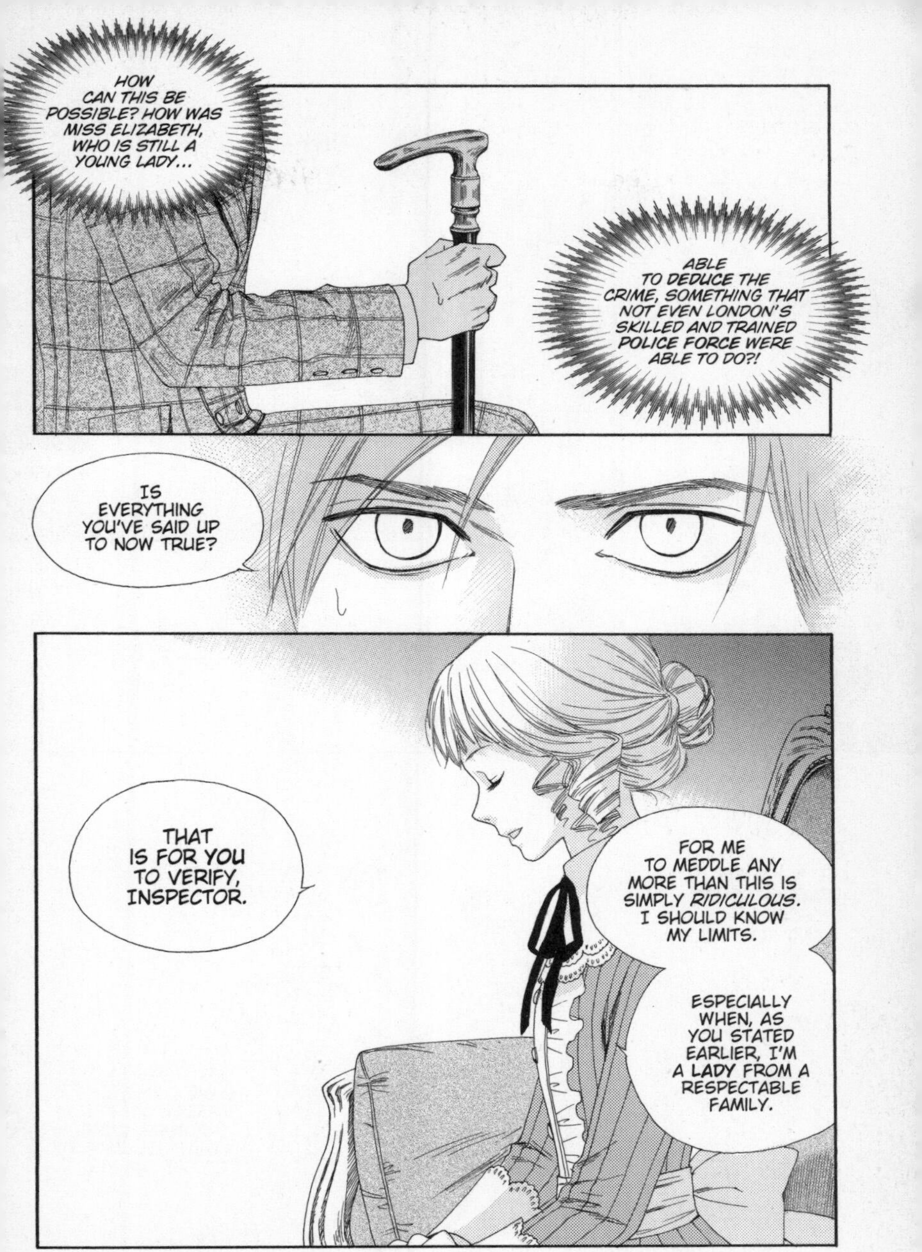
HOW CAN THIS BE POSSIBLE? HOW WAS MISS ELIZABETH, WHO IS STILL A YOUNG LADY...
ABLE TO DEDUCE THE CRIME, SOMETHING THAT NOT EVEN LONDON'S SKILLED AND TRAINED POLICE FORCE WERE ABLE TO DO?!
IS EVERYTHING YOU'VE SAID UP TO NOW TRUE?
THAT IS FOR YOU TO VERIFY, INSPECTOR.
FOR ME TO MEDDLE ANY MORE THAN THIS IS SIMPLY *RIDICULOUS*. I SHOULD KNOW MY LIMITS.
ESPECIALLY WHEN, AS YOU STATED EARLIER, I'M A **LADY** FROM A RESPECTABLE FAMILY.

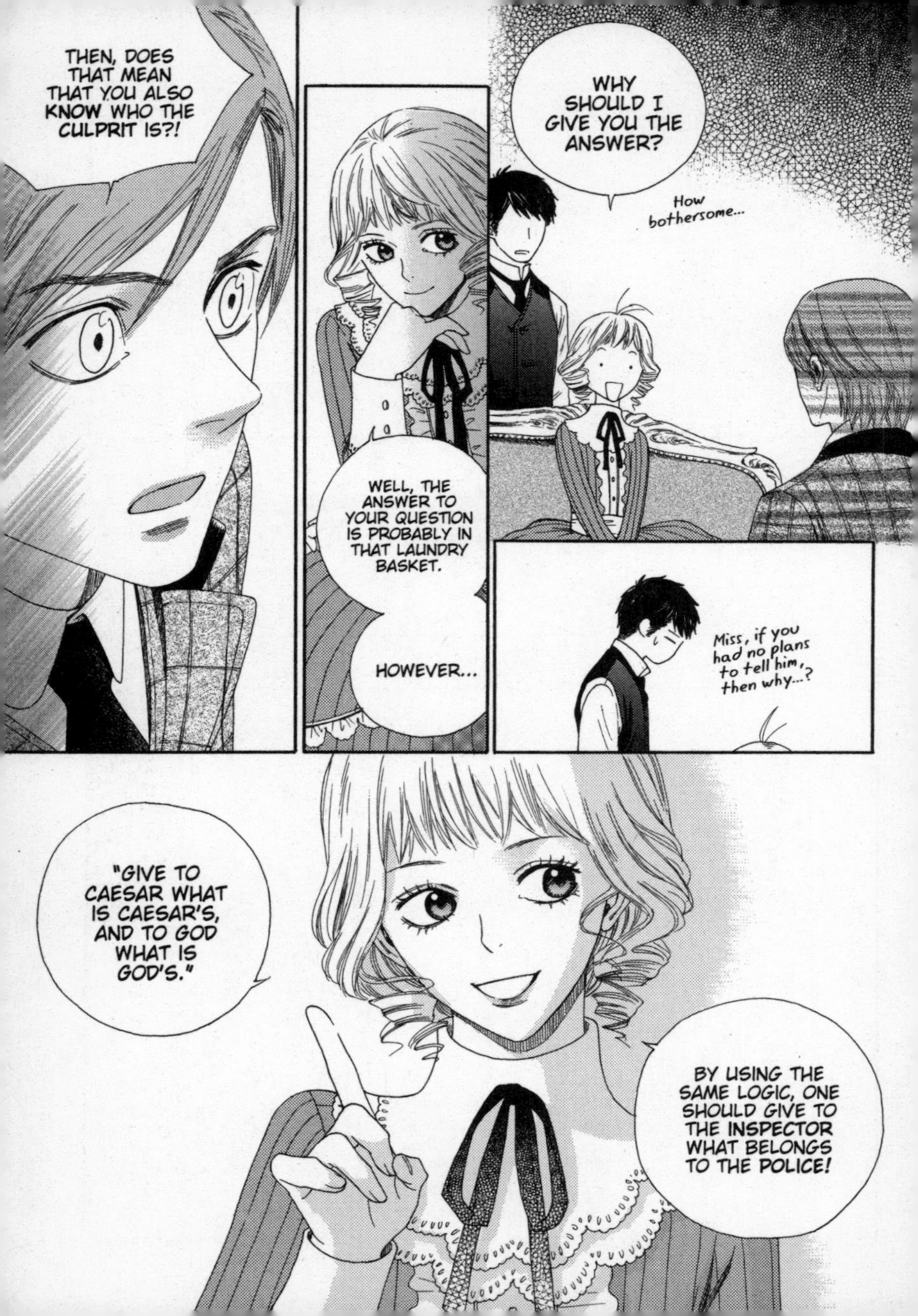
THEN, DOES THAT MEAN THAT YOU ALSO KNOW WHO THE CULPRIT IS?!
WELL, THE ANSWER TO YOUR QUESTION IS PROBABLY IN THAT LAUNDRY BASKET.
HOWEVER...
WHY SHOULD I GIVE YOU THE ANSWER?
How bothersome...
Miss, if you had no plans to tell him, then why...?
"GIVE TO CAESAR WHAT IS CAESAR'S, AND TO GOD WHAT IS GOD'S."
BY USING THE SAME LOGIC, ONE SHOULD GIVE TO THE INSPECTOR WHAT BELONGS TO THE POLICE!

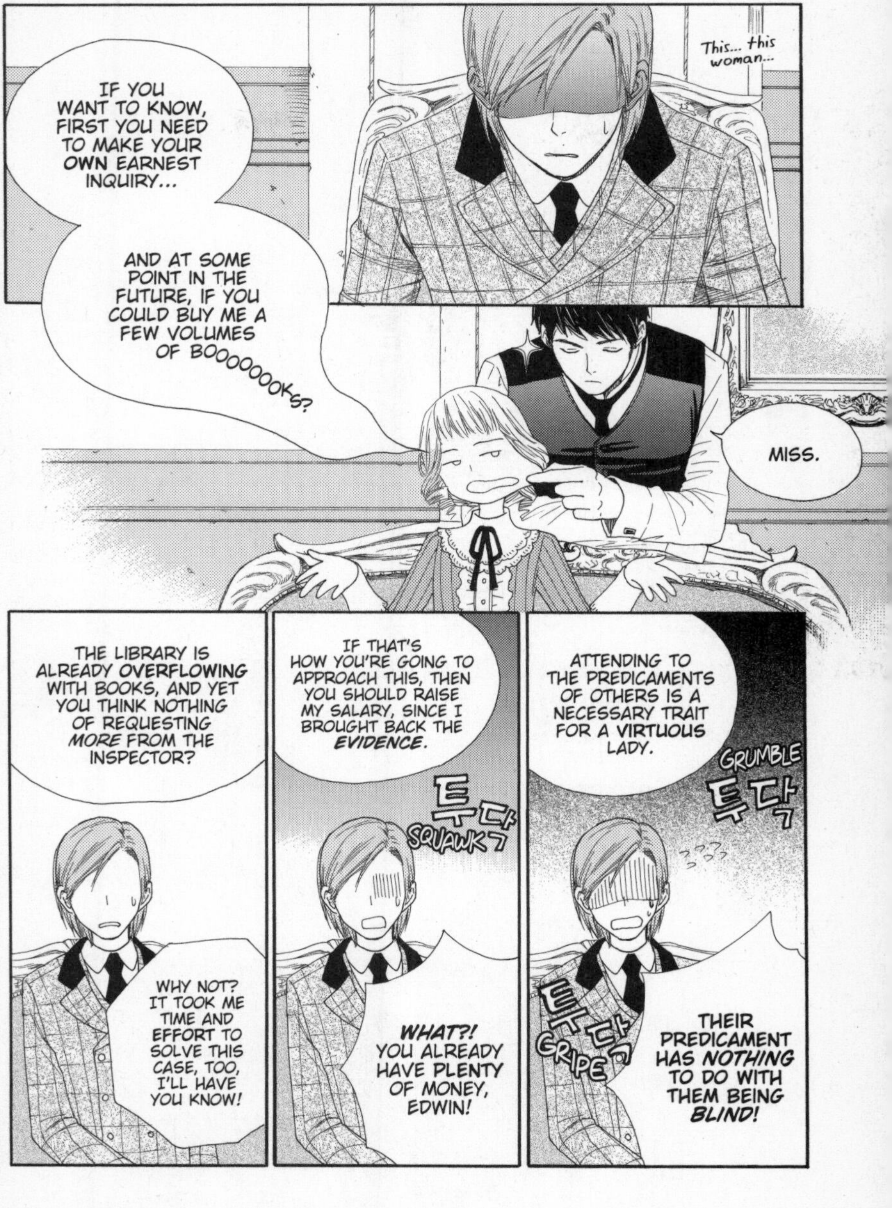

IF YOU WANT TO KNOW, FIRST YOU NEED TO MAKE YOUR OWN EARNEST INQUIRY...
This... this woman...
AND AT SOME POINT IN THE FUTURE, IF YOU COULD BUY ME A FEW VOLUMES OF BOOOOOOOKS?
MISS.
THE LIBRARY IS ALREADY OVERFLOWING WITH BOOKS, AND YET YOU THINK NOTHING OF REQUESTING MORE FROM THE INSPECTOR?
WHY NOT? IT TOOK ME TIME AND EFFORT TO SOLVE THIS CASE, TOO, I'LL HAVE YOU KNOW!
IF THAT'S HOW YOU'RE GOING TO APPROACH THIS, THEN YOU SHOULD RAISE MY SALARY, SINCE I BROUGHT BACK THE EVIDENCE.
투닥
SQUAWK
WHAT?! YOU ALREADY HAVE PLENTY OF MONEY, EDWIN!
ATTENDING TO THE PREDICAMENTS OF OTHERS IS A NECESSARY TRAIT FOR A VIRTUOUS LADY.
GRUMBLE
투닥
투닥
GRIPE
THEIR PREDICAMENT HAS NOTHING TO DO WITH THEM BEING BLIND!

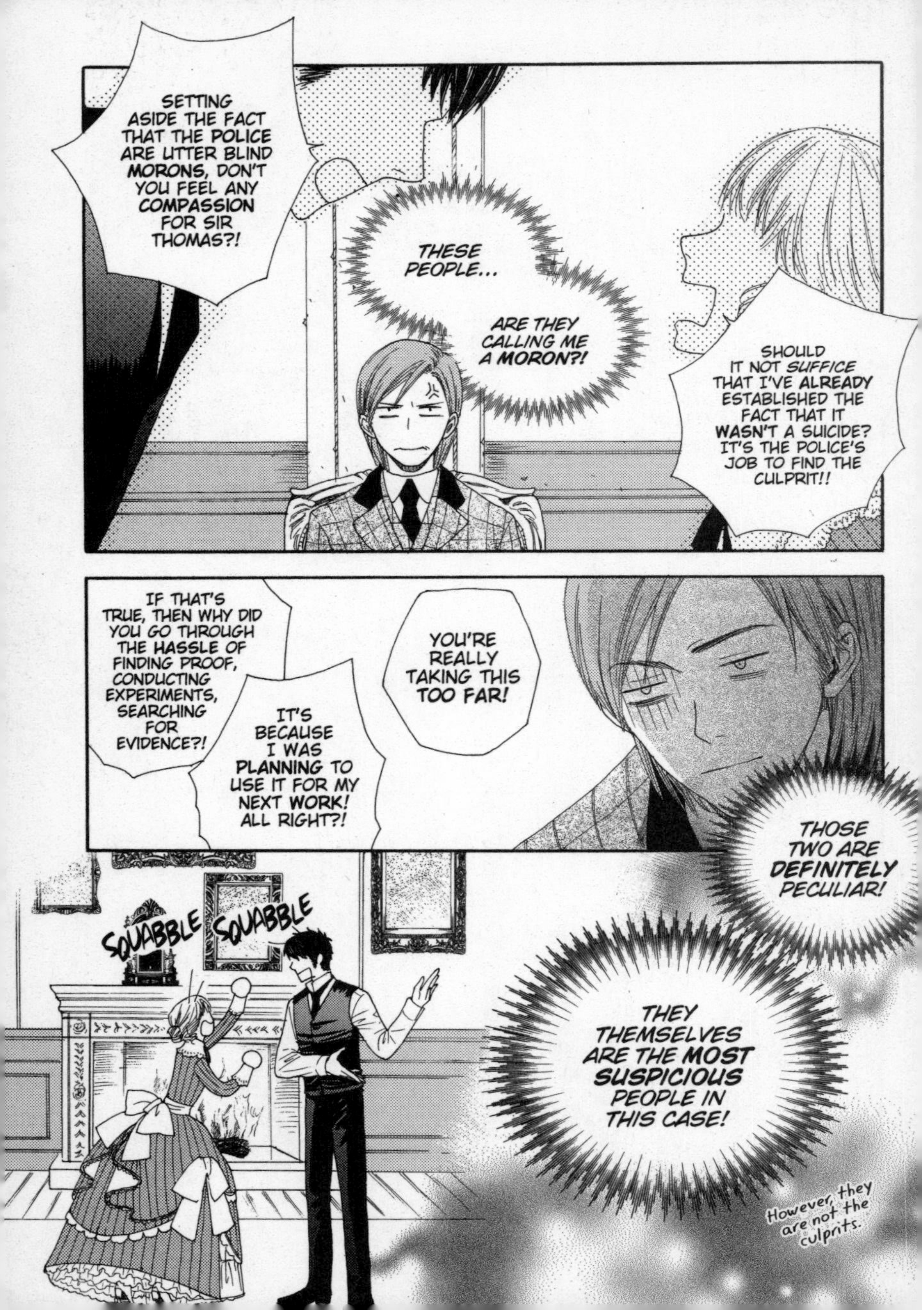

SETTING ASIDE THE FACT THAT THE POLICE ARE UTTER BLIND MORONS, DON'T YOU FEEL ANY COMPASSION FOR SIR THOMAS?!
THESE PEOPLE...
ARE THEY CALLING ME A MORON?!
SHOULD IT NOT SUFFICE THAT I'VE ALREADY ESTABLISHED THE FACT THAT IT WASN'T A SUICIDE? IT'S THE POLICE'S JOB TO FIND THE CULPRIT!!
IF THAT'S TRUE, THEN WHY DID YOU GO THROUGH THE HASSLE OF FINDING PROOF, CONDUCTING EXPERIMENTS, SEARCHING FOR EVIDENCE?!
IT'S BECAUSE I WAS PLANNING TO USE IT FOR MY NEXT WORK! ALL RIGHT?!
YOU'RE REALLY TAKING THIS TOO FAR!
THOSE TWO ARE DEFINITELY PECULIAR!
SQUABBLE
SQUABBLE
THEY THEMSELVES ARE THE MOST SUSPICIOUS PEOPLE IN THIS CASE!
However, they are not the culprits.

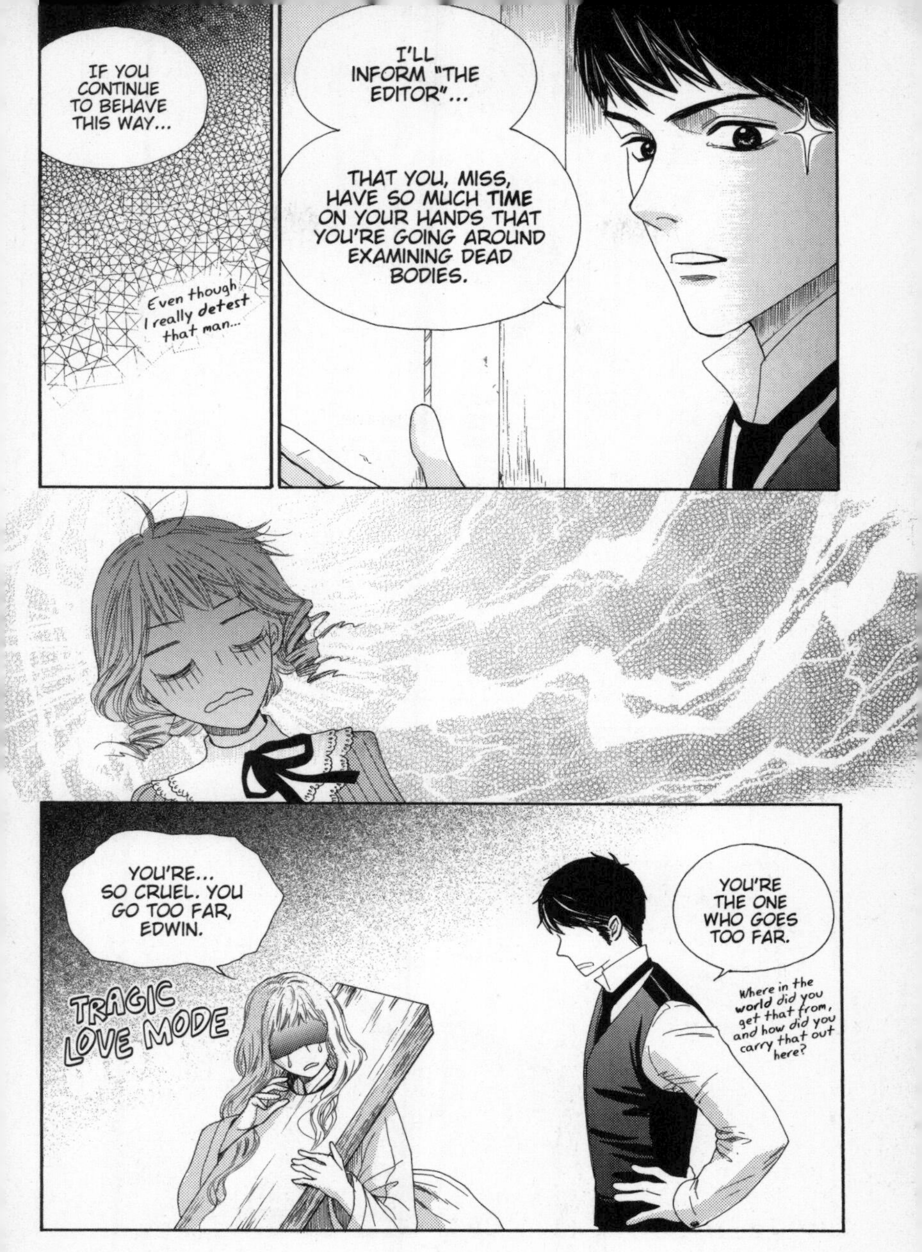
IF YOU CONTINUE TO BEHAVE THIS WAY...
Even though I really detest that man...
I'LL INFORM "THE EDITOR"...
THAT YOU, MISS, HAVE SO MUCH TIME ON YOUR HANDS THAT YOU'RE GOING AROUND EXAMINING DEAD BODIES.
YOU'RE... SO CRUEL. YOU GO TOO FAR, EDWIN.
TRAGIC LOVE MODE
YOU'RE THE ONE WHO GOES TOO FAR.
Where in the world did you get that from, and how did you carry that out here?

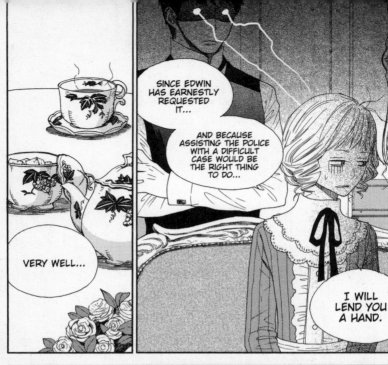

SINCE EDWIN HAS EARNESTLY REQUESTED IT...

AND BECAUSE ASSISTING THE POLICE WITH A DIFFICULT CASE WOULD BE THE RIGHT THING TO DO...

VERY WELL...

I WILL LEND YOU A HAND.

If you hadn't requested books, I would have let you continue lording it over him.

FIRST AND FOREMOST, THESE LEGAL DOCUMENTS...

DETAIL THE TRICK USED TO LOCK THE ROOM, HER OBSERVATIONS, AND SO FORTH. THIS IS OUR MISS' TESTIMONY, REGARDING HER DEDUCTIONS.

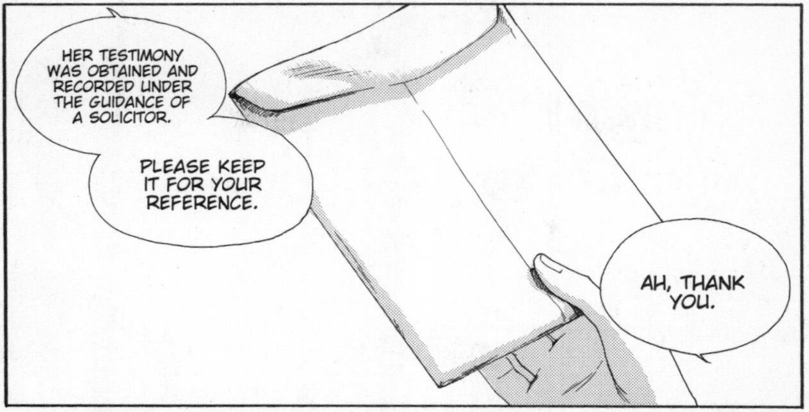
HER TESTIMONY WAS OBTAINED AND RECORDED UNDER THE GUIDANCE OF A SOLICITOR.
PLEASE KEEP IT FOR YOUR REFERENCE.
AH, THANK YOU.

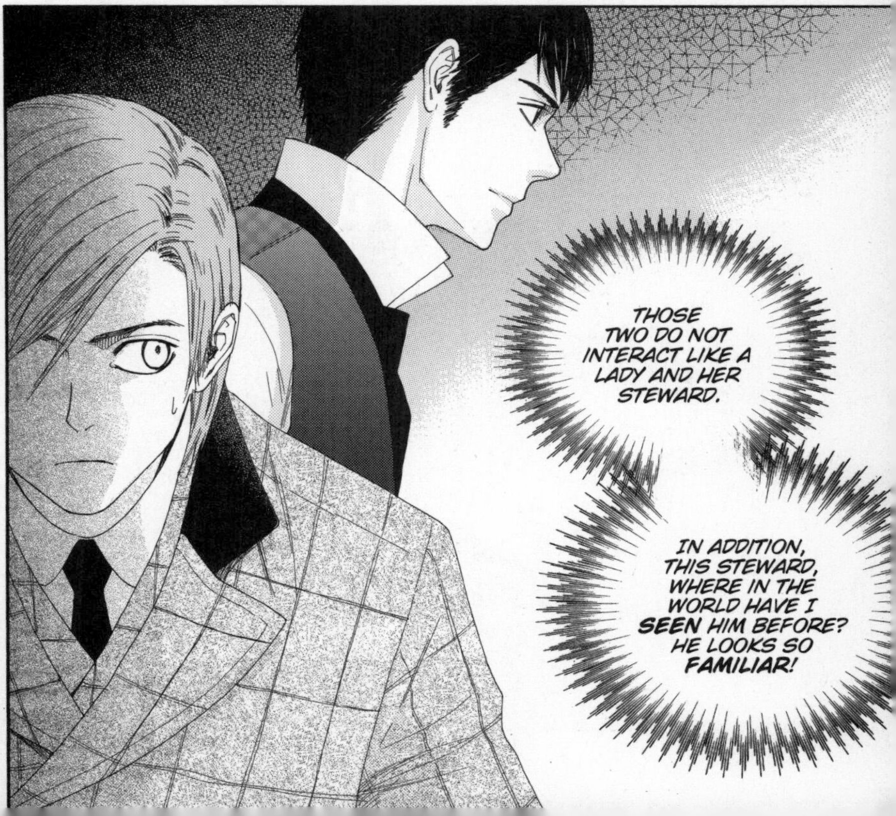
THOSE TWO DO NOT INTERACT LIKE A LADY AND HER STEWARD.
IN ADDITION, THIS STEWARD, WHERE IN THE WORLD HAVE I **SEEN** HIM BEFORE? HE LOOKS SO **FAMILIAR!**

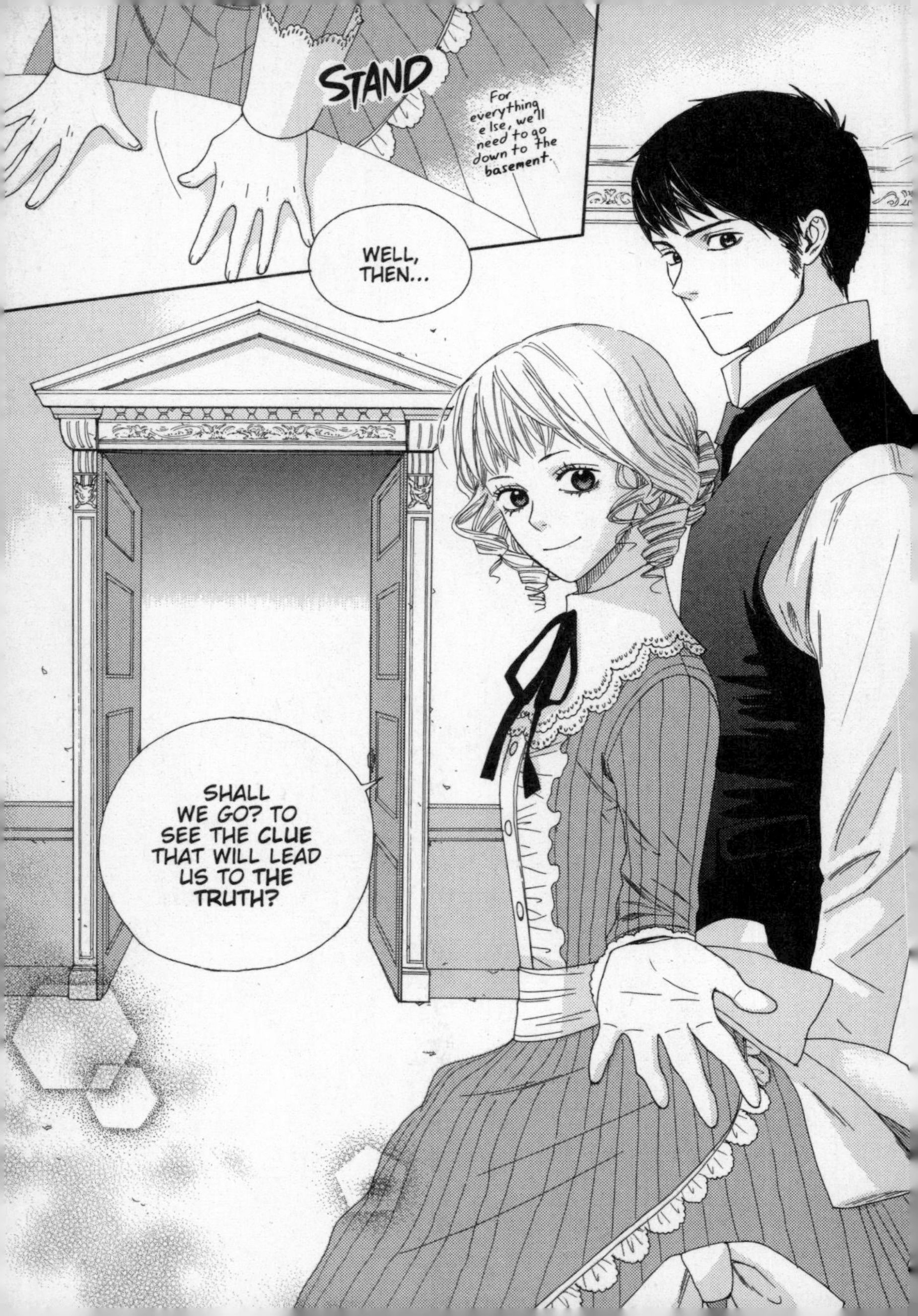
STAND
For everything else, we'll need to go down to the basement.
WELL, THEN...
SHALL WE GO? TO SEE THE CLUE THAT WILL LEAD US TO THE TRUTH?

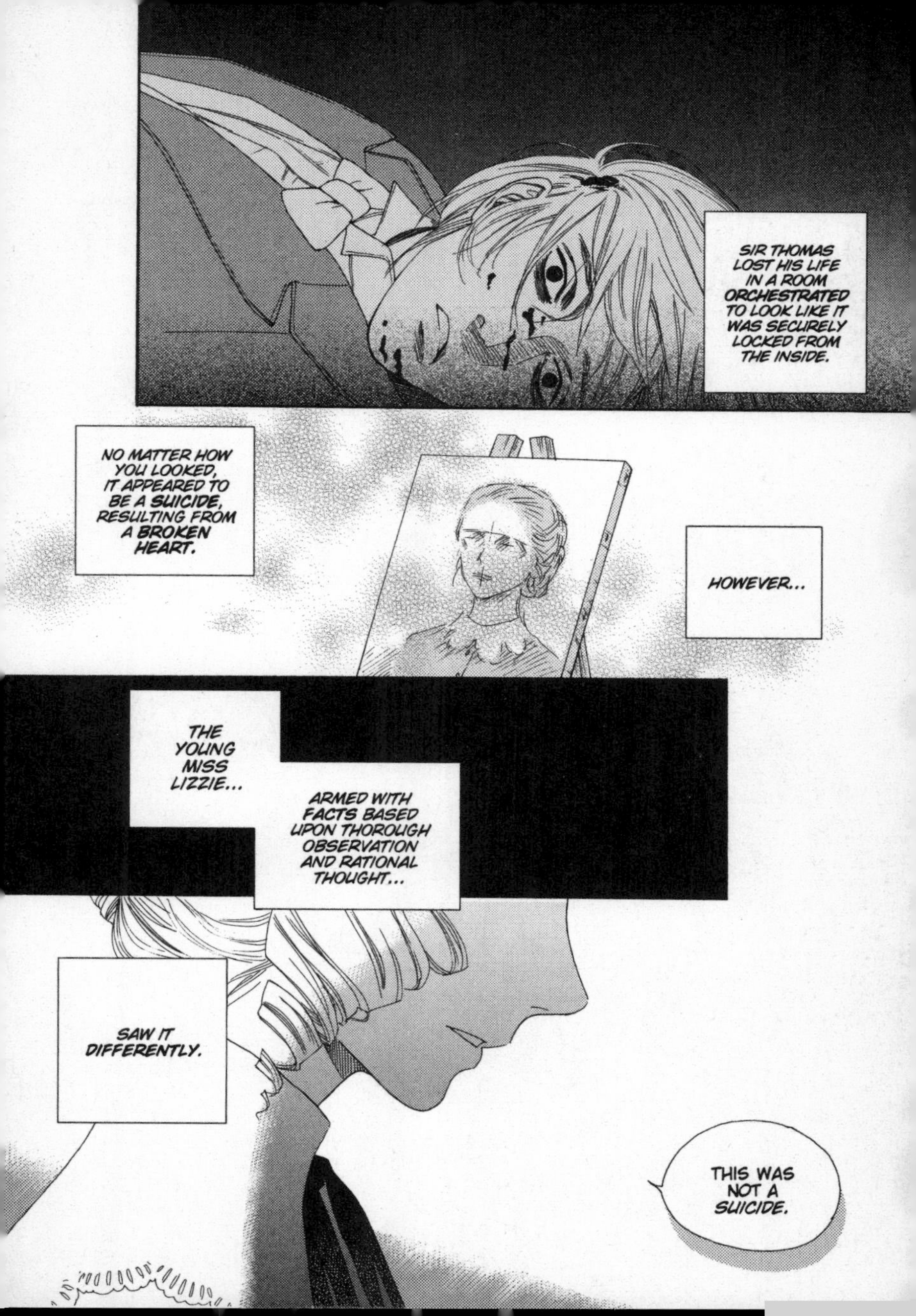
SIR THOMAS LOST HIS LIFE IN A ROOM ORCHESTRATED TO LOOK LIKE IT WAS SECURELY LOCKED FROM THE INSIDE.
NO MATTER HOW YOU LOOKED, IT APPEARED TO BE A SUICIDE, RESULTING FROM A BROKEN HEART.
HOWEVER...
THE YOUNG MISS LIZZIE...
ARMED WITH FACTS BASED UPON THOROUGH OBSERVATION AND RATIONAL THOUGHT...
SAW IT DIFFERENTLY.
THIS WAS NOT A SUICIDE.

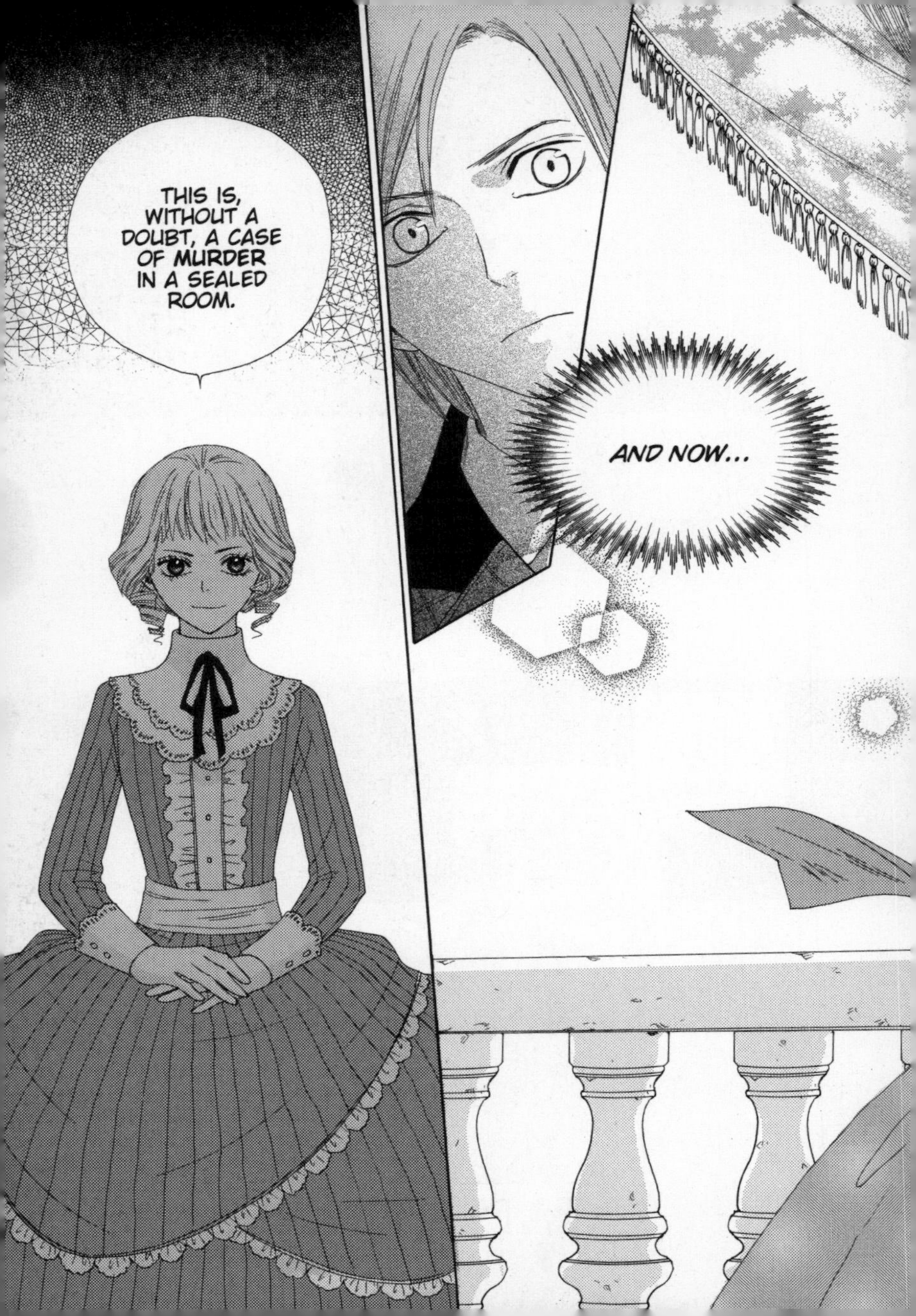
THIS IS, WITHOUT A DOUBT, A CASE OF MURDER IN A SEALED ROOM.
AND NOW...

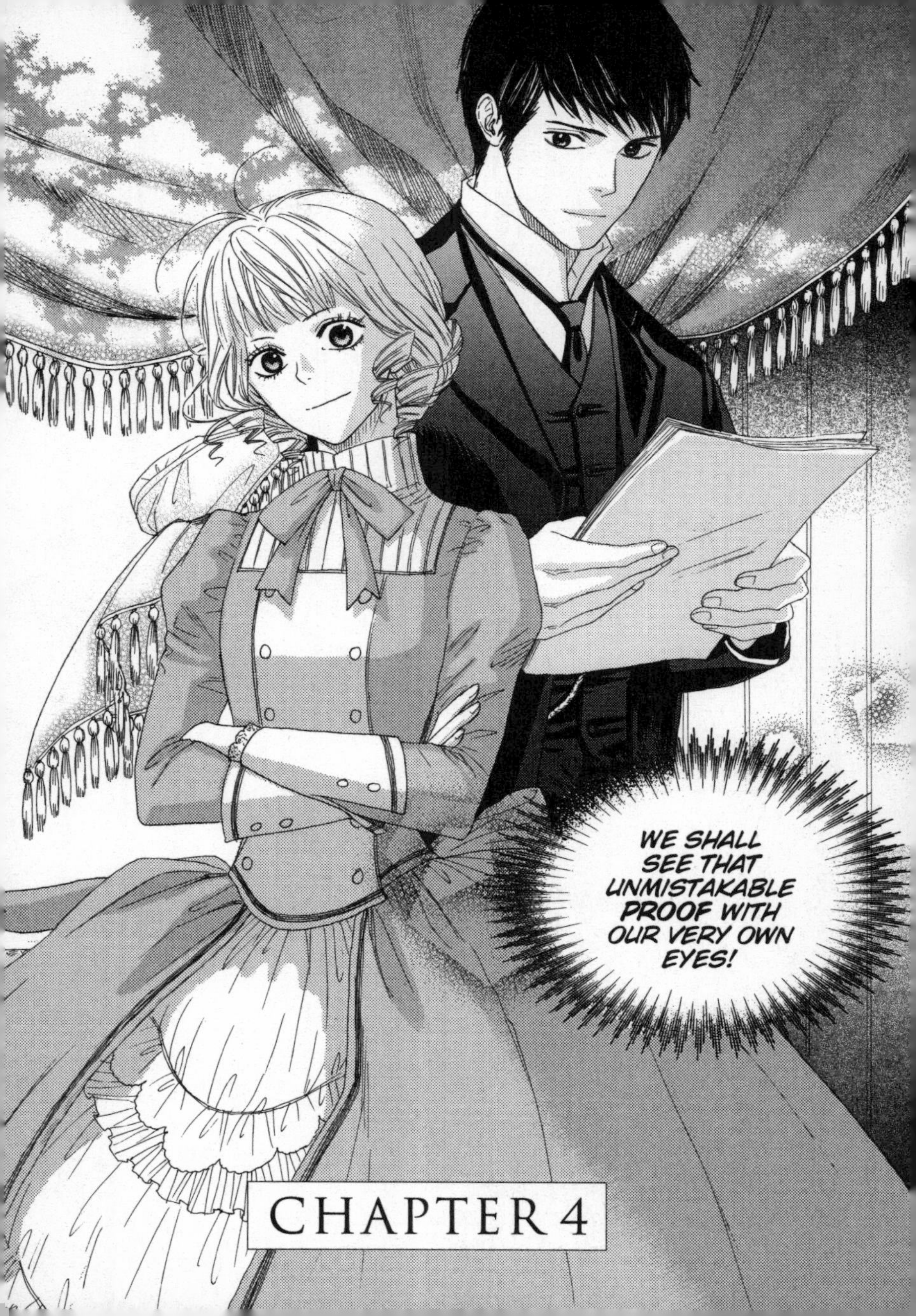
WE SHALL SEE THAT UNMISTAKABLE PROOF WITH OUR VERY OWN EYES!
CHAPTER 4

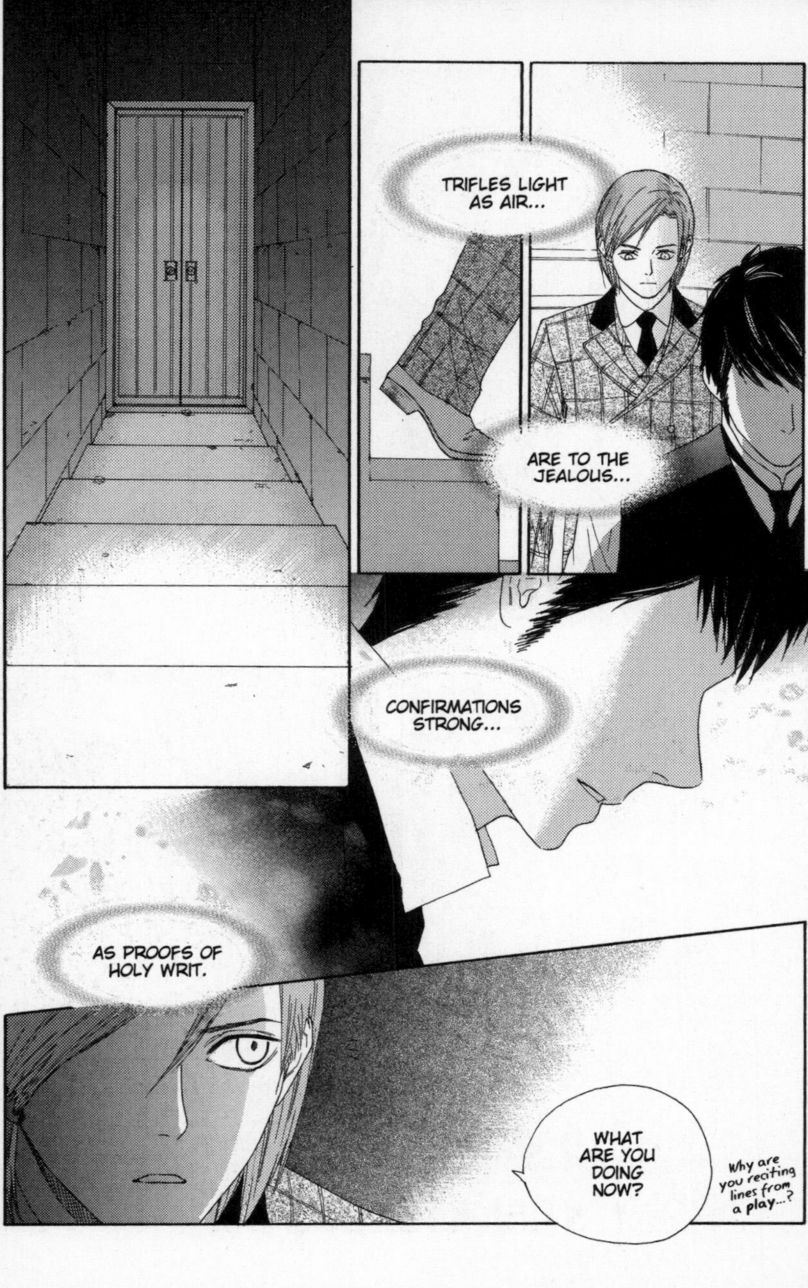
TRIFLES LIGHT AS AIR...
ARE TO THE JEALOUS...
CONFIRMATIONS STRONG...
AS PROOFS OF HOLY WRIT.
WHAT ARE YOU DOING NOW?
Why are you reciting lines from a play...?

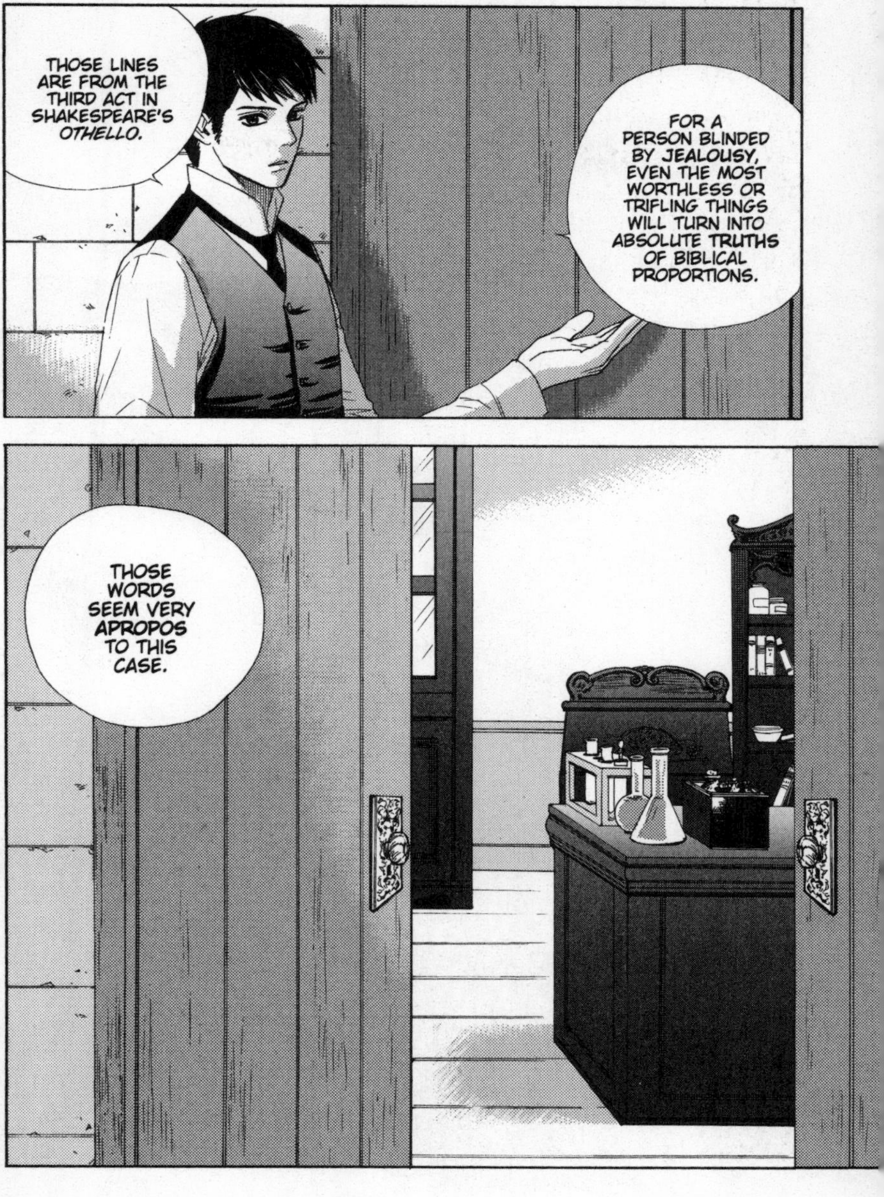
THOSE LINES ARE FROM THE THIRD ACT IN SHAKESPEARE'S *OTHELLO.*
FOR A PERSON BLINDED BY JEALOUSY, EVEN THE MOST WORTHLESS OR TRIFLING THINGS WILL TURN INTO ABSOLUTE TRUTHS OF BIBLICAL PROPORTIONS.
THOSE WORDS SEEM VERY APROPOS TO THIS CASE.

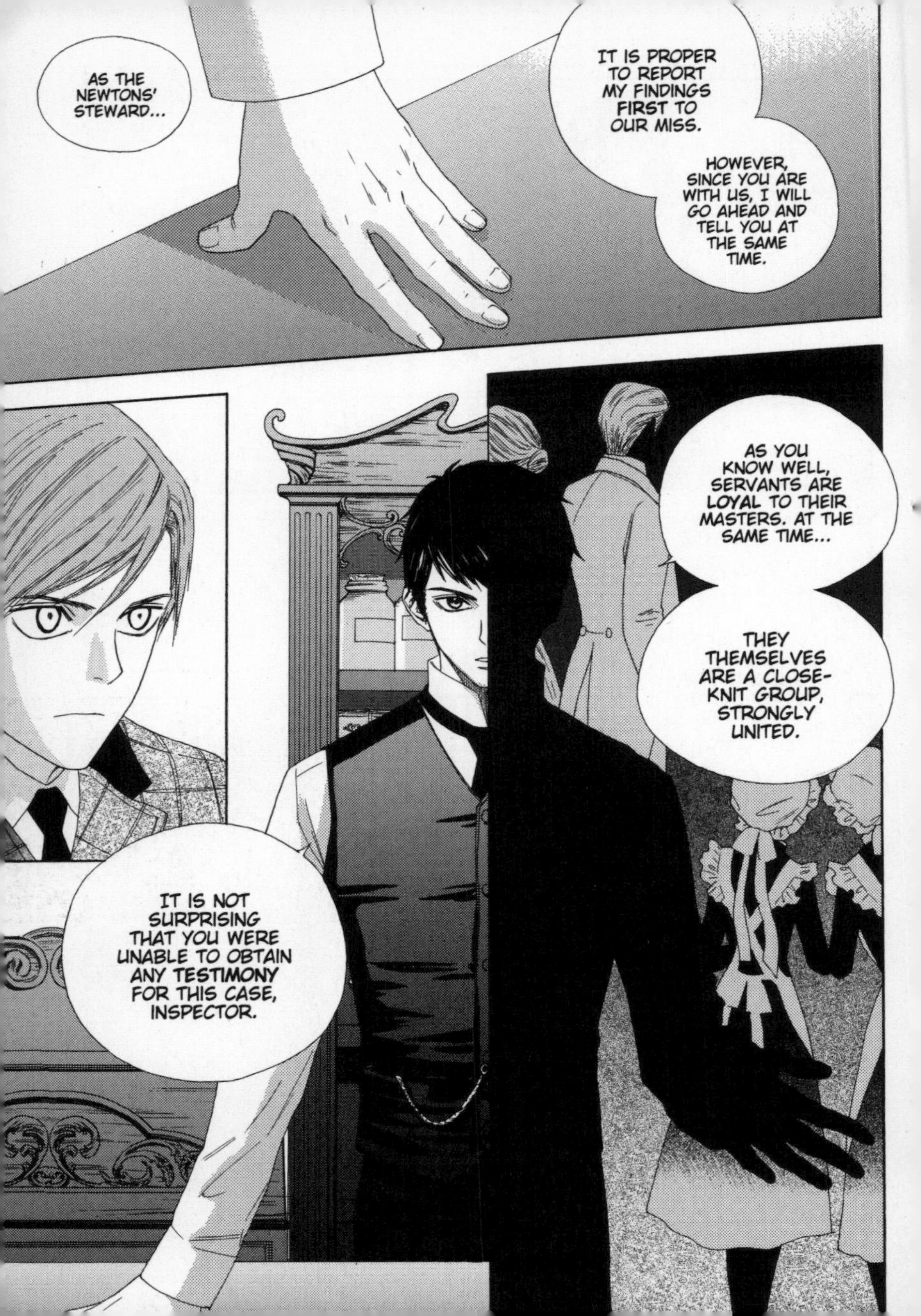
AS THE NEWTONS' STEWARD...
IT IS PROPER TO REPORT MY FINDINGS FIRST TO OUR MISS.
HOWEVER, SINCE YOU ARE WITH US, I WILL GO AHEAD AND TELL YOU AT THE SAME TIME.
AS YOU KNOW WELL, SERVANTS ARE LOYAL TO THEIR MASTERS. AT THE SAME TIME...
THEY THEMSELVES ARE A CLOSE-KNIT GROUP, STRONGLY UNITED.
IT IS NOT SURPRISING THAT YOU WERE UNABLE TO OBTAIN ANY TESTIMONY FOR THIS CASE, INSPECTOR.

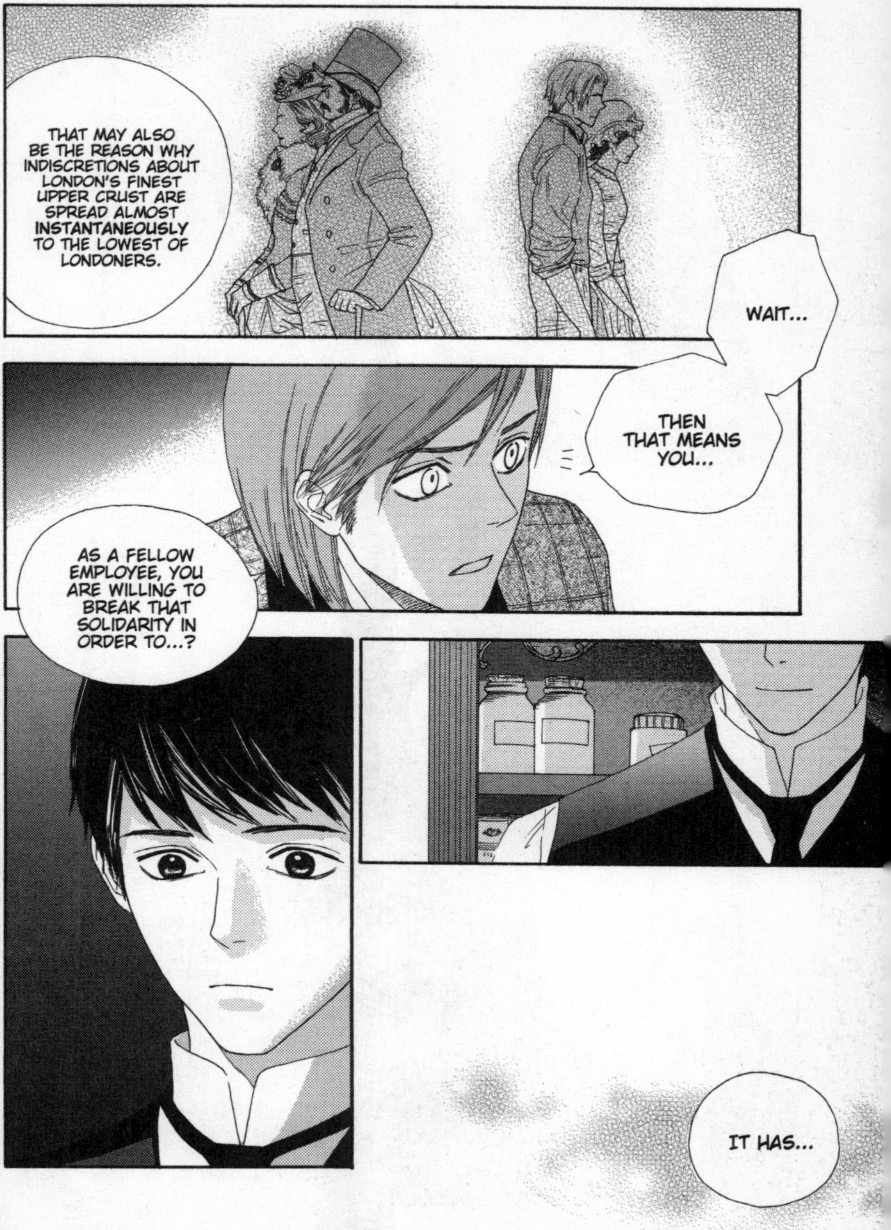
THAT MAY ALSO BE THE REASON WHY INDISCRETIONS ABOUT LONDON'S FINEST UPPER CRUST ARE SPREAD ALMOST INSTANTANEOUSLY TO THE LOWEST OF LONDONERS.
WAIT...
THEN THAT MEANS YOU...
AS A FELLOW EMPLOYEE, YOU ARE WILLING TO BREAK THAT SOLIDARITY IN ORDER TO...?
IT HAS...

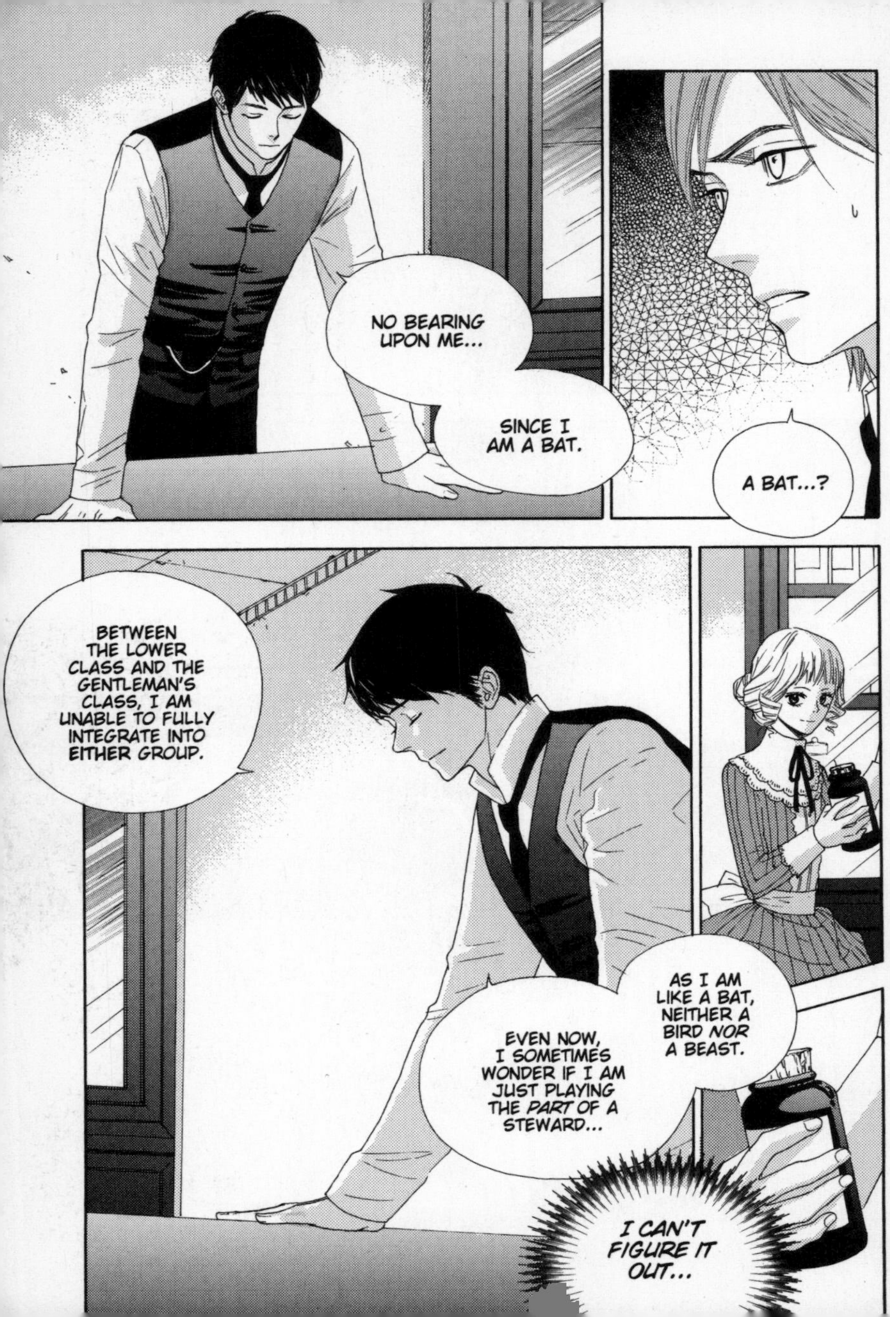
NO BEARING UPON ME...
SINCE I AM A BAT.
A BAT...?
BETWEEN THE LOWER CLASS AND THE GENTLEMAN'S CLASS, I AM UNABLE TO FULLY INTEGRATE INTO EITHER GROUP.
EVEN NOW, I SOMETIMES WONDER IF I AM JUST PLAYING THE *PART* OF A STEWARD...
AS I AM LIKE A BAT, NEITHER A BIRD *NOR* A BEAST.
I CAN'T FIGURE IT OUT...

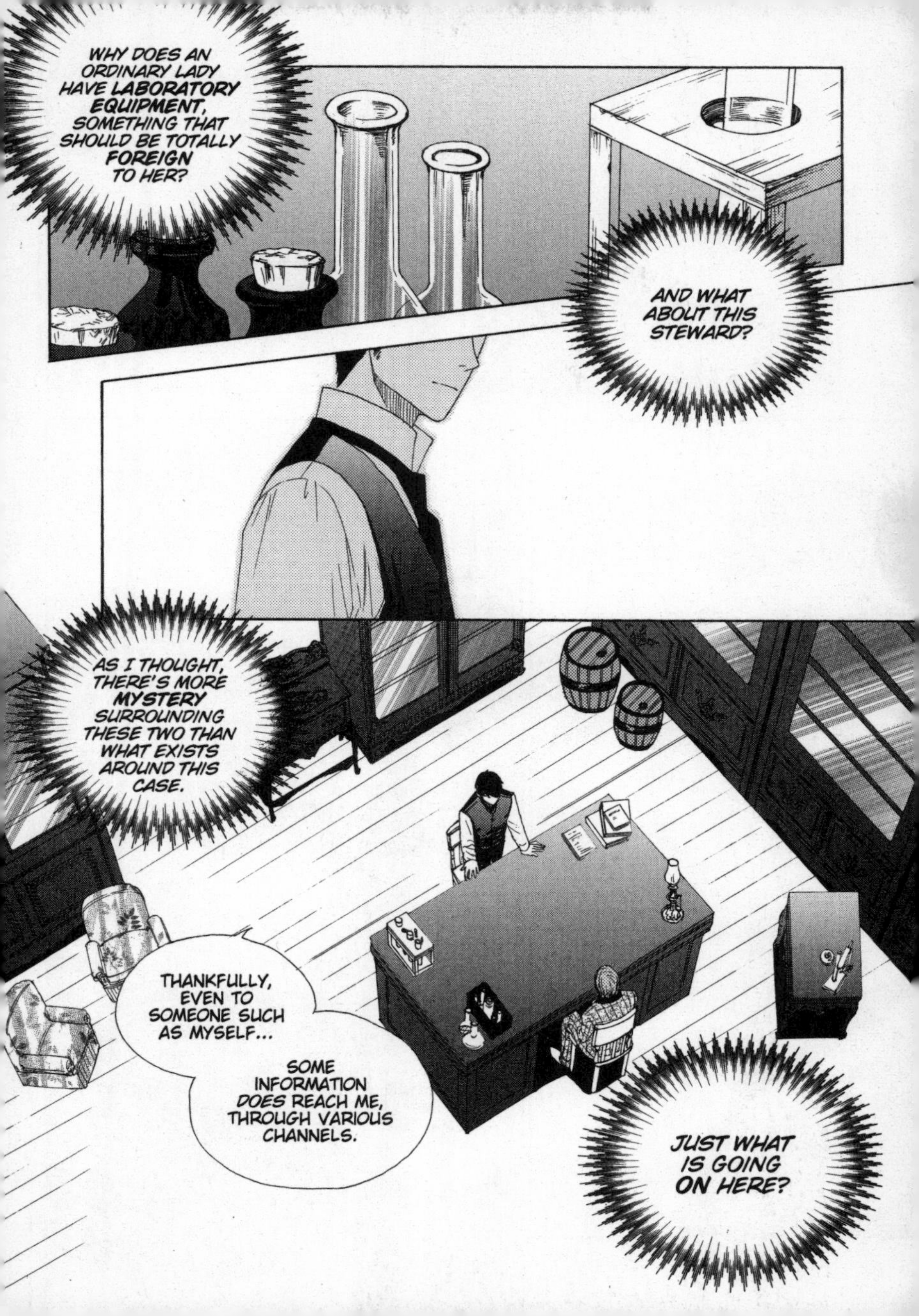
WHY DOES AN ORDINARY LADY HAVE LABORATORY EQUIPMENT, SOMETHING THAT SHOULD BE TOTALLY FOREIGN TO HER?
AND WHAT ABOUT THIS STEWARD?
AS I THOUGHT, THERE'S MORE MYSTERY SURROUNDING THESE TWO THAN WHAT EXISTS AROUND THIS CASE.
THANKFULLY, EVEN TO SOMEONE SUCH AS MYSELF...
SOME INFORMATION DOES REACH ME, THROUGH VARIOUS CHANNELS.
JUST WHAT IS GOING ON HERE?

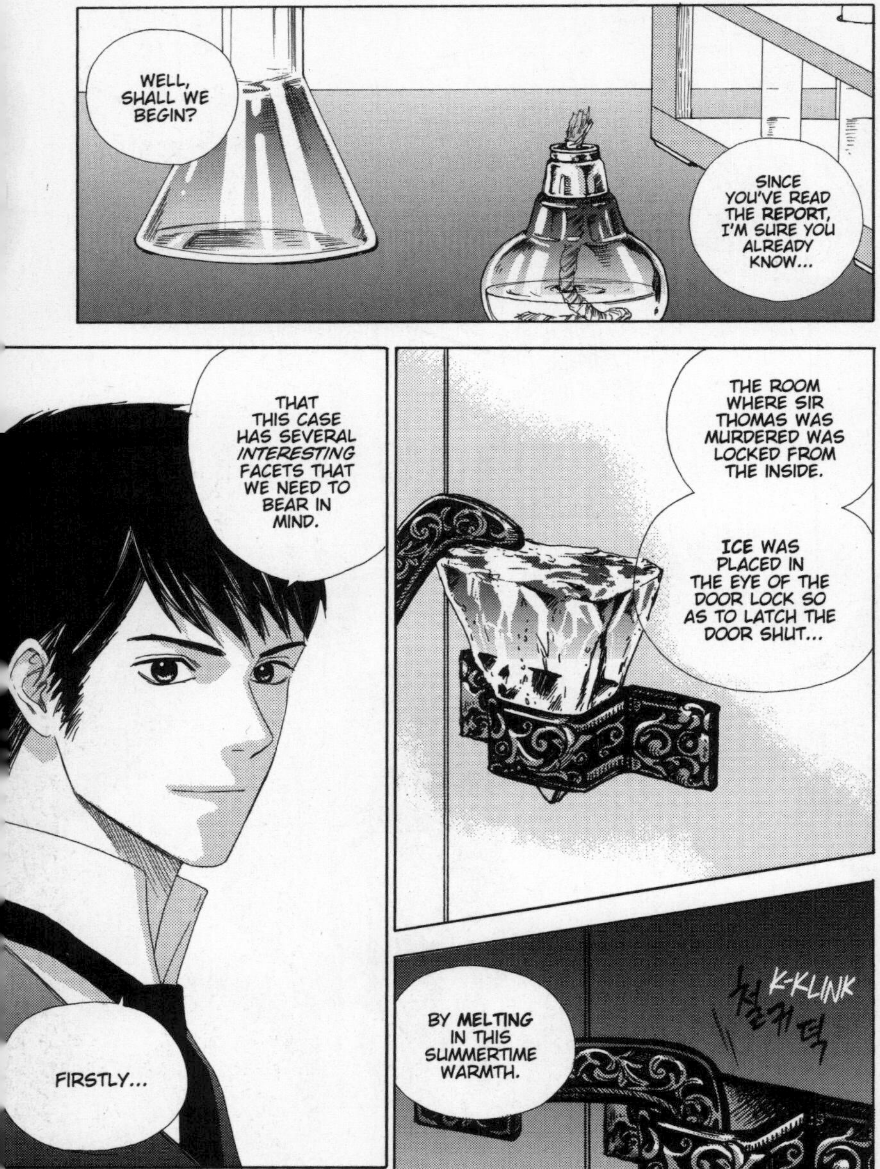
WELL, SHALL WE BEGIN?
SINCE YOU'VE READ THE REPORT, I'M SURE YOU ALREADY KNOW...
THAT THIS CASE HAS SEVERAL *INTERESTING* FACETS THAT WE NEED TO BEAR IN MIND.
FIRSTLY...
THE ROOM WHERE SIR THOMAS WAS MURDERED WAS LOCKED FROM THE INSIDE.
ICE WAS PLACED IN THE EYE OF THE DOOR LOCK SO AS TO LATCH THE DOOR SHUT...
BY MELTING IN THIS SUMMERTIME WARMTH.
K-KLINK
철커덕

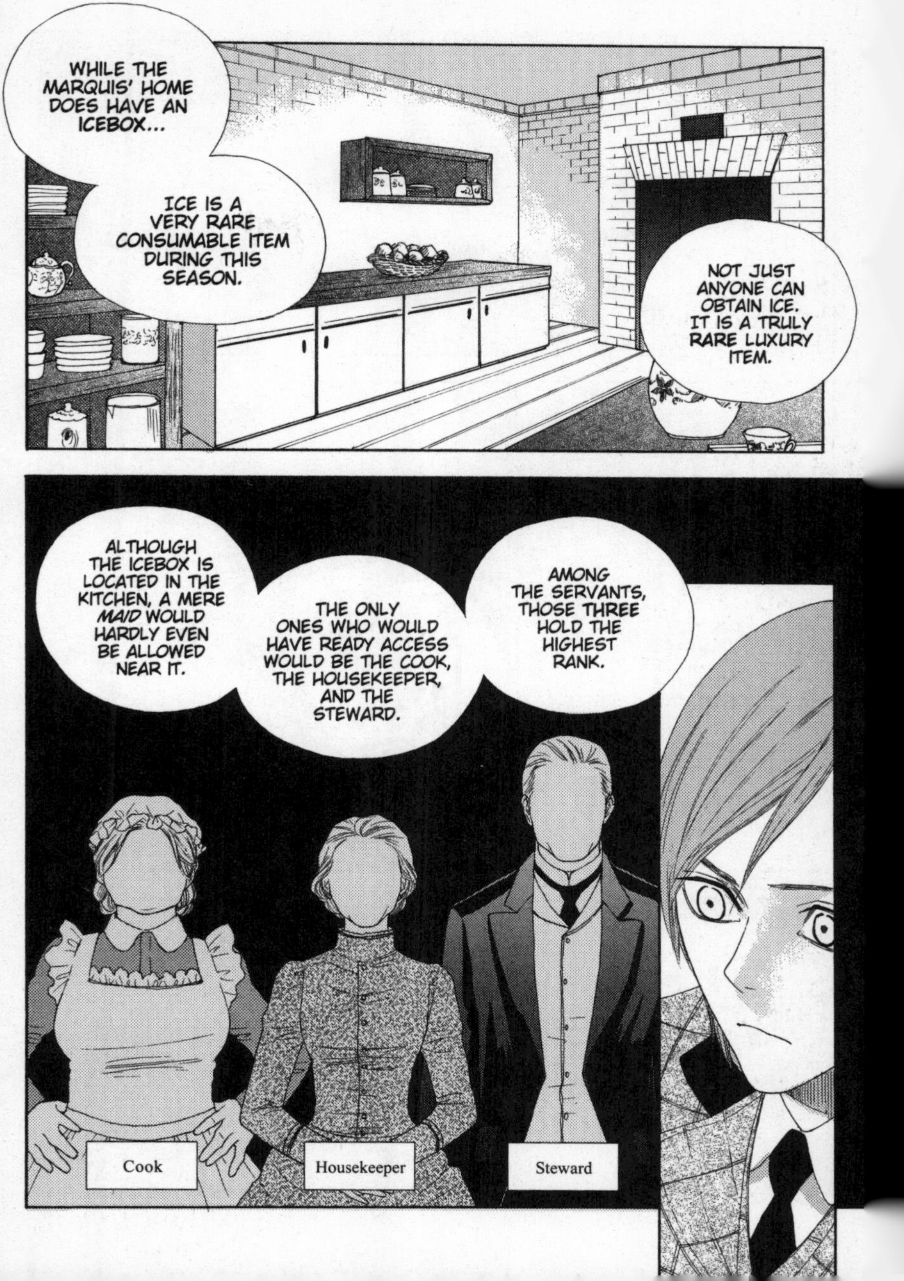
WHILE THE MARQUIS' HOME DOES HAVE AN ICEBOX...
ICE IS A VERY RARE CONSUMABLE ITEM DURING THIS SEASON.
NOT JUST ANYONE CAN OBTAIN ICE. IT IS A TRULY RARE LUXURY ITEM.
ALTHOUGH THE ICEBOX IS LOCATED IN THE KITCHEN, A MERE *MAID* WOULD HARDLY EVEN BE ALLOWED NEAR IT.
THE ONLY ONES WHO WOULD HAVE READY ACCESS WOULD BE THE COOK, THE HOUSEKEEPER, AND THE STEWARD.
AMONG THE SERVANTS, THOSE THREE HOLD THE HIGHEST RANK.
Cook
Housekeeper
Steward

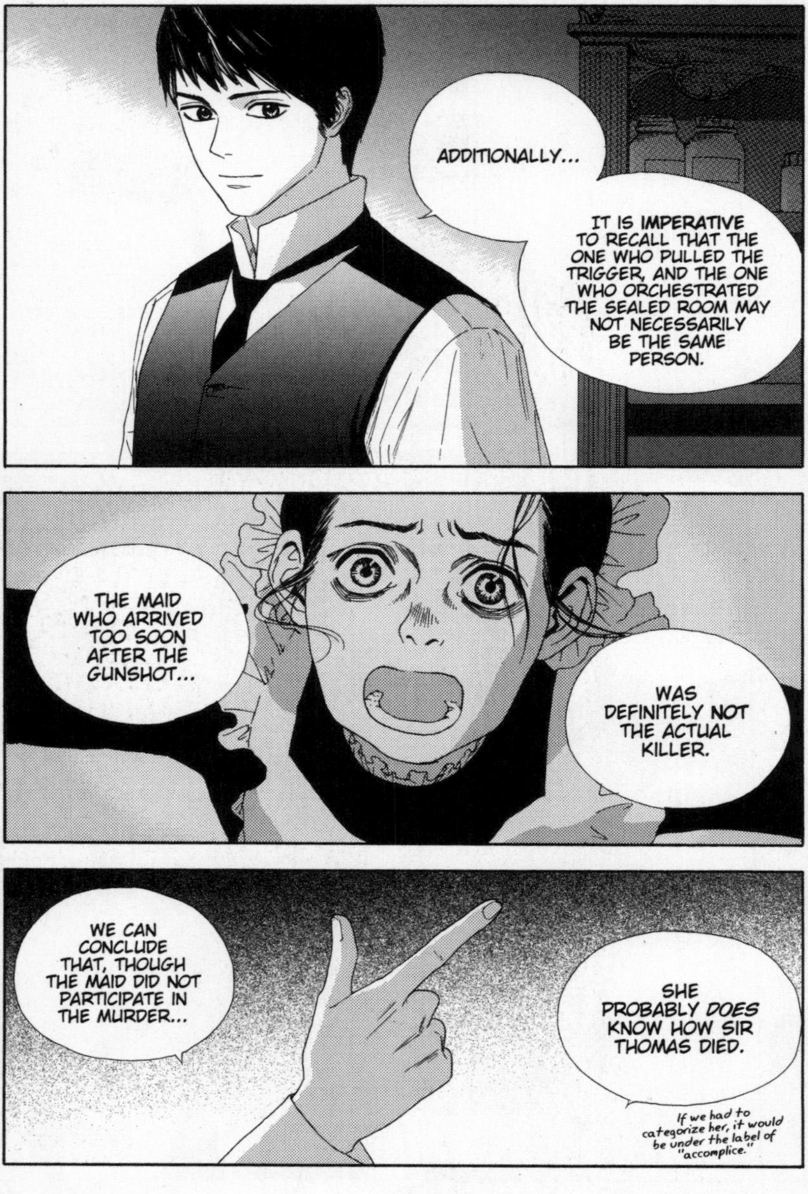
ADDITIONALLY...
IT IS IMPERATIVE TO RECALL THAT THE ONE WHO PULLED THE TRIGGER, AND THE ONE WHO ORCHESTRATED THE SEALED ROOM MAY NOT NECESSARILY BE THE SAME PERSON.
THE MAID WHO ARRIVED TOO SOON AFTER THE GUNSHOT...
WAS DEFINITELY NOT THE ACTUAL KILLER.
WE CAN CONCLUDE THAT, THOUGH THE MAID DID NOT PARTICIPATE IN THE MURDER...
SHE PROBABLY *DOES* KNOW HOW SIR THOMAS DIED.
If we had to categorize her, it would be under the label of "accomplice."

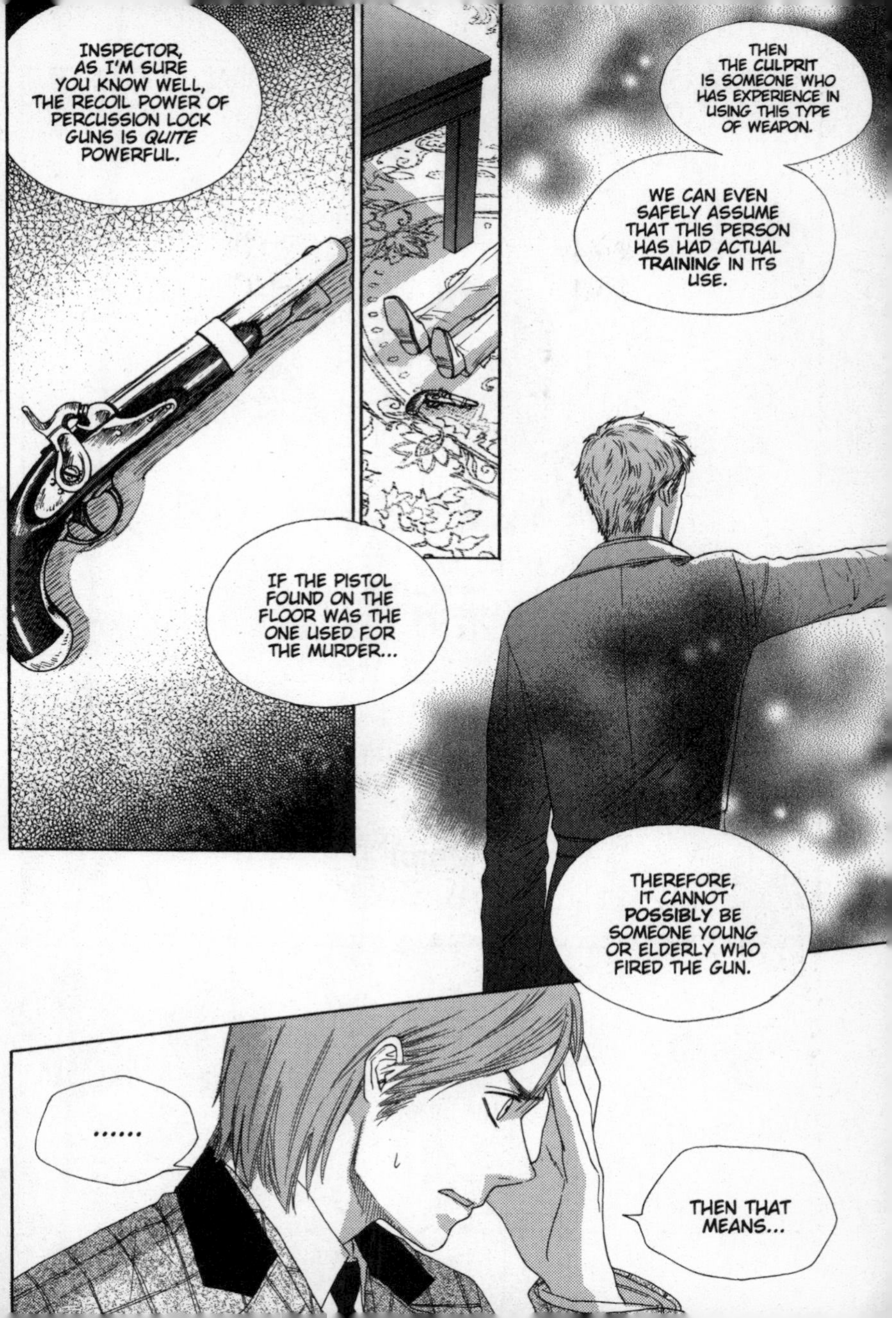
INSPECTOR, AS I'M SURE YOU KNOW WELL, THE RECOIL POWER OF PERCUSSION LOCK GUNS IS *QUITE* POWERFUL.
THEN THE CULPRIT IS SOMEONE WHO HAS EXPERIENCE IN USING THIS TYPE OF WEAPON.
WE CAN EVEN SAFELY ASSUME THAT THIS PERSON HAS HAD ACTUAL TRAINING IN ITS USE.
IF THE PISTOL FOUND ON THE FLOOR WAS THE ONE USED FOR THE MURDER...
THEREFORE, IT CANNOT POSSIBLY BE SOMEONE YOUNG OR ELDERLY WHO FIRED THE GUN.
......
THEN THAT MEANS...

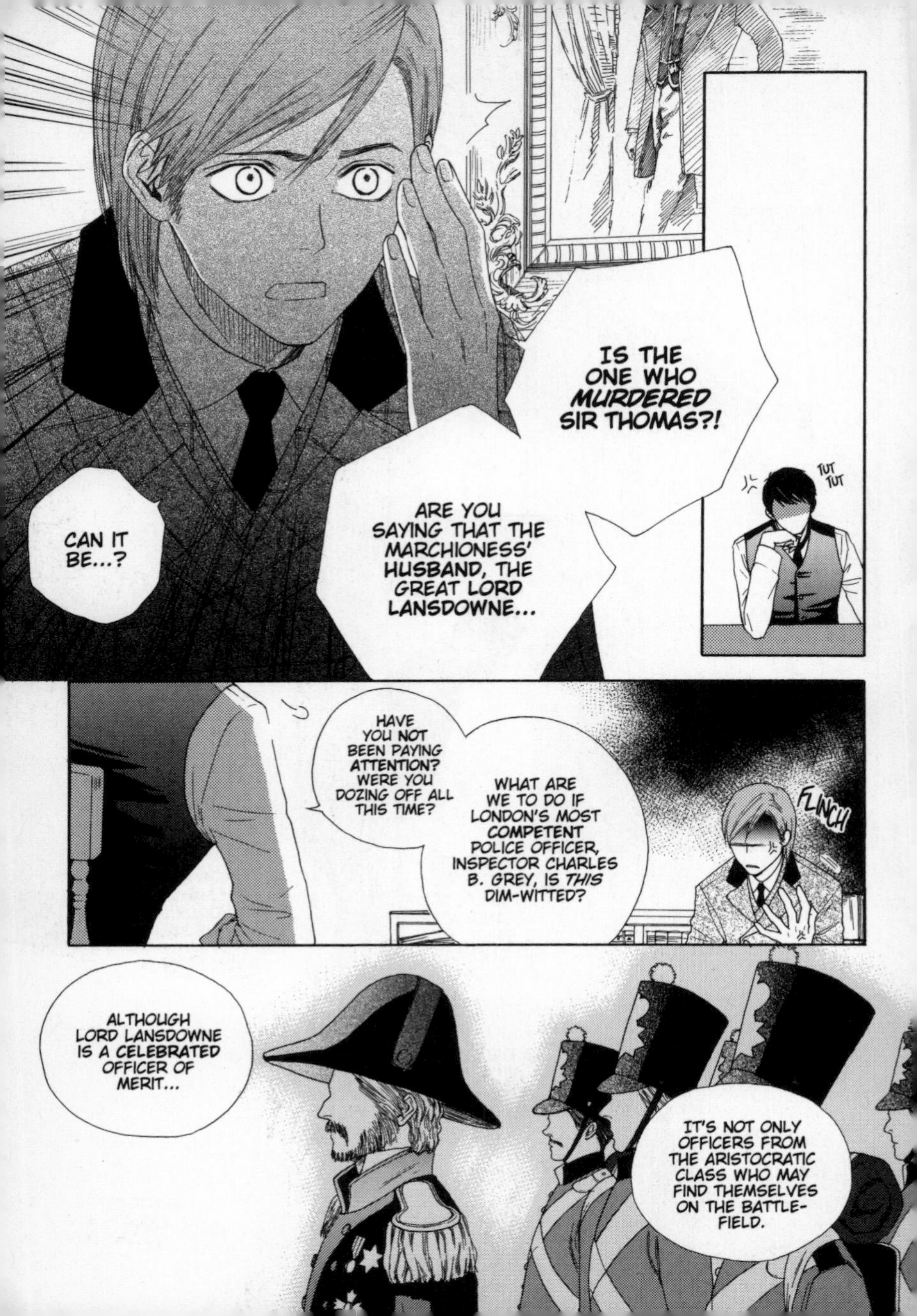
CAN IT BE...?
ARE YOU SAYING THAT THE MARCHIONESS' HUSBAND, THE GREAT LORD LANSDOWNE...
IS THE ONE WHO *MURDERED* SIR THOMAS?!
TUT TUT
HAVE YOU NOT BEEN PAYING ATTENTION? WERE YOU DOZING OFF ALL THIS TIME?
WHAT ARE WE TO DO IF LONDON'S MOST COMPETENT POLICE OFFICER, INSPECTOR CHARLES B. GREY, IS *THIS* DIM-WITTED?
FLINCH
ALTHOUGH LORD LANSDOWNE IS A CELEBRATED OFFICER OF MERIT...
IT'S NOT ONLY OFFICERS FROM THE ARISTOCRATIC CLASS WHO MAY FIND THEMSELVES ON THE BATTLE-FIELD.

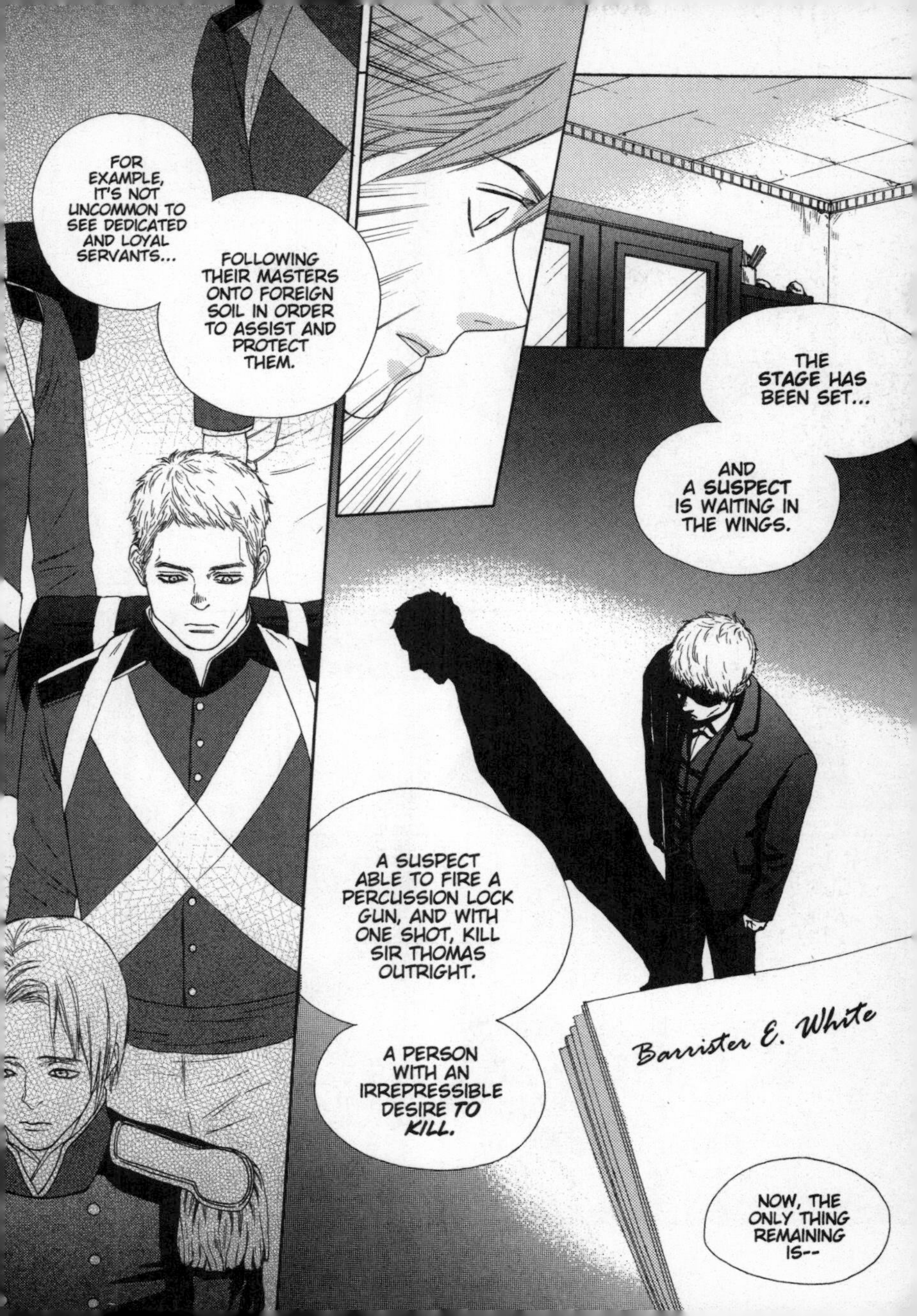
FOR EXAMPLE, IT'S NOT UNCOMMON TO SEE DEDICATED AND LOYAL SERVANTS...
FOLLOWING THEIR MASTERS ONTO FOREIGN SOIL IN ORDER TO ASSIST AND PROTECT THEM.
THE STAGE HAS BEEN SET...
AND A SUSPECT IS WAITING IN THE WINGS.
A SUSPECT ABLE TO FIRE A PERCUSSION LOCK GUN, AND WITH ONE SHOT, KILL SIR THOMAS OUTRIGHT.
A PERSON WITH AN IRREPRESSIBLE DESIRE TO KILL.
Barrister E. White
NOW, THE ONLY THING REMAINING IS--

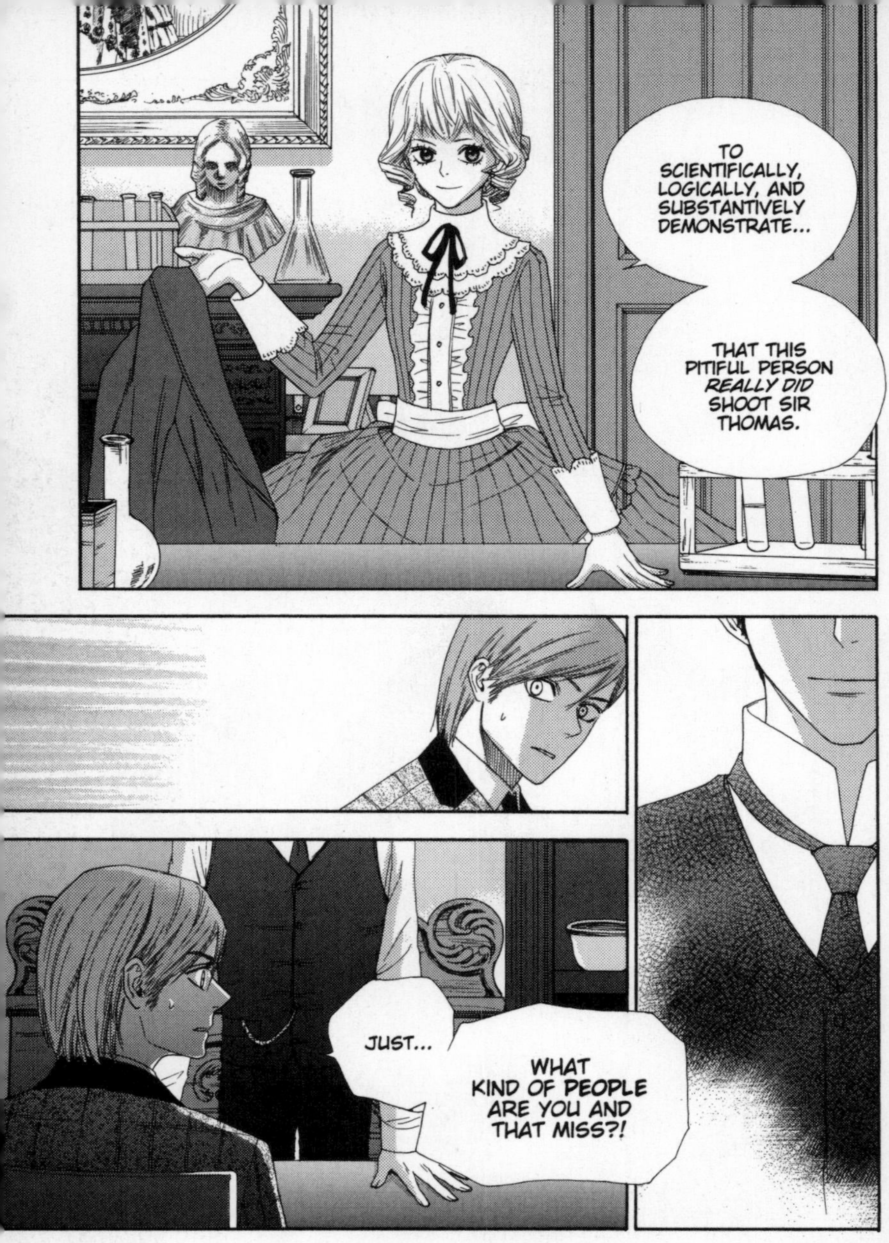
TO SCIENTIFICALLY, LOGICALLY, AND SUBSTANTIVELY DEMONSTRATE...
THAT THIS PITIFUL PERSON *REALLY DID* SHOOT SIR THOMAS.
JUST...
WHAT KIND OF PEOPLE ARE YOU AND THAT MISS?!

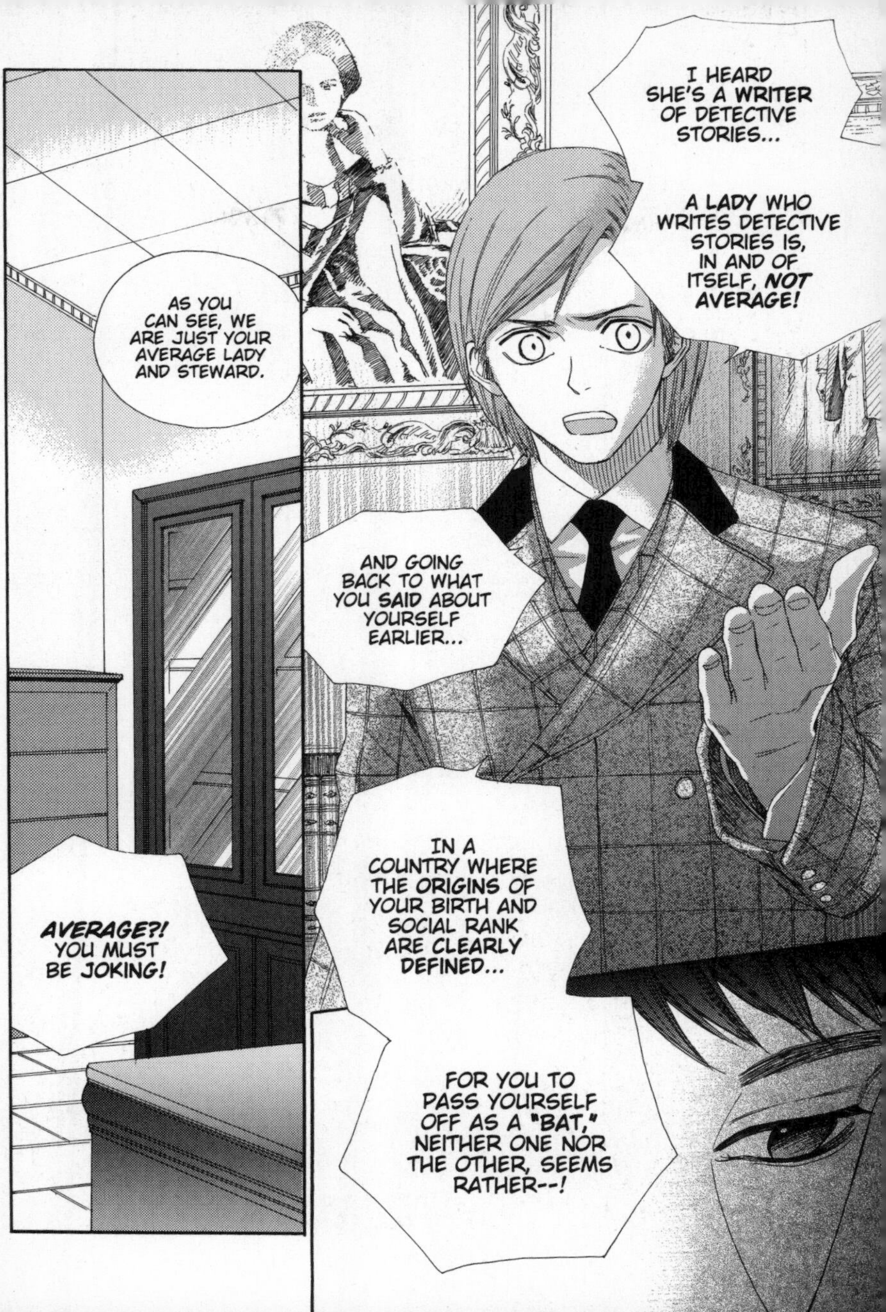
AS YOU CAN SEE, WE ARE JUST YOUR AVERAGE LADY AND STEWARD.
AVERAGE?! YOU MUST BE JOKING!
I HEARD SHE'S A WRITER OF DETECTIVE STORIES...
A LADY WHO WRITES DETECTIVE STORIES IS, IN AND OF ITSELF, NOT AVERAGE!
AND GOING BACK TO WHAT YOU SAID ABOUT YOURSELF EARLIER...
IN A COUNTRY WHERE THE ORIGINS OF YOUR BIRTH AND SOCIAL RANK ARE CLEARLY DEFINED...
FOR YOU TO PASS YOURSELF OFF AS A "BAT," NEITHER ONE NOR THE OTHER, SEEMS RATHER--!

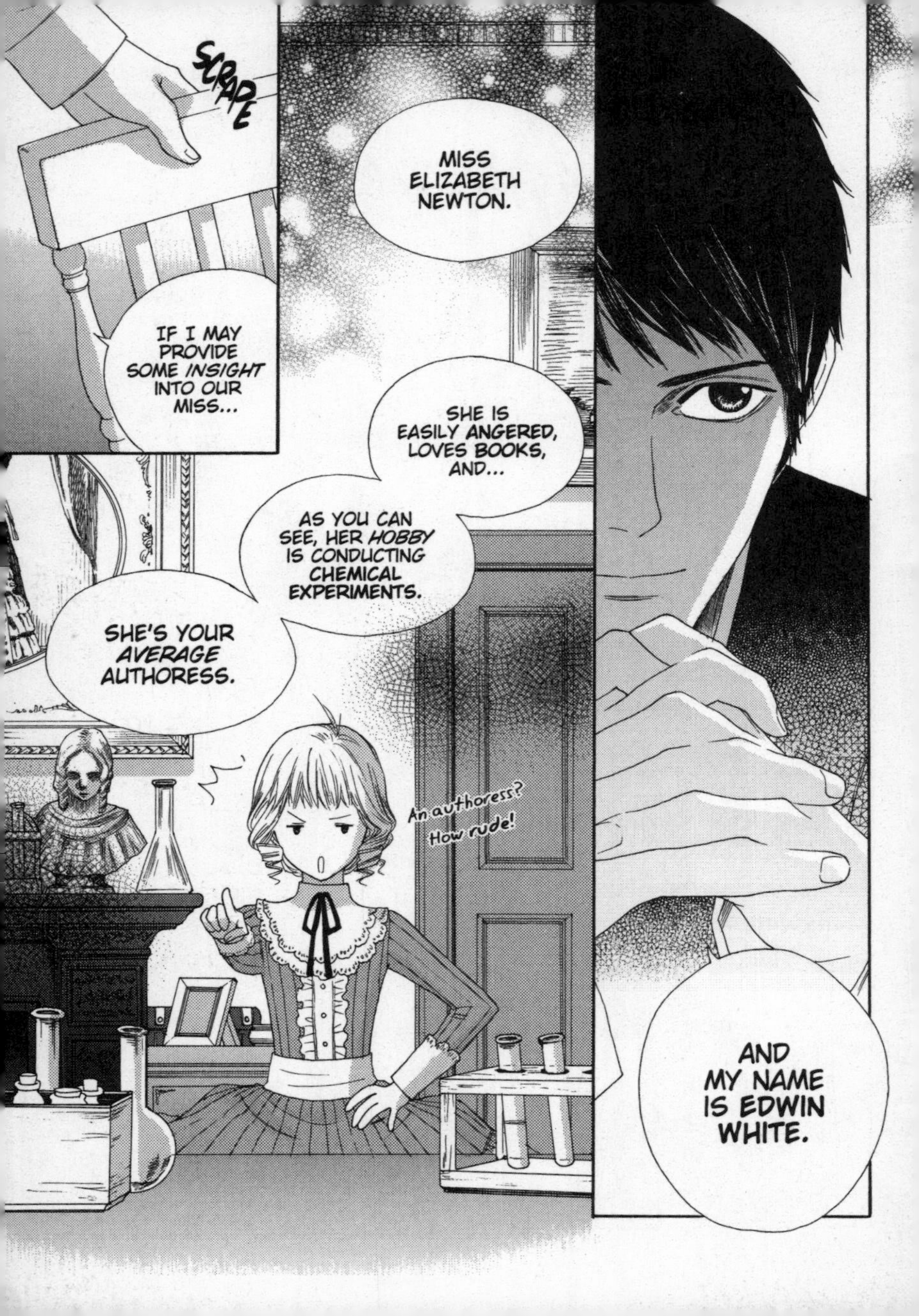
SCRAPE
MISS ELIZABETH NEWTON.
IF I MAY PROVIDE SOME *INSIGHT* INTO OUR MISS...
SHE IS EASILY ANGERED, LOVES BOOKS, AND...
AS YOU CAN SEE, HER *HOBBY* IS CONDUCTING CHEMICAL EXPERIMENTS.
SHE'S YOUR *AVERAGE* AUTHORESS.
An authoress? How rude!
AND MY NAME IS EDWIN WHITE.

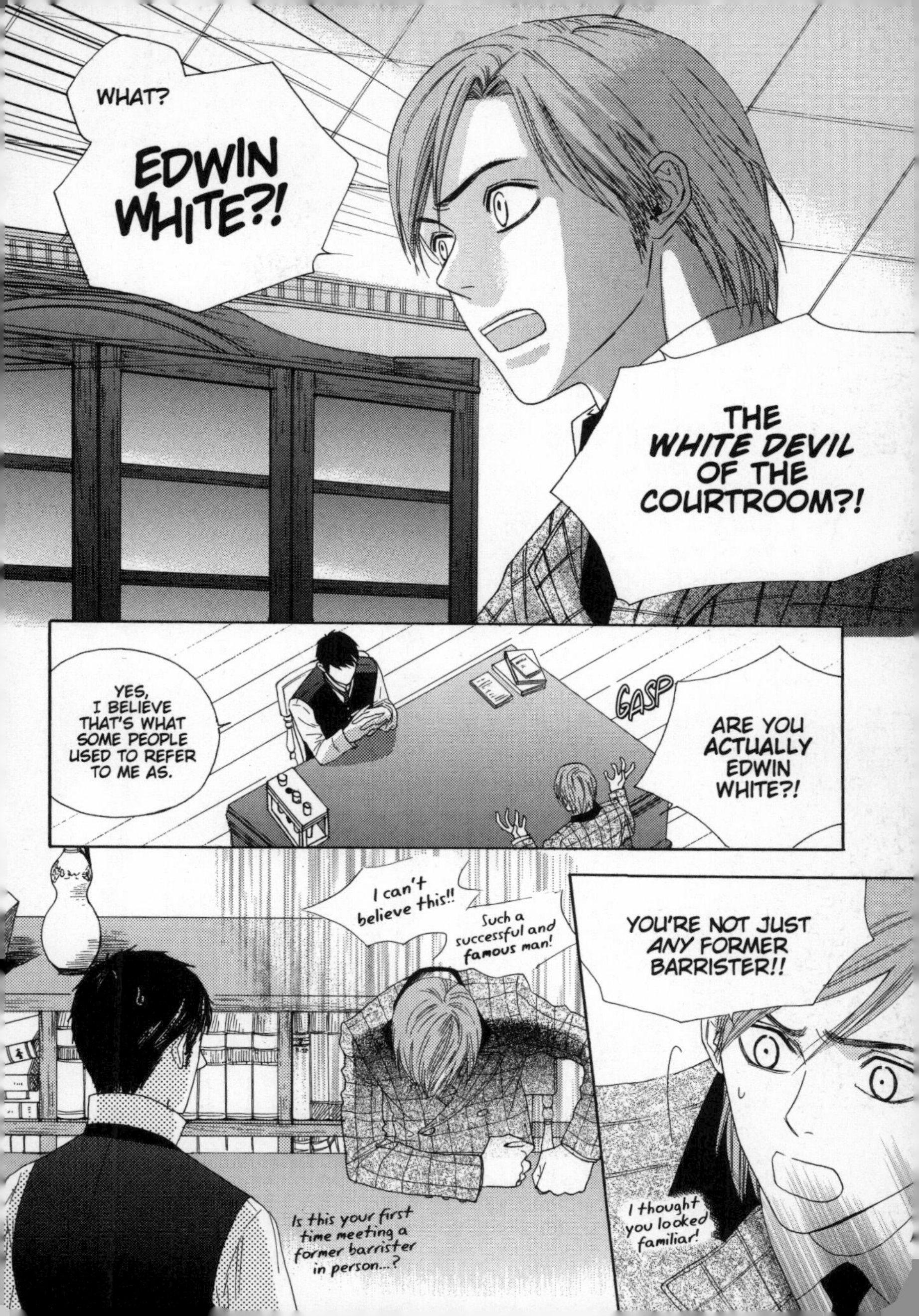
WHAT?
EDWIN WHITE?!
THE WHITE DEVIL OF THE COURTROOM?!
YES, I BELIEVE THAT'S WHAT SOME PEOPLE USED TO REFER TO ME AS.
GASP
ARE YOU ACTUALLY EDWIN WHITE?!
I can't believe this!!
Such a successful and famous man!
Is this your first time meeting a former barrister in person...?
YOU'RE NOT JUST ANY FORMER BARRISTER!!
I thought you looked familiar!

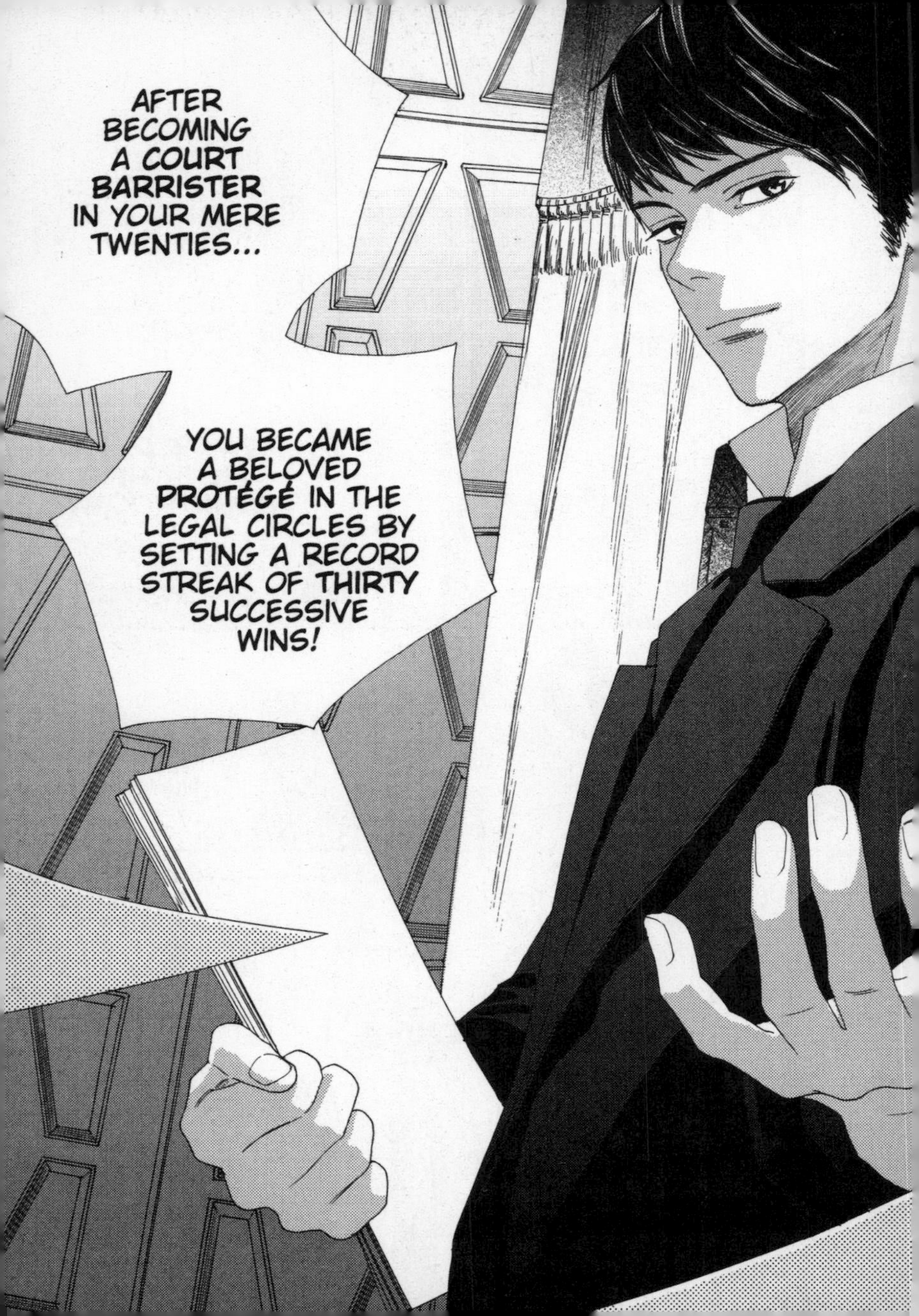
AFTER BECOMING A COURT BARRISTER IN YOUR MERE TWENTIES...
YOU BECAME A BELOVED PROTÉGÉ IN THE LEGAL CIRCLES BY SETTING A RECORD STREAK OF THIRTY SUCCESSIVE WINS!

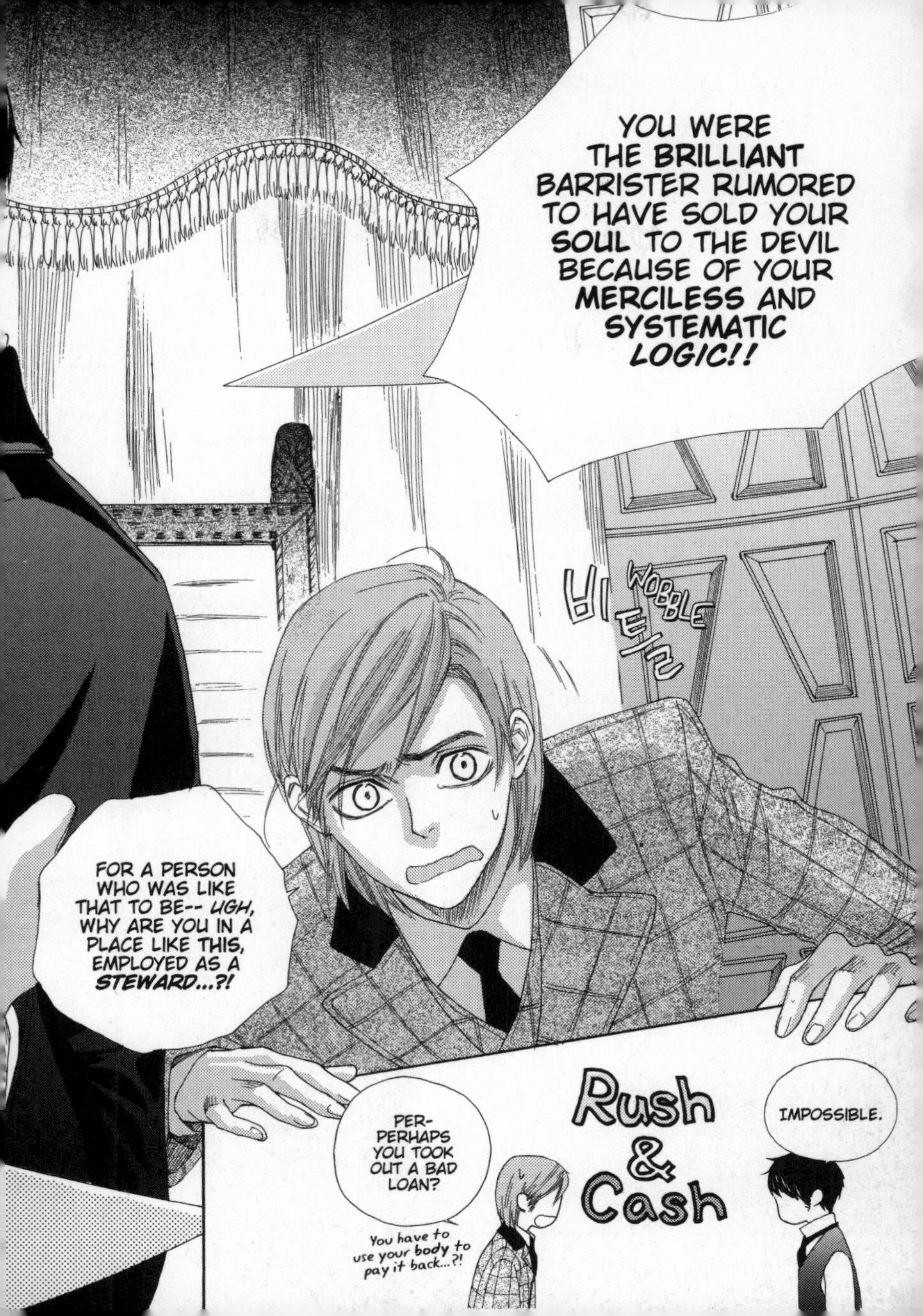
YOU WERE THE BRILLIANT BARRISTER RUMORED TO HAVE SOLD YOUR SOUL TO THE DEVIL BECAUSE OF YOUR MERCILESS AND SYSTEMATIC *LOGIC!!*
WOBBLE
FOR A PERSON WHO WAS LIKE THAT TO BE-- *UGH*, WHY ARE YOU IN A PLACE LIKE THIS, EMPLOYED AS A *STEWARD...?!*
Rush & Cash
PER- PERHAPS YOU TOOK OUT A BAD LOAN?
You have to use your body to pay it back...?!
IMPOSSIBLE.

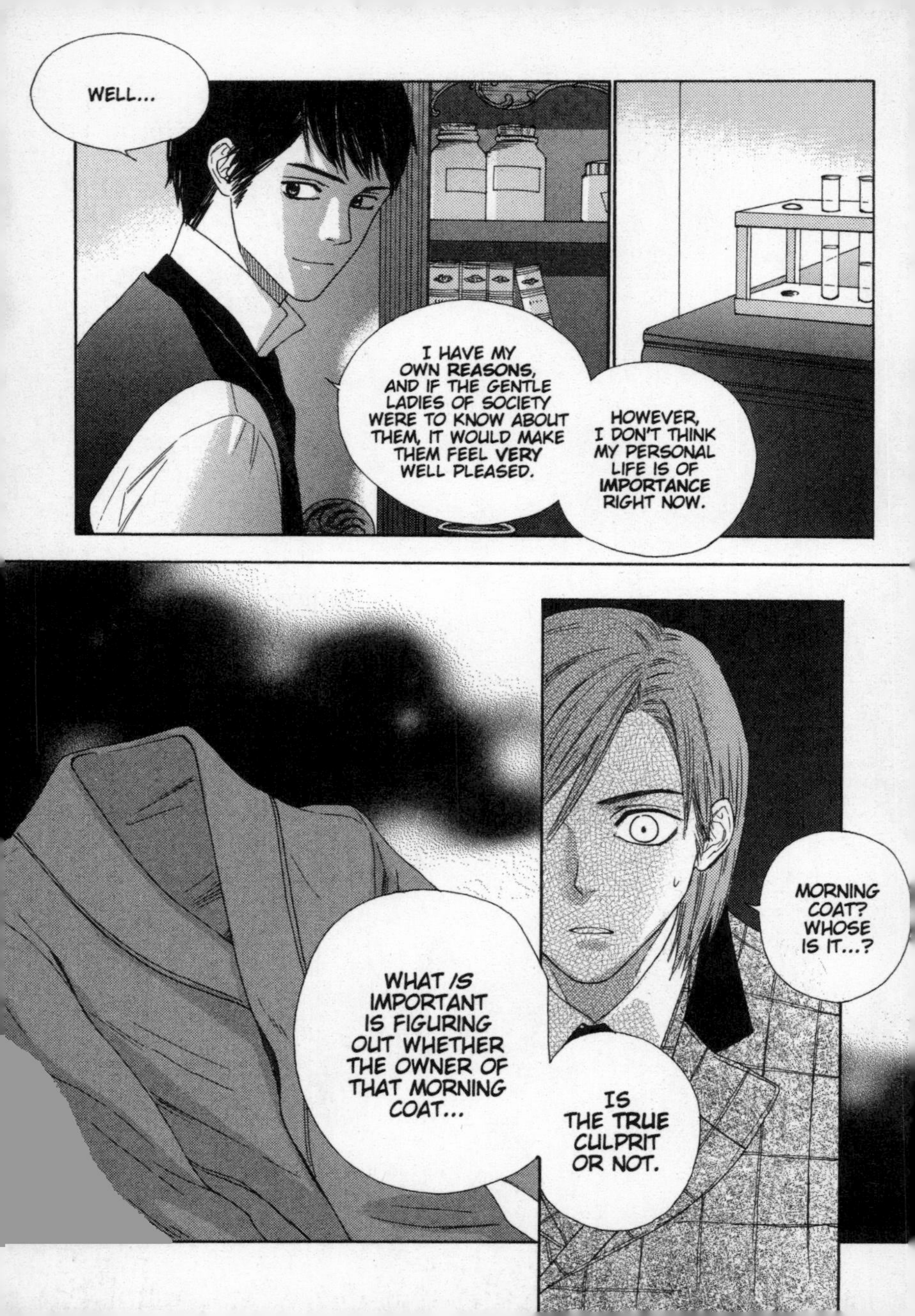
WELL...
I HAVE MY OWN REASONS, AND IF THE GENTLE LADIES OF SOCIETY WERE TO KNOW ABOUT THEM, IT WOULD MAKE THEM FEEL VERY WELL PLEASED.
HOWEVER, I DON'T THINK MY PERSONAL LIFE IS OF IMPORTANCE RIGHT NOW.
MORNING COAT? WHOSE IS IT...?
WHAT *IS* IMPORTANT IS FIGURING OUT WHETHER THE OWNER OF THAT MORNING COAT...
IS THE TRUE CULPRIT OR NOT.

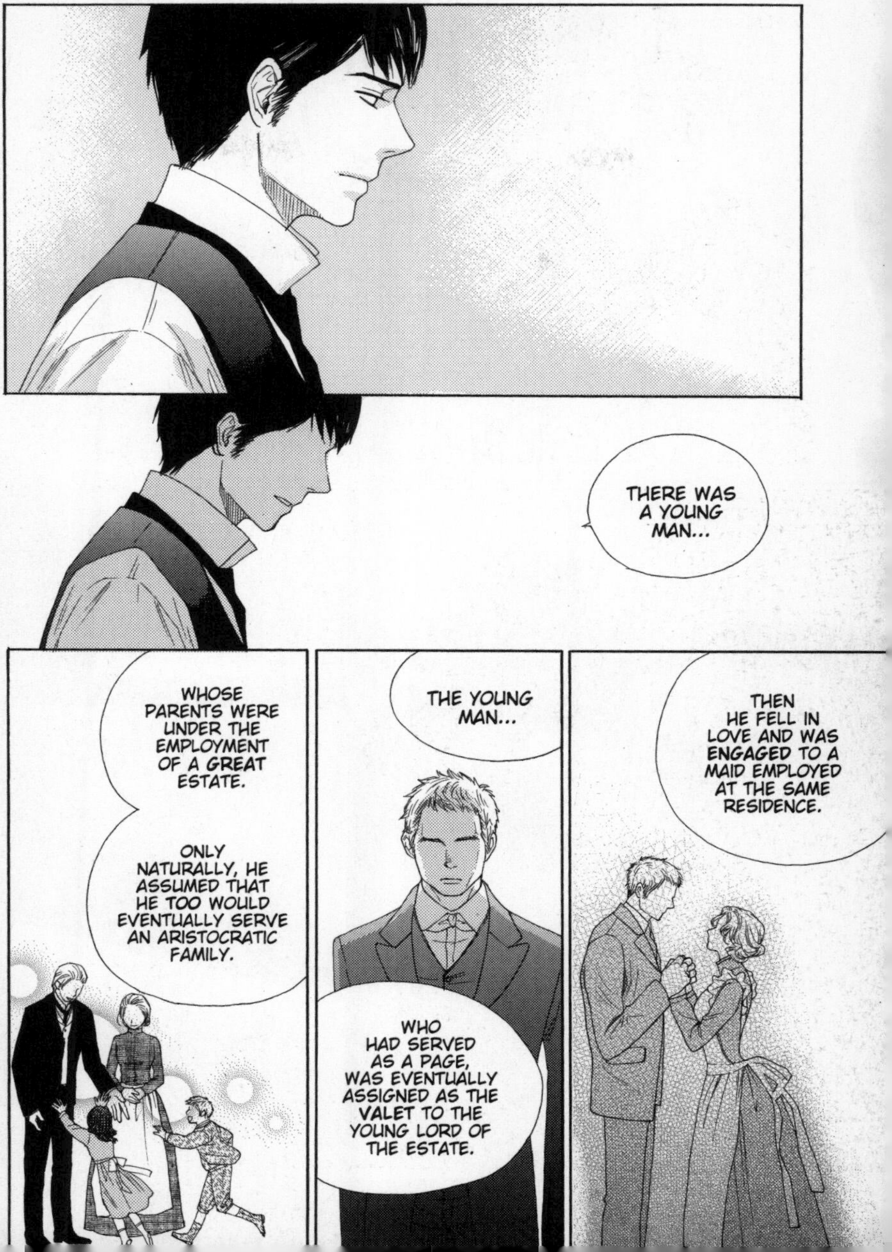
THERE WAS A YOUNG MAN...
WHOSE PARENTS WERE UNDER THE EMPLOYMENT OF A GREAT ESTATE.
ONLY NATURALLY, HE ASSUMED THAT HE TOO WOULD EVENTUALLY SERVE AN ARISTOCRATIC FAMILY.
THE YOUNG MAN...
WHO HAD SERVED AS A PAGE, WAS EVENTUALLY ASSIGNED AS THE VALET TO THE YOUNG LORD OF THE ESTATE.
THEN HE FELL IN LOVE AND WAS ENGAGED TO A MAID EMPLOYED AT THE SAME RESIDENCE.

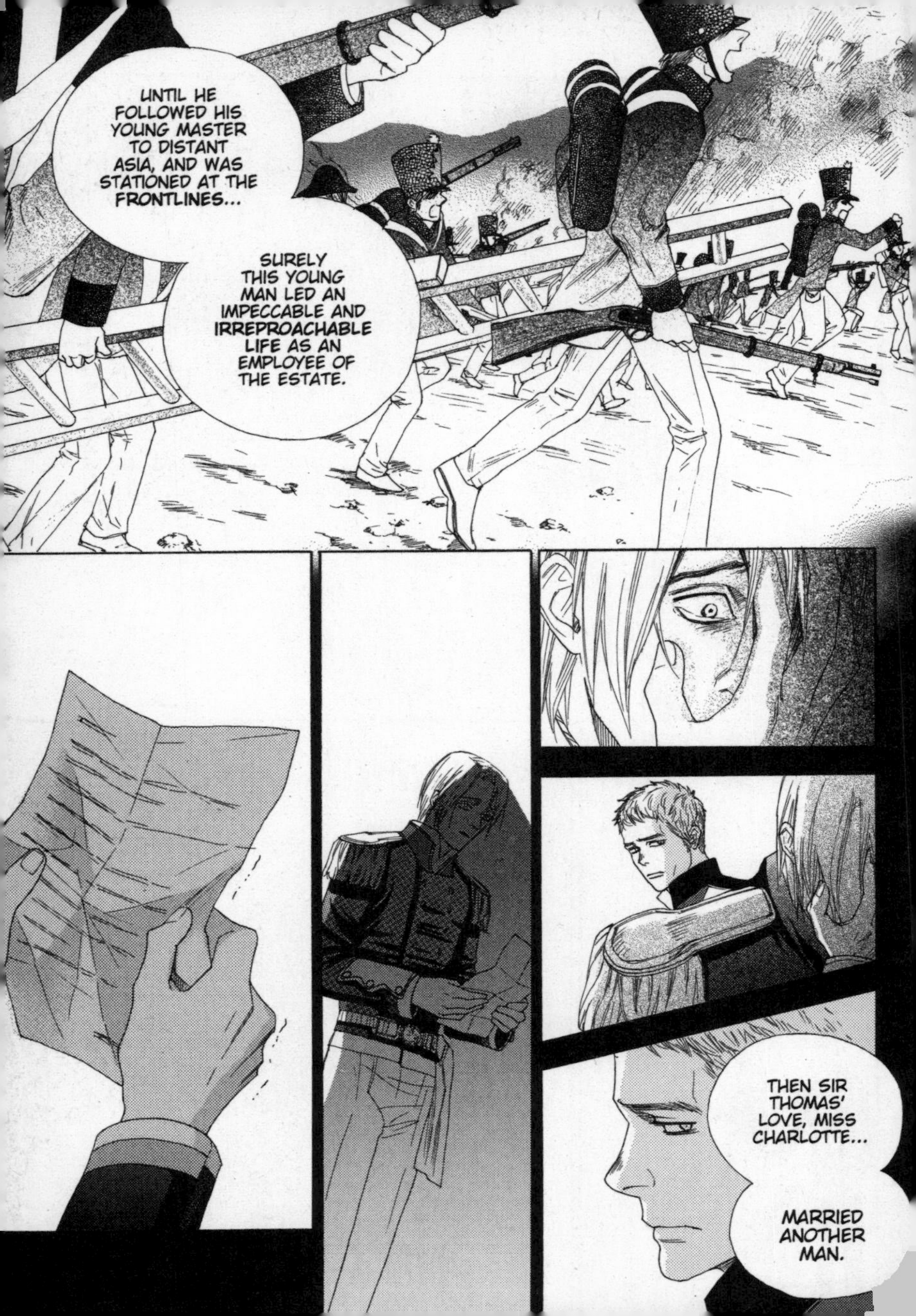
UNTIL HE FOLLOWED HIS YOUNG MASTER TO DISTANT ASIA, AND WAS STATIONED AT THE FRONTLINES...
SURELY THIS YOUNG MAN LED AN IMPECCABLE AND **IRREPROACHABLE** LIFE AS AN EMPLOYEE OF THE ESTATE.
THEN SIR THOMAS' LOVE, MISS CHARLOTTE...
MARRIED ANOTHER MAN.

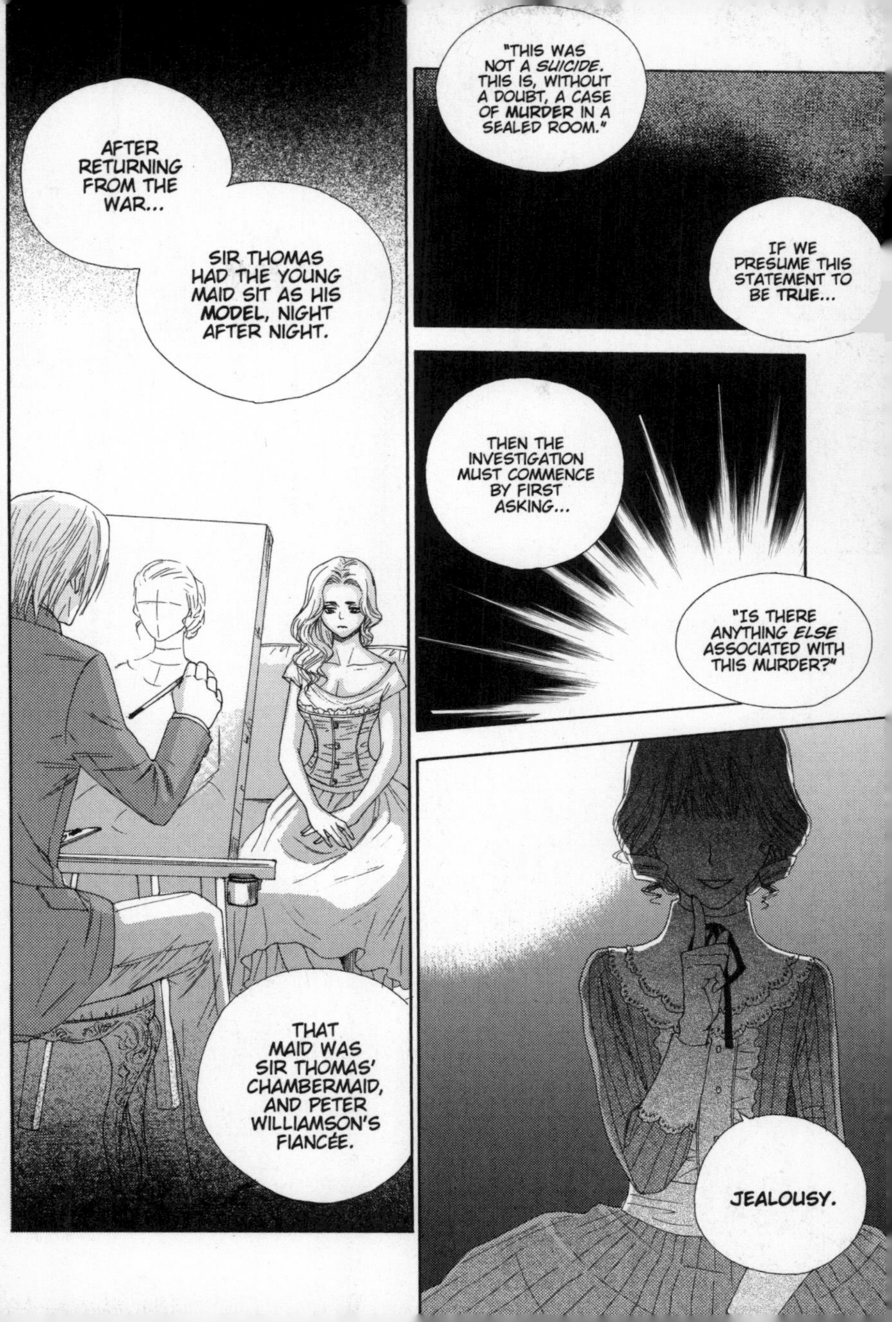
AFTER RETURNING FROM THE WAR...
SIR THOMAS HAD THE YOUNG MAID SIT AS HIS MODEL, NIGHT AFTER NIGHT.
THAT MAID WAS SIR THOMAS' CHAMBERMAID, AND PETER WILLIAMSON'S FIANCÉE.
"THIS WAS NOT A *SUICIDE*. THIS IS, WITHOUT A DOUBT, A CASE OF **MURDER** IN A SEALED ROOM."
IF WE PRESUME THIS STATEMENT TO BE TRUE...
THEN THE INVESTIGATION MUST COMMENCE BY FIRST ASKING...
"IS THERE ANYTHING *ELSE* ASSOCIATED WITH THIS MURDER?"
JEALOUSY.

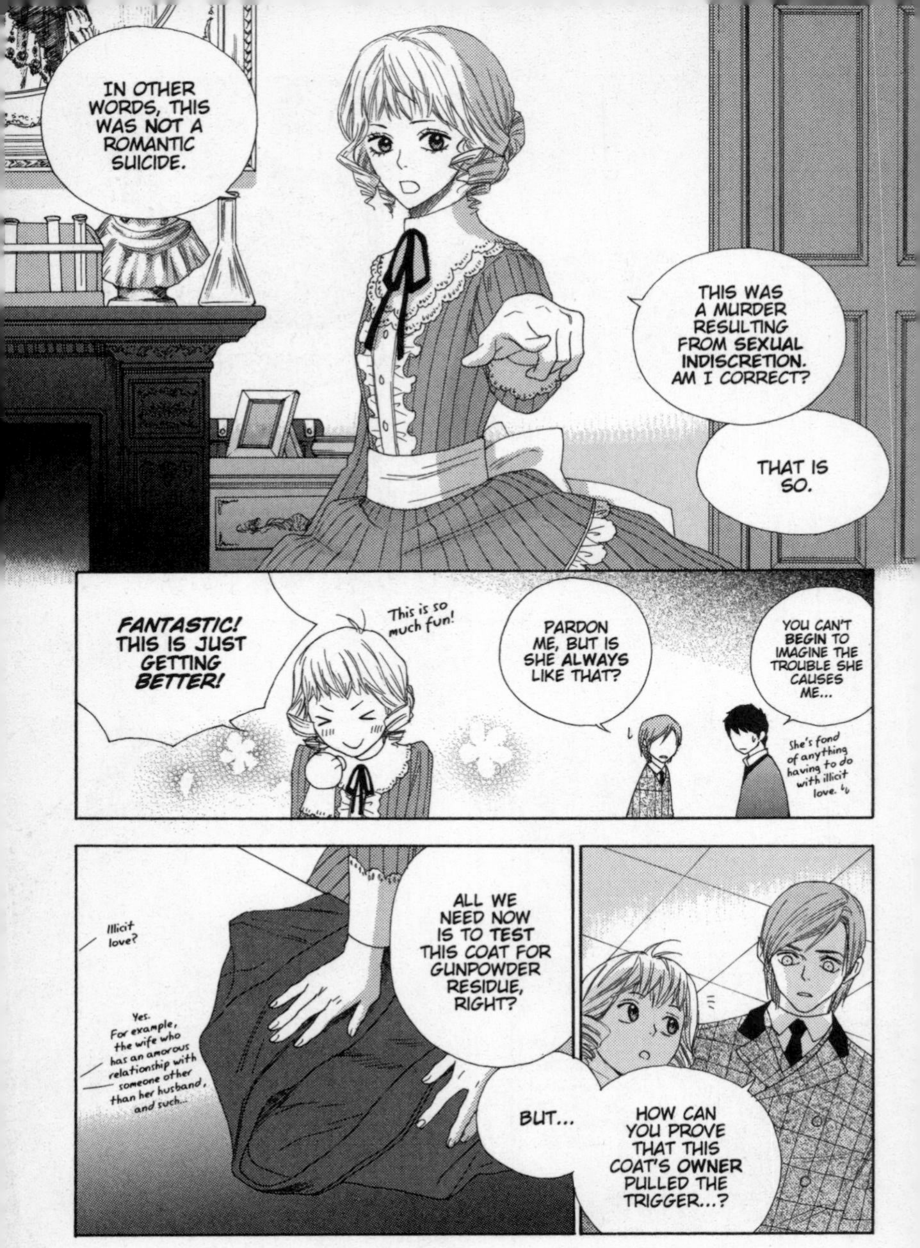
IN OTHER WORDS, THIS WAS NOT A ROMANTIC SUICIDE.
THIS WAS A MURDER RESULTING FROM SEXUAL INDISCRETION. AM I CORRECT?
THAT IS SO.
FANTASTIC! THIS IS JUST GETTING BETTER!
This is so much fun!
PARDON ME, BUT IS SHE ALWAYS LIKE THAT?
YOU CAN'T BEGIN TO IMAGINE THE TROUBLE SHE CAUSES ME...
She's fond of anything having to do with illicit love.
Illicit love?
Yes. For example, the wife who has an amorous relationship with someone other than her husband, and such...
ALL WE NEED NOW IS TO TEST THIS COAT FOR GUNPOWDER RESIDUE, RIGHT?
BUT...
HOW CAN YOU PROVE THAT THIS COAT'S OWNER PULLED THE TRIGGER...?

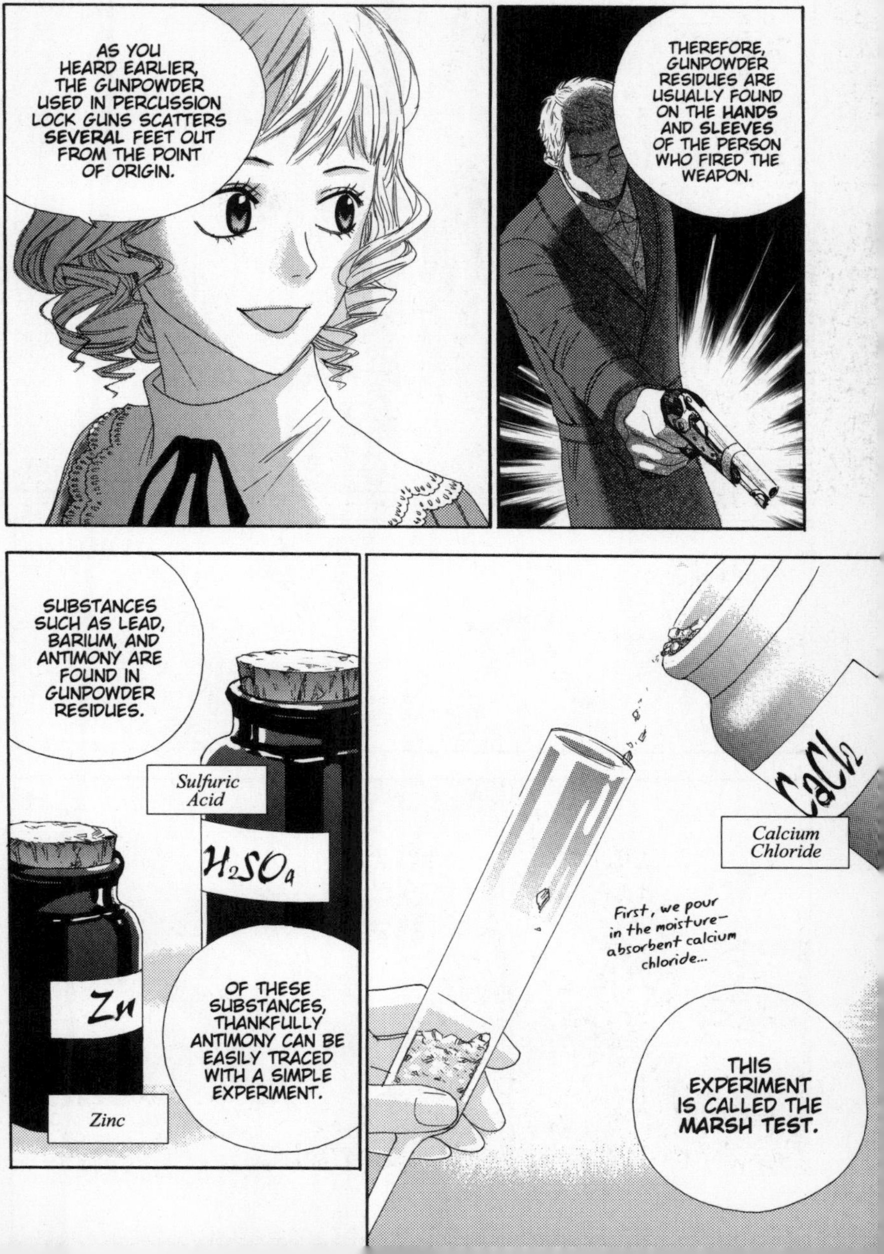
AS YOU HEARD EARLIER, THE GUNPOWDER USED IN PERCUSSION LOCK GUNS SCATTERS SEVERAL FEET OUT FROM THE POINT OF ORIGIN.
THEREFORE, GUNPOWDER RESIDUES ARE USUALLY FOUND ON THE HANDS AND SLEEVES OF THE PERSON WHO FIRED THE WEAPON.
SUBSTANCES SUCH AS LEAD, BARIUM, AND ANTIMONY ARE FOUND IN GUNPOWDER RESIDUES.
Sulfuric Acid
H2SO4
Zn
Zinc
OF THESE SUBSTANCES, THANKFULLY ANTIMONY CAN BE EASILY TRACED WITH A SIMPLE EXPERIMENT.
CaCl2
Calcium Chloride
First, we pour in the moisture-absorbent calcium chloride...
THIS EXPERIMENT IS CALLED THE MARSH TEST.

YOU BEGIN BY ADDING ZINC TO SULFURIC ACID. THIS BRINGS FORTH SULFURIC ACID ZINC HYDROXIDE.

THEN WE ADD A SOLUTION THAT HAS BEEN PRESOAKED IN A PORTION OF THE COAT'S SLEEVE. IF OUR ASSUMPTIONS ARE CORRECT, HYDROGEN ANTIMONY WILL BE THE REMAINING SUBSTANCE. WHEN WE DETECT ANTIMONY, OUR PROOF HAS BEEN FOUND!

IMPOSSIBLE! CAN THEY REALLY PROVE...

With the moisture-absorbent calcium chloride, we can extract the air.

WHO THE MURDERER IS BY THIS METHOD?

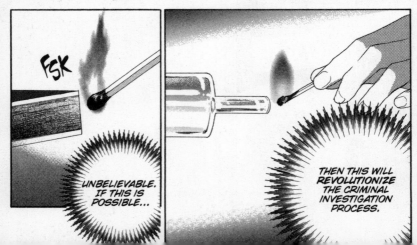

FSK

UNBELIEVABLE. IF THIS IS POSSIBLE...

THEN THIS WILL REVOLUTIONIZE THE CRIMINAL INVESTIGATION PROCESS.

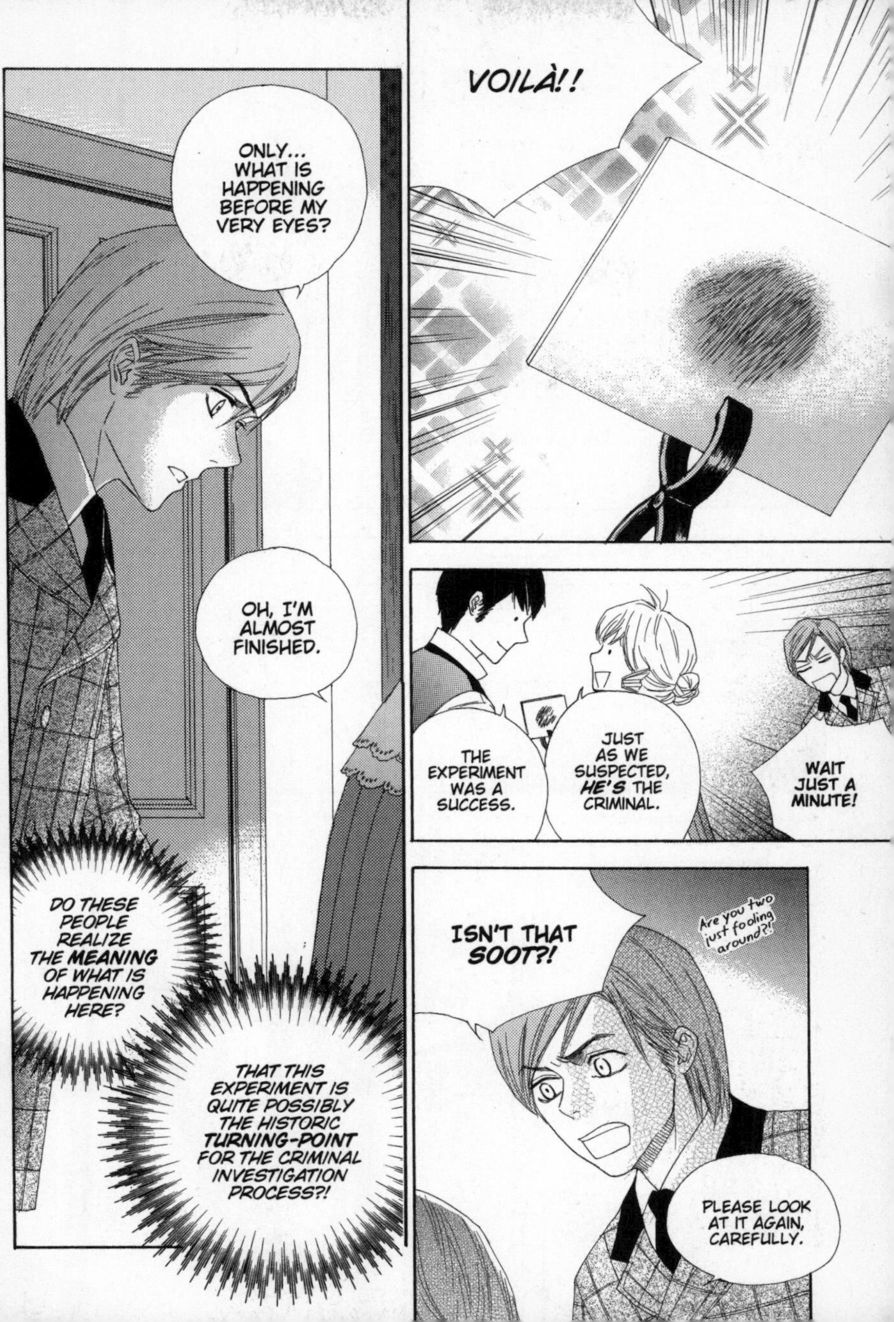
ONLY... WHAT IS HAPPENING BEFORE MY VERY EYES?
OH, I'M ALMOST FINISHED.
DO THESE PEOPLE REALIZE THE **MEANING** OF WHAT IS HAPPENING HERE?
THAT THIS EXPERIMENT IS QUITE POSSIBLY THE HISTORIC **TURNING-POINT** FOR THE CRIMINAL INVESTIGATION PROCESS?!
VOILÀ!!
THE EXPERIMENT WAS A SUCCESS.
JUST AS WE SUSPECTED, ***HE'S*** THE CRIMINAL.
WAIT JUST A MINUTE!
ISN'T THAT ***SOOT?!***
Are you two just fooling around?!
PLEASE LOOK AT IT AGAIN, CAREFULLY.

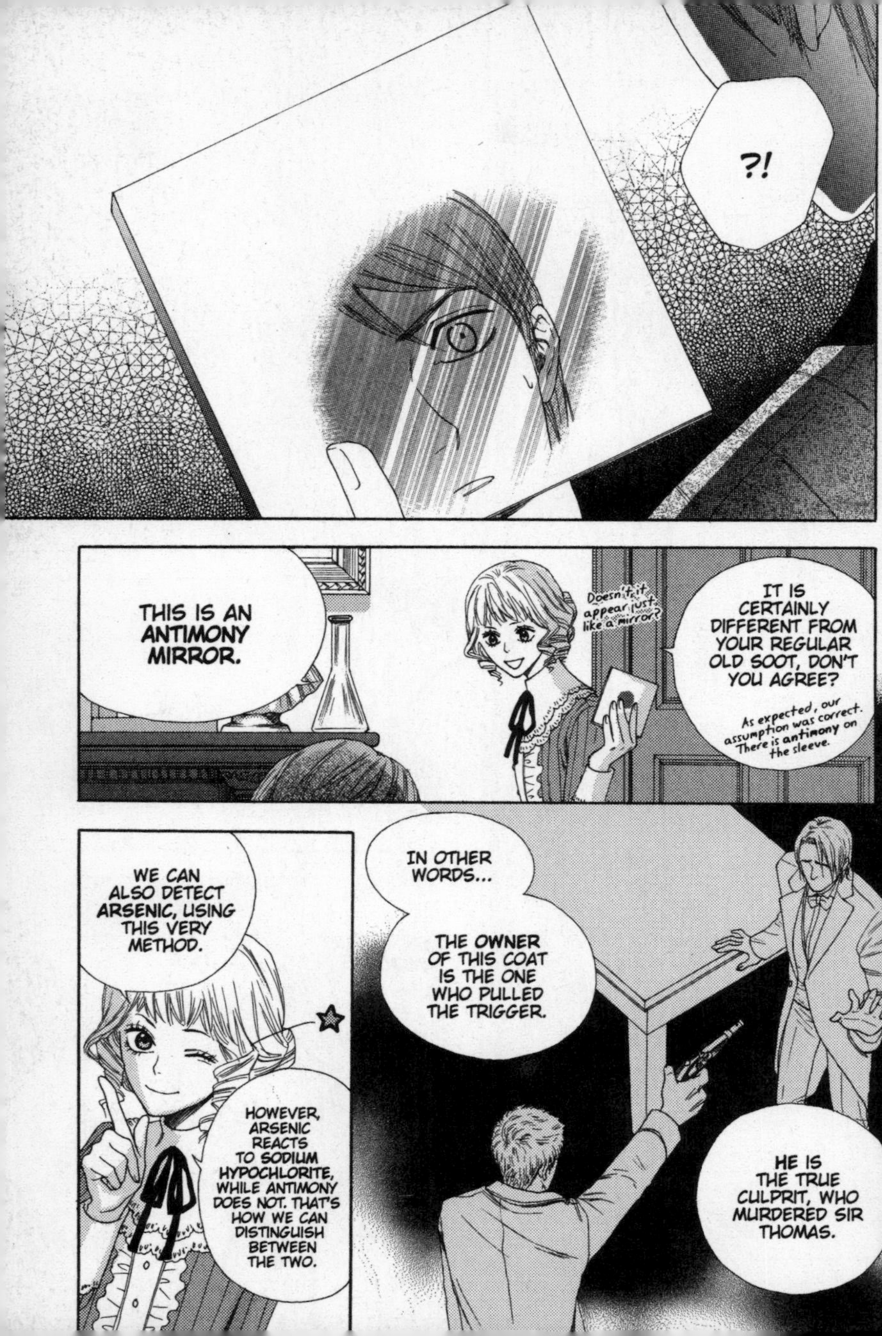
?!
THIS IS AN ANTIMONY MIRROR.
Doesn't it appear just like a mirror?
IT IS CERTAINLY DIFFERENT FROM YOUR REGULAR OLD SOOT, DON'T YOU AGREE?
As expected, our assumption was correct. There is antimony on the sleeve.
WE CAN ALSO DETECT ARSENIC, USING THIS VERY METHOD.
HOWEVER, ARSENIC REACTS TO SODIUM HYPOCHLORITE, WHILE ANTIMONY DOES NOT. THAT'S HOW WE CAN DISTINGUISH BETWEEN THE TWO.
IN OTHER WORDS...
THE OWNER OF THIS COAT IS THE ONE WHO PULLED THE TRIGGER.
HE IS THE TRUE CULPRIT, WHO MURDERED SIR THOMAS.

HIS LOVE, LUCY, IS CALLED INTO SIR THOMAS' ROOM, EVERY NIGHT.
HE'S SUSPICIOUS...
JEALOUS EVEN...
AND EVENTUALLY, HE PULLS THE TRIGGER.
HE PROBABLY DIDN'T EVEN CHECK TO SEE WHETHER SIR THOMAS HAD ACTUALLY *TOUCHED* LUCY.

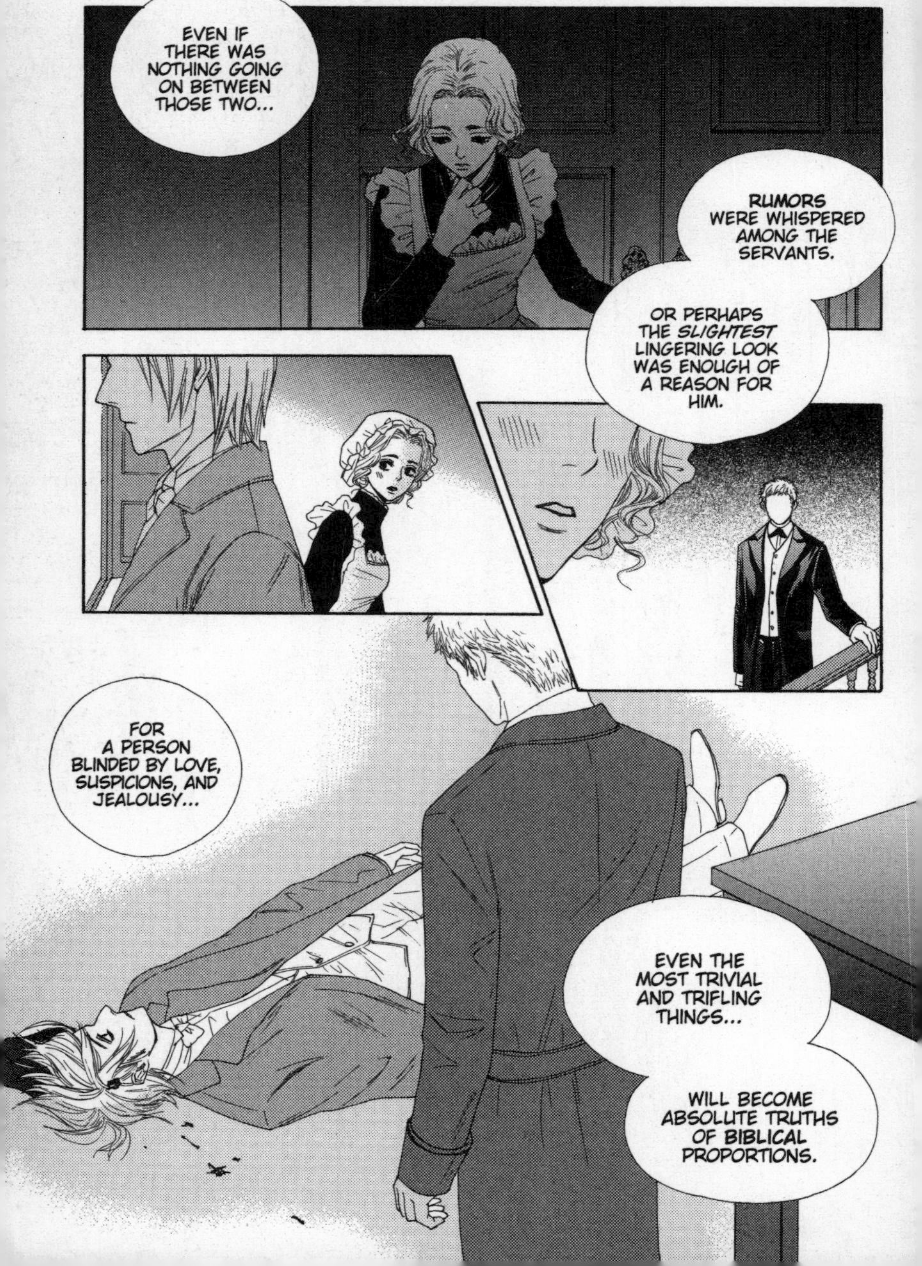
EVEN IF THERE WAS NOTHING GOING ON BETWEEN THOSE TWO...
RUMORS WERE WHISPERED AMONG THE SERVANTS.
OR PERHAPS THE *SLIGHTEST* LINGERING LOOK WAS ENOUGH OF A REASON FOR HIM.
FOR A PERSON BLINDED BY LOVE, SUSPICIONS, AND JEALOUSY...
EVEN THE MOST TRIVIAL AND TRIFLING THINGS...
WILL BECOME ABSOLUTE TRUTHS OF BIBLICAL PROPORTIONS.

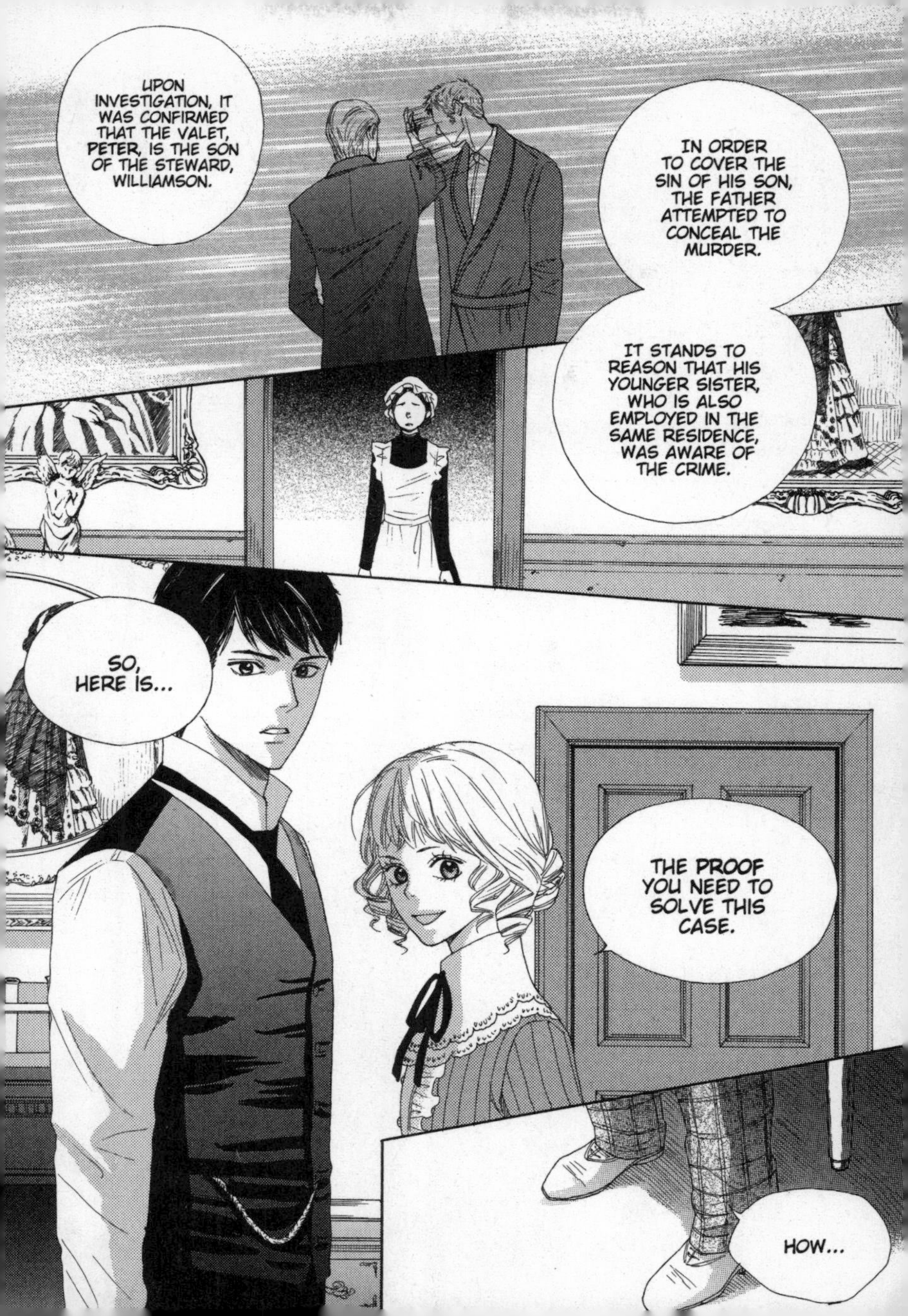
UPON INVESTIGATION, IT WAS CONFIRMED THAT THE VALET, PETER, IS THE SON OF THE STEWARD, WILLIAMSON.
IN ORDER TO COVER THE SIN OF HIS SON, THE FATHER ATTEMPTED TO CONCEAL THE MURDER.
IT STANDS TO REASON THAT HIS YOUNGER SISTER, WHO IS ALSO EMPLOYED IN THE SAME RESIDENCE, WAS AWARE OF THE CRIME.
SO, HERE IS...
THE PROOF YOU NEED TO SOLVE THIS CASE.
HOW...

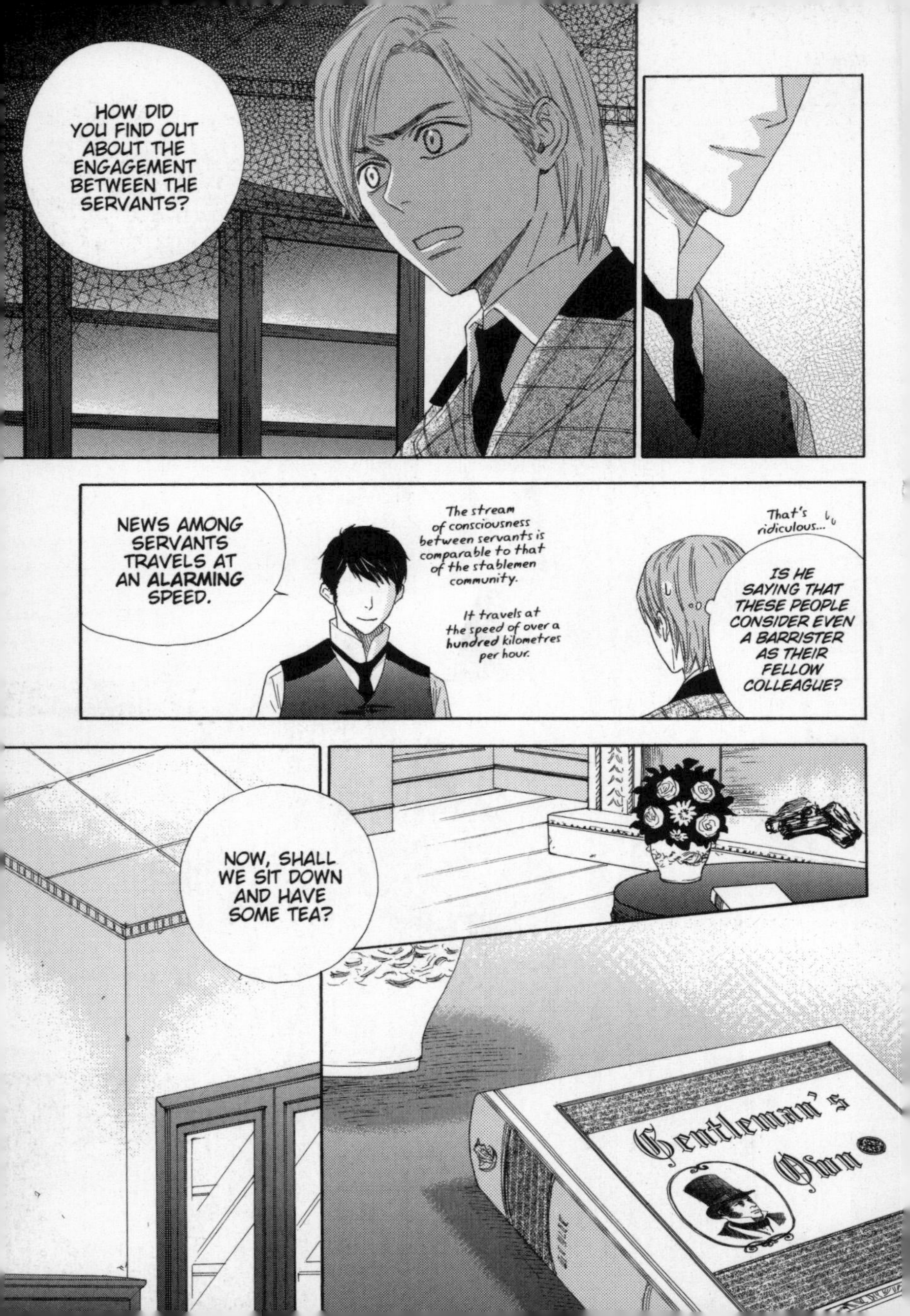
HOW DID YOU FIND OUT ABOUT THE ENGAGEMENT BETWEEN THE SERVANTS?
NEWS AMONG SERVANTS TRAVELS AT AN ALARMING SPEED.
The stream of consciousness between servants is comparable to that of the stablemen community.
It travels at the speed of over a hundred kilometres per hour.
That's ridiculous...
IS HE SAYING THAT THESE PEOPLE CONSIDER EVEN A BARRISTER AS THEIR FELLOW COLLEAGUE?
NOW, SHALL WE SIT DOWN AND HAVE SOME TEA?
Gentleman's Own

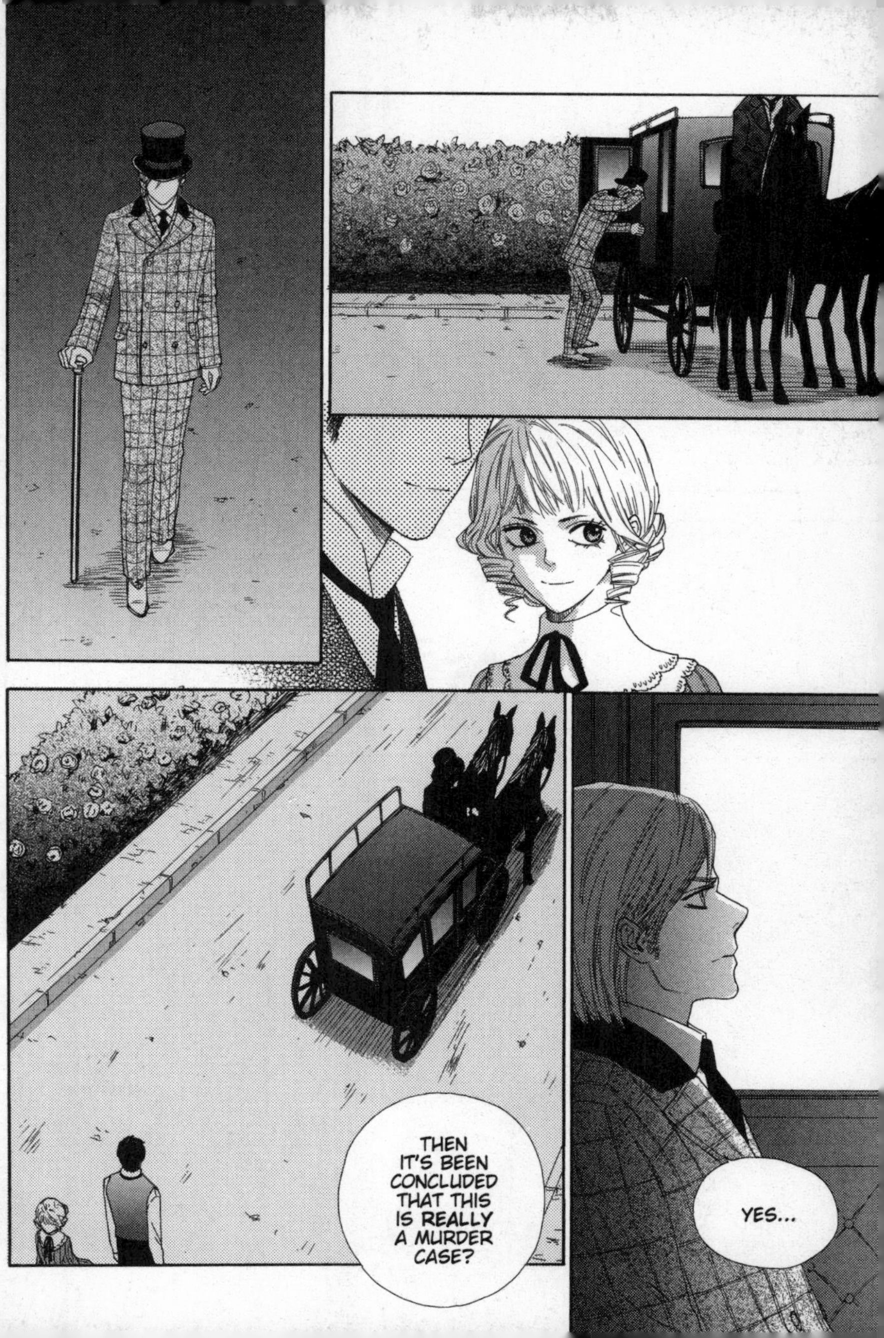
THEN IT'S BEEN CONCLUDED THAT THIS IS REALLY A MURDER CASE?
YES...

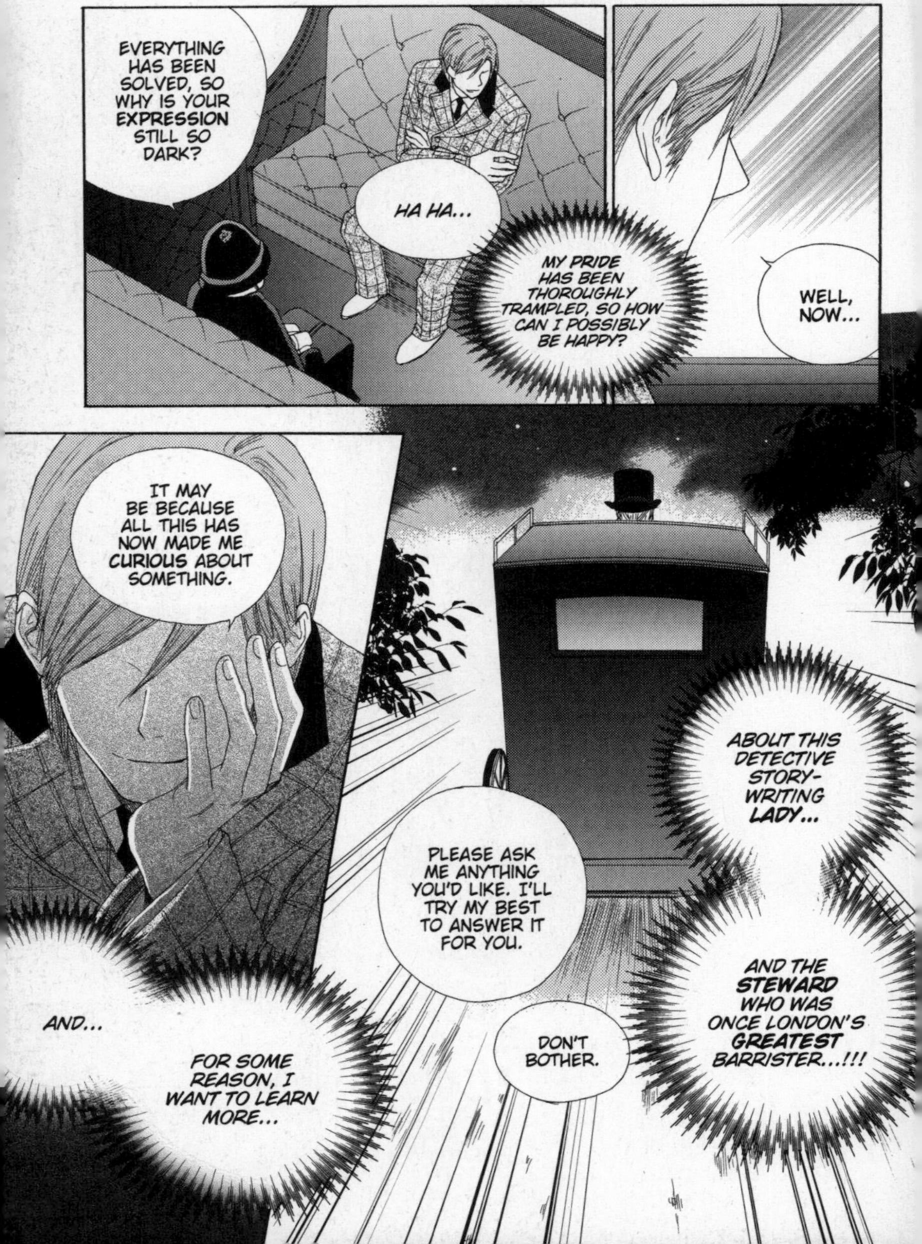
EVERYTHING HAS BEEN SOLVED, SO WHY IS YOUR EXPRESSION STILL SO DARK?
HA HA...
MY PRIDE HAS BEEN THOROUGHLY TRAMPLED, SO HOW CAN I POSSIBLY BE HAPPY?
WELL, NOW...
IT MAY BE BECAUSE ALL THIS HAS NOW MADE ME CURIOUS ABOUT SOMETHING.
AND...
FOR SOME REASON, I WANT TO LEARN MORE...
ABOUT THIS DETECTIVE STORY-WRITING LADY...
PLEASE ASK ME ANYTHING YOU'D LIKE. I'LL TRY MY BEST TO ANSWER IT FOR YOU.
AND THE STEWARD WHO WAS ONCE LONDON'S GREATEST BARRISTER...!!!
DON'T BOTHER.

To be continued...

HELLO. I AM OFFICER LESTRADE OF SCOTLAND YARD, LONDON'S METROPOLITAN POLICE SERVICE.

You can just call me Lele. Aha ha ha!

OUR SPLENDID AND MAGNIFICENT INSPECTOR, ONE OF LONDON'S GREATEST POLICE OFFICERS, SUCCESSFULLY SOLVES YET ANOTHER CASE.

Although it seemed as if he encountered something strange at the Newton Residence, it's not related to this case at all.

NOW, LET'S LEARN MORE ABOUT THE MARSH TEST THAT HELPED TO SUCCESSFULLY SOLVE THIS CASE.

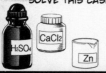

We can also check for arsenic by using the same test.

FIRST, WE POUR SULFURIC ACID ONTO ZINC.

FIZZLE~

Zn (zinc) + H2SO4 (sulfuric acid)
→ ZnSO4 (zinc sulfate)
+ H2 (hydrogen)

NEXT, WE TAKE THE SOLUTION THAT WE HAVE SOAKED THE CULPRIT'S JACKET IN, AND COMBINE IT WITH THE ZINC SULFATE.

BUBBLE~

Sb2O3 (antimony trioxide)
+ 6Zn (zinc) + 6H2SO4 (sulfuric acid)
6ZnSO4 + 6H2 + Sb2O3
6ZnSO4 (zinc sulfate)
+ 2SbH3 (covalent hydride of antimony, commonly called stibine)
+ 3H2O (water)

DISREGARDING THE ZINC SULFATE REMAINING IN THE FLASK, WE CREATE A PASSAGEWAY FOR THE GAS TO REACH A TUBE OF CALCIUM CHLORIDE (CaCl2). CALCIUM CHLORIDE ABSORBS MOISTURE (H2O), THEREFORE, IN THE CONNECTING TUBE, WE WILL HAVE ONLY STIBINE (SbH3) REMAINING.

CaCl2

Hee hee hee!

H2O

SbH3

SQUEEZE

HEAT THE STIBINE (SbH3) REMAINING IN THE TUBE. THE HEAT WILL SEPARATE OUT THE HYDROGEN, LEAVING US WITH ANTIMONY. WHEN A PORCELAIN PLATE IS PLACED BEFORE THE FUMES EMITTED WHEN THE TUBE IS HEATED, A MIRROR IS CREATED ON THE PLATE. IF THIS OCCURS, THEN WE CAN CORRECTLY SURMISE THAT WE HAVE DETECTED ANTIMONY ON THE JACKET, ONE OF THE SUBSTANCES FOUND IN PERCUSSION LOCK GUNPOWDER.

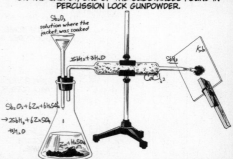

Sb2O3 solution where the jacket was soaked

2SbH3 + 3H2O

SbH3

Sb2O3 + 6Zn + 6H2SO4
→ 2SbH3 + 6ZnSO4
+ 3H2O

Zn + H2SO4

CONSIDER THIS AS MORE OF A LEARNING OPPORTUNITY IN COMIC FORM, AND LESS OF AN AUTHOR'S REVIEW

This is my third manhwa, but my first serialized work in a manhwa magazine. However, this is actually the sixth work in my career. There is no one who didn't like Holmes when they were younger; that is why I naturally came to the Victorian period. That being said, Holmes is still just a boy here because this story takes place seventeen years before Holmes and Watson would live together on Baker Street. I think this is a really fascinating period to be telling a whodunit story in, notwithstanding the fact that we can only use logic and don't have the help of CSI. Also, in terms of dresses... This is the period right before the popularity of crinolines faded and when bustles became the rage, although I'm not the one who's drawing it.

Please look forward to our brilliant Inspector in action again in the next volume!

So now, this **Victorian** science-loving **mystery** romance will begin...

Special thanks to all my current editors, my very first editor, teacher Lee Ki-ha, the readers, and to Ssay, whom I've neglected for several days. Although I will be faithful in adhering to the scientific advances and historical facts of the period, I may span across fifteen years when it comes to criminal investigation methodology and fashion.

Hey-jin:
*IF THE YEAR IS 1864, THEN SHERLOCK HOLMES
IS STILL ONLY A LITTLE BOY IN PRIMARY SCHOOL!!
"CALL ME BIG SISTER, SHERLOCK!" >_<*

Ki-ha:
HEH HEH HEH... TEACHER HEY-JIN, YOU
SHOULDN'T TEASE AN ELEMENTARY SCHOOLBOY
LIKE THAT. *"SHERLOCK, RUN AWAY!"*

Hey-jin:
OH MY GOODNESS! BUT TO HAVE A DETECTIVE
STORY SET IN THE 19TH CENTURY, IT'S FANTASTIC!

Ki-ha:
IT IS, ISN'T IT?! WE CAN HAVE THREE-PIECE
SUITS! SUSPENDERS! BOWTIES!

Hey-jin:
AND ARSENIC! CANES WITH
HIDDEN BLADES! CORPSES!

Ki-ha:
BUT DO YOU THINK IT'S OKAY TO START OFF
OUR FIRST VOLUME LIKE THAT? I CAN SEE
THE EDITOR CRYING UP A STORM ALREADY.

Hey-jin:
SHALL WE START OFF WITH SOMETHING
TAMER? DO YOU HAVE A *GOOD* IDEA IN MIND?

Ki-ha:
WELL, SOMETHING TAMER WOULD
BE, *"PLEASE BUY TWO COPIES."*

Hey-jin:
HEH HEH HEH. LET'S CAPTURE
THIS EXCHANGE AND INCLUDE
IT IN OUR FIRST VOLUME.

Ki-ha:
HEH HEH... WHAT? NOW,
WAIT A MINUTE! *HA HA HA!*

Hey-jin Jeon
http://hamadris.com

Ki-ha Lee
http://skiha.ivy.ro

Counterattack from Tools of the Trade

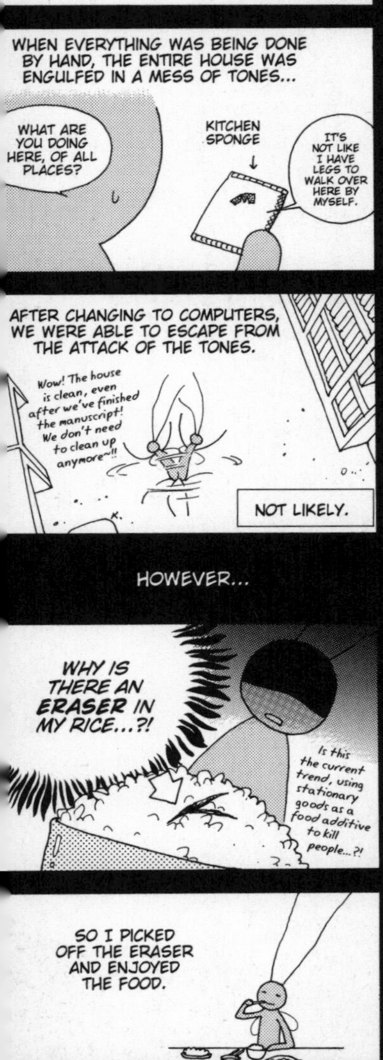

WHEN EVERYTHING WAS BEING DONE BY HAND, THE ENTIRE HOUSE WAS ENGULFED IN A MESS OF TONES...
WHAT ARE YOU DOING HERE, OF ALL PLACES?
KITCHEN SPONGE
IT'S NOT LIKE I HAVE LEGS TO WALK OVER HERE BY MYSELF.
AFTER CHANGING TO COMPUTERS, WE WERE ABLE TO ESCAPE FROM THE ATTACK OF THE TONES.
Wow! The house is clean, even after we've finished the manuscript! We don't need to clean up anymore~!!
NOT LIKELY.
HOWEVER...
WHY IS THERE AN ERASER IN MY RICE...?!
Is this the current trend, using stationary goods as a food additive to kill people...?!
SO I PICKED OFF THE ERASER AND ENJOYED THE FOOD.

Not Likely

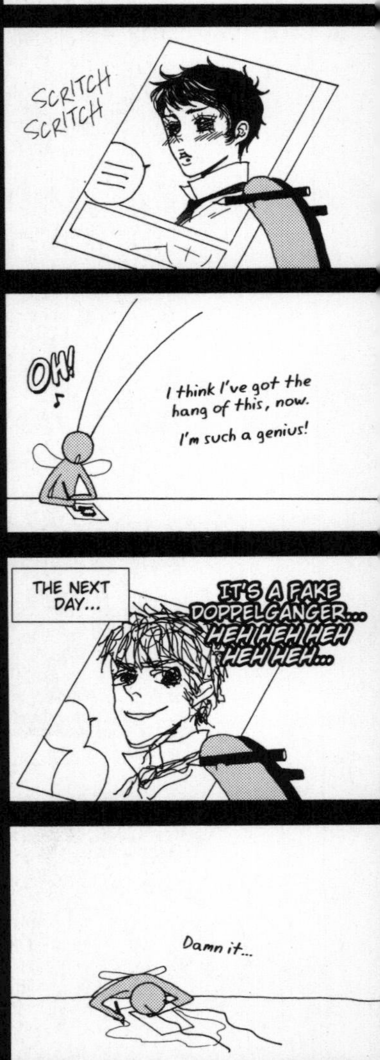

SCRITCH SCRITCH
OH!
I think I've got the hang of this, now.
I'm such a genius!
THE NEXT DAY...
IT'S A FAKE DOPPELGANGER... HEH HEH HEH HEH HEH...
Damn it...

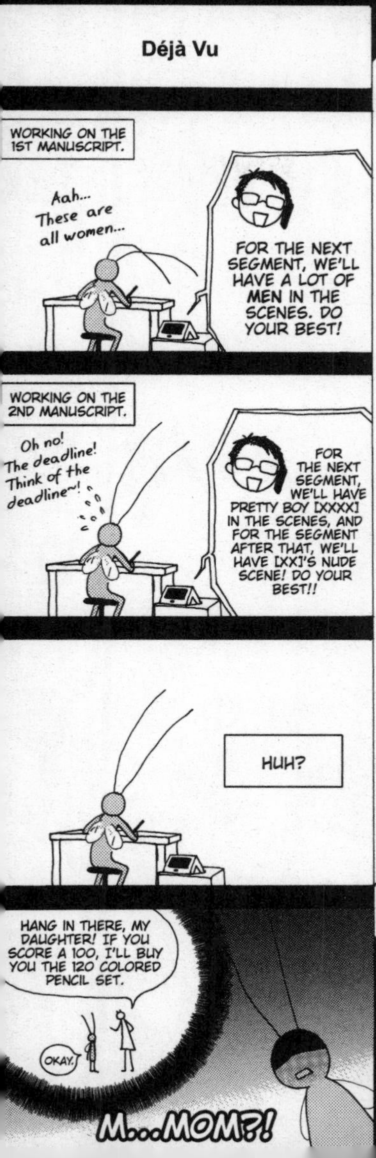
Déjà Vu
WORKING ON THE 1ST MANUSCRIPT.
Aah... These are all women...
FOR THE NEXT SEGMENT, WE'LL HAVE A LOT OF MEN IN THE SCENES. DO YOUR BEST!
WORKING ON THE 2ND MANUSCRIPT.
Oh no! The deadline! Think of the deadline~!
FOR THE NEXT SEGMENT, WE'LL HAVE PRETTY BOY [XXXXX] IN THE SCENES, AND FOR THE SEGMENT AFTER THAT, WE'LL HAVE [XX]'S NUDE SCENE! DO YOUR BEST!!
HUH?
HANG IN THERE, MY DAUGHTER! IF YOU SCORE A 100, I'LL BUY YOU THE 120 COLORED PENCIL SET.
OKAY.
M...MOM?!

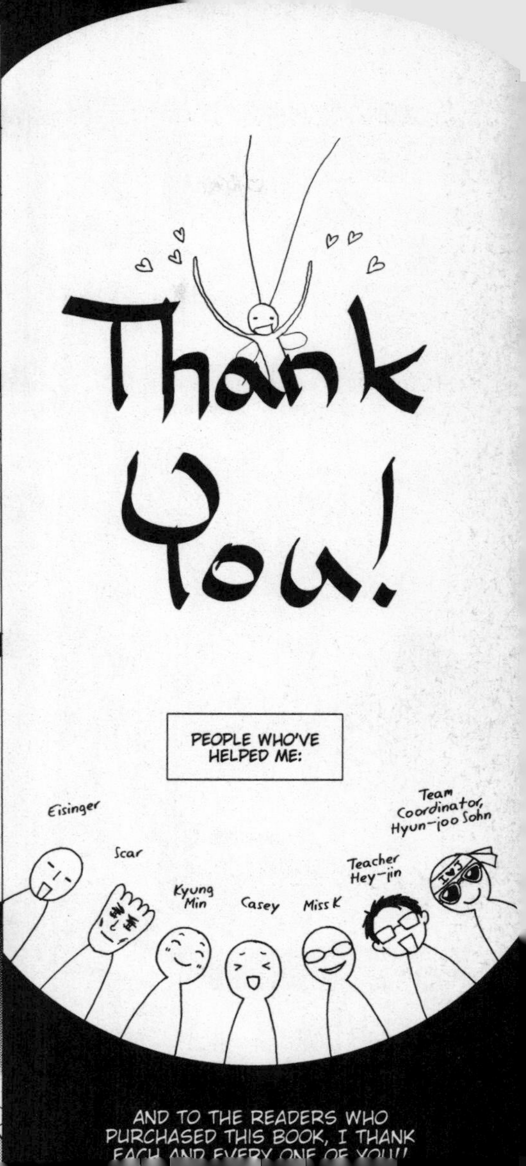
Thank You!
PEOPLE WHO'VE HELPED ME:
Eisinger
Scar
Kyung Min
Casey
Miss K
Teacher Hey-jin
Team Coordinator, Hyun-joo Sohn
AND TO THE READERS WHO PURCHASED THIS BOOK, I THANK EACH AND EVERY ONE OF YOU!!

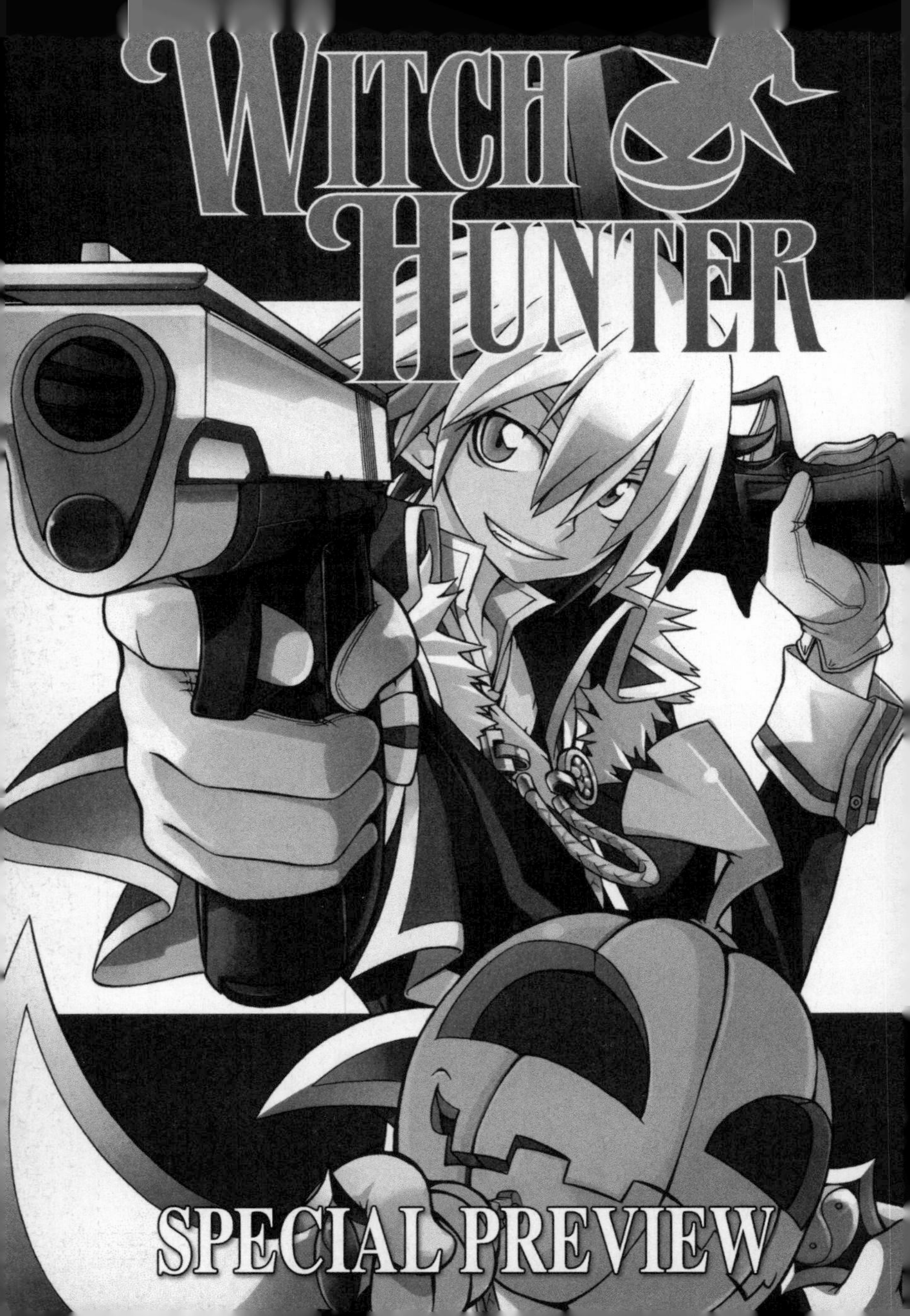
WITCH HUNTER
SPECIAL PREVIEW

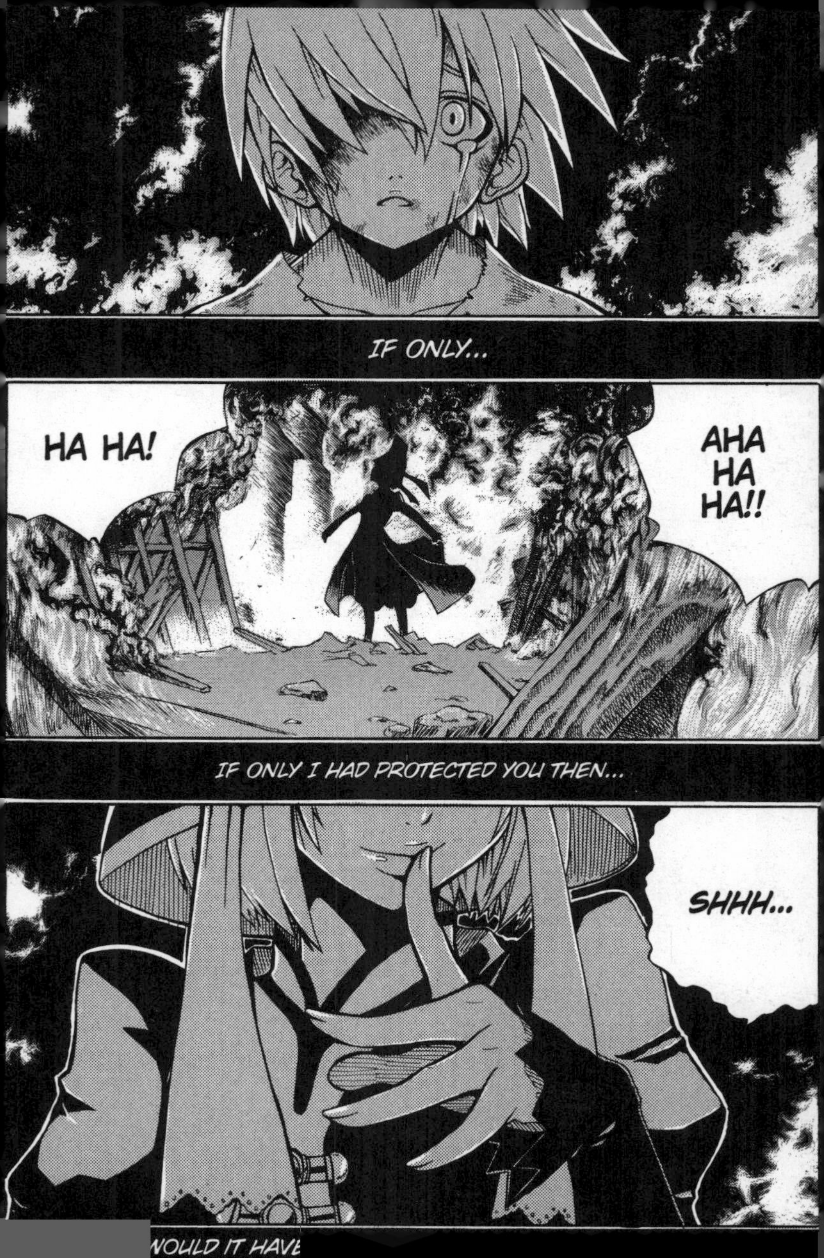
IF ONLY...
HA HA!
AHA HA HA!!
IF ONLY I HAD PROTECTED YOU THEN...
SHHH...
WOULD IT HAVE

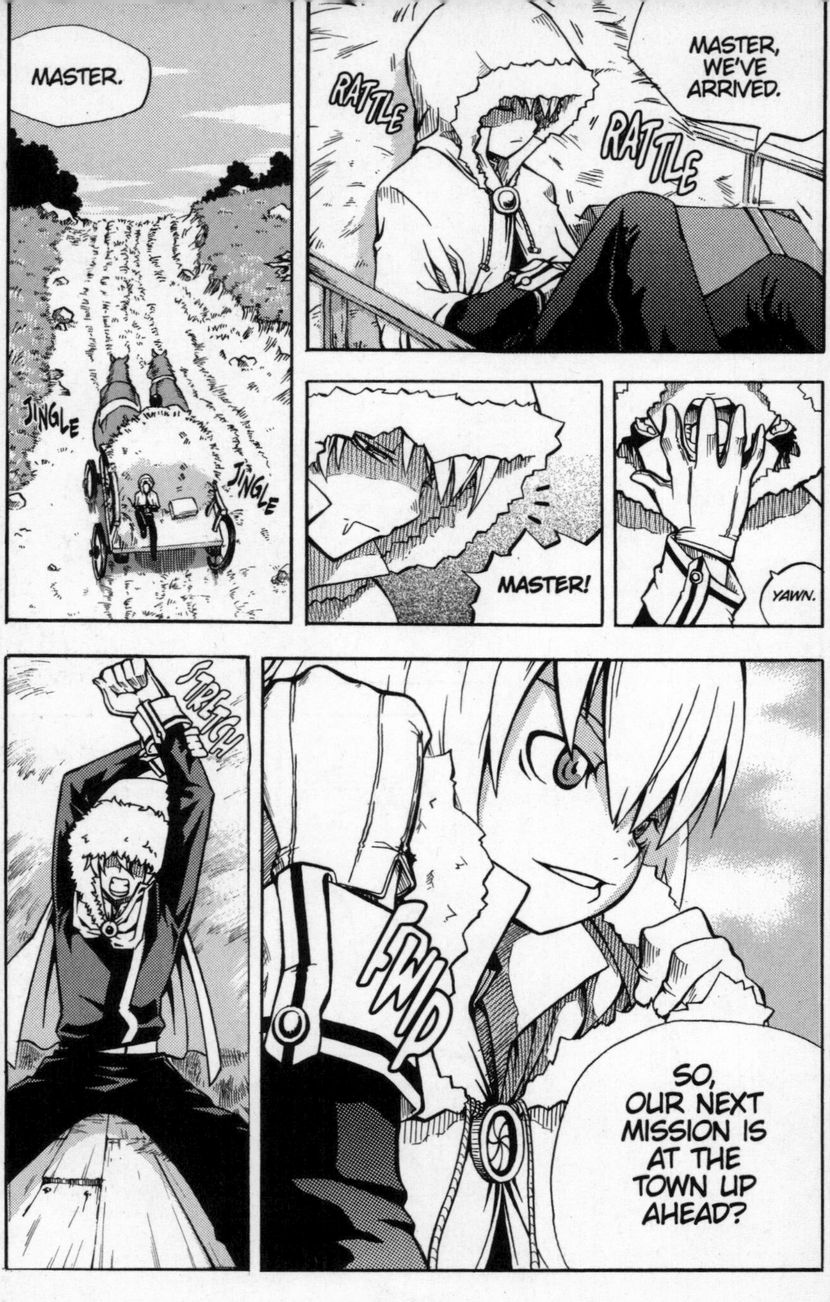
MASTER.
JINGLE
JINGLE
RATTLE
MASTER, WE'VE ARRIVED.
RATTLE
MASTER!
YAWN.
STRETCH
FWIP
SO, OUR NEXT MISSION IS AT THE TOWN UP AHEAD?

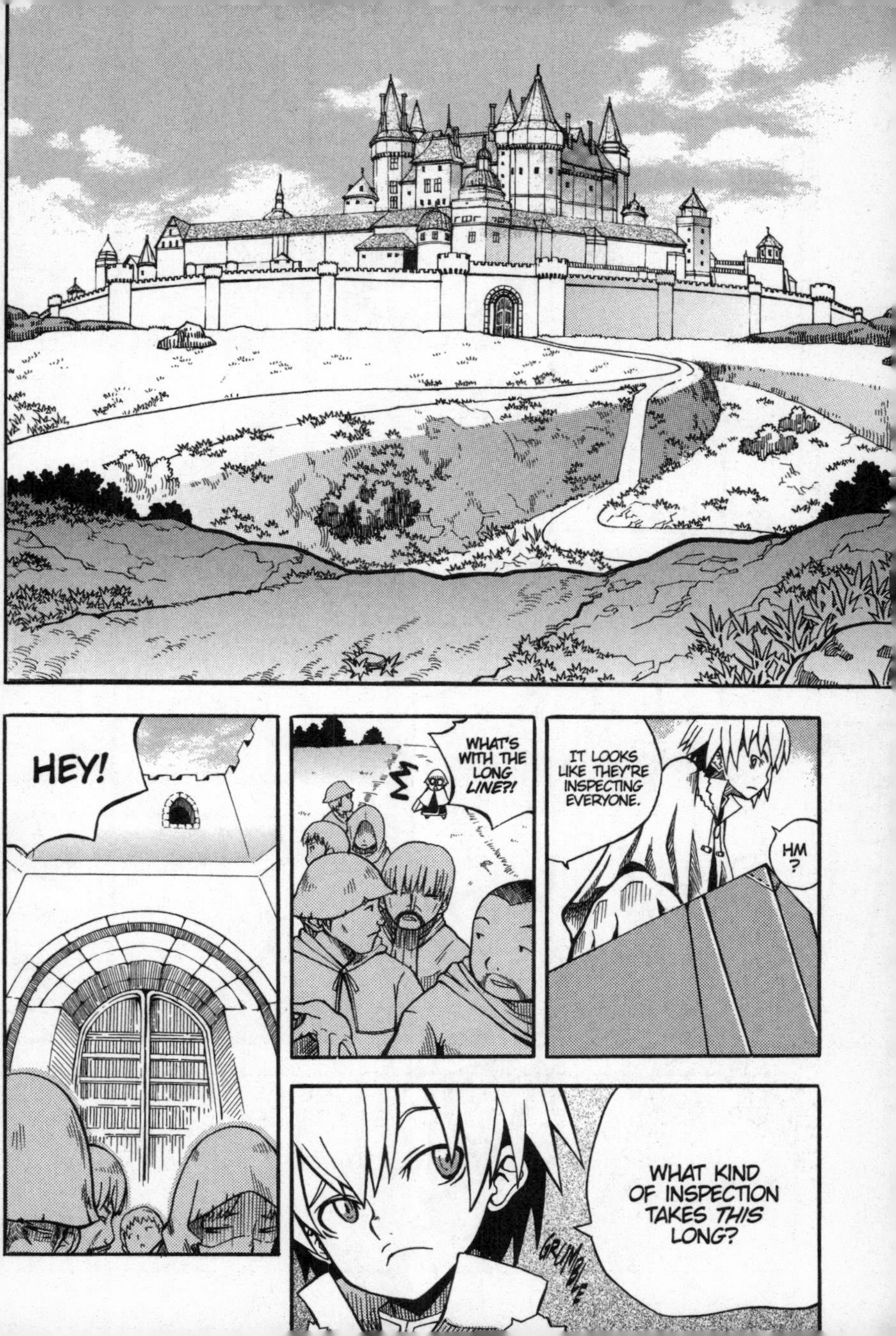
HEY!
WHAT'S WITH THE LONG LINE?!
IT LOOKS LIKE THEY'RE INSPECTING EVERYONE.
HM?
WHAT KIND OF INSPECTION TAKES THIS LONG?
GRUMBLE

PLEASE OPEN YOUR BAGS AND EMPTY OUT ALL YOUR BELONGINGS.

YOU WON'T NEED TO INSPECT ME.

HUH?

I'M A TRAVELING ARTIST. FOR A *TRUE* ARTIST, POSSESSIONS ARE MEANING-LESS.

AS ONE IN PURSUIT OF ARTISTIC PERFECTION, I FIND EARTHLY POSSESSIONS SERVE ONLY AS OBSTACLES IN MY JOURNEY.

IN OTHER WORDS, I OWN *ABSOLUTELY* NOTHING...

Ahh, the world is just so beautiful!

TWITCH

WE HAVE NO USE FOR STARVING ARTISTS! BE GONE!

POINT

BUT, SIR, WAIT! I HAVE A SECRET WAY OF MAKING *LOADS OF MONEY!* (EVEN I HAVE TO EAT!)

REALLY...? HOW?

PREPARE TO BE AMAZED...

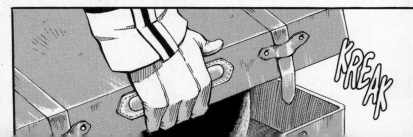

KREAK

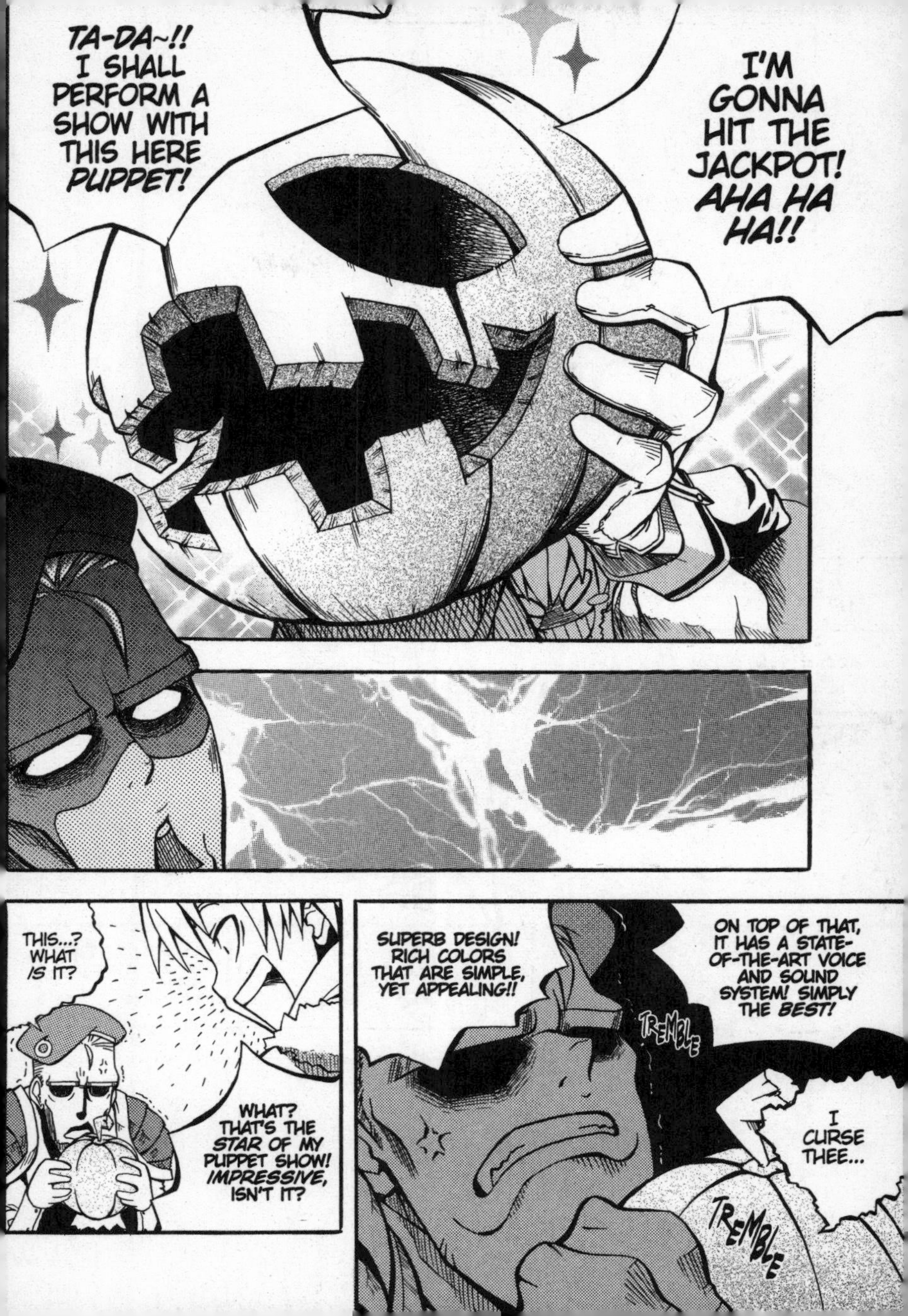
TA-DA~!! I SHALL PERFORM A SHOW WITH THIS HERE PUPPET!
I'M GONNA HIT THE JACKPOT! AHA HA HA!!
THIS...? WHAT IS IT?
WHAT? THAT'S THE STAR OF MY PUPPET SHOW! IMPRESSIVE, ISN'T IT?
SUPERB DESIGN! RICH COLORS THAT ARE SIMPLE, YET APPEALING!!
ON TOP OF THAT, IT HAS A STATE-OF-THE-ART VOICE AND SOUND SYSTEM! SIMPLY THE BEST!
TREMBLE
I CURSE THEE...
TREMBLE

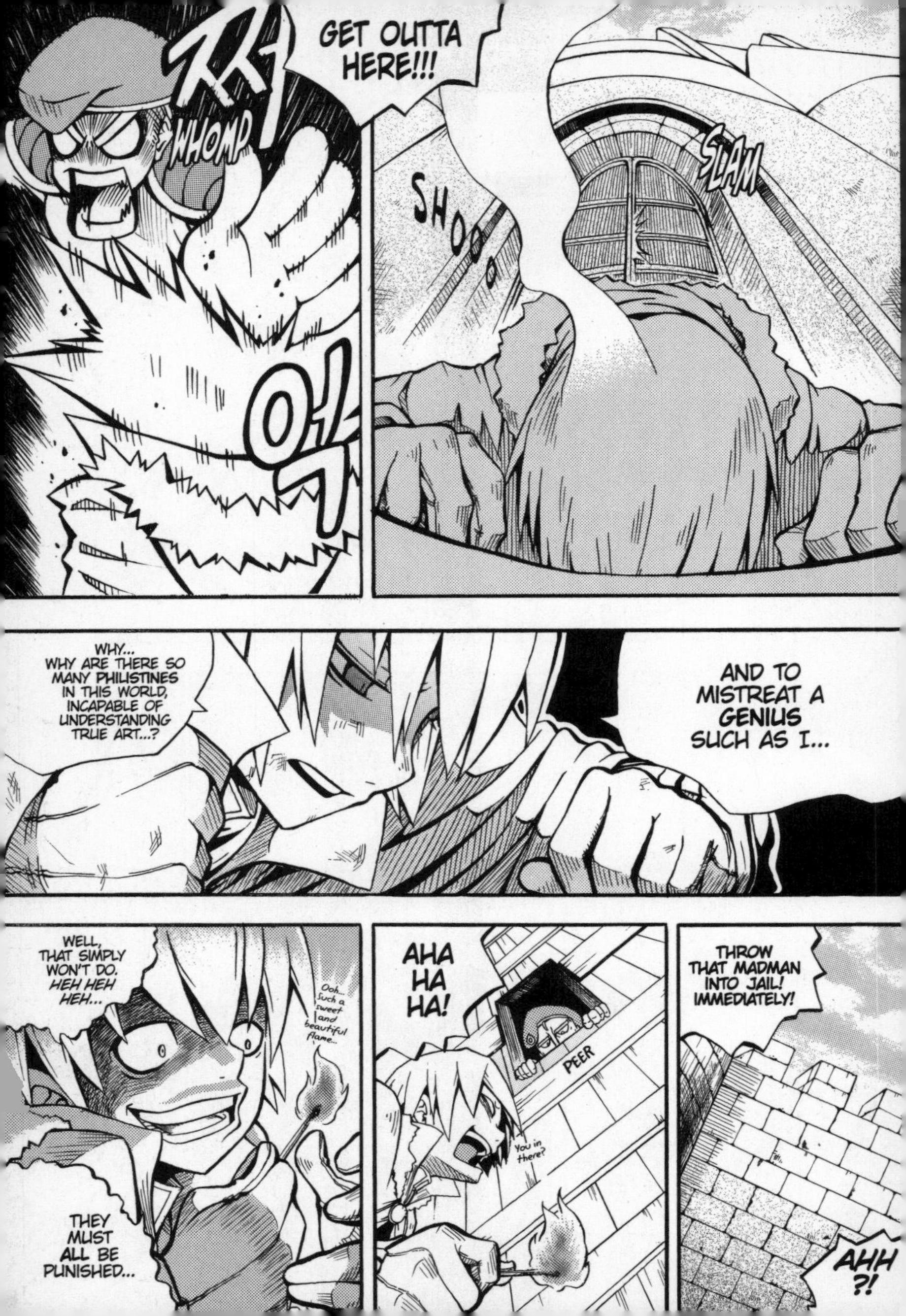
WHOMP
GET OUTTA HERE!!!
SHOOO
SLAM
WHY... WHY ARE THERE SO MANY PHILISTINES IN THIS WORLD, INCAPABLE OF UNDERSTANDING TRUE ART...?
AND TO MISTREAT A GENIUS SUCH AS I...
WELL, THAT SIMPLY WON'T DO. HEH HEH HEH...
Ooh... Such a sweet and beautiful flame...
THEY MUST ALL BE PUNISHED...
AHA HA HA!
PEER
You in there?
THROW THAT MADMAN INTO JAIL! IMMEDIATELY!
AHH ?!

I'VE DONE *NOTHING WRONG*, I TELL YOU! I'M INNOCENT!!!

TWITCH

URK!

GRAB

INNOCENT? *REALLY?!* I CAUGHT YOU RED-HANDED!

OH, DON'T MIND ME... I ALWAYS WANTED TO SAY SOMETHING LIKE THAT INSIDE A JAIL CELL, JUST ONCE...

THANK YOU FOR ALL YOUR HARD WORK!

HEY... ARE YOU JUST *STUPID?*

WHAT DID YOU SAY?!

TWIST

WHY ARE YOU ACTING LIKE A *MORON?* IT'S EMBAR-RASSING.

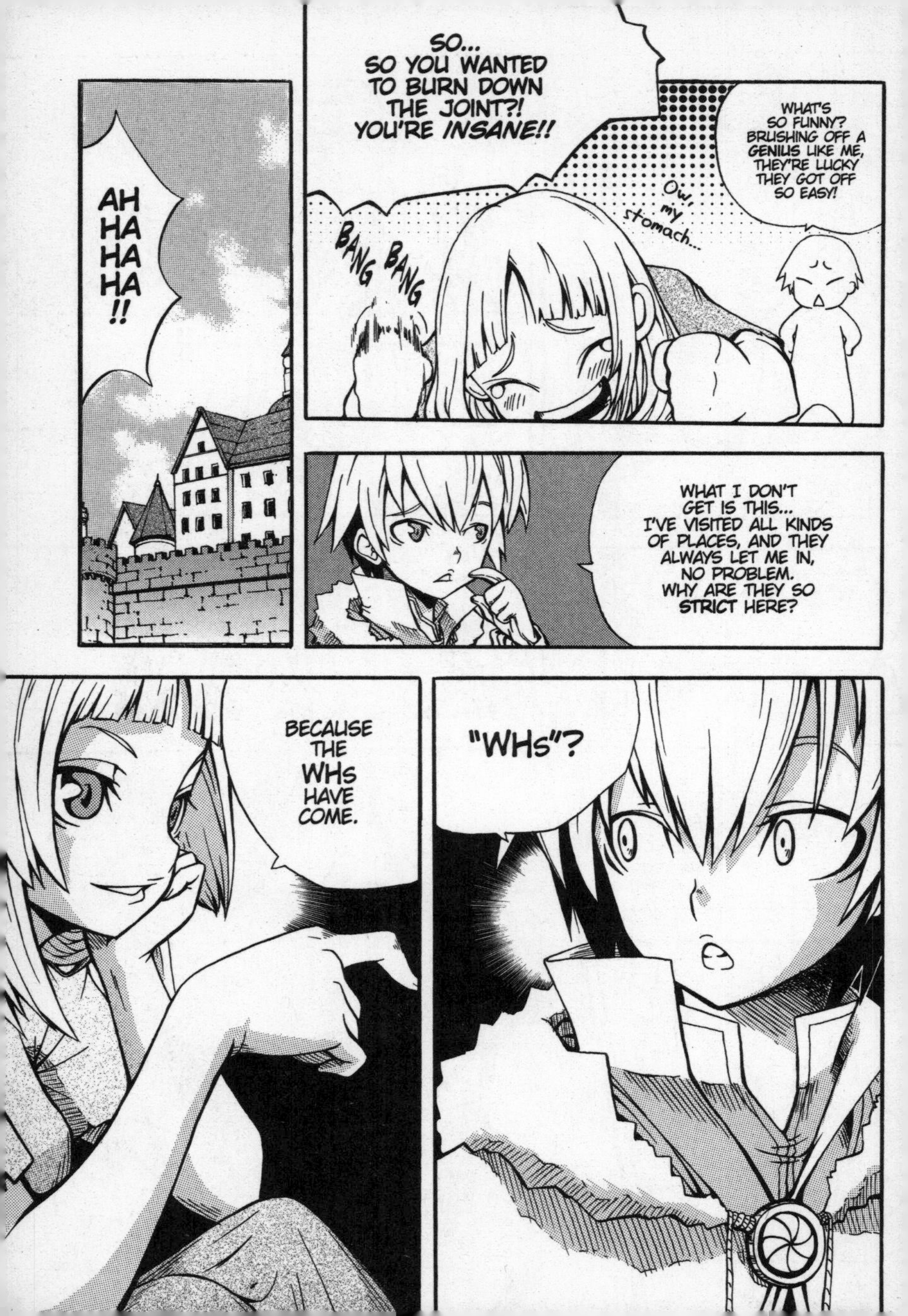
AH HA HA HA!!
SO... SO YOU WANTED TO BURN DOWN THE JOINT?! YOU'RE INSANE!!
BANG BANG
Ow, my stomach...
WHAT'S SO FUNNY? BRUSHING OFF A GENIUS LIKE ME, THEY'RE LUCKY THEY GOT OFF SO EASY!
WHAT I DON'T GET IS THIS... I'VE VISITED ALL KINDS OF PLACES, AND THEY ALWAYS LET ME IN, NO PROBLEM. WHY ARE THEY SO STRICT HERE?
BECAUSE THE WHs HAVE COME.
"WHs"?

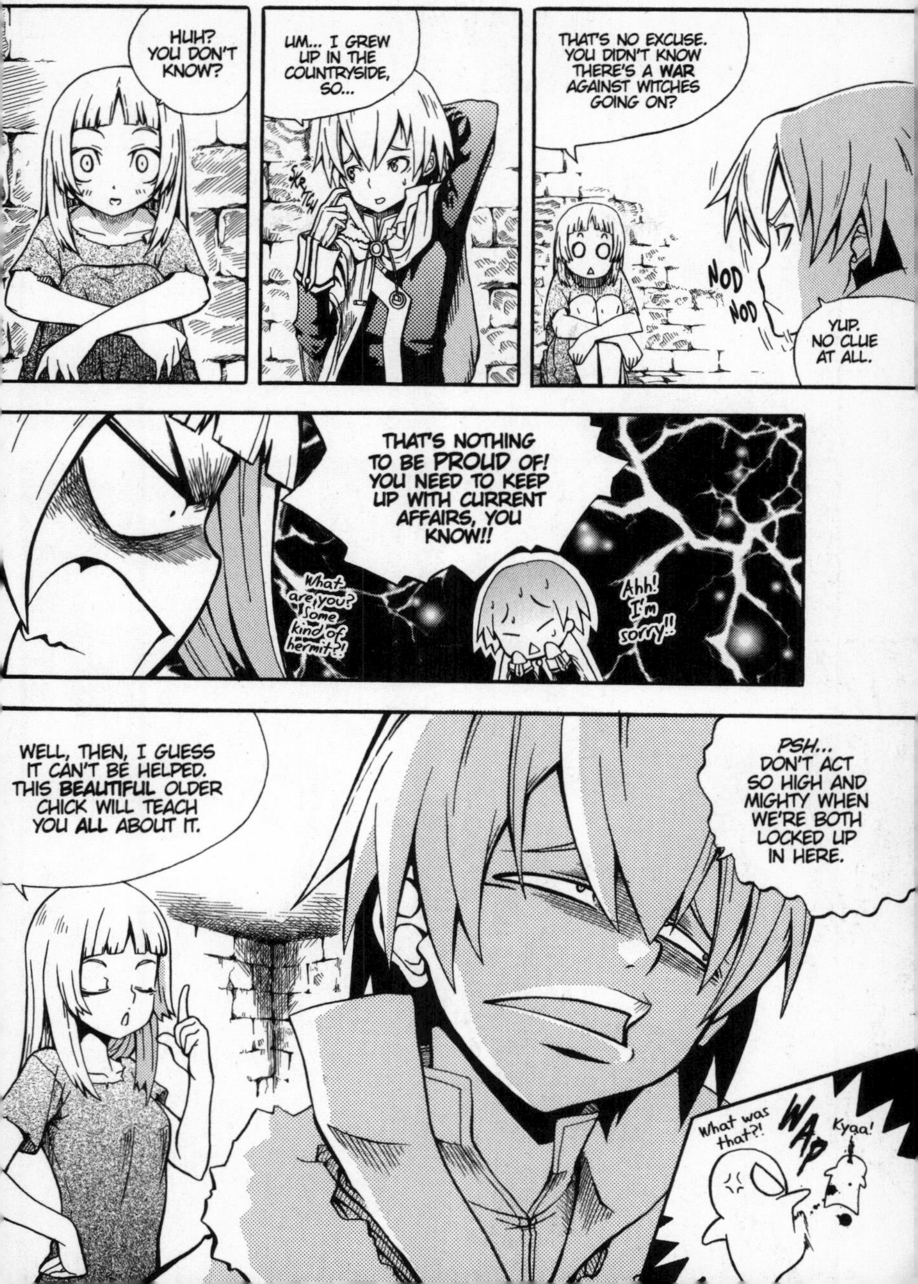
HUH? YOU DON'T KNOW?
UM... I GREW UP IN THE COUNTRYSIDE, SO...
SKRITCH
THAT'S NO EXCUSE. YOU DIDN'T KNOW THERE'S A WAR AGAINST WITCHES GOING ON?
NOD NOD
YUP. NO CLUE AT ALL.
THAT'S NOTHING TO BE PROUD OF! YOU NEED TO KEEP UP WITH CURRENT AFFAIRS, YOU KNOW!!
What are you? Some kind of hermit?!
Ahh! I'm sorry!!
WELL, THEN, I GUESS IT CAN'T BE HELPED. THIS BEAUTIFUL OLDER CHICK WILL TEACH YOU ALL ABOUT IT.
PSH... DON'T ACT SO HIGH AND MIGHTY WHEN WE'RE BOTH LOCKED UP IN HERE.
What was that?!
WAP
Kyaa!

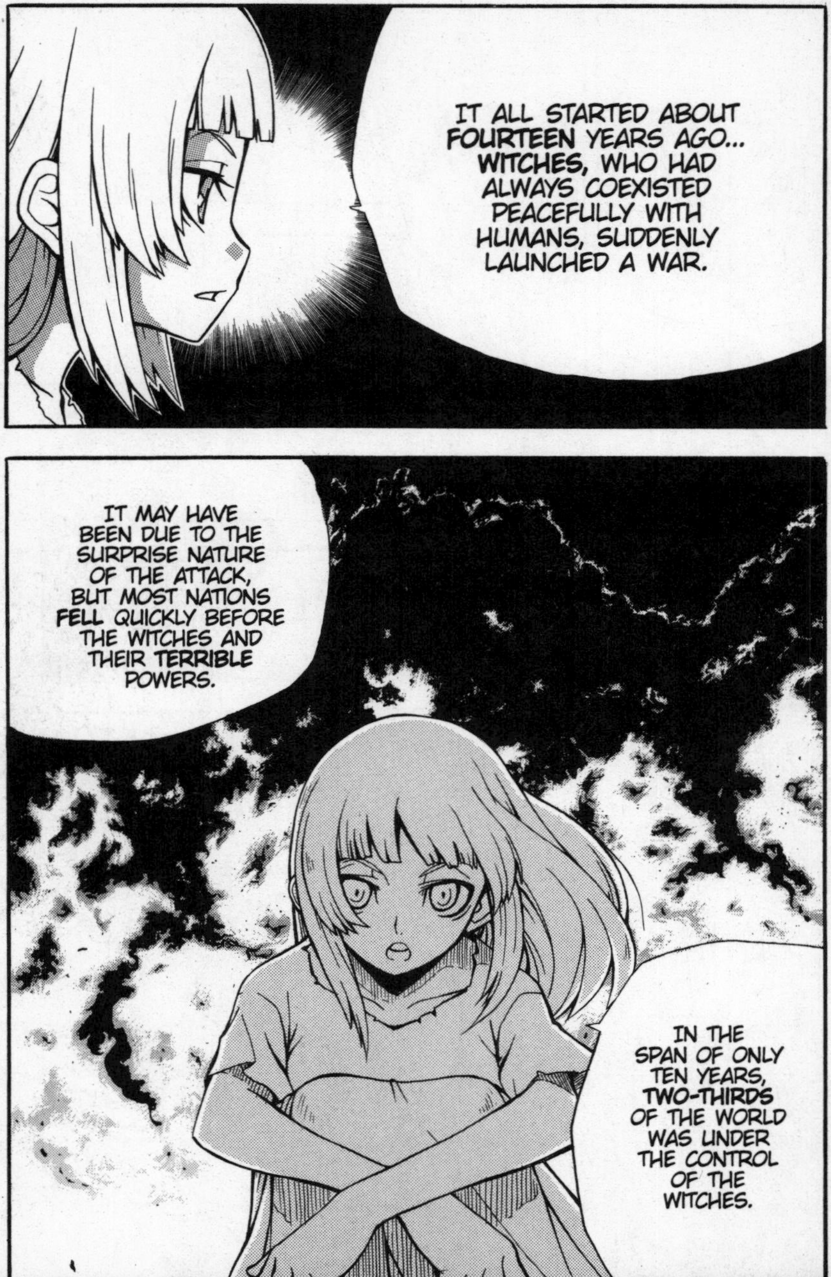
IT ALL STARTED ABOUT FOURTEEN YEARS AGO... WITCHES, WHO HAD ALWAYS COEXISTED PEACEFULLY WITH HUMANS, SUDDENLY LAUNCHED A WAR.
IT MAY HAVE BEEN DUE TO THE SURPRISE NATURE OF THE ATTACK, BUT MOST NATIONS FELL QUICKLY BEFORE THE WITCHES AND THEIR TERRIBLE POWERS.
IN THE SPAN OF ONLY TEN YEARS, TWO-THIRDS OF THE WORLD WAS UNDER THE CONTROL OF THE WITCHES.

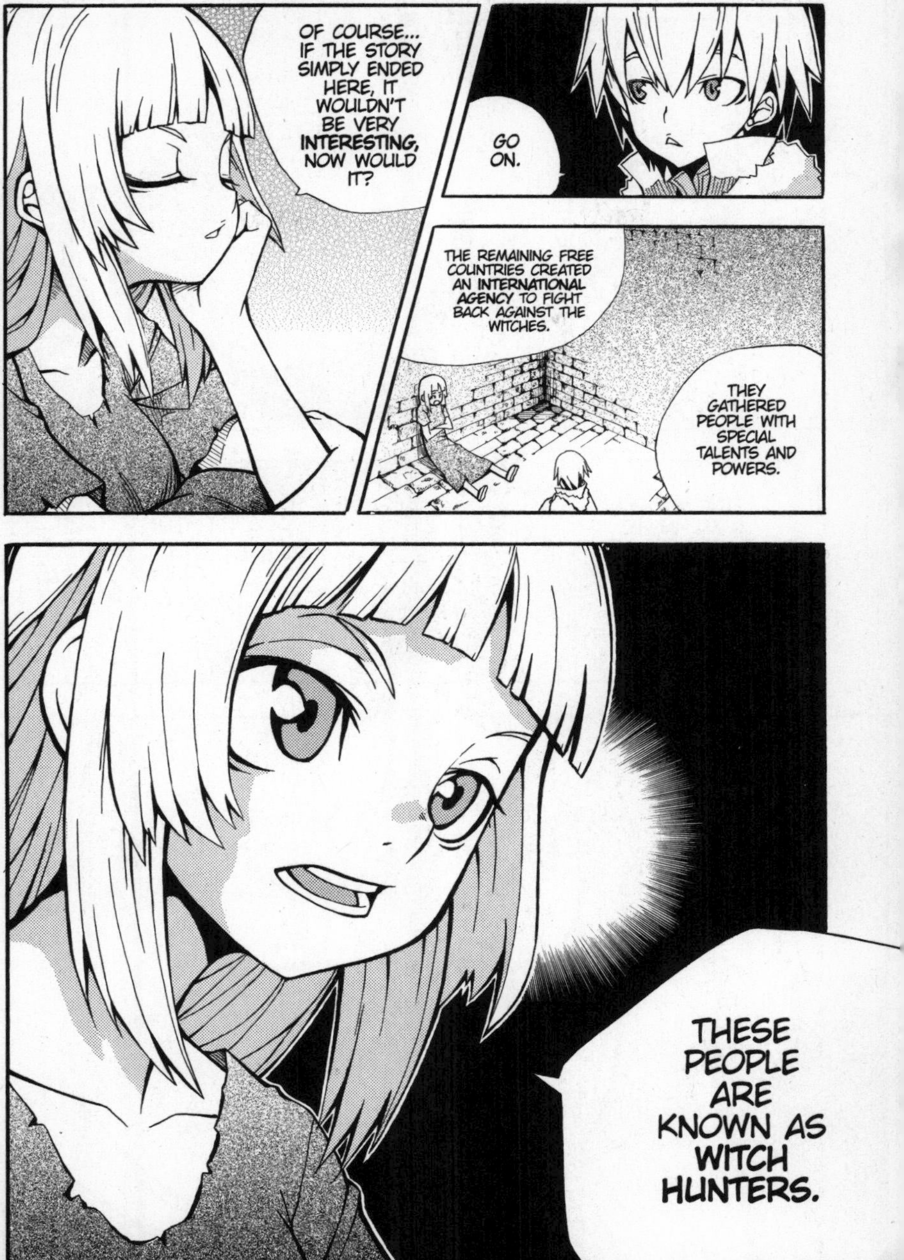
OF COURSE... IF THE STORY SIMPLY ENDED HERE, IT WOULDN'T BE VERY INTERESTING, NOW WOULD IT?
GO ON.
THE REMAINING FREE COUNTRIES CREATED AN INTERNATIONAL AGENCY TO FIGHT BACK AGAINST THE WITCHES.
THEY GATHERED PEOPLE WITH SPECIAL TALENTS AND POWERS.
THESE PEOPLE ARE KNOWN AS WITCH HUNTERS.

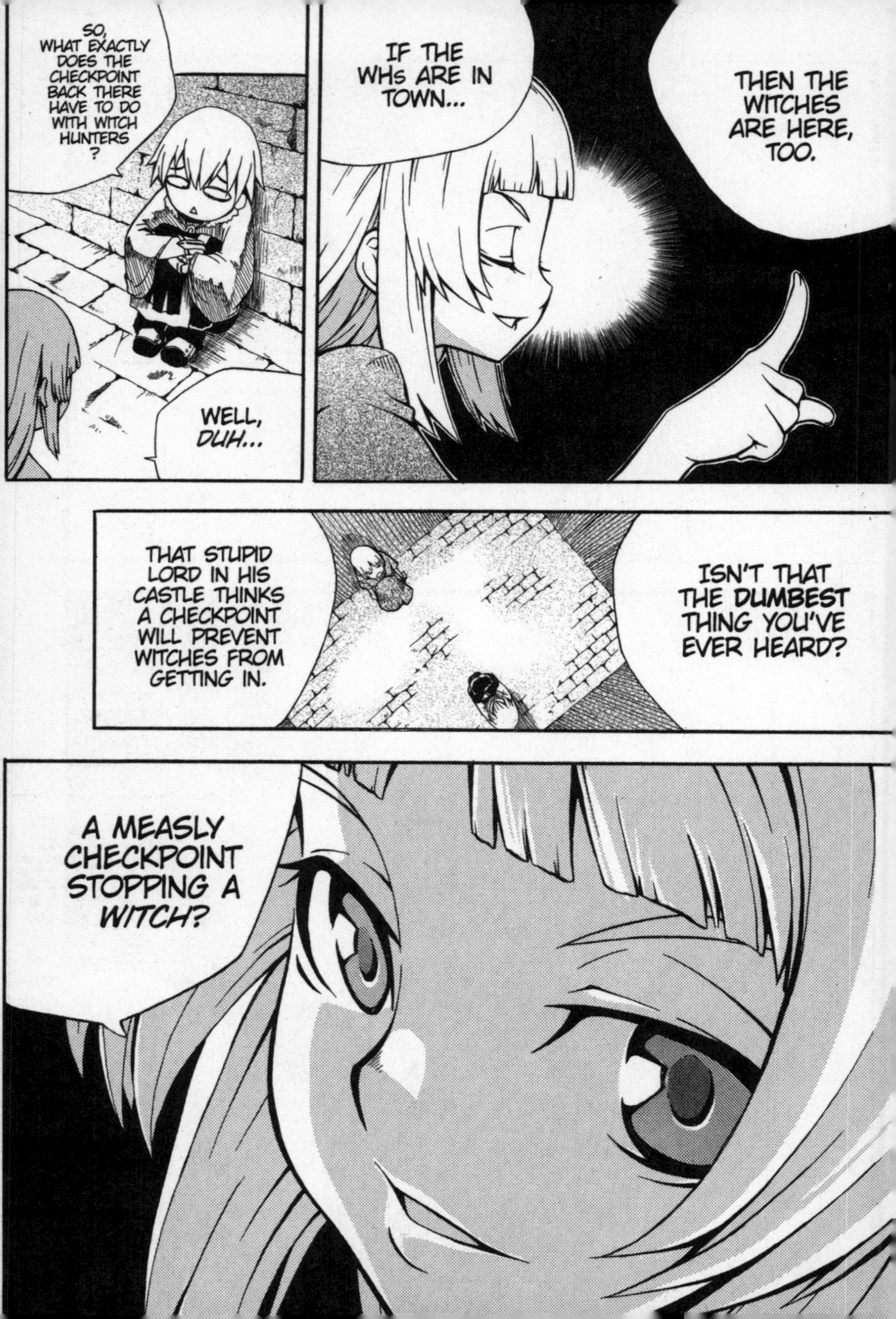
SO, WHAT EXACTLY DOES THE CHECKPOINT BACK THERE HAVE TO DO WITH WITCH HUNTERS ?
WELL, DUH...
IF THE WHs ARE IN TOWN...
THEN THE WITCHES ARE HERE, TOO.
THAT STUPID LORD IN HIS CASTLE THINKS A CHECKPOINT WILL PREVENT WITCHES FROM GETTING IN.
ISN'T THAT THE DUMBEST THING YOU'VE EVER HEARD?
A MEASLY CHECKPOINT STOPPING A WITCH?

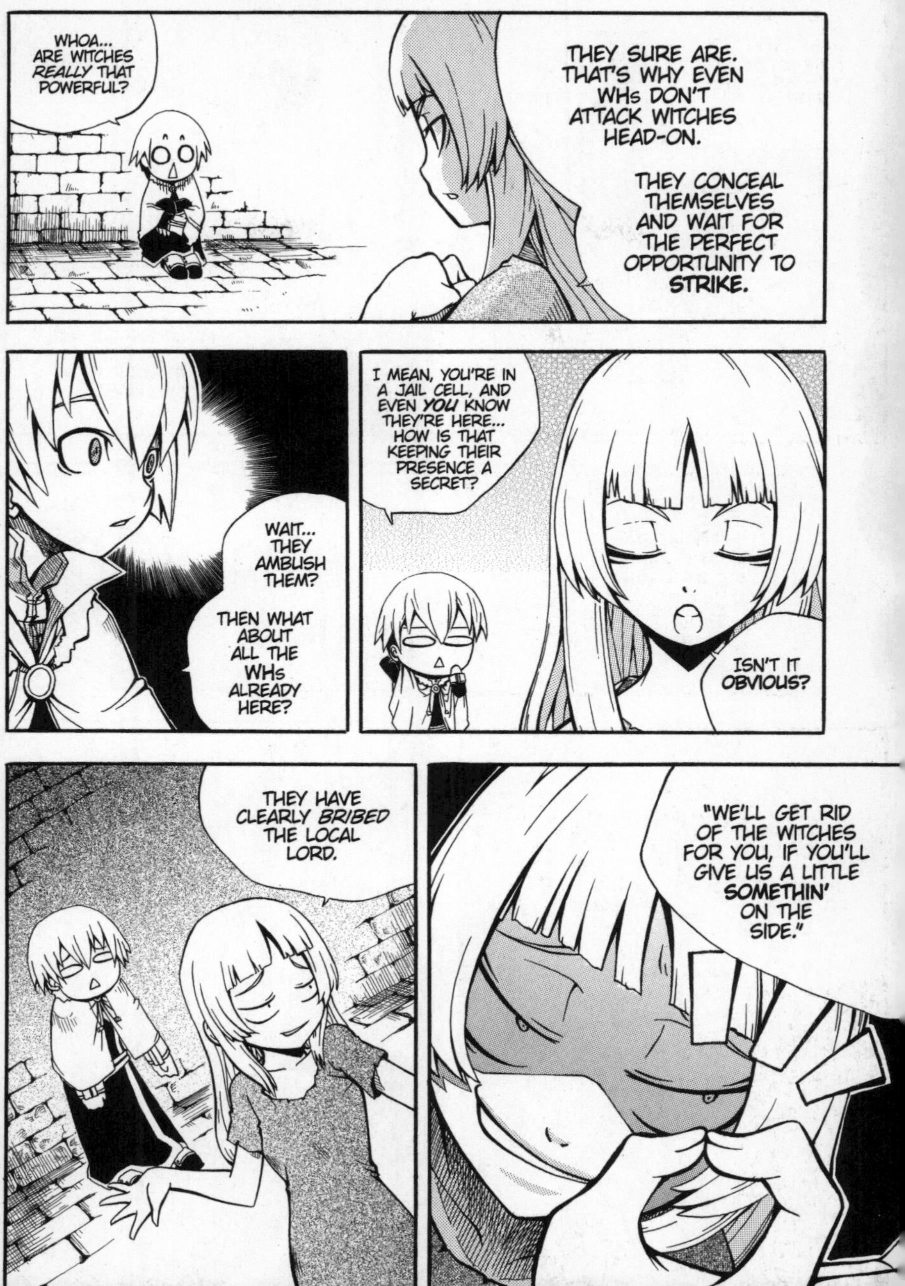
WHOA... ARE WITCHES *REALLY* THAT POWERFUL?
THEY SURE ARE. THAT'S WHY EVEN WHs DON'T ATTACK WITCHES HEAD-ON.
THEY CONCEAL THEMSELVES AND WAIT FOR THE PERFECT OPPORTUNITY TO **STRIKE.**
WAIT... THEY AMBUSH THEM?
THEN WHAT ABOUT ALL THE WHs ALREADY HERE?
I MEAN, YOU'RE IN A JAIL CELL, AND EVEN *YOU* KNOW THEY'RE HERE... HOW IS THAT KEEPING THEIR PRESENCE A SECRET?
ISN'T IT OBVIOUS?
THEY HAVE CLEARLY *BRIBED* THE LOCAL LORD.
"WE'LL GET RID OF THE WITCHES FOR YOU, IF YOU'LL GIVE US A LITTLE **SOMETHIN'** ON THE SIDE."

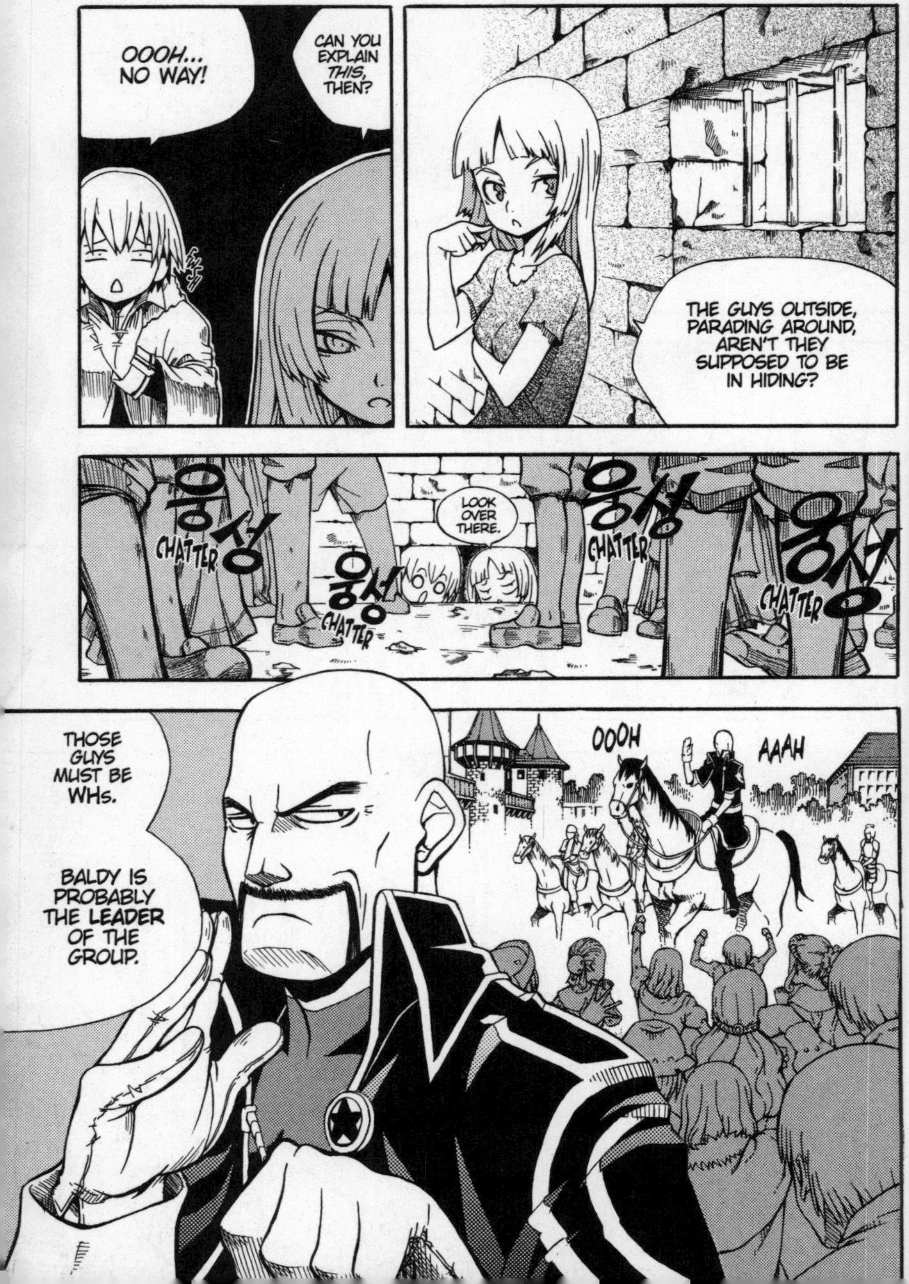
OOOH... NO WAY!
CAN YOU EXPLAIN THIS, THEN?
THE GUYS OUTSIDE, PARADING AROUND, AREN'T THEY SUPPOSED TO BE IN HIDING?
웅성
CHATTER
웅성
CHATTER
LOOK OVER THERE.
웅성
CHATTER
웅성
CHATTER
THOSE GUYS MUST BE WHs.
BALDY IS PROBABLY THE LEADER OF THE GROUP.
OOOH
AAAH

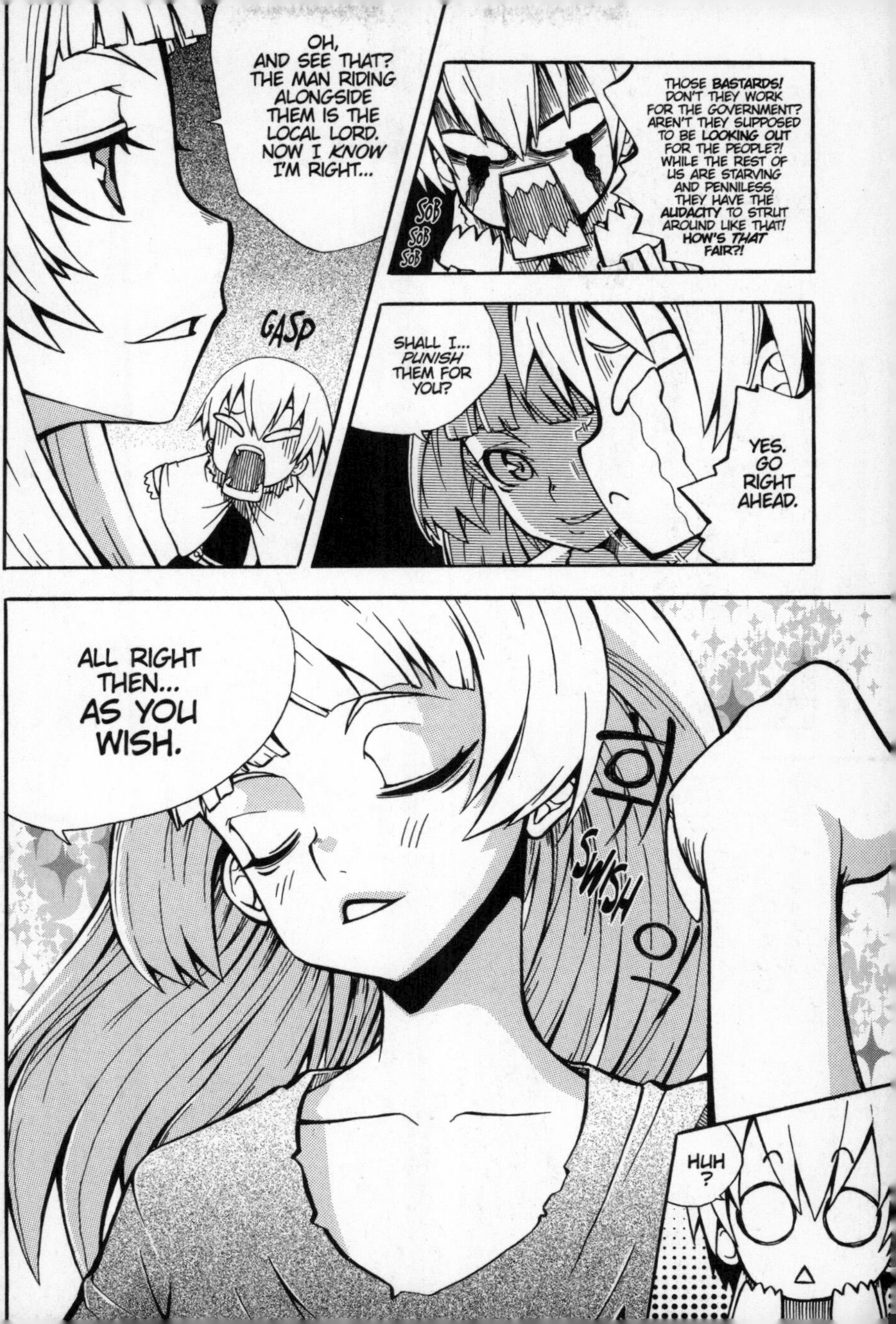
OH, AND SEE THAT? THE MAN RIDING ALONGSIDE THEM IS THE LOCAL LORD. NOW I KNOW I'M RIGHT...
GASP
SOB SOB SOB
THOSE BASTARDS! DON'T THEY WORK FOR THE GOVERNMENT? AREN'T THEY SUPPOSED TO BE LOOKING OUT FOR THE PEOPLE?! WHILE THE REST OF US ARE STARVING AND PENNILESS, THEY HAVE THE AUDACITY TO STRUT AROUND LIKE THAT! HOW'S THAT FAIR?!
SHALL I... PUNISH THEM FOR YOU?
YES. GO RIGHT AHEAD.
ALL RIGHT THEN... AS YOU WISH.
SWISH
HUH?

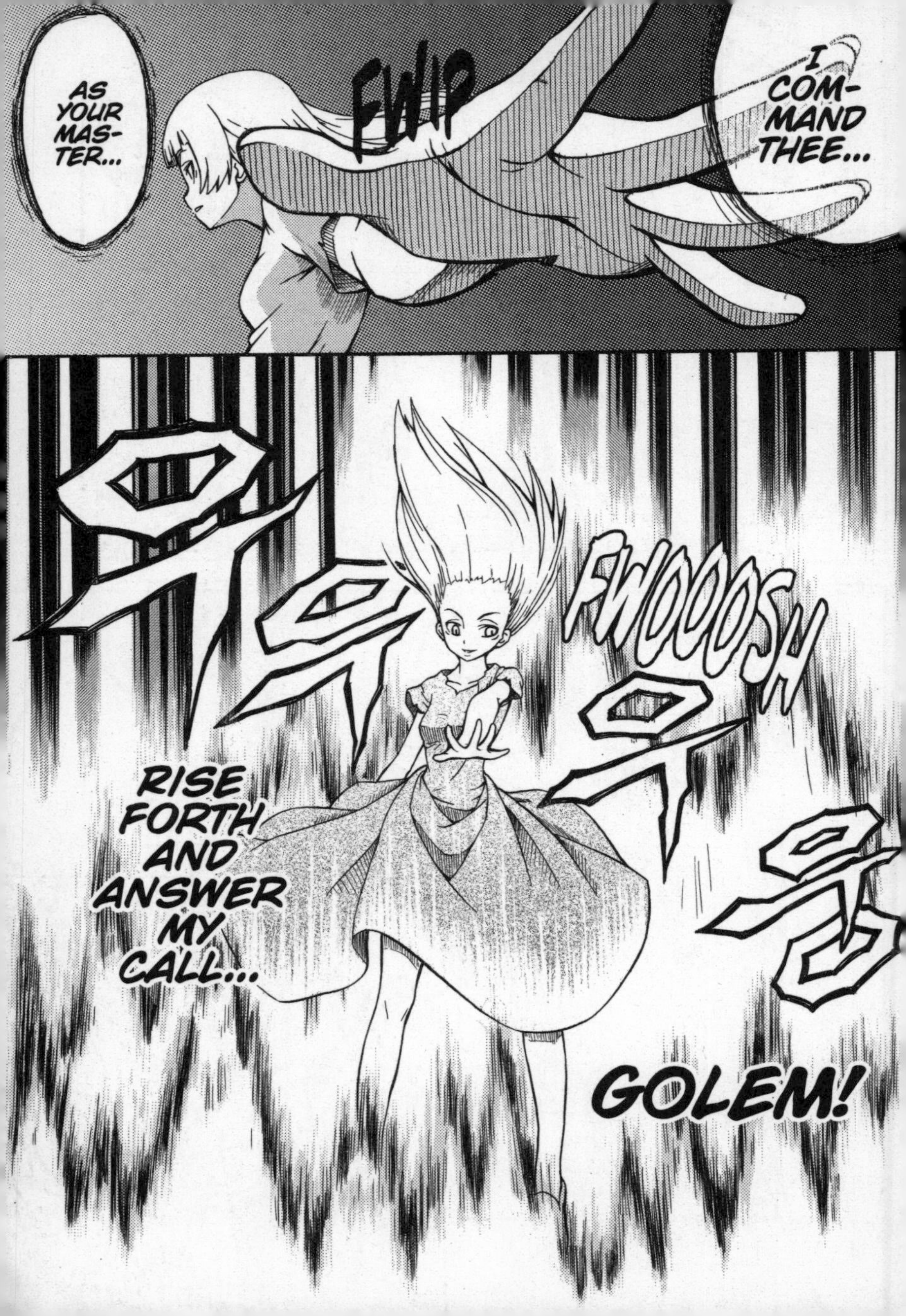
AS YOUR MAS-TER...
FWIP
I COM-MAND THEE...
FWOOOSH
RISE FORTH AND ANSWER MY CALL...
GOLEM!

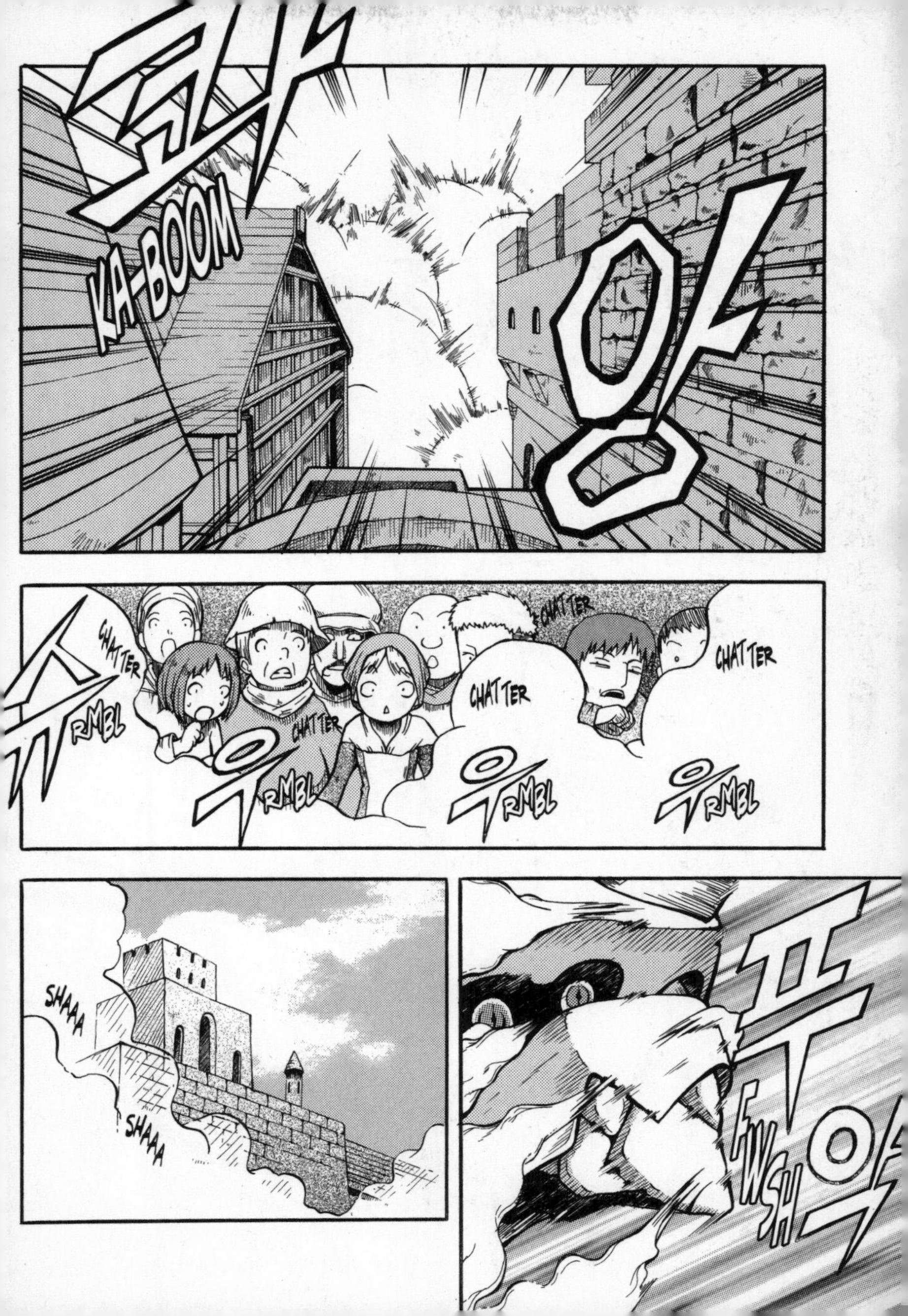
KA-BOOM
CHATTER
RMBL
CHATTER
CHATTER
CHATTER
CHATTER
RMBL
RMBL
RMBL
SHAAA
SHAAA
FWSH

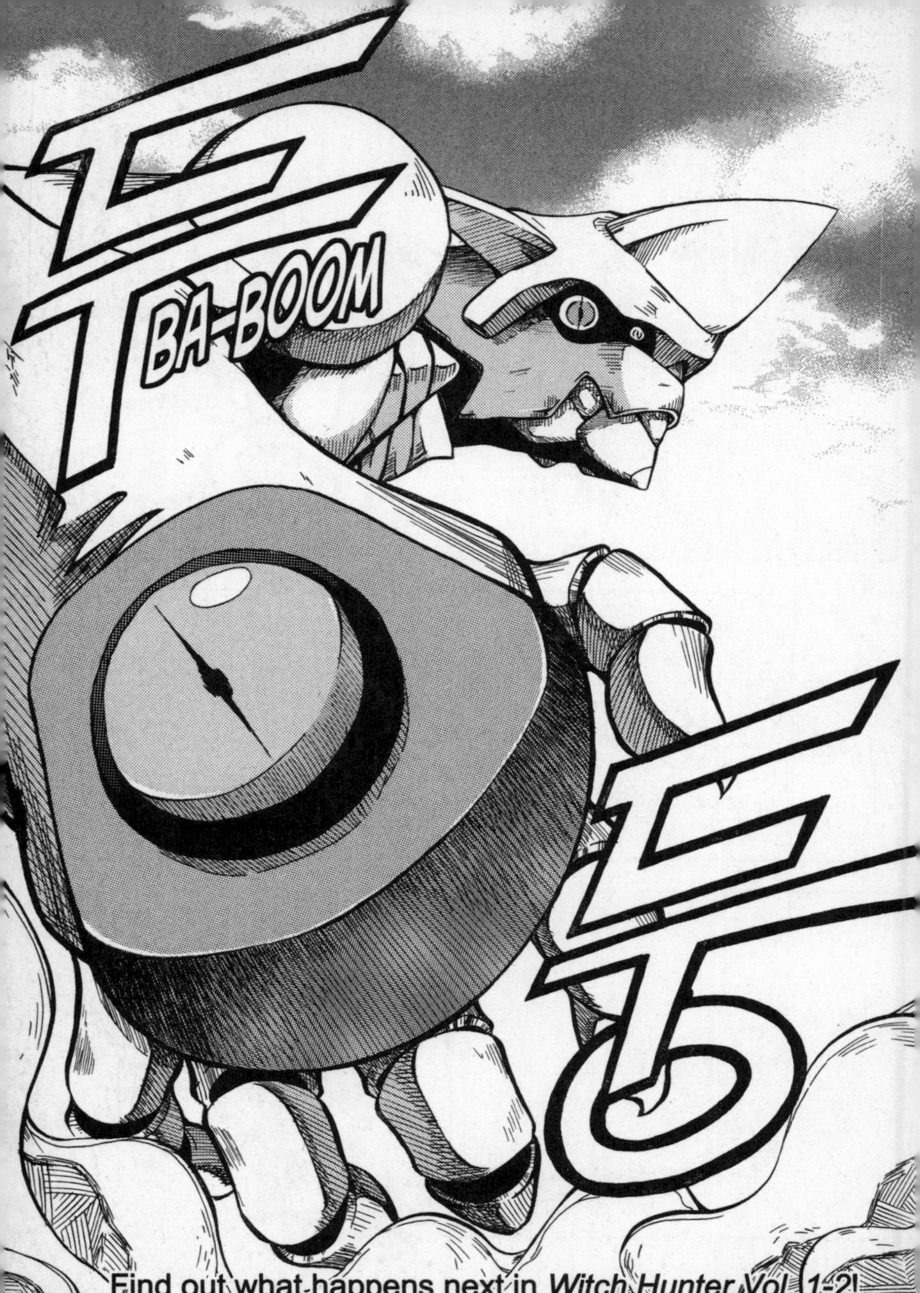
BA-BOOM

Find out what happens next in *Witch Hunter Vol. 1-2!*

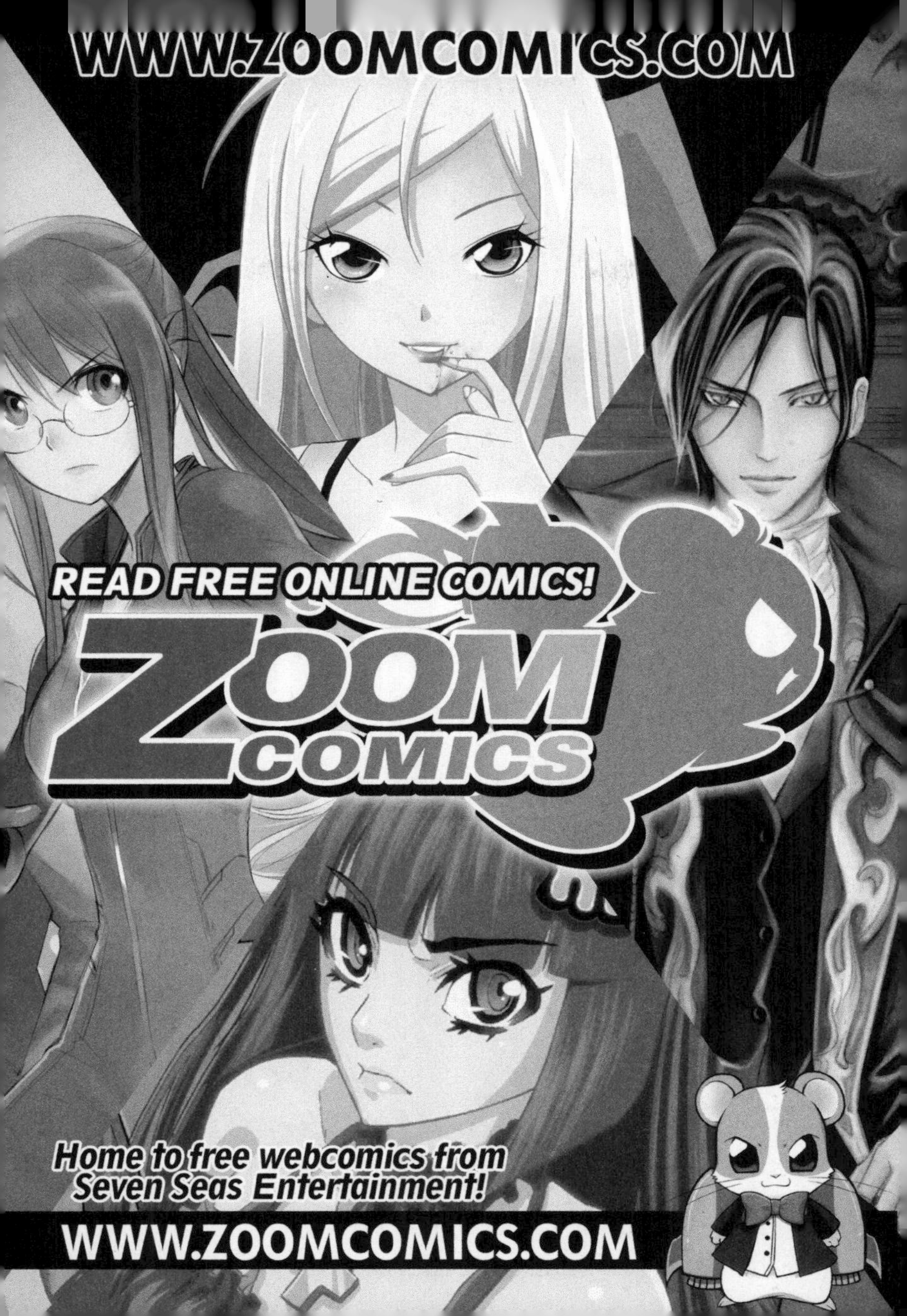

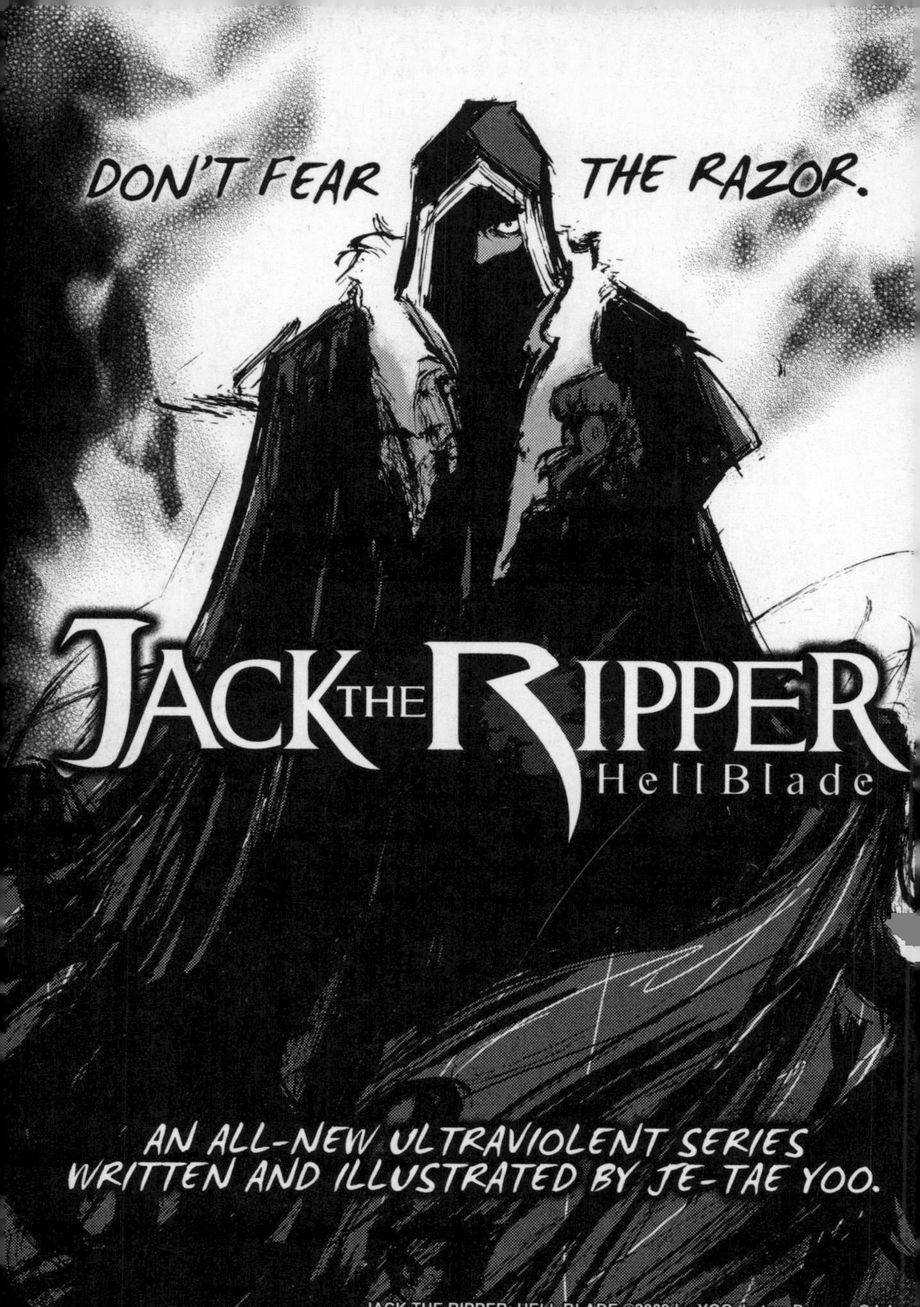
DON'T FEAR THE RAZOR.
JACK THE RIPPER
Hell Blade
AN ALL-NEW ULTRAVIOLENT SERIES
WRITTEN AND ILLUSTRATED BY JE-TAE YOO.

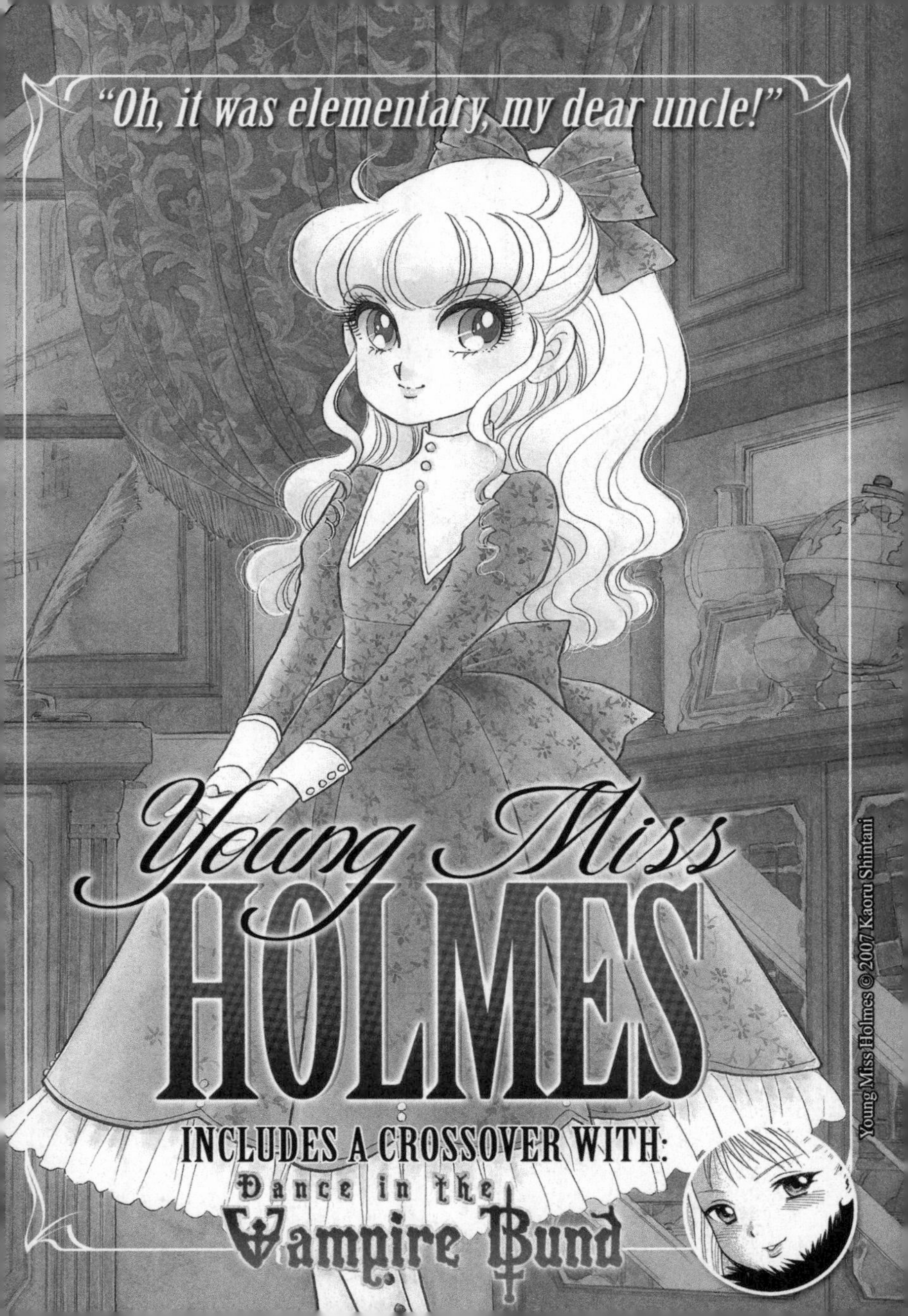
"Oh, it was elementary, my dear uncle!"
Young Miss
HOLMES
INCLUDES A CROSSOVER WITH:
Dance in the
Vampire Bund
Young Miss Holmes © 2007 Kaoru Shintani